CW01309754

Me 262

VOLUME TWO

Me 262

VOLUME TWO

J. Richard Smith
AND
Eddie J. Creek

With Contributions by
WILLY RADINGER
MIKE NORTON
STEPHEN RANSOM
JÜRGEN ROSENSTOCK

Technical Drawings by
ARTHUR L. BENTLEY
With Additional Line Drawings by
EDDIE J. CREEK AND GÜNTER SENGFELDER

Colour Artwork
TOM TULLIS AND EDDIE J. CREEK

CLASSIC
PUBLICATIONS

An imprint of
Ian Allan Publishing

www.ianallanpublishing.com

J. Richard Smith is indisputedly one of the world's foremost authorities on the history of the Luftwaffe. His works include the landmark publication *Jet Planes of the Third Reich* as well as *Arado 234 Blitz, Luftwaffe Camouflage & Markings 1935-45* and numerous other leading aviation titles including several studies in the acclaimed *Close Up* series.

Eddie J. Creek, a qualified architect, has for many years worked in partnership with Richard Smith producing a wealth of the most historically accurate line drawings and colour artwork so far published on aviation in the Third Reich. As a historian and enthusiast, he has been actively collecting documents and photographs relative to the history of the Luftwaffe for over 30 years. He is co-author of *Jet Planes of the Third Reich, Arado 234 Blitz* and other highly regarded works.

The authors would like to thank the following individuals for their kind assistance in the preparation of this volume:

Nick Beale	Alfred Krüger	Jürgen Rosenstock	The Staff of the
Arthur Bentley	Tony Landis	Walter Schick	Department of
Ken Bokelman	Dieter Lukesch	Günther Sengfelder	Documents at the
Steve Coates	Richard Lutz	Erich Sommer	Imperial War
Jerry Crandall	Perry Manley	Werner Stocker	Museum, London.
Jim Crow	Ken Merrick	Chris Thomas	Maj Gen P Pretorius
Robert Forsyth	Mike Norton	Ken Thompson	of the South African
Horst Geyer	Peter Petrick	Dave Wadman	National Museum of
Manfred Griehl	Alfred Price	USAF Flight Test	Military History.
Horst Götz	Willy Radinger	Center, Edwards AFB,	
Peter Kappus	Stephen Ransom	USA.	

First published in Great Britain in 1998 by **Classic Publications**, Quarry Ridge House, 7 Quarry Close, Burgess Hill, West Sussex RH15 0TJ, England.

Project Editor - Robert Forsyth

© 1998 Colour Illustrations - Thomas Tullis & Eddie J. Creek

© 1998 Line Drawings - Arthur Bentley, Eddie J. Creek & Günter Sengfelder

All rights reserved. No part of this book may be reproduced or transmitted in any form or by any means, electronic or mechanical including photocopying, recording, chemical, optical or otherwise without prior written permission from the publisher. All enquiries should be addressed to the publisher.

ISBN (10) 09526867 32
ISBN (13) 978 09526867 36
Book and jacket design by Colin Woodman Graphic Design

An imprint of Ian Allan Publishing Ltd, Hersham, Surrey KT12 4RG.
Printed in England by Ian Allan Printing Ltd, Hersham, Surrey KT12 4RG.
Visit the Ian Allan publishing website at www.ianallanpublishing.com

CONTENTS

CHAPTER EIGHT
"THE AIRCRAFT IS SIMPLY WONDERFUL"
Page 230

CHAPTER NINE
Me 262 VARIANTS
Page 266

CHAPTER TEN
"THE CRUCIAL FACTOR"
Page 312

CHAPTER ELEVEN
"MY GOD, WHAT WAS THAT?"
Page 358

CHAPTER TWELVE
"IN ACCORDANCE WITH THE FÜHRER'S ORDERS"
Page 380

CHAPTER THIRTEEN
"CARELESSNESS AND INADEQUATE TRAINING"
Page 406

APPENDIX FIVE
CAMOUFLAGE AND MARKINGS
Page 438

APPENDIX SIX
LUFTWAFFE RANKS AND FLYING UNITS
Page 440

APPENDIX SEVEN
MESSERSCHMITT Me 262 SPECIFICATION FIGURES
Page 442

GLOSSARY
INDEX

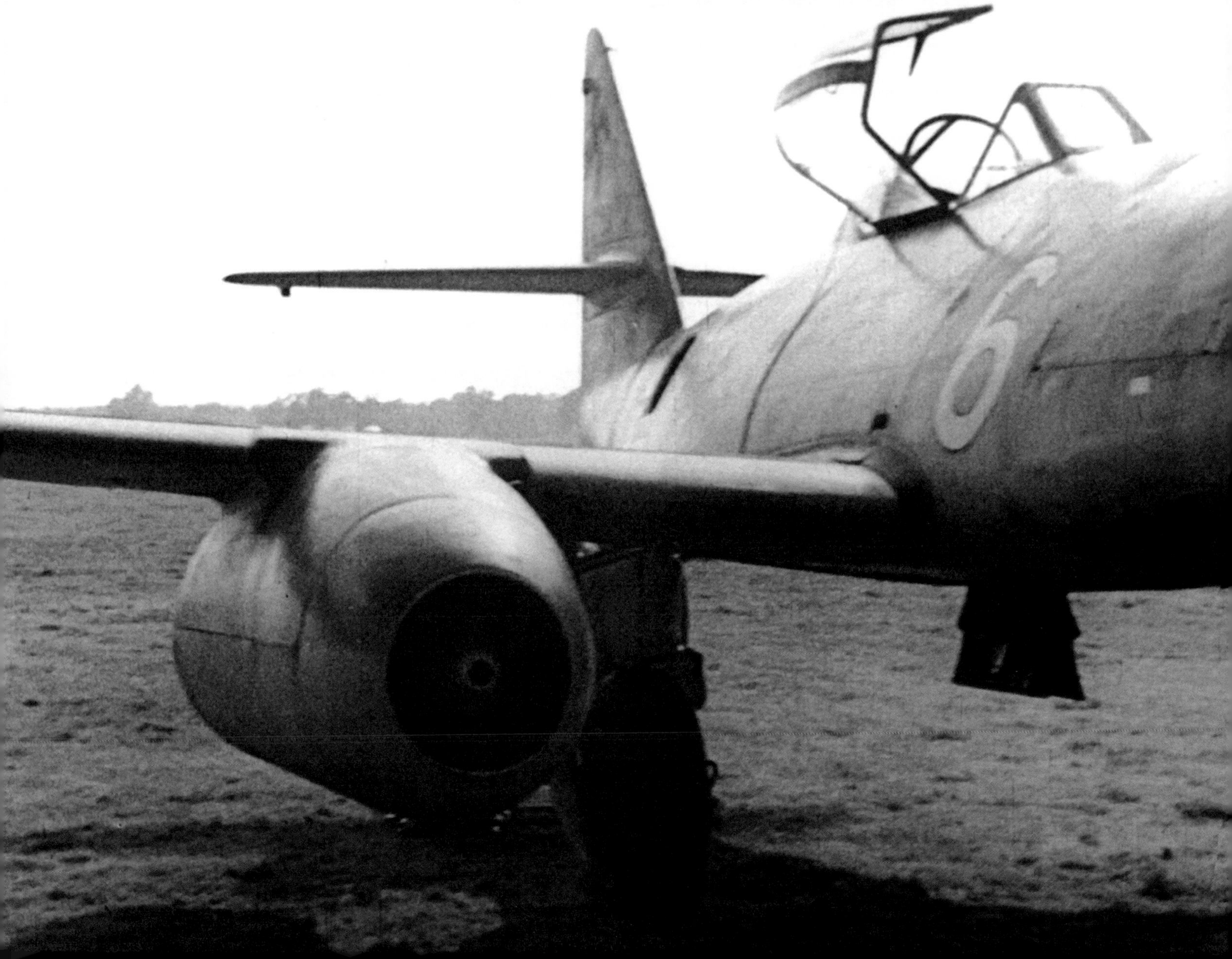

CHAPTER EIGHT
"THE AIRCRAFT IS SIMPLY WONDERFUL"

By the second half of 1943, the air war over north-west Europe had reached a new level of intensity with both the Allies and the *Luftwaffe* refining and expanding their respective strategies and operational assets. During hours of daylight the American Eighth Air Force, although still nowhere near the size and might of RAF Bomber Command, was determined to compete with its British partner in terms of operational success and effectiveness. On 17 August, a day that would commemorate the USAAF's first anniversary of heavy bomber operations from England, a force of more than 350 B-17 Flying Fortresses penetrated deep into southern Germany for the first time to attack the Messerschmitt aircraft manufacturing plant at Regensburg and a vital ball-bearing plant at Schweinfurt.

In response, the *Luftwaffe* fighter force, benefiting from a major reorganisation of its fighter control system and strengthened by increased aircraft availability, struck hard and violently. Sixty Fortresses were shot down in generally well-coordinated and aggressive

Smoke coils to the sky from the Messerschmitt production plant at Regensburg as B-17 Flying Fortresses of the US Eighth Air Force's 390th Bomb Group move away from their target on 17 August 1943. This was the Eighth's first deep penetration raid into southern Germany.

Below: Map of southern Germany showing main Me 262 production sites.

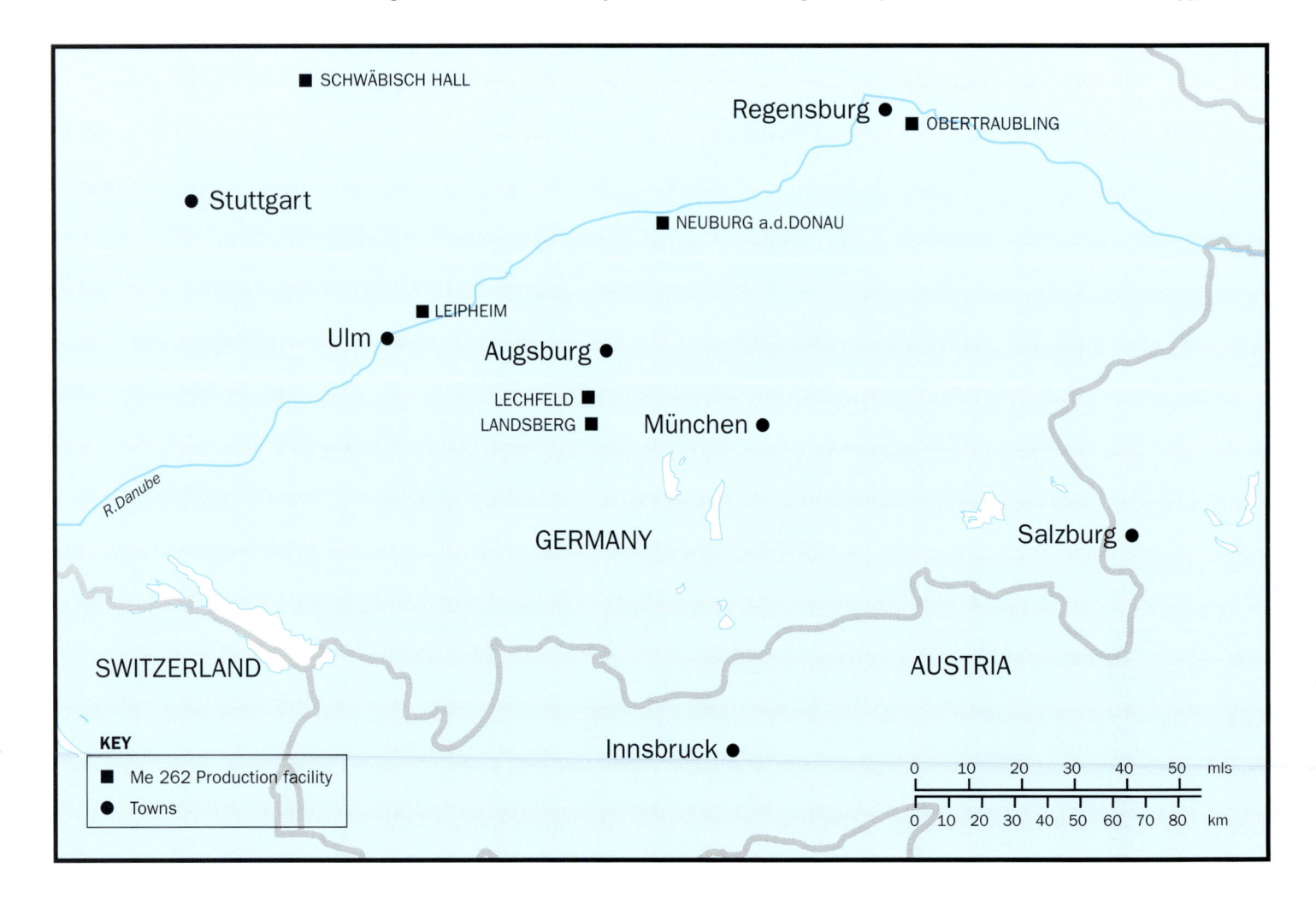

attacks. The Americans, scathed but unbowed, would return throughout September and October when, once again, the battles over Frankfurt, Bremen, Vegesack and Münster raged with ever-increasing attrition as the *Luftwaffe* was forced to tackle growing numbers of long-range P-47 Thunderbolt fighter escorts. Losses began to climb steadily.

The damage caused by the August raid against the Messerschmitt plant at Regensburg had dealt a severe blow to one of Germany's most secret development projects. When German officials inspected the factory after the raid, they discovered much to their relief, that despite the virtual destruction of Regensburg's flimsy single story workshops, many of the valuable machine tools remained intact and useable. However, it was with horror that they also realised that a large number of fuselage jigs and acceptance gauges for the new Me 262 jet fighter had been destroyed. One railway worker emerging from his air-raid shelter later told his family: "This is the end of the road - we have as good as lost the war. If they can come all the way here in broad daylight, we have no chance."

Recognising such an awful scenario, Messerschmitt worked urgently to minimise the delay to the Me 262 development programme.

By late 1943 only four prototypes of the Me 262 were flying, the V1, V3, V6 and V7. These were being tested at Lechfeld, a *Luftwaffe* airfield used by Messerschmitt, located some 20 km (12 miles) due south of Augsburg on the east side of the Augsburg-Landsberg highway in Bavaria. The company's flight test department, based on the western perimeter of the airfield,

The heavy damage inflicted on Regensburg can clearly be seen from this USAAF photo taken a few hours after the 17 August raid. Many of the fuselage jigs and acceptance gauges used in producing the Me 262 were destroyed during the attack.

Left: The remains of early production Me 262 airframes lie amidst the wreckage of the Messerschmitt Regensburg factory following the USAAF raid on 17 August 1943. In the middle distance is the old Zeppelin hangar, whilst behind that is the fuselage and wing assembly hall.

Below left: The Me 262 V3 commences its take-off run on the occasion of its first flight at Leiphem, 18 July 1942, with Messerschmitt test pilot Fritz Wendel at the controls. The first four Me 262s had tailwheel undercarriages which necessitated the pilot briefly applying the brakes to bring the tail up when attempting to takeoff. If this was not done the airframe would continue to mask the elevators, rendering them ineffective. Using this technique, Wendel lifted the V3 off the runway at Leipheim to complete a 12-minute trouble free test. This aircraft, along with the V1, V6 and V7 would still be test flying over a year later.

was led by *Dipl.-Ing.* Gerhard Caroli and given the code name *Autobedarf Lechfeld*. Although *Hptm.* Wolfgang Späte of the Me 163 test unit, *Erprobungskommando 16*, had flown the type, it was not until 9 December that the first experimental operational development unit was formed. Designated *Erprobungskommando (EKdo) 262*, the unit was to be led by an experienced combat pilot with considerable technical ability who had previously led 4./ZG 2, *Hptm.* Werner Thierfelder.

On 21 December he and another accomplished fighter pilot, *Maj.* Egon Mayer, commander of JG 2, made their first flights in an Me 262, the V6. A day previously, *Oberst* Dietrich Peltz, Inspector of Bombers, also flew the V6.

Although Thierfelder began jet training at Lechfeld in December, it was not until 20 January 1944, that he was joined by three other pilots, *Fw.* Helmut Baudach and *Fw.* Erwin Eichhorn from JG 2 and *Fw.* Helmut Lennartz from JG 11, with *Oblt.* Wörner arriving from ZG 101 at the end of February. On 1 February, Thierfelder escaped unhurt when the repaired Me 262 V5, which he was testing, crashed and was destroyed.

Erprobungskommando 262 did not receive its first aircraft until 19 April when the Me 262 V8 arrived, Lennartz making his first jet flight on that day. Then, early in May, 14 pilots from III./ZG 26 (minus the 7.*Staffel*), which had been flying Bf 110s against USAAF bombers from Königsberg-Neumark, were ordered to transfer

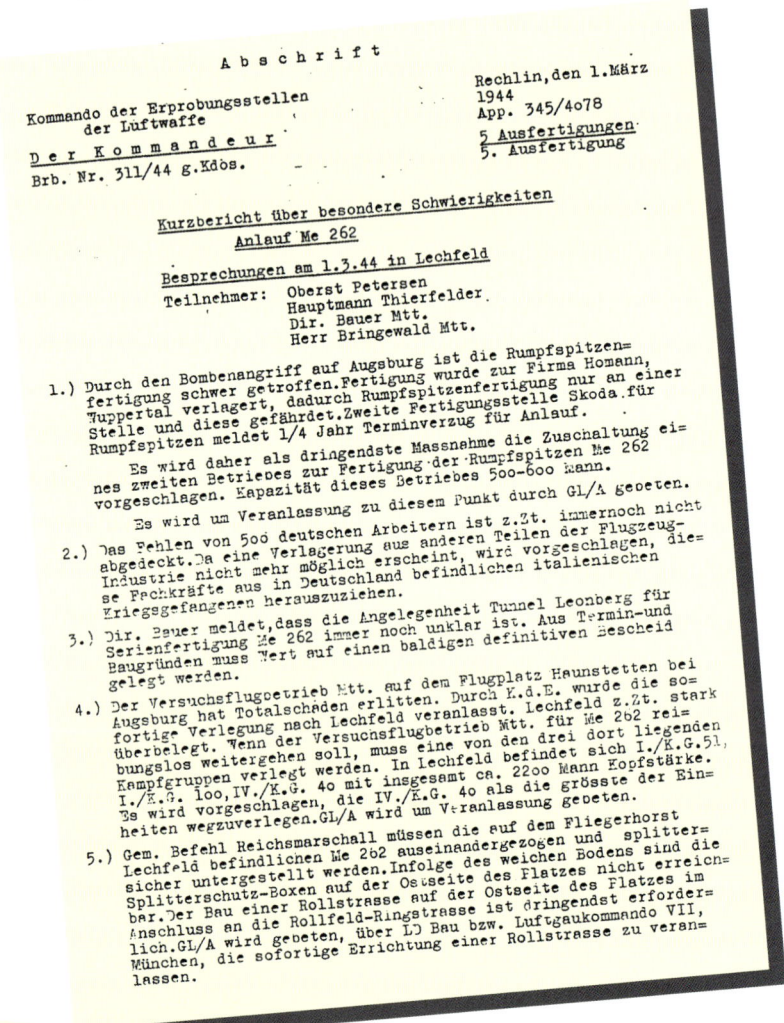

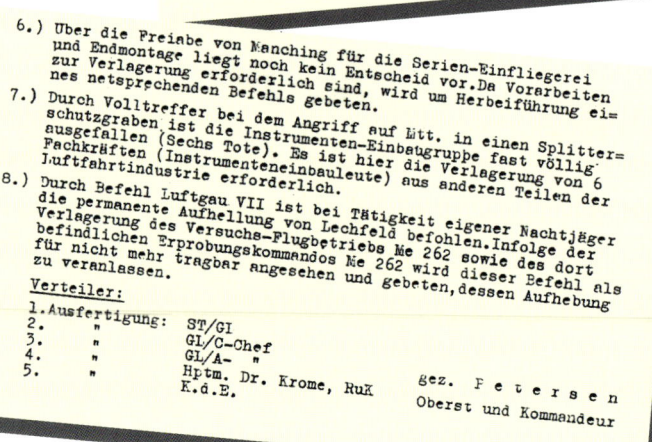

Following the American "Big Week" raid on Augsburg on 25 February 1944, thirty of its buildings and a third of its machine tools were damaged. In this document, Edgar Petersen, head of the KdE, Werner Thierfelder of the fledgling Erprobungskommando 262, Hubert Bauer and August Bringewalde of Messerschmitt, discussed the raid and how the difficulties it had caused could be overcome.

WERNER THIERFELDER

Born on 24 December 1915 in Berlin but brought up in South West Africa (now Namibia). Thierfelder studied at Göttingen University before joining II./ZG 26, part of the famous Horst Wessel Geschwader, at the beginning of the war. He flew in combat during the battles for France and Britain and then in the Balkans and Crete. He was awarded the Knight's Cross on 10 October 1941 for 14 aerial victories and the destruction of 41 aircraft and six trains on the ground, flying the Messerschmitt Bf 110 Zerstörer. He joined II./ZG 2 in May 1942 and was promoted to Staffelkapitän of 4./ZG 2. On 1 October 1942 he transferred to the General der Jagdflieger where much use was made of his extensive technical knowledge. He was appointed to lead Erprobungskommando 262 on 15 December 1943, and became, at the same time, commander of III./ZG 26. By this time he had destroyed 27 aircraft in the air plus 41 on the ground.

Four key figures in the story of the Me 262 photographed during the summer of 1944 at Lechfeld. From left: Gerd Lindner who was to become the most experienced Me 262 test pilot; Professor Willy Messerschmitt, the aircraft's designer; Hptm. Werner Thierfelder, commander of Erprobungskommando 262 and Gerhard Caroli who headed Messerschmitt's flight test department. Caroli is seen holding a winch rope which is being used to salvage a Me 262 apparently suffering from a collapsed nose wheel. It is thought that this aircraft is the S6, the machine in which Thierfelder was killed on 18 July 1944. At the time of this photograph, the aircraft had been fitted with a tube which extended from the nose. This is thought to have been used for stability trials.
Below: The Me 262 V5, PC+UE, W.Nr. 262 00 005, was the first prototype to be fitted with a tricycle undercarriage. On 1 February 1944, Werner Thierfelder, commander of Ekdo 262, escaped from the aircraft when it crashed and was destroyed during a test flight.

to Lechfeld for conversion to the Me 262. Advanced detachments arrived on 10 May, ground staff from 8./ZG 26 going to the Messerschmitt assembly plant at Leipheim, those from 9./ZG 26 to Schwäbisch Hall for technical familiarisation. During the middle of May two Me 262s, the S3 and S4, were delivered to the unit. Ten pilots are known to have begun conversion training. They were: *Oblt.* Hans-Günther Müller (*Staffelkapitän* of 8./ZG 26), *Oblt.* Paul Bley (*Staffelkapitän* of 9./ZG 26), *Oblt.* Günther Wegmann, *Lt.* Joachim Weber, *Lt.* Alfred Schreiber, *Ofw.* Hubert Göbel, *Ofw.* Helmut Recker, *Ofw.* Strathmann, *Fw.* Heinz Herlitzius and *Uffz.* Hans Flachs.

A problem then arose at the end of May with Hitler's directive that the Me 262 was in future to be referred to as a bomber. At this stage, all delivery of new aircraft to the fighter units ceased. In a report written for the Allies shortly after the end of the war, the then head of the *Luftwaffe* Operations Staff, *General der Flieger* Karl Koller, commented revealingly on Hitler's intransigence over the deployment of the Me 262 as a fighter: "The fuss began in April 1944 when the *Führer* wanted the Me 262 to be used as a fighter-bomber and he kept agitating about this until late autumn. Göring was very depressed and embittered; he frequently opposed this idea, but perhaps he did not do so strongly enough. In any case, if the *Führer* was as unpleasant to him as he was to me, to Christian,

Erprobungskommando 262
The first jet pilots

Below: Oberleutnant Ernst Wörner, (centre holding a fir wreath), was amongst the first group of Luftwaffe pilots to fly the Me 262 with Thierfelder's experimental unit. Wörner had come from the twin-engined, heavy fighter operational training unit, ZG 101.
He is seen here having completed his first flight in a Me 262. To Wörner's left in this photograph is Gerd Linder, the Messerschmitt test pilot and to his right, Oberleutnant Ernst Tesch who conducted bomb carrying tests in the Me 262 V10 in June 1944 (see Me 262 Volume One).

Above: Fw. Helmut Lennartz, seen here at Lechfeld in September 1944 shortly after joining the fledgling Kommando Nowotny. Lennartz was one of the first pilots to join Erprobungskommando 262, having previously served with the Bf 109-equipped 5./JG 11 in the defence of the Reich. On 14 May 1943, he claimed a B-17 brought down by air-to-air bombing, a tactic with which his unit briefly experimented at that time.

Fw. Erwin Eichhorn (2nd from left) and Fw Helmut Lennartz (3rd from left) of Erprobungskommando 262 at Lechfeld, summer 1944. With them are Fhr. Kaser and Fw. Oppers.

"THE AIRCRAFT IS SIMPLY WONDERFUL" • 237

Oblt. Günther Wegmann flew the Me 262 with Erprobungskommando 262, Kommando Nowotny and finally with III./JG 7. He is seen here at Schwabstadl, near Lechfeld in July 1944 whilst serving with Erprobungskommando 262. He was wounded in an attack on a formation of B-17s near Berlin on 18 March 1945. After being hit by machine-gun fire from a P-51 his aircraft caught fire and he was forced to bail out. His wounds were tended by a Red Cross nurse, but this did not save his leg which was amputated a few hours later.

Below: Lt Alfred "Bubi" Schreiber who flew with both Erprobungskommando 262 and JG 7. He claimed the Erprobungskommando's first victory on 26 July 1944, possibly the Mosquito piloted by Flt. Lt. Wall. After being transferred to 9./JG 7 he was lost on 26 November 1944 when his aircraft crashed near Lechfeld.

Personnel from Erprobungskommando 262 steal a ride on a Zündapp motorcycle combination at Lechfeld, 1944. From left: Fw. Paul Ziesch (signals), Lt. Hans-Günther Müller and Lt. Joachim Weber. Following Hitler's decision on the role of the Me 262, Müller was transferred to Leipheim as a delivery pilot. Weber went on to fly the Me 262 with JG 7 but was killed in action on 21 March 1945, having claimed seven victories whilst flying the jet.

Above: Fw. Heinz Herlitzius, spent a brief time with Erprobungskommando 262 before being transferred to Messerschmitt's flight test division at Lechfeld as a result of Hitler's directive that the Me 262 was to be deployed in the bomber role, thus curtailing fighter development.

Above: On 3 August 1944 Oblt. Hans-Günter Müller of Erprobungskommando 262 flew this Me 262, W.Nr. 170059, from Leipheim to Lechfeld. He is seen here standing on the wing just prior to the flight and before operational markings had been applied to the aircraft. The Me 262 immediately behind, W.Nr. 170045, was unusual in having a white swastika applied to its tail. It was also delivered to Erprobungskommando 262 as "White 5" and flown in combat by Fw. Helmut Lennartz in August 1944. *Above right*: General der Flieger Karl Koller, Luftwaffe Chief of Operations Staff, was forbidden to mention the Me 262 to Hitler. He wrote: "The Führer's attitude to this whole business was inconceivably obstinate…"

Below and other officers who recommended that the Me 262 should be used as a fighter aircraft, then one can understand his attitude, even though one cannot excuse it. The *Führer's* attitude to this whole business was inconceivably obstinate and he heaped curses upon the heads of those who stood in his way. Most people were afraid of him and obeyed him blindly."

"When, on the Führer's instructions, I was sent to the West on 13 August 1944 to gain a picture of the air situation there and to make a report on it, I again took the opportunity of championing the cause of the Me 262 being used as a fighter aircraft. Amongst many other brief teleprinter messages which I sent to OKH and to the *Luftwaffe* Chief of Staff, I sent the following one, which I wanted submitted to the *Führer*: *"Me 262s should be sent to the front-line as fighter aircraft as soon as possible."* This message was not submitted to the *Führer* because it was feared it would cause him to have a dangerous breakdown."

"Before I was due to report to the *Führer* on my return, the then *Luftwaffe* Chief of Staff, *General* Kreipe, who was acting on Göring's instructions, expressly forbade me to mention to Hitler the subject of the Me 262 being used as a fighter. I was told that this was in the interests of the relationship between OKL and the *Führer* and in my own interest. I did mention it nevertheless. *Generalfeldmarschall* Keitel was there at the time. On this occasion the *Führer* listened quietly for the first time. He showed that he did not agree with the idea, but did not express any personal opinion on the subject. I think that I penetrated his obstinate shell of resistance on the subject for the first time then."

Hans-Günther Müller and Paul Bley however were reduced to the role of delivery pilots at

Eight Me 262s are seen here recently arrived at Lechfeld from Leiphem and now carrying the white tactical numerals of Erprobungskommando 262 on their noses. The three aircraft in the foreground are "White 2", W.Nr. 170071, "White 3", W.Nr. 170067 and "White 5", W.Nr. 170045. Additionally, many of the Kommando's aircraft had yellow recognition bands applied to the fuselage forward of the Balkenkreuz.

Messerschmitt Me 262 A-1a W.Nr. 170071 "White 2" Erprobungskommando 262

With its undercarriage retracting, Me 262 A-1a "White 2", W.Nr. 170071 of Erprobungskommando 262 climbs away from Lechfeld at the start of another flight. This aircraft was later flown by Major Erich Hohagen before being found abandoned by the side of an autobahn at the end of the war.

Below: The same aircraft returns from its flight and taxies past the camera.

Leipheim and Schwäbisch Hall respectively, and Herlitzius and Flachs were later seconded to Messerschmitt's flight test division at Lechfeld. Other pilots, including Strathmann, returned to ZG 26. Thierfelder was now left with 6 to 8 aircraft and about eight pilots with which to develop operational tactics for the Me 262.

In addition to lack of aircraft, the unit was also experiencing many problems with lack of quality control on the production line. A large number of faults were registered by the *Kommando* on receiving their aircraft. For example flaps were distorted, there was a considerable amount of faulty spot welding, there were cracks in the elevator push rods, oil levels were wrong, etc., etc. However, these faults seemed to be common to the German aircraft industry at this time as many other operational units reported such problems. *EKdo 262* could correct the faults, but this took time which could have been better spent on training and developing operational tactics.

Because of the high speed of the Me 262, the unit developed the tactic of 'bouncing' its target from above and behind, then streaking ahead before the enemy could bring his guns to bear. It would then make a turn out of range so that the attacked aircraft would not benefit by its superior turning circle, and return for another quick 'bounce'. These tactics seemed to prove satisfactory and were witnessed by *Reichsminister* Albert Speer, Germany's Armaments Minister and *Generalfeldmarschall* Albert Kesselring, Commander-in-Chief of German forces in Italy, during a demonstration held at Lechfeld in which an Me 262 repeatedly 'shot down' a Bf 109. An interesting insight into the state of the aircraft at this time was given by a previous commander of III./ZG 26, *Obstlt.* Johann Kogler,[1] during a lecture clandestinely recorded by Allied intelligence, to his fellow officers in a prisoner of war camp on 15 March 1945:

"The aircraft is simply wonderful from the point of view of flying. Of course with its speed the take-off presents difficulties, as does the landing, because it needs a very long run. So we put all our hopes on this type of aircraft and kept hoping that when it went into operation it would finally turn the scales of the air war again.

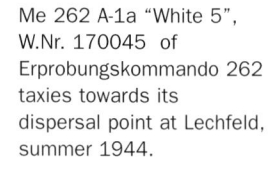

Obstlt. Johann Kogler, one-time Gruppenkommandeur of III./ZG 26 and later Geschwader Kommodore of JG 6. Pilots from the former Gruppe formed the nucleus of Erprobungskommando 262. In Kogler's opinion, the Me 262 was ".. simply wonderful from the point of view of flying."

Me 262 A-1a "White 5", W.Nr. 170045 of Erprobungskommando 262 taxies towards its dispersal point at Lechfeld, summer 1944.

After servicing Me 262 A-1a "White 3", W.Nr. 170067 of Erprobungs-kommando 262 a mechanic makes a final inspection of the aircraft's access panels and latches to make sure that all have been securely fastened. Note that the outer leading edge slot is in the open position, normal for a Me 262 on the ground while the inboard leading edge slot is stuck in the closed position.

The mechanic discovers the stuck automatic leading edge slot and proceeds carefully to rectify the problem using a pair of grips until the slot opens and shuts freely. Note the wire basket fitted to the engine intake intended to prevent the accidental ingestion of foreign objects during an engine run-up. All of Erprobungs-kommando 262's aircraft had white numbers painted on the fuselage just in front of the wing leading edge and outlined in black.

As luck would have it, my *Gruppe* was chosen to be retrained on this type of aircraft in May 1944. Unfortunately, I was unable to accompany them, because then I had to take over command of the *Geschwader*. After the *Gruppe* started retraining with some pilots already having become accustomed to this type of aircraft and others still being trained, an order was suddenly received from Supreme Command *'The Me 262 will not be employed as a fighter but as a bomber'*. So, after we were already up to our necks in trouble this type of aircraft began to be tried out as a bomber, as a fast bomber to be exact. A fierce struggle went on between *General* Galland, the *Reichsmarschall* and the *Führer*. But they stuck to it at the time, that the aircraft was to be tried out as a bomber. It was badly suited to that or not suited at all; its maximum load was one 500 kg bomb, and its flying time barely an hour."

When asked how the fuel consumption compared with that of a Messerschmitt 109, Kogler replied: "Of course with these turbine aircraft the consumption of fuel is terrific, corresponding with the performance. The aircraft needs about 1,800 litres of fuel to be able to fly for two hours, that's to say about twice as much as an ordinary twin-engined aircraft. But then you can fill it up with anything combustible such as Diesel or crude oil. This therefore obviates the need for various steps in industrial development such as the distillation of all kinds of fuel etc. In May last year there was still no acute shortage of petrol, there was still sufficient petrol available. Meanwhile the aircraft was actually employed as a bomber and dropped an odd 500 kg bomb here and there. As there was also no bomb sight for use at this speed, they didn't hit anything and now they have reached the point of saying that the aircraft is to be employed solely as a fighter, now when it is already too late."

Meanwhile, on 18 July, *EKdo 262* had suffered a severe blow when *Hptm.* Thierfelder was killed. There is some mystery surrounding the circumstances of his death. He had taken off in the Me 262 S6 to engage a formation of US bombers near Kaufering, 5 km (3 miles) north of Landsberg/Lech but failed to return. One report stated that he was shot down by about 15 P-51 Mustangs, probably from the US Fifteenth Air Force, but the more likely cause was a technical failure, possibly the ripping away of the stator rings in both engines. Thierfelder managed to bail out, but he was too low for his parachute to open.

Seven days later, a photographic reconnaissance Mosquito from 544 Squadron RAF piloted by Flt. Lt. A.E.Wall was intercepted by an Me 262 from *EKdo 262* near Munich. The RAF machine was flying at 30,000 ft (10,000 m) when the observer, Flg Off. A.S. Lobban was surprised to see it being rapidly overhauled by a twin-engined aircraft. He shouted a warning to Wall who pushed open the throttles, but the Me 262 continued to close at high speed. With great skill, Wall waited until the jet was within firing range, then wrenched the Mosquito into a tight turn so that the cannon shells passed harmlessly. After this manoeuvre had been repeated four times, the German pilot attempted an attack from below, but again Wall evaded him and dived for the safety of a cloud bank. After about three minutes he cautiously edged the Mosquito from the cloud cover over the Tyrol to find, to his relief, that there was no sign of the Me 262. The Mosquito landed safely at Fermo in Italy some three and a half hours after leaving Benson in southern England. No record of this action

Ground crew check the engine control switches of Me 262 A-1a "White 6" W.Nr. 170063 belonging to Erprobungskommando 262.

of
nal jet
l. In the
ost-flight

Me 262 A-1a W.Nr. 170063 "White 6", Erprobungskommando 262

The number "White 6" and yellow fuselage band was applied to this aircraft after it was delivered to Erprobungskommando 262 at Lechfeld, summer 1944. Similarly camouflaged to the other aircraft of Ekdo 262, this machine was assembled at Schwäbisch Hall. It was transferred to Kommando Nowotny at Hesepe in October 1944, suffering an accident on 6 November with Ofw. Helmut Baudach at the controls. This may also have been the aircraft in which Ofw. Helmut Lennartz of JG 7 crashed at Kolberg in April 1945. It is reported to have been test flown later in 1945 by Andrei Kochetov of the Soviet Air Force.

Me 262 A-1a W.Nr. 170067 "White 3", Erprobungskommando 262

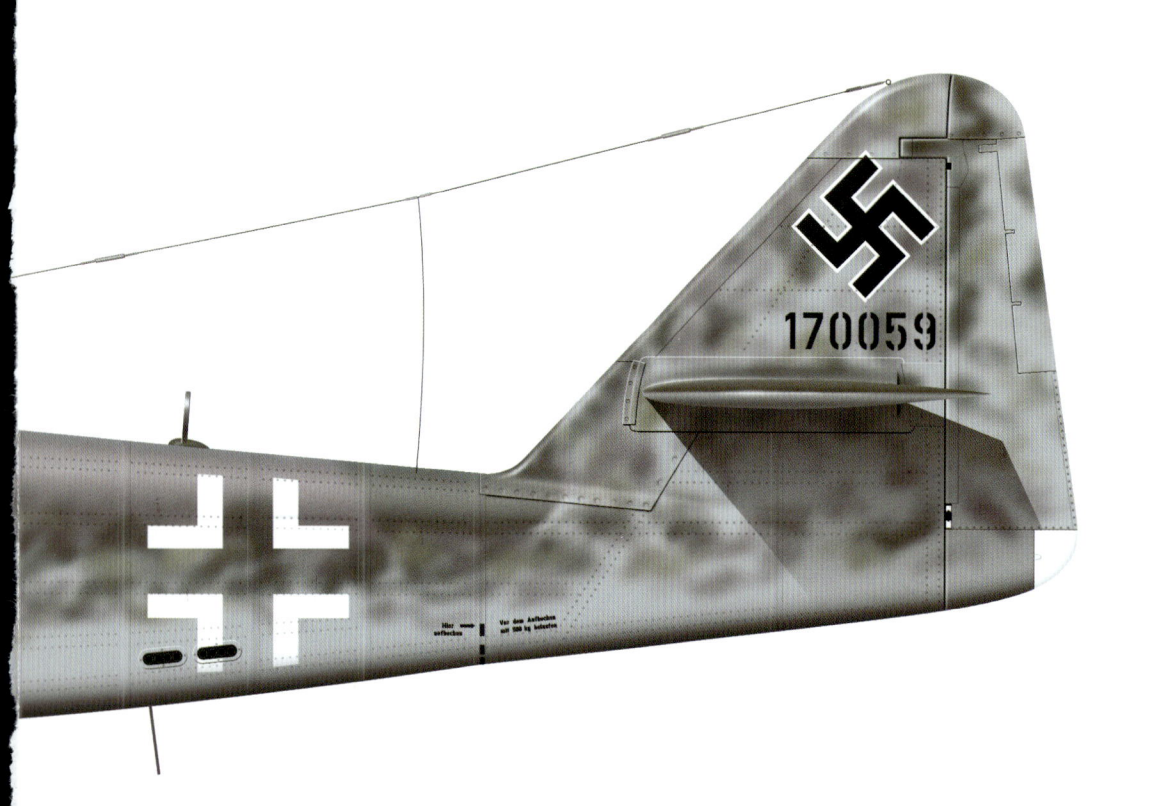

Me 262 A-1a W.Nr. 170059, Erpobungskommando 262

Shown here as it was delivered to Erprobungskommando 262 at Lechfeld, early July 1944. This aircraft was finished in dark grey (74) and medium grey (75) upper surfaces with pale blue grey (76) beneath with mottling down the fuselage sides and at this time no markings had been applied. The aircraft was later damaged due to a technical fault, the pilot, Lt. Hans Günter Müller, being unhurt. After being repaired, the aircraft was passed to KG 51.

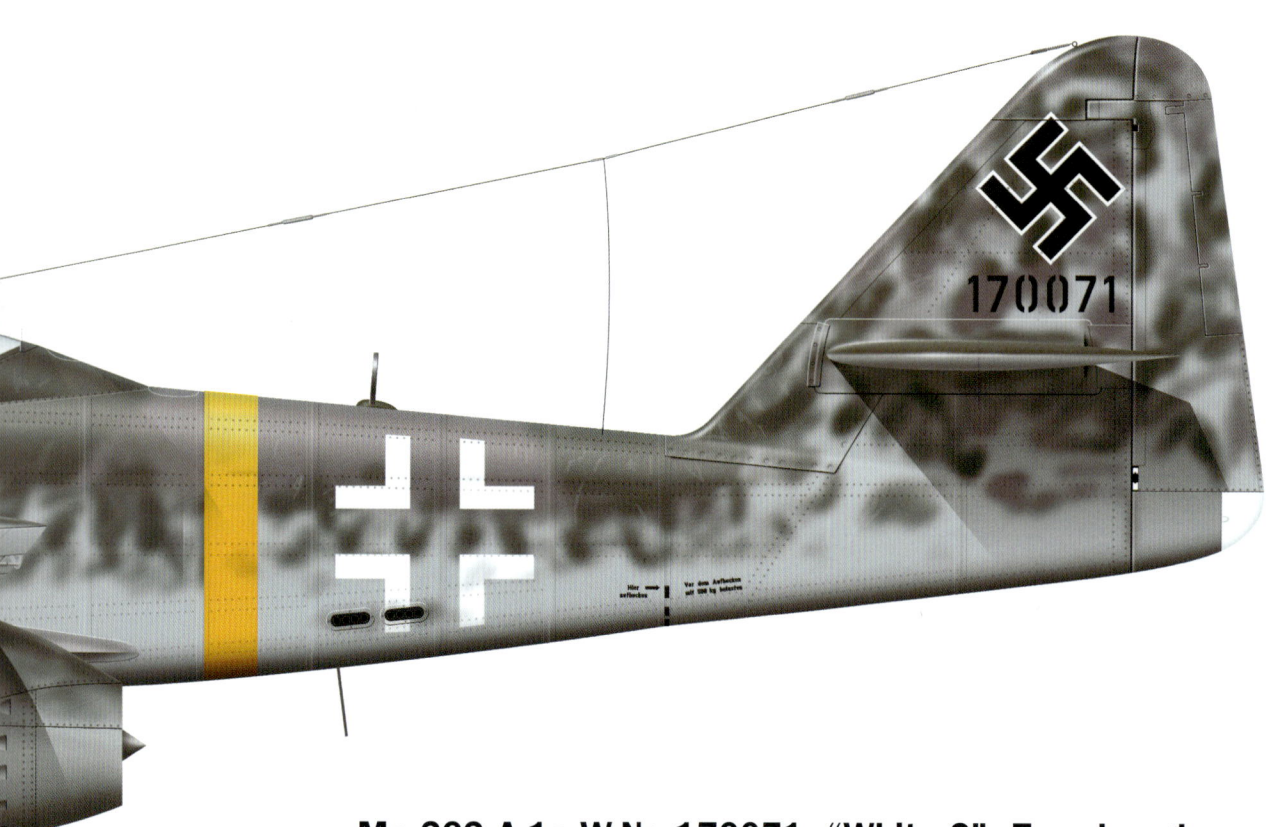

Me 262 A-1a W.Nr. 170071, "White 2", Erprobungkommando 262

The aircraft is shown here shortly after delivery to Erprobungskommando 262 at Lechfeld, in July 1944. It was similarly camouflaged to W.Nr. 170059, and carried a white number "2", thinly outlined in black, on the nose.
In common with other Ekdo 262 aircraft, a thin yellow (27) band (approximately 150 mm wide) was applied around the rear fuselage. This feature was later also carried by many Me 262s of Kommando Nowotny and EJG 2. "White 2" was later transferred to EJG 2 and flown by Maj. Erich Hohagen who abandoned it on an autobahn near Lechfeld in 1945.
Note the aircraft only has two gun ports.

170067

Vor dem Auftanken mit 100 kg betanken

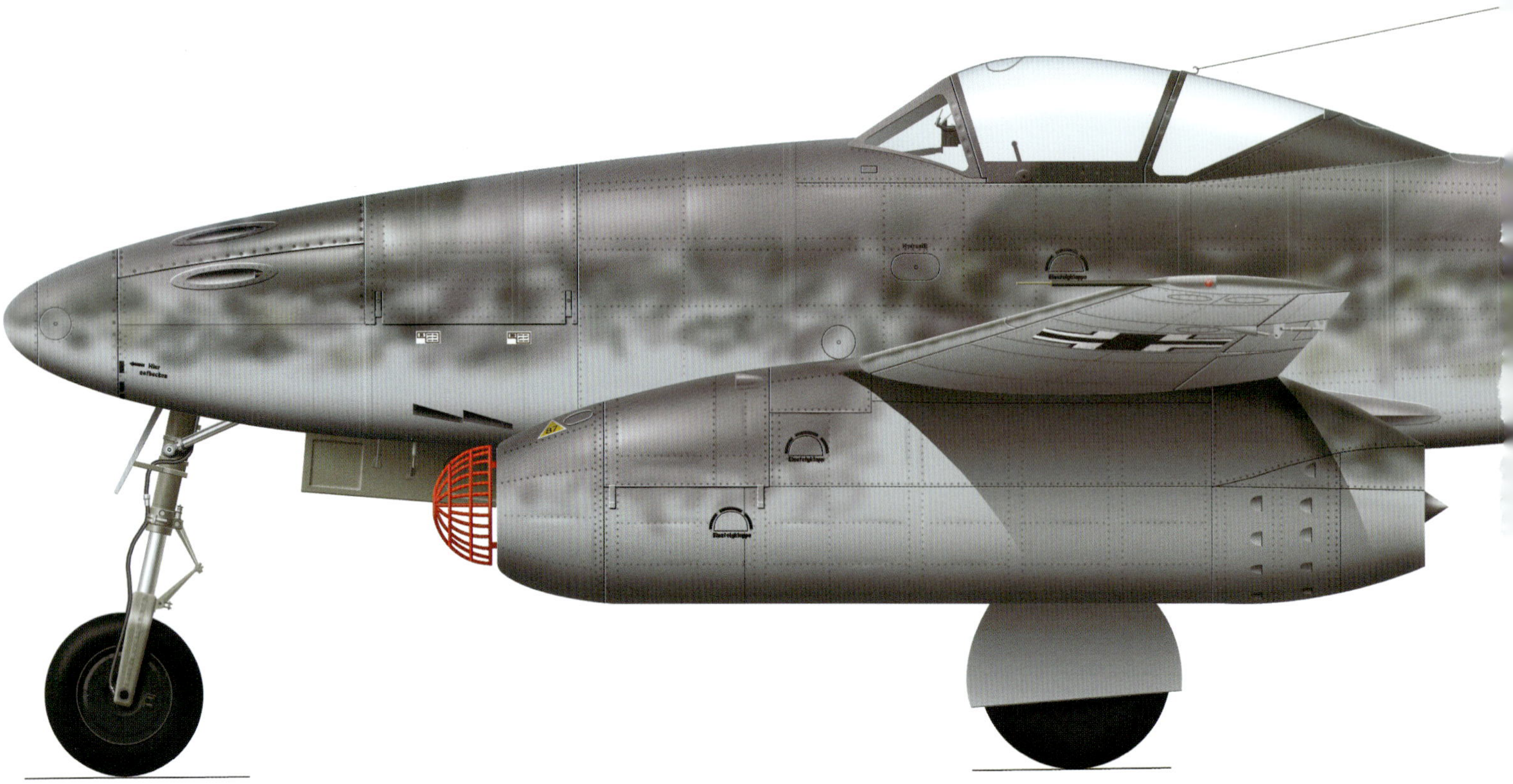

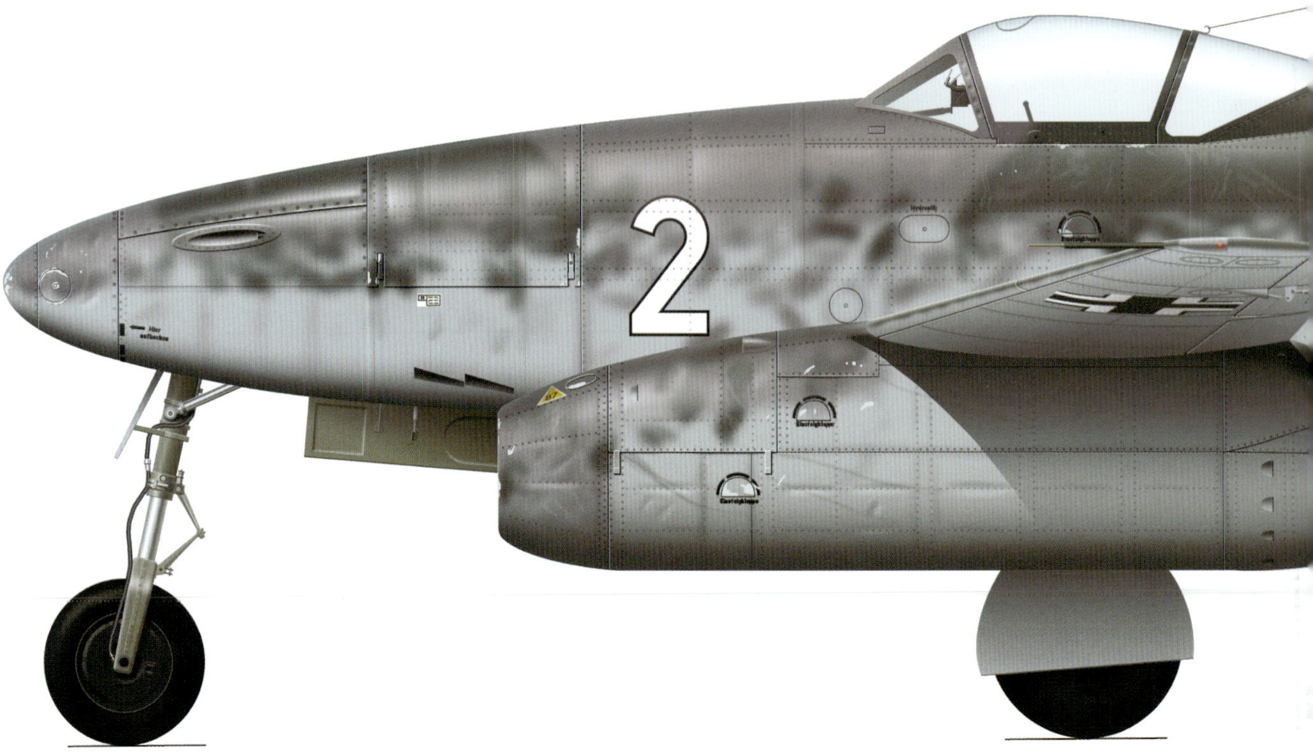
2

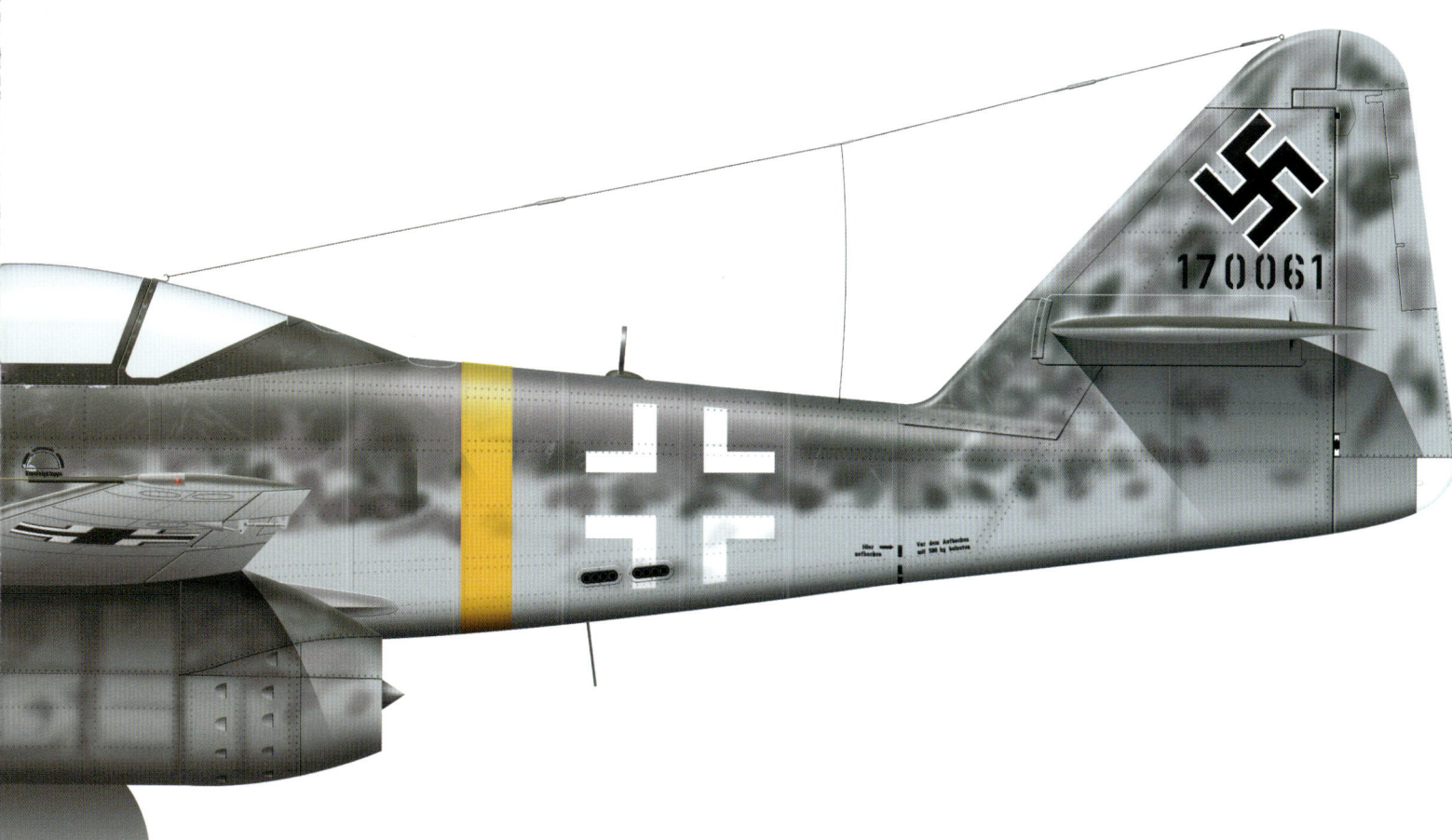

Me 262 A-1a W.Nr. 170061, "White 11", Erprobungskommando 262

Lechfeld summer 1944 and like many other Ekdo 262 aircraft, this A-1a was later transferred to III./EJG 2 where Lt. Harbot flew it in combat operation on 28 February 1945, then carrying the number "White 4". The aircraft was finally taken over by JV 44 on 26 April 1945 and was found at Innsbruck in May 1945

Lechfeld – Summer 1944 …

Accompanied by what was to become the familiar high pitched whine
turbojet engines, a Me 262, "White 5", from the world's first operatic
fighter unit, Erprobungskommando 262, taxies in towards its dispersa
foreground "White 6" and "White 3" undergo maintenance and pre-/p
checks. Note the variety of ground support equipment used.

"THE AIRCRAFT IS SIMPLY WONDERFUL" • 247

Continuing his checks, the mechanic examines the rear Zwiebel (onion) cone which could be adjusted in flight to increase and decrease the jet flow from the turbojet.

This close-up of the Jumo 004 B turbojet shows the intake cone with, in its centre, the pull ring for the Riedel two-stroke starter motor.

The yellow 87 octane triangle denotes the fuel filler point for the Riedel starter motor.

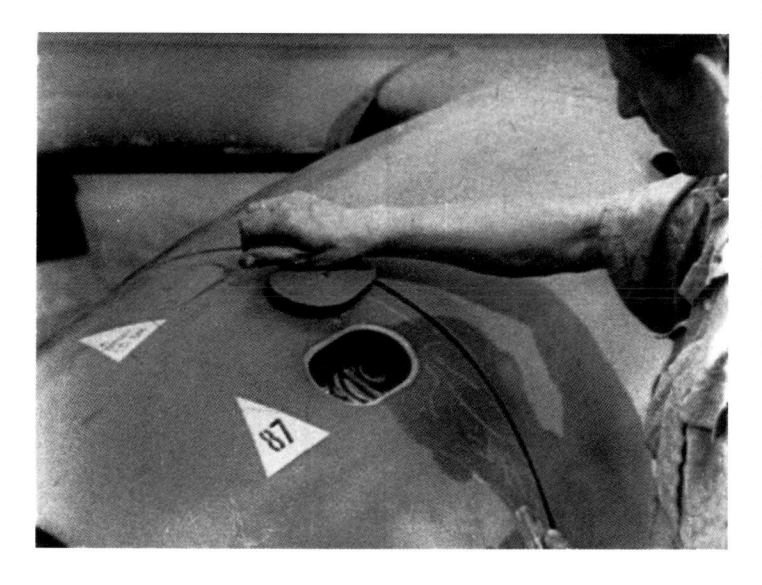

Above: In this sequence the mechanic removes the access cover to the Me 262's port engine and carries out routine checks. Note again the wire basket protecting the intake of the engine. The designs of these baskets and cover plates varied considerably. A case was reported of a ground crewman being almost suffocated by standing too close to the engine intake while it was being run up.

appears in the war diary of *EKdo 262*, but on the next day, *Lt.* Alfred 'Bubi' Schreiber, flying an Me 262 coded 'White 4' (W.Nr. 130017), claimed the destruction of a Mosquito over Bavaria. This was the first claim to be registered by an Me 262. Strangely, no indication of an RAF Mosquito having been lost on this day appears in RAF records and it is possible that the two dates have become confused, a not uncommon occurrence. It would have been easy for the *Luftwaffe* pilot to think that he had destroyed Wall's aircraft when it disappeared into the cloud bank.

By flying these operations, the Me 262 had claimed the distinction of becoming the world's first operational jet fighter and already, through their intelligence sources, some far-sighted Allied air commanders recognised the threat of German jet fighter development. As early as April 1944, Air Marshal Sir Arthur Coningham, commander of the British 2nd Tactical Air Force, whose responsibility it would be to provide close support to Montgomery's armies in north-west Europe following the Invasion, expressed his concern to a close friend: *"I'm getting into a private flurry at our delay in producing jet-propelled aircraft,"* wrote the tough New Zealander. *"(German) jets could wash away our great air superiority tomorrow."* The following month, Coningham told Air Chief Marshal Sir Trafford Leigh-Mallory, head of the Allied Expeditionary Air Force, that the introduction of German jet fighters would give the *Luftwaffe* "an immense advantage" and that all possible pressure must be brought to bear to assure early production of British jets. However, two months later, on 27 July, the British Gloster Meteor jet fighter flew its first sorties against V-1 flying bombs.

British jet research could be traced back to 1929 when a young RAF officer, Frank Whittle, put forward the first practical proposal for a turbojet engine. He filed his Provisional Patent Application on 6 January 1930, the Patent being granted 18 months later. Sadly for Whittle he met with much apathy and downright disinterest and it was not until July 1939 that the first official contract was placed for an aircraft to be powered by one of his engines. This machine, the Gloster E.28/39, made its first flight on 15 May 1941, powered by the Whittle W1 turbojet which produced 860 lbs (390 kg) thrust at 17,750 rpm. Even this early prototype outperformed the Spitfire and was successfully demonstrated before Winston Churchill a little later.

Owing to the problems being experienced with German air attacks, Sir Henry Tizard of the British Air Ministry and General 'Hap' Arnold of the USAAF decided that domestic turbojet construction should be supplemented by production from the General Electric company in the USA. On 1 October 1941, the disassembled W1X engine and a team from Frank Whittle's Power Jets company were flown to the USA in a B-24 Liberator. A set of drawings of the new Whittle W2B was also sent to the USA and by April 1942 General Electric were already bench testing the engine under the designation I-14. The turbojet was used to power America's first jet aircraft, the Bell XP-59 A Airacomet which flew for the first time on 2 October 1942, at Muroc Lake in California.

Even before the E.28/39 had made its first flight, a contract had been awarded by the British Air Ministry for a twin jet fighter under the designation F.9/40 that later became the Meteor. Because the Rover built W2B engines were only producing 1,000 lbs (450 kg) thrust at the time, the first prototype Meteor to fly was

Air Marshal Sir Arthur Coningham (left), commander of the British 2nd Tactical Air Force, warned fellow officers that the Me 262 could "wash away" Allied air superiority, giving the Luftwaffe an "immense advantage". Coningham is seen here in Normandy in June 1944 with Air Vice Marshal Harry Broadhurst (centre), commander 83 Group, 2nd TAF and Air Chief Marshal Sir Arthur Tedder, (right) deputy Allied Supreme Commander.

powered by Halford H.1 units. This event occurred on 15 March 1943, at Cranwell.

Many problems associated with the W2B engines were overcome after transfer of manufacture from Rover to Rolls Royce. The Meteor first flew with these engines, which were then renamed Welland, in June 1943. These units, which soon attained their design thrust of 1,700 lbs (770 kg), were chosen to power the first production model which received the designation Meteor I.

The first two production Meteor Is were delivered to 616 Squadron at Culmhead on 12 July 1944, and by the end of the month the unit had become operational at Manston in Kent with a mixture of Spitfires and seven Meteors. The initial operations against V-1 flying bombs met with little success because of problems with the guns jamming. The first success against a V-1 came on 4 August when Flg.Off. Dean eased the wingtip of his Meteor under the wing of a flying bomb and tipped it over so that it crashed in open country. Minutes later, a second kill was claimed by Flg. Off. Roger who shot down a V-1 in a more conventional manner. These were the first Allied claims by jet fighters.

Meanwhile *EKdo 262* continued operations with the Me 262. On 30 July, *Fhr.* Herbert Kaiser bailed out of W.Nr. 170058 due to an engine fire near Biberbach at 09.58 hours but he survived unhurt. Three days later the unit claimed its second victory, a reconnaissance Spitfire also destroyed by *Lt.* Schreiber.

On 5 August Thierfelder's place as commander of *EKdo 262* was taken by *Hptm.* Horst Geyer. Before taking over the Me 262 unit, Geyer had commanded *Erprobungskommando 25* (later JGr. 10), another experimental unit which was developing various weapons for use against

In England, Group Captain Frank Whittle put forward the first practical proposal for a turbojet engine, but due to lack of interest on the part of the British Air Ministry it was not until July 1939 that the first contract was placed for an aircraft powered by one of his engines.

Britain's first jet aircraft was the Gloster E28/39 Pioneer which first flew on 15 May 1941 powered by a Whittle W1 engine developing 860 lbs (390 kg) thrust.

Two Bell XP-59A Airacomets, America's first jet propelled aircraft. The upper aircraft shows the P-59A with the P-59B below. Following a visit by General Hap Arnold to Britain in June 1941, General Electric acquired the drawings of Whittle's W2B jet engine and built it under licence with the designation 1A. This engine, which produced 1,250 lbs (570 kg) thrust was used to power the Airacomet which made its first flight on 1 October 1942. Although the performance of the Airacomet was disappointing, two additional prototypes, thirteen pre-production and fifty production aircraft were built.

The Gloster E28/39, S/N W4041/G, takes off from the Royal Aircraft Establishment at Farnborough, England sometime in June 1944. The "G" element of the serial number denoted that the aircraft was to be kept under armed guard at all times whilst at the Farnborough testing and evaluation centre.

Right: The Gloster F.9/40, S/N DG204; this was the third prototype aircraft and was used to test the Metro-Vickers (Metrovick) F-2/2 and F-2/4 2,000 lb. (907 kg) thrust axial-flow units. It is interesting to note that like the Me 262, the British axial-flow engines were slung under the wing.

Left: The Gloster F.9/40, S/N DG202/G, was the first prototype interceptor but the fifth to fly. It was powered by two 1,000 lb. (454 kg) thrust Rover-built W.2B engines and was later used extensively to test the Rolls-Royce B.23 engine.

Allied heavy bomber formations. The *Kommando* also exchanged several other personnel with JGr. 10 at Parchim. At this stage the key personnel of *EKdo 262* were:

Kommandeur:	*Hptm.* Horst Geyer
Adjutant:	*Oblt.* Günther Wegmann
Major beim Stab:	*Hptm.* Heinrich Richter (JGr. 10)
Technical Officer:	*Oblt.* Georg Wiing (JGr. 10)
Signals Officer:	*Oblt.* Leitner
Ib/Wa. (weapons specialist):	*Oberinsp.* Tietze (JGr. 10)
IVa (administrative officer):	*Obzm.* König
IVb (medical officer):	*Oberarzt* Dr. Debus
Staffelkapitän of 8./ZG 26:	*Oblt.* Hans-Günther Müller
Staffelkapitän of 9./ZG 26:	*Oblt.* Paul Bley

On 8 August *Lt.* Joachim Weber of *EKdo 262* shot down the unit's second Mosquito, an aircraft from the US 802nd Reconnaissance Group, over the Ammer see, south-west of Munich. The report of this action was intercepted and decoded by the Allied 'Ultra'[2] code breaking team at Bletchley Park north of London. It was reported as follows: *"EKdo 262 at Lechfeld claims one Allied aircraft shot down. The headquarters of the Test Group at Rechlin communicated to Luftgau West France a list of Me 262 parts known to be scarce and says that it hasn't enough experience to show which parts are subject to wear and tear. It adds that any further questions about employment of the Me 262 should be addressed to the General of the Bomber Force."*

Seven days after Weber's victory, on 15 August, a Mosquito crewed by Capt. Saloman Pienaar and Lt. Archie Lockhart-Ross of 60 Squadron, South African Air Force, took off from San Severo in Italy to photograph Leipheim airfield. After flying up the Adriatic coast toward Prague, they turned to approach Munich from the north east. As Pienaar recalled: "I wasn't due to fly at all that day. Intelligence had called for a quick urgent flight over the Black Forest area. Normally you would never volunteer for another man's flight; it was considered very unlucky. But the pilot due to fly that day had a rotten cold and the other who might have stood in for him was at the end of his tour, so we were keeping him for the milk runs which was the squadron tradition. We were at 30,000 ft. Nice afternoon it was too,

The Gloster Meteor F-1 was the second production Meteor and was powered by two 2,600 lb. (1,179 kg) thrust Rolls-Royce Welland jet units and later by W2/700 engines. The aircraft was finally broken up in April 1956. Some of the first missions flown by the RAF's Gloster Meteor-equipped 616 Squadron involved the interception of German high-speed V-1 flying bombs (*inset*) which had been launched from bases in France across the Channel against southern England.

A Mosquito piloted by Captain Saloman 'Pi' Pienaar, 60 Squadron, SAAF, encountered a Me 262, probably from Erprobungskommando 262, whilst photographing airfields in southern Germany on 15 August 1944. Pienaar recalled: "I took my eyes off that speck for only a few seconds, but when I glanced again, he was right on my tail, climbing into the attack ..." The Me 262 attacked the Mosquito several times shooting away the port flap, port aileron and the mainspar of the port elevator. Despite this, Pienaar and his navigator/observer Lt. Archie Lockhart-Ross, returned to their base in San Severo, Italy and their aircraft was subsequently deemed unserviceable as a result of the damage inflicted by the German jet. Pienaar (right) and Lockhart-Ross are seen here at San Severo beside their damaged aircraft

In August 1944, Hptm. Horst Geyer (centre) took over command of Erprobungskommando 262 following Werner Thierfelder's death. He is seen here in 1943, wearing a highly prized USAAF flying jacket whilst commander of Erprobungskommando 25, the Luftwaffe's air-to-air weapons testing and evaluation unit based at Achmer.

warm with a little broken cloud as we headed up the Adriatic towards Prague.

"We turned off north-north-east of Munich and flew over an airfield named Memmingen, but I wasn't feeling very happy at all; it was too quiet, no flak, no enemy fighters. We knew the enemy fighters well and they were no match for the Mossie, but the word was that this new fighter that they had was something else again.

"Archie was over the bomb-sight directing things for the six-inch and 12-inch mapping cameras, but we were also carrying the big 36-inch camera, which is for detail, and with that camera in operation you have to fly dead straight and level, otherwise you blur the photographs.

"At the next airfield, just a strip in fact, and very well camouflaged, Archie shouted: *"I can see it ... There's a fighter taking off at a helluva speed!"* I asked Archie to keep an eye on it because I was going nice and straight and level but a few minutes later I picked up a speck in my rear-vision mirrors, directly behind the tail, but just a speck.

"Up to that time nothing could get at the Mossies, but this fighter must have climbed at well over 5,000 ft per minute, so I didn't dismiss this from my mind at all, especially when Archie said: *"That's the fighter!"*

"I took my eyes off that speck for only a few seconds, but when I glanced again there he was right on my tail, climbing into the attack a little and it didn't look like a normal aeroplane - that's for sure. This wasn't a normal fighter at all.

"So instead of turning left, I took the throttles, pitch levers and at the same time I hit the drop tank button and then I turned it to starboard. Just as I did so he fired and he hit the left aileron and blew it away completely. I was still in the turn to the right when this lot came off. I could see it out of the corner of my eye but I didn't want to look too closely. Suddenly the aeroplane flicked left - it was losing all that lift on the left aileron, and the next moment I was in a spiral. In a spiral normally, the first thing to do is to roll it and get the power off, and I had the throttles right back, but it didn't make any difference; the boost was way up there and I could hear the engines screaming, but the plane was still going. I had full right rudder and when I pushed the stick forward, it just made a little ripple ... that's all.

"It was down, down and when I heard the high blowers cut out I knew I must have been down to 19,000 ft. Then I saw the two throttles way back and the two pitch levers way up forward, so I pulled back the starboard engine pitch lever, and as I did so I could hear the revs come down and the plane just came back. So I was flying it with the stick right over to the right,

Me 262 A-1a W.Nr. 170045 'White 5' of Erprobungskommando 262 at Lechfeld, August 1944

Similarly camouflaged to the other aircraft of Erprobungskommando 262, this machine was assembled at Schwäbisch Hall. It was transferred to Kommando Nowotny at Hesepe in October 1944, suffering an accident on 6 November with Ofw. Helmut Baudach at the controls. After repair it was delivered to I./KG(J) 54.

Above: An Erprobungskommando 262 mechanic checks the instrumentation in the cockpit of a Me 262. Note the thickness of the frontal armoured glass windscreen panel.

In the above sequence of photographs Me 262 A-1a, W.Nr. 170045, "White 5" is seen here shortly after landing at Lechfeld. One member of the ground crew has climbed on to the wing to assist the pilot in opening the aircraft's canopy and to unfasten his harness straps. Simultaneously, another mechanic approaches to attach a wire "basket" over the port-side turbojet intake and fits chocks to the mainwheel.

The instrument panel of an Me 262 A-1a showing the six major instruments at top left: airspeed indicator, artificial horizon, rate of climb indicator, altimeter, compass and AFN2 blind landing indicator. To the right are the engine instruments, one for each turbojet comprising tachometers, temperature, fuel and oil pressure gauges.

"THE AIRCRAFT IS SIMPLY WONDERFUL" • 255

A sequence of photographs showing the refuelling of Erprobungskommando 262's Me 262 A-1a, "White 6", possibly W.Nr. 170063, at Lechfeld, summer, 1944.

An airfield control officer watches as an Opel Blitz fuel truck approaches. Note the dark sand and green camouflage pattern applied to the truck and the clearly marked "J2" fuel tank; J2 was a low-grade fuel similar to diesel oil and usually readily available during 1944 despite the transport and production difficulties facing the Third Reich at the time.

As the truck halts, a mechanic takes the pump hose and fits the nozzle into the aircraft's fuel intake. The Me 262 A-1a held a total of 2,570 litres (565 Imp gallons) of fuel in its four tanks, providing it with a range of 845 km (525 miles) at 6,000 m (19,686 ft).

Me 262 A-1a, W.Nr. 170061 "White 11" of Erprobungs-kommando 262 at Lechfeld, summer 1944. Most of the unit's aircraft all had narrow yellow bands painted around the fuselage, forward of the national insignia. The inset photograph shows ground crew working on the tail elevator mechanism of "White 11".

right rudder full on and the left engine screaming its head off and boiling. The right engine revs had fallen, but the boost was still way up at the top.

"I was still trying to get things straight when Archie shouted: *"Look out, here he comes again!"* So all I did was to let go of everything and the aeroplane just flicked, to the left this time, and I saw him go past. I could see the Me 262 pilot was looking back at us ... He was a smart flyer and every time he made a pass he pulled up into the sun. He really was playing around with us with his enormous speed, but Archie was a wonderful fellow in these moments. He kept calling out when the Me 262 was a thousand yards away... firing range... but every time I turned to stay inside him I had to lose a bit of height.

"The third really concentrated attack was made when I was down to seven or eight thousand feet, but I was already making a little progress towards Switzerland and there was some low cloud, so I dived into it. But I realised that each time I evaded I had to lose some altitude, so that as he made his second run in, I said to Archie: *"Well, here goes..."* and I flipped the aircraft round and headed straight for the Me 262. After all, if we had to go, we might as well have taken him with us! I saw him go straight over me ... I could just see his belly ... Then I dived into low cloud again. This was somewhere near Lake Constance. The head-on gave me a little more time, because the Me 262 had quite a wide radius of turn, but when I got into the clouds and looked at the artificial horizon it was perpendicular.

"The final attack came at 500 ft, but I think by then this chap was running short of fuel and I just saw him go over me and break off. It was just as well because I couldn't fly the Mossie above 500 ft or the left the engine would boil. The throttle was jammed full on and the linkage was damaged by that shell in the main spar. The right engine was still at full boost, but we reduced revs and that's the way we made it out, just skimming the hills and then losing altitude."

Eventually the crippled Mosquito managed to land back at San Severo where both crew members were awarded the DFC. Although the aircraft was written off, the mission did achieve one conspicuous success as its cameras managed to record some clear views of the Me 262.

On the same day, *Fw.* Helmut Lennartz and *Ofw.* Kreutzberg of *EKdo 262* were scrambled from Lechfeld to intercept a B-17 near Stuttgart. It was attacked by Lennartz who blew off its port wing with his 30 mm cannon. Three days later, on 18 August, a Mosquito of 544 Squadron piloted by Flt. Lt. F.L. Dodd was intercepted by an Me 262 of *EKdo 262* over Giebelstadt but this time the British aircraft managed to escape without damage.

On 18 August, the 8. *Staffel* of ZG 26 moved to Rechlin-Lärz to form the first *Einsatzkommando* for operations against Allied reconnaissance aircraft. The unit's pilots were *Oblt.* Müller, *Lt.* Weber and *Fw.* Lennartz with *Lt.* Preusker as fighter controller.

Two days later an American fighter pilot reported on an encounter he had with a Me 262. It was obvious that the jet was still very new to Allied pilots: *"Blue Flight was flying top cover at 13,000 feet while we had two flights on the deck. We were flying north when I saw a ship very similar to an A-20 at 3 o'clock down sun. This ship seemed to be trying for a position to make a pass on us. I turned into the sun from 6 o'clock. We turned into this attack, but due to the tremendous speed of the E/A, I was unable to get my guns on him. He started firing at about 1,000 yards range. We easily outmanoeuvred him and when he dived passed us, I realised the E/A was jet-propelled. Although the fuselage and tail were the same as the Me 262, the wings and turbo nacelles were different. The wing has a definite taper on the trailing edge and the turbo nacelles do not extend past the trailing edge as does the Me 262. The speed of this E/A makes it possible for one ship to be in the sun and another ship on the down sun side at all times. When we turned into the attack from the sun the stooge ship attacked from 6 o'clock. In this manner the E/A exchanged positions for another pass. The ship started firing at estimated 1,000 yards and seemed to have from six to eight guns in the nose. It is this pilot's opinion that this aircraft has no guns in the wings. All passes made on us by this aircraft were from a dive of between 45 and 69 degrees. The dive was held until he was approximately 7,000 feet below us, at which time he resumed straight and level for approximately 10 miles before pulling the nose up to regain altitude. The pattern of this pass was very big and we had not wanted to stay with this aircraft. I am certain we could have lost them by diving to the deck. Either of the two ships would attack if the other was not in the perfect position. The attacks were well co-ordinated. They did not try to turn with us, they continued their dive after we had easily evaded their guns. Care should be taken when breaking into this type of aircraft. The break should start much sooner than is necessary when fighting Bf 109s or Fw 190s. This is due to the tremendous speed of the E/A. The fight lasted about 10 minutes. We had no casualties or*

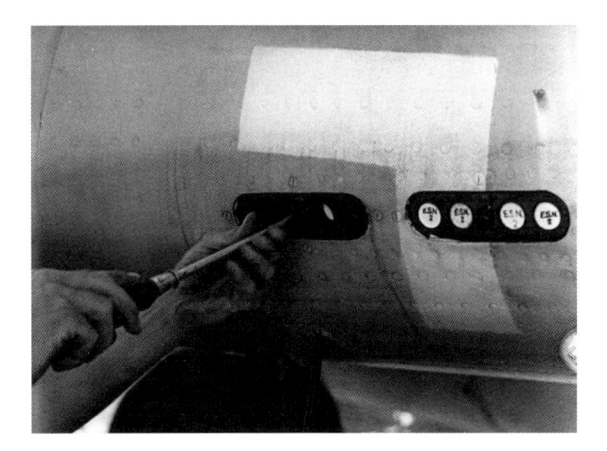

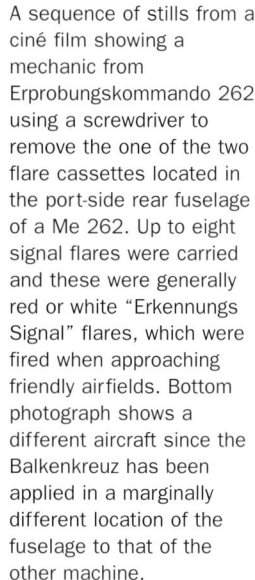

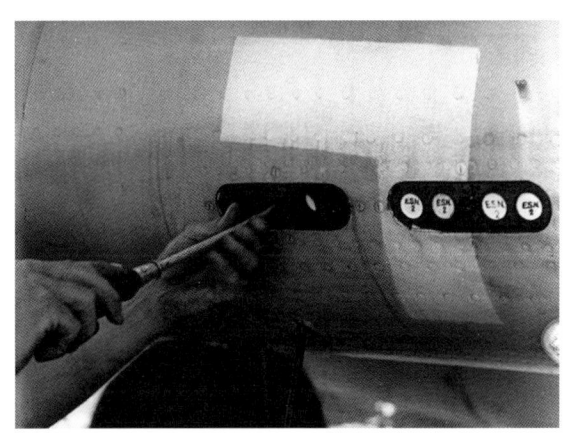

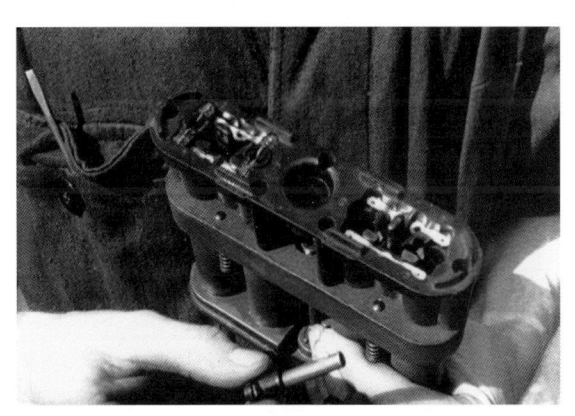

A sequence of stills from a ciné film showing a mechanic from Erprobungskommando 262 using a screwdriver to remove the one of the two flare cassettes located in the port-side rear fuselage of a Me 262. Up to eight signal flares were carried and these were generally red or white "Erkennungs Signal" flares, which were fired when approaching friendly airfields. Bottom photograph shows a different aircraft since the Balkenkreuz has been applied in a marginally different location of the fuselage to that of the other machine.

damage to the E/A and they, none to us. The E/A started to fly away. I chased with an airspeed of 350 mph indicated to 15,000 feet. The E/A was out of sight at about 10,000 feet in approximately five seconds time."

On 24 August, *Ofw.* Helmut Baudach of *EKdo 262* claimed an F-5 Lightning[3] reconnaissance aircraft although, unaccountably, this was described as the third Me 262 victory in a letter from Professor Messerschmitt to Baudach written on 4 September:

> *"You have flown our latest jet fighter in its first engagements, and under your control the Me 262 has victoriously withstood its baptism of fire.*
>
> *"I congratulate you on this great success which for me too means the joy of knowing that our latest design has been proved, and the certainty that air supremacy over our homeland can be regained.*
>
> *"In this sense I couple with my congratulations on the third victory in the Me 262 my best wishes for many further successful air battles."*

Two days later *Lt.* Schreiber shot down a 60 Squadron Mosquito and *Ofw.* Recker a Spitfire, possibly from 683 Squadron. Also on 26 August, the German army were issued with the first aircraft recognition details of the Me 262:

Subject: New operational aircraft type
Gen.Kdo.LXIV.A.K. informs via telex:

> *"New operational aircraft type Me 262*
>
> *Rough description:*
>
> *Monoplane two engines, single tail fin, no undercarriage, rectangular centre section, horizontal tailplanes placed high, no engine noise, strong whistling sound."*

At the end of August 1944 a document was issued by the *General der Jagdflieger* detailing the proposed fighter training programme for the Me 262. Three *Einsatzkommandos* were to be established at Lechfeld, Rechlin-Lärz and Erfurt-Bindersleben, each being led by an officer with the powers of a *Staffelkapitän*. They were to iron out technical problems, develop tactical procedures and evolve a training programme for the Me 262 fighter which could be used by single aircraft, and on *Rotte*, *Schwarm*, *Staffel* and *Gruppe* operations. At the same time III./ZG 26, comprising the *Stabskompanie* and the 8. and 9. *Staffeln*, was to continue training under Messerschmitt's aegis at Leipheim, Schwäbisch

The Kettenkrad semi-tracked motor cycle was widely used to tow the Me 262 when on the ground. Here, an aircraft of Erprobungskommando 262 is towed under its camouflaged dispersal at Lechfeld during the summer of 1944.

A typical scene at Lechfeld during the summer of 1944. Pilots and ground personnel of Erprobungskommando 262 use landlines to communicate with other members of the unit elsewhere on the airfield. Third from left on the telephone is Lt. Alfred "Bubi" Schreiber whilst to his left is Lt Joachim Weber. At left is one of the unit's signals NCOs, Fw. Puttkammer.

Hall and Lechfeld. The role of *Gruppenkommandeur*, was to be undertaken by the *Kommandoführer* of *EKdo 262*, Hptm. Geyer. 7./ZG 26 was incorporated into II./ZG 1.

A list of all ground equipment to be delivered to the unit, including radar, radio and associated apparatus was given and the following pilot training programme proposed:

a) *A-Schule* (preliminary flying training)
b) *Jagdschule* (fighter training)
c) *Jagdergänzungsgruppe* (operational fighter training)
d) Specialist Me 262 training using such aircraft as the Si 204, Bf 110 or Me 210. The Ta 154 and Me 262 were to be used for final jet fighter training. (The Ta 154 was proposed mainly because it, like the Me 262, was a twin-engined aircraft with a tricycle undercarriage).
e) Front-line training with the Me 262.

The tactical development sections of the *Kommando* were to be placed under the command of *Maj.* Walter Nowotny, a 23 year-old Austrian fighter ace who had already claimed 255 victories on the Eastern Front with JG 54 and was one of the *Luftwaffe's* most popular young pilots. The authors consider that although an excellent combat pilot of rare ability, Nowotny was perhaps entirely the wrong type of person to oversee the introduction of such a radical aircraft as the Me 262 into operational service. An older and more technically qualified pilot would have been a better choice.

One of Nowotny's great friends at this time was *Lt.* Karl 'Quax' Schnörrer, a pilot who initially had great difficulty in handling the Bf 109 during landing, damaging no fewer than three such machines in his early career. Nicknamed somewhat unfairly after an accident-prone cartoon character, "*Quax der Bruchpilot*", Schnörrer had been Nowotny's wingman in Russia with JG 54 for a considerable time and eventually won the *Ritterkreuz* in recognition of his 46 aerial victories. In November 1943, he was badly injured when his Fw 190 A-5 was shot down by flak. As he recalled:

"On 12 November 1943, after shooting down by 36th Russian aircraft, I was shot down and badly injured when I bailed out too low for my parachute to open. I suffered concussion, my ribs were broken, both knees broken, arms broken. A German infantry unit rescued me from no-man's land. General Ritter von Greim[4] ordered that I should be flown back to Germany in his personal He 111 to receive the best treatment that was possible. Nowotny escorted me back. Once every three weeks he would visit me in hospital and bring me food, drink and

WALTER NOWOTNY

Born on 7 December 1920 at Gmünd in Austria, Nowotny joined the Luftwaffe on 1 October 1939 but did not fly his first operational missions until February 1941 with 9./JG 54. He claimed his first victories on 19 July 1941, shooting down three Soviet I-153s. He was awarded the Knight's Cross after scoring his 56th victory on 4 September 1942, and took over command of 9./JG 54 on 25 October. During the month of June 1943 he shot down no fewer than 41 aircraft, with another nine on 13 August and a further seven on 21st. On this day he took over command of I./JG 54, and on 4 September he became only the fourth pilot in the world to claim 200 victories. In September he was awarded the Oakleaves *and* Swords to the Knight's Cross and his victory tally increased to 250 less than a month later. On 19 October he became only the eighth person to be awarded the Diamonds to the Knight's Cross. His operational career then came to a temporary halt when he was transferred to take over command of the fighter training unit, JG 101 in February 1944.

Major Walter Nowotny (right) seen here with Professor Kurt Tank, chief designer of the Focke-Wulf company, during a high-profile visit to the Focke-Wulf factory at Bad Eilsen, 21 December 1943.

Lt. Karl "Quax" Schnörrer (right) talks tactics with Walter Nowotny in Russia in 1943, whilst both men were serving with JG 54. Schnörrer would go on to fly with Erprobungskommando 262, Kommando Nowotny and JG 7. He would claim 11 jet "kills" before being injured on 30 March 1945 whilst bailing out of his jet fighter. Eight days earlier he received the Ritterkreuz.

cigarettes. One day Nowotny said to me: *'Quax, we are going to get a very new aircraft, a jet fighter'*. I later made my first flight in the Me 262 in June 1944, still with my legs in plaster. There were no two-seaters at that time, but I did do some flying with the Bf 110 to become familiar with a twin-engined aircraft. The first flight gave me a wonderful feeling of effortless speed and power.

"Before flying the Me 262 I had three to four days at a ground school learning about the new engines followed by fourteen days of theory. The early engines only flew for about twelve hours before the turbines had to be changed. We had to be very careful with handling the throttles. We had to advance them only very slowly or there was a risk of fire. The Riedel starter would run the engine up to 1,800 rpm then we would use C-3 fuel to light up the Jumo. Then we had to advance the throttles slowly until 3,000 rpm was reached and we could switch to J-2 fuel. Between 6,000 and 8,000 rpm the throttles could be moved a little faster. When 8,400 rpm was reached, we released the brakes and off we went. With fuel for only 40 to 60 minutes the Me 262s were usually started up in position to begin the take-off run. We certainly could not spend ten minutes on the ground taxying. When we were off the ground we had to retract the undercarriage.

"The other pilots advised me that flying was not difficult, *but* to do everything in the climb, not in the descent. They told me that if you got into a dive and let the speed rise above 1,000 km/h (620 km/h) you would not get out of it. Later, between March and April 1945, a new type of control column was fitted to all Me 262s. The other problem was that you had to be careful not to throttle back too far when flying at altitude or the engines would flame out."

By the end of August 1944 the two *Einsatzkommando* at Lechfeld and Lärz were already operational, the third unit, under the command of *Oblt.* Günther Wegmann, leaving for Erfurt-Bindersleben on 22 September. Four days later the *General der Jagdflieger* issued an order which revised the earlier proposals. Firstly, III./ZG 26 was to be renamed III./JG 6. At the same time: *"...the Kommando at Schwäbisch Hall, Leipheim, Erfurt-Bindersleben and Lärz together with elements of the Stabskompanie, the entire signals platoon and part of EKdo 262 were to form a new Gruppe under the command of Major Nowotny. On 27 September this Gruppe would transfer from its former bases to Achmer near Osnabrück. The remaining elements of III./ZG 26 and EKdo 262 would be combined into one unit which, with the assignment of new personnel, would form the new Erprobungskommando 262."*

Previously, on 5 September, *Lt.* Schreiber from *EKdo 262* at Lechfeld had shot down an American Spitfire XI flown by Lt. Robert Hilborn of the 7th Photo Recon Group based at Mount Farm. He was attacked over Stuttgart and 'shredded' by 30 mm cannon fire from the Me 262. He bailed out and was taken prisoner. Next day *Ofw.* Göbel intercepted a RAF Mosquito which he claimed destroyed. This may have been a 540 Squadron aircraft piloted by Sqd. Ldr. Fleming which was reported missing. The unit intercepted another Me 262 over Aschaffenburg on 9 September and two days later US heavy bombers reported the first engagement with jet fighters when an Eighth Air Force formation was attacked near Leipzig. In fact the German aircraft were Me 163 rocket fighters from I./JG 400 based at Brandis but a P-51 Mustang piloted by Lt. William A Jones of the US 339th Fighter Group was shot down by *Ofw.* Helmut Baudach of *EKdo 262*.

On 13 September 1944 the second US Eighth Air Force claim was made against a jet when Lt. John A. Walker flying a P-51 of the 364th Fighter Group, damaged an Me 262 south of Stralsund. This was probably an aircraft from the Lärz *Kommando*. *Lt.* Joachim Weber claimed two Mosquitoes (his second and third jet victories) one on 14 September and one on the 18th. These were probably aircraft from 540 and 544 Squadron respectively.

On 23 September *Erprobungskommando 262* declared a strength of 12 aircraft and 17 crews. Four days later, in what appears to have been a mainly paper transaction, the unit was redesignated 10./EJG 2. Horst Geyer, the commander of the unit, remembered nothing of this redesignation, and even *Luftwaffe* records seem confused. On 14 October a pilot from the

Me 262s of Erprobungskommando 262 lined up at Lechfeld, September 1944. Nearest the camera, an NCO pilot and member of the ground crew are in discussion on the nose of Me 262 A-1a "White 2", W.Nr. 170071, whilst "White 3", W.Nr. 170087 and W.Nr. 170045, "White 5" can be seen parked in the next positions. Note that "White 2" only has two gun ports but four shell cartridge ejection chutes.

Major Georg-Peter Eder, former Kommandeur of II./JG 26, was appointed commander of 3. Staffel, Kommando Nowotny in October 1944. Awarded the Eichenlaub to the Ritterkreuz in November 1944, he would become one of the Luftwaffe's leading jet aces.

Lt. Urban L. Drew of the US 361st Fighter Group became the first American pilot to score two jet "kills" in one day when he shot down the Me 262s piloted by Oblt. Paul Bley and Lt. Gerhard Kobert. This took place on 7 October 1944.

unit, *Ofäh*. Erich Haffke, was killed in a crash at Hochstadt/Donau. Different sources give his unit as *Erprobungskommando 262* and 10./EJG 2.

By this time the establishment of the new *Kommando Nowotny* had been set at three *Staffeln* of 16 aircraft each, with four machines allocated to the *Gruppenstab*.

The leading unit personnel were:

KOMMANDOFÜHRER	*Maj.* Walter Nowotny
ADJUTANT	*Oblt.* Günther Wegmann
TECHNICAL OFFICER	*Hptm.* Streicher
1. STAFFELKAPITÄN	*Oblt.* Paul Bley
2. STAFFELKAPITÄN	*Oblt.* Alfred Teumer
3. STAFFELKAPITÄN	*Hptm.* Georg-Peter Eder

Eder, who had been awarded the *Ritterkreuz* in June 1944 and was to receive the Oak Leaves in November, was an experienced fighter pilot who had previously commanded II./JG 26. He did not transfer to *3./Kommando Nowotny* until 8 October but then led this unit and 11./JG 7 until February 1945. On 27 September *Kommando Nowotny* received orders to transfer to Achmer and Hesepe near Osnabrück for operations against Allied bomber formations. By this time the unit had about thirty Me 262s divided between the three *Staffeln*. The unit actually moved to its new bases on 3 and 4 October, but on the second day the engine of *Hptm.* Teumer's aircraft, W.Nr. 170044, flamed out as he attempted to land at Hesepe and he was killed in the resulting crash and fire. His place as commander of *2./Kommando Nowotny* was taken by *Lt.* Franz Schall. On the same day this pilot escaped unhurt when his aircraft crashed on landing at Waggum owing to a technical failure.

The unit flew its first operational sortie on 7 October when it intercepted four USAAF bomber formations attacking targets in the Magdeburg area. The first force was to bomb Pölitz, the second Ruhland, the third Böhlen, Lützkendorf, Merseberg and Leuna and the fourth Magdeburg and Kassel. *Lt.* Schall and *Fw.* Heinz Lennartz of the *2. Staffel* took off from Hesepe and each destroyed a B-24, but the *1. Staffel* was not so lucky. As *Oblt.* Bley, *Lt.* Gerhard Kobert and *Ofäh.* Heinz Russel began their take-off runs from Achmer they were spotted by Lt. Urban L. Drew of the US 361st Fighter Group flying a P-51 Mustang *"Detroit Miss"*. Diving from 5,000 metres (16,000 ft) the American fighter opened fire first on Russel's aircraft which resulted in the collapse of the undercarriage and the Me 262 skidding along the runway on its engines. Russel escaped unhurt, but Kobert and Bley were not so fortunate. At 300 metres (1,000 ft) both were hit by a hail of machine-gun fire, the former's Me 262 (W.Nr. 110405) exploding in a ball of flame, the latter (W.Nr. 170307), its controls shot away, also crashing but not before Bley managed to bail out at low altitude. Drew thus became the first pilot to score two jet "kills" in one day.

This disaster led Nowotny to request conventional fighter cover for the *Kommando's* bases, and shortly afterwards, III./JG 54 under *Hptm*. Robert Weiss was transferred to nearby Oldenburg. This unit had just re-equipped with the new long-nose Fw 190 D-9 powered by a Jumo 213 A engine. Its arrival prevented a repetition of the disaster, but Weiss's unit often had to fight off determined attacks by Allied fighter-bombers. During one of the first of these actions, on 15 October, 9./JG 54 lost four Fw 190s.

By this time the appearance of the Me 262 and Me 163 jet and rocket fighters was beginning to worry the leaders of the USAAF daylight bombing offensive. To give their bombers some experience in combating the menace, a series of tactical trials, organised by the US 65th Fighter Wing and RAF Fighter Command, were carried out between 10 and 17 October 1944. For these trials four RAF Meteor jets were flown to the USAAF base at Debden under the command of W/Cmdr. Andrew McDowell of 616 Squadron.

During the first trial, on 10 October 120 B-24s from the 2nd Bombardment Group rendezvoused with a fighter screen provided by the US 4th Fighter Group. Two missions were flown by the Meteors. During the first, two types of attacks were made; from head-on and from 4 o'clock astern. On the second mission attacks were made from head-on and dead astern. These revealed three main points. The first was that close escort was useless due to the high speed of the jet aircraft. The second suggested that the defending fighters should fly at least 5,000 feet (1,500 m) above the bombers and at the same distance to the side to give them time to intercept. The third showed that the lead elements of the bomber formation should have their escort positioned well above them to allow defence against head-on attacks. The trials were to prove that hit and run tactics by the jet fighters were very effective, and even in a dogfight the Meteor was well able to look after itself.

After the trials had been completed, a series of reports were made on their progress by the pilots concerned. A Captain from Red Flight of the US 4th Fighter Group recounted: "Six to eight sightings of the jets were made and a similar number of attempts were made to intercept. The jet passes were very good from the attack point of view and were made from 12 and 6 o'clock. Red flight was positioned 5,000 feet (1,500 m) above and half a mile (8,000 m) out in front. The jets came in on a 10 or 15 degree dive through the bomber formation. The escort fighters rolled over in a dive to try to get enough speed to intercept. For all interceptions except one we began too late. Once I got up to 500 mph (800 km/h) in a dive but I overshot, getting in front of the jet, but the rest of the flight were behind it."

Another pilot, from White Flight of the US 355th Fighter Group reported: "Approximately eight sightings of the jets were made with seven attempts to intercept. The jet approach was good, but in combat, they would undoubtedly use more evasive action on the attack run. The jet attacks were made from 2, 4, 6, 8, 10, and 12 o'clock. Our flight was positioned 3,000 to 5,000 ft above the bombers, on the left rear of the last box. Most of the jet attacks were made from 6 or 12 o'clock level. One jet however made attacks from 2, 4, 8 or 10 o'clock. After each attack he pulled up sharply in a climbing turn. Our flight tactics were to half roll and make a 60 degree diving turn. The half roll was not too successful because of blanking the jet out at some part of the manoeuvre. Also we miscalculated speed. Head-on passes seemed more successful as the jet could be kept in sight and the interception made easier. I noticed

During the autumn of 1944, the Fw 190 D-9-equipped III./JG 54 under Hptm. Robert "Bazi" Weiss, was moved to Oldenburg to offer conventional fighter protection to the Me 262s of Kommando Nowotny at Achmer but losses sustained during such operations were critically high. Weiss is seen here during an airfield briefing.

Right: A Meteor makes its landing approach at Manston, summer 1944. The Meteor III with engines of approximately the same power as the Jumo 004, possessed an inferior performance to the Me 262 mainly because of its more conservative design.

Right: As the Me 262s of Erprobungs-kommando 262 and Kommando Nowotny mounted the first German jet fighter operations during the summer and autumn of 1944, so the RAF's 616 Squadron began to convert from the Spitfire VII to the Gloster Meteor and by August was fully equipped with the type. This sequence of photographs shows freshly delivered Meteors of 616 Squadron at Manston, Kent from where the first British jet sorties were flown.

Below: The Meteor like the Me 262 A-1a, carried four cannon in its nose (20 mm Hispano Mk IIs with a total of 700 rounds).

Below: It is interesting to compare these views of Meteors being refuelled with those of Erprobungs-kommando 262's Me 262 A-1a "White 6" at Lechfeld on page 255. Similarly, the photos showing the servicing of Meteors should be compared to the sequence relating to Me 262 A-1a "White 3" on page 246–247.

that several other flights half rolled but were generally out distanced."

A Meteor pilot from 616 Squadron commented: "With the four 20 mm cannon in the nose, I was not worried about head-on attacks against the bombers. I had no blanking out trouble, and had good visibility." When asked if he could get a good burst on a 12 o'clock pass, the pilot replied: "Yes, by firing early in the attack, I could get in a couple of seconds burst from 1,000 yards before I had to break off." Commenting on the defensive fighter tactics he said: "I believe that the escort rolls off too slowly. Jerry would come in faster than we did today. If we had more height we would have come down through the fighters." He was then asked if this problem could have been solved by having another group of escort fighters at 10,000 feet above to warn those at 5,000 feet. "No," he replied, "The service ceiling of the bombers would not allow the 10,000 feet differential."

On the 27th, in Germany, an OKL[5] order was issued stating that, "for reasons of security", the following code names are to be used for the new aircraft types in use, or in the experimental stage: *Silber* (Silver) for the Me 262, *Zinn* (Tin) for the Ar 234, *Blei* (Lead) for the Me 163 and *Kupfer* (Copper) for the Do 335. In fact, two code names were used for the Me 262, the other being *Ahorn* or Maple. Two official names were allocated to the Me 262, *Schwalbe* or Swallow (this being confirmed by an official memo) and *Sturmvogel* or Stormy Petrel (the name preferred by Hitler). This last name was changed to *Blitzbomber* on 17 June 1944, but after 26 November, it was decided to revert to the original name.

Meanwhile, following their disastrous first action, *Kommando Nowotny* continued to fly operations from Achmer and Hesepe.

On 10 October Bley claimed a P-51 but two days later he was forced to make an emergency landing at Steenwijk, his Me 262 suffering light damage. After claiming the destruction of another P-51, *Fw.* Lennartz of *1./Kdo Nowotny* was also compelled to make an emergency landing near Bramel. On the 13th, *Obering.* Lüthner's aircraft crashed on take-off from Achmer and was destroyed and *Ofäh.* Heinz Russel's Me 262 was heavily damaged attempting to make an emergency landing at Hesepe. Bad weather then prevented further operations by *Kdo Nowotny* until 28 October.

When the unit returned to operations it attempted to intercept a US Eighth Air Force raid on Hamm. Two pilots, *Lt.* Schall and *Lt.* Schreiber, claimed victories (a P-51 and a P-38 respectively), but *Oblt.* Bley's aircraft struck a flock of birds on take-off from Achmer, and he was killed. The nosewheel of *Lt.* Franz Schall's Me 262 also collapsed as he landed at the same airfield, but he was unhurt. Bley's place as commander of *1./Kdo Nowotny* was taken by *Oblt.* Joachim Weber. Next day *Lt.* Schreiber claimed an F-5 Lightning of the US 7th Photo Recon Group. He later rammed a Spitfire near Nordhorn, possibly that piloted by Flt. Lt. Wilkins of 4 Squadron, but he bailed out and was unhurt. *Fw.* Büttner and *Ofw.* Göbel of *Kommando Nowotny* engaged a flight of P-47s, each claiming one destroyed.

---

1 Kogler, who was then Geschwader Kommodore of JG 6, was shot down on 1 January 1945 during the Luftwaffe attack on Allied airfields in Holland, Belgium and France mounted that day. He was flying a Fw 190 A-9, W.Nr. 980543 which carried a single chevron and horizontal bar forward of the fuselage cross, with a further horizontal bar aft and red/white/red JG 6 tail bands.

2 "Ultra" was the British code name adopted, from June 1941, for all high grade signals intelligence derived from the German Enigma (Morse) and Geheimschreiber (telex) encoding machines and hand ciphers. The importance of the Allied ability to break the German code system on the outcome of the Second World War is only just being realised.

3 The F-5 was a reconnaissance version of the P-38 Lightning.

4 Robert Ritter von Greim had won the Pour le Mérite as a fighter pilot in the First World War, flying Hitler to Berlin to witness the outcome of the Kapp Putsch there in 1920. He then stayed closely connected to Hitler and the Nazi Party and when the Luftwaffe was revealed in 1935, he was placed in command of the first fighter squadron, the Reklamestaffel Mitteldeutschland. He was given command of Luftflotte 6 in Central Russia in 1943 and in April 1945, flew to Hitler's bunker where he was appointed to succeed Göring as commander of the Luftwaffe. The was taken prisoner by the Americans, but took poison and died in Salzburg in May 1945.

5 OKL = Oberkommando der Luftwaffe (the High Command of the Luftwaffe).

6 OKH = Oberkommando des Heeres - High Command of the Armed Forces.

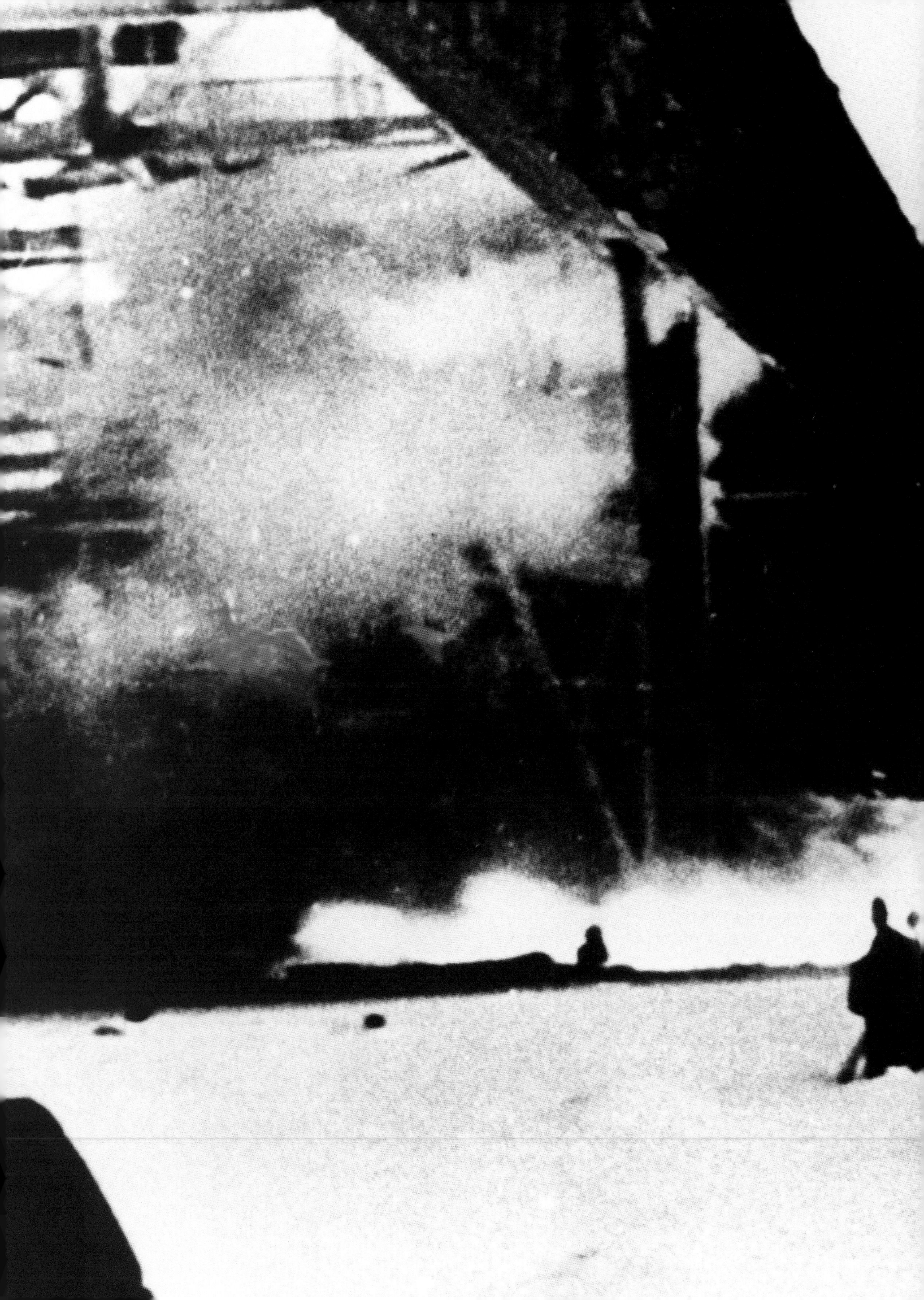

CHAPTER NINE
Me 262 VARIANTS

By the end of 1944, a large diversity of variants had been proposed for the Me 262. Occasionally aircraft were redesignated several times. The following chapter comprises details of all known variants.

Me 262 A-1a JÄGER (FIGHTER)

The Me 262 A-1a was the standard fighter variant with an armament of four 30 mm MK 108 cannon (two with 100 rounds and two with 80) aimed with the aid of a *Revi* 16b gunsight. It was hoped that this would be replaced by the EZ 42 *Adler* (Eagle) gyroscopic sight from early 1945. Armour comprised a steel plate behind the pilot, a 90 mm armoured glass windshield and protection for the ammunition boxes in the nose. The variant was provided with a FuG 16 ZY transmitter/receiver and a FuG 25a IFF set. Standard fuel tankage comprised 2,570 ltrs (680 Imp gals) of J2 fuel in four internal tanks with provision for two ETC 503[1] or *Wikingerschiff* racks each carrying a 300 ltr (80 Imp gal) drop tank.

The Revi *(Reflexvisier)* 16B, the standard gunsight fitted to the Me 262

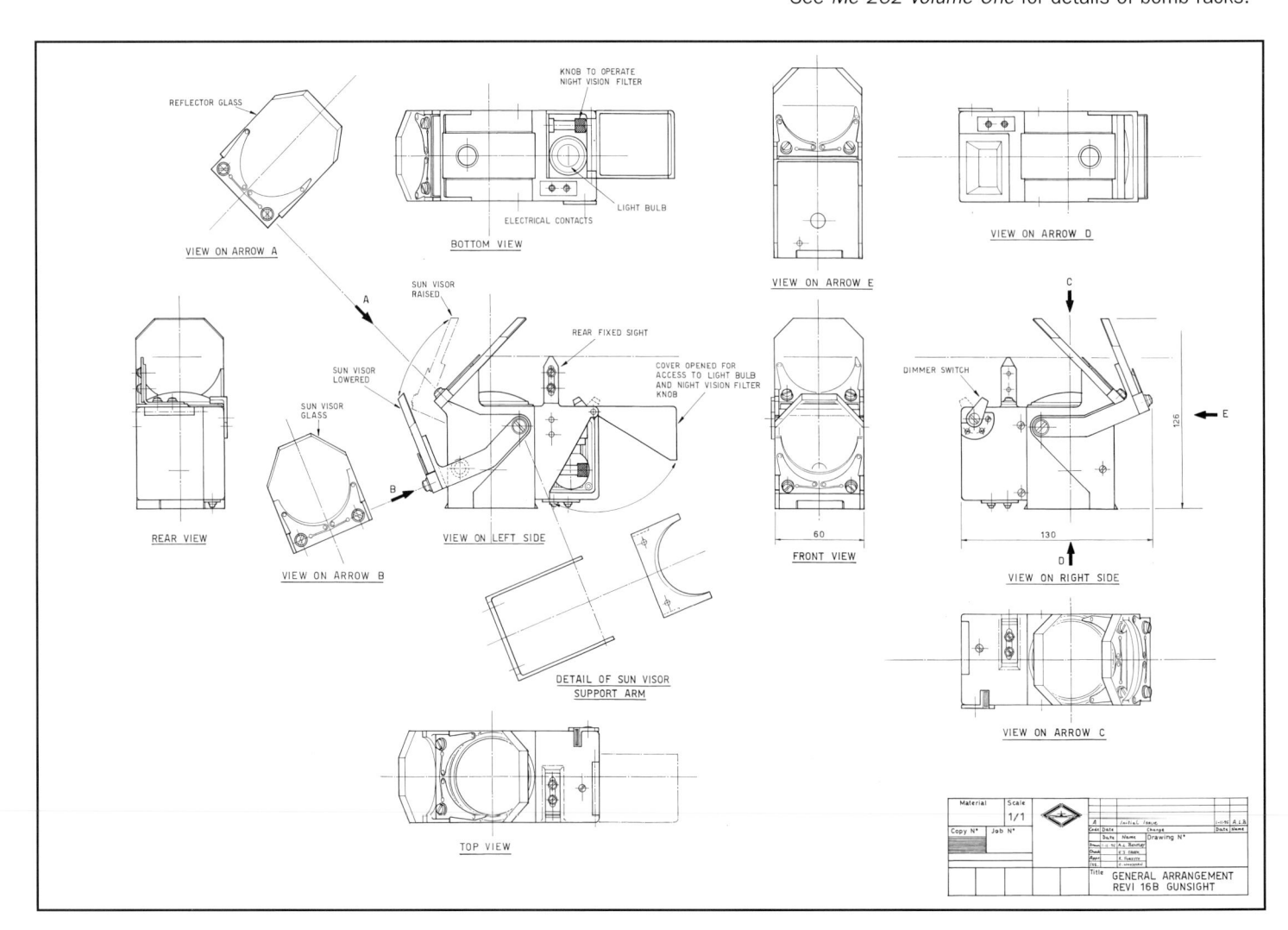

Me 262 A-1a JABO (FIGHTER-BOMBER)

A fighter-bomber version of the A-1a, but carrying either one or two SC 250 or SD 250 or one SC 500 or SD 500 bombs on the ETC 503 or *Wikingerschiff* racks. The designation 'SC' *(Splitterbomben, cylindrisch)* indicated a thin cased blast bomb, 'SD' *(Splitterbomben, Dickwand)* a semi-armour piercing/ fragmentation weapon. The figure indicated the weight: 250 kg (550 lbs) or 500 kg (1,100 lbs). The Me 262 experienced the following loss of speed with each type of bomb load:

One SC 250	3.6% loss
Two SC 250	7.3% loss
One SC 500	4.6% loss
One SD 500	3.3% loss

See *Me 262 Volume One* for details of bomb racks.

Me 262 A-1a/U1 JÄGER (FIGHTER)

Similar to the Me 262 A-1a, this variant carried an armament of two 30 mm MK 103 cannon with 72 rounds each – the barrels of which protruded from either side of the nose (see photograph to right); two 20 mm MG 151/20 with 146 rounds mounted into the uppermost part of the nose assembly and two MK 108 with 65 rounds in the centre. The MK 103 gun was a slower firing weapon than the MK 108, but had a longer range.

As far as is known only one prototype of the A-1a/U1 was built. It was hoped that the MK 103 guns would be replaced eventually by the remarkable 30 mm MK 213 weapon which had a rate of fire of no less than 1,100 rounds per minute and a muzzle velocity about the same as the MK 108.

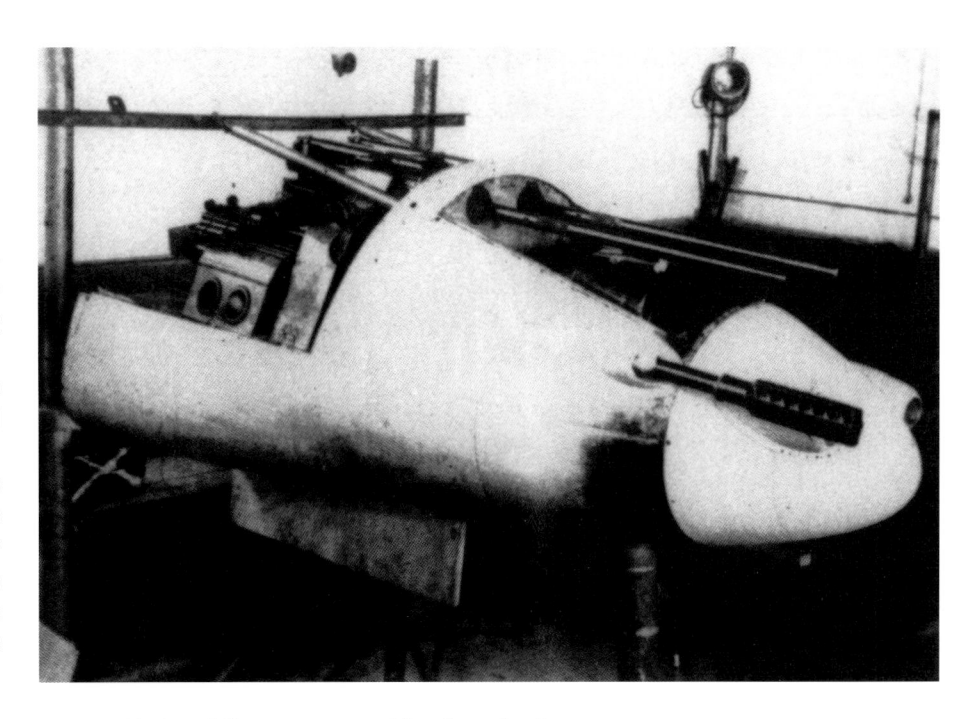

	Weight	Length	Rate of fire	Muzzle velocity
MK 103	145 kg (320 lbs)	2,335 mm (7 ft 8 ins)	420 rounds/minute	940 m/sec (3,084 ft/sec)
MK 108	58 kg (128 lbs)	1,050 mm (3 ft 4 ins)	600 rounds/minute	520 m/sec (1,706 ft/sec)

The 20 mm Rheinmetall-Borsig MG 151/20 cannon, a pair of which were to be fitted to the Me 262 A-1a/U1.

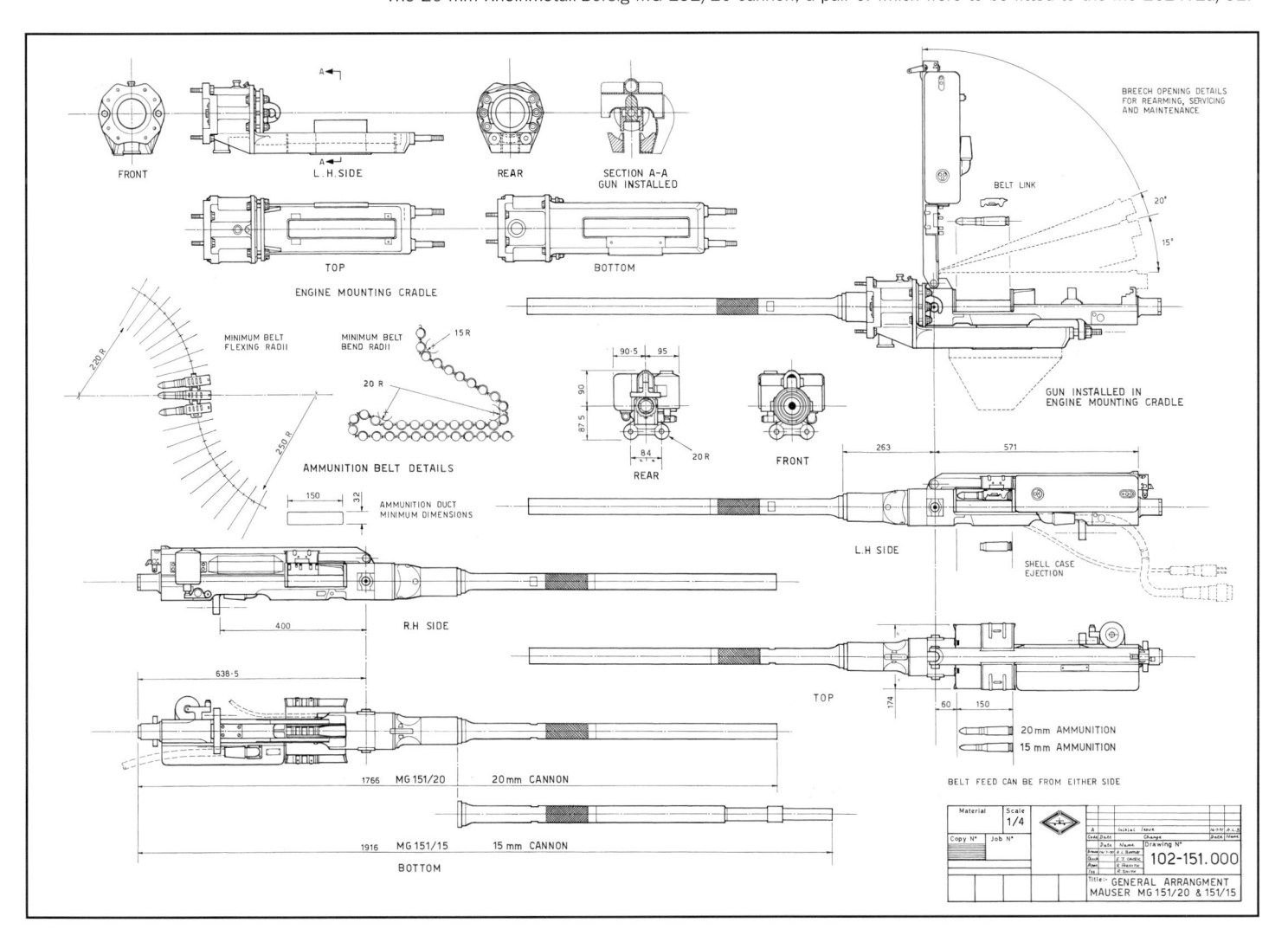

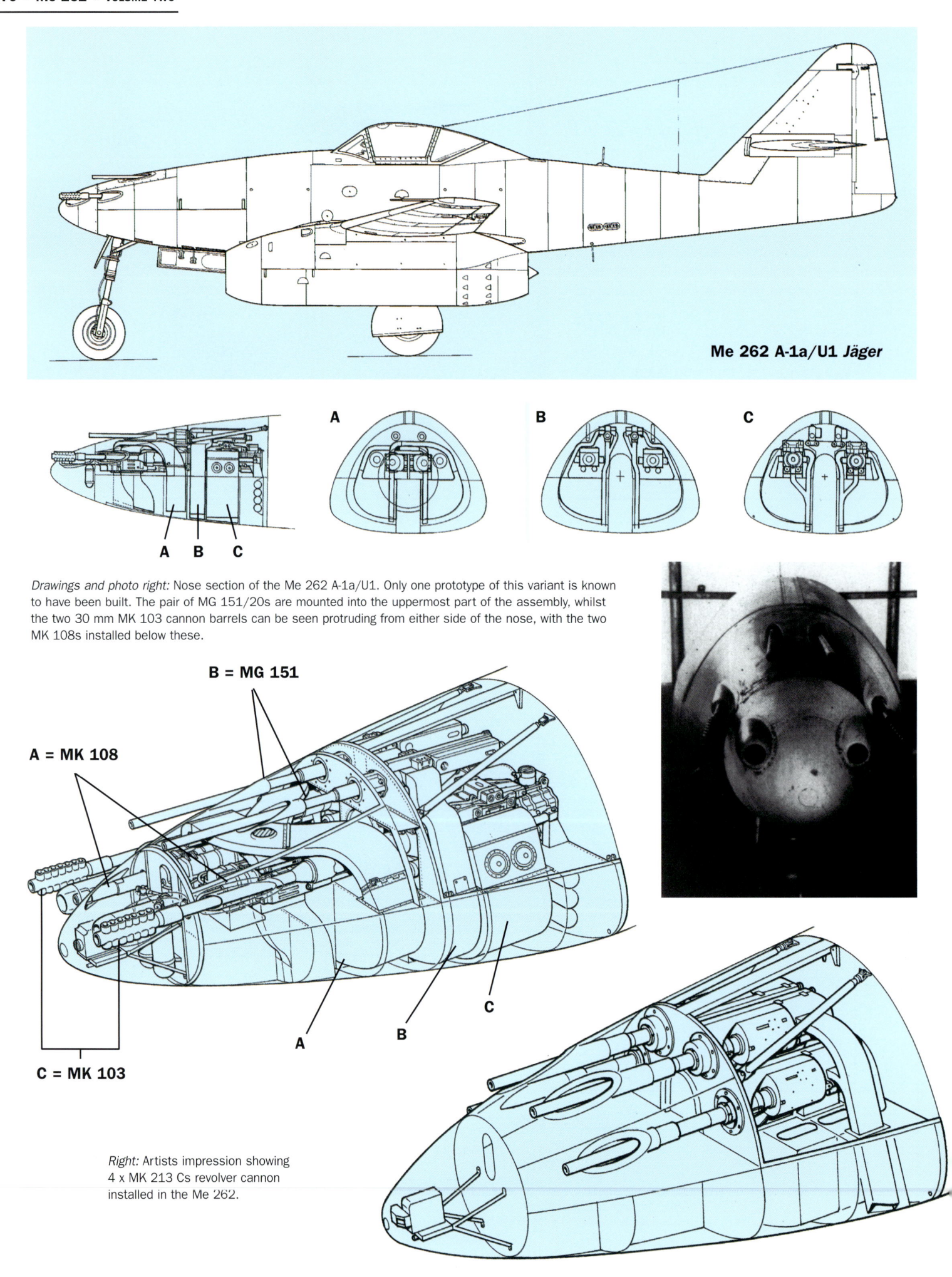

Me 262 A-1a/U1 Jäger

Drawings and photo right: Nose section of the Me 262 A-1a/U1. Only one prototype of this variant is known to have been built. The pair of MG 151/20s are mounted into the uppermost part of the assembly, whilst the two 30 mm MK 103 cannon barrels can be seen protruding from either side of the nose, with the two MK 108s installed below these.

A = MK 108
B = MG 151
C = MK 103

Right: Artists impression showing 4 x MK 213 Cs revolver cannon installed in the Me 262.

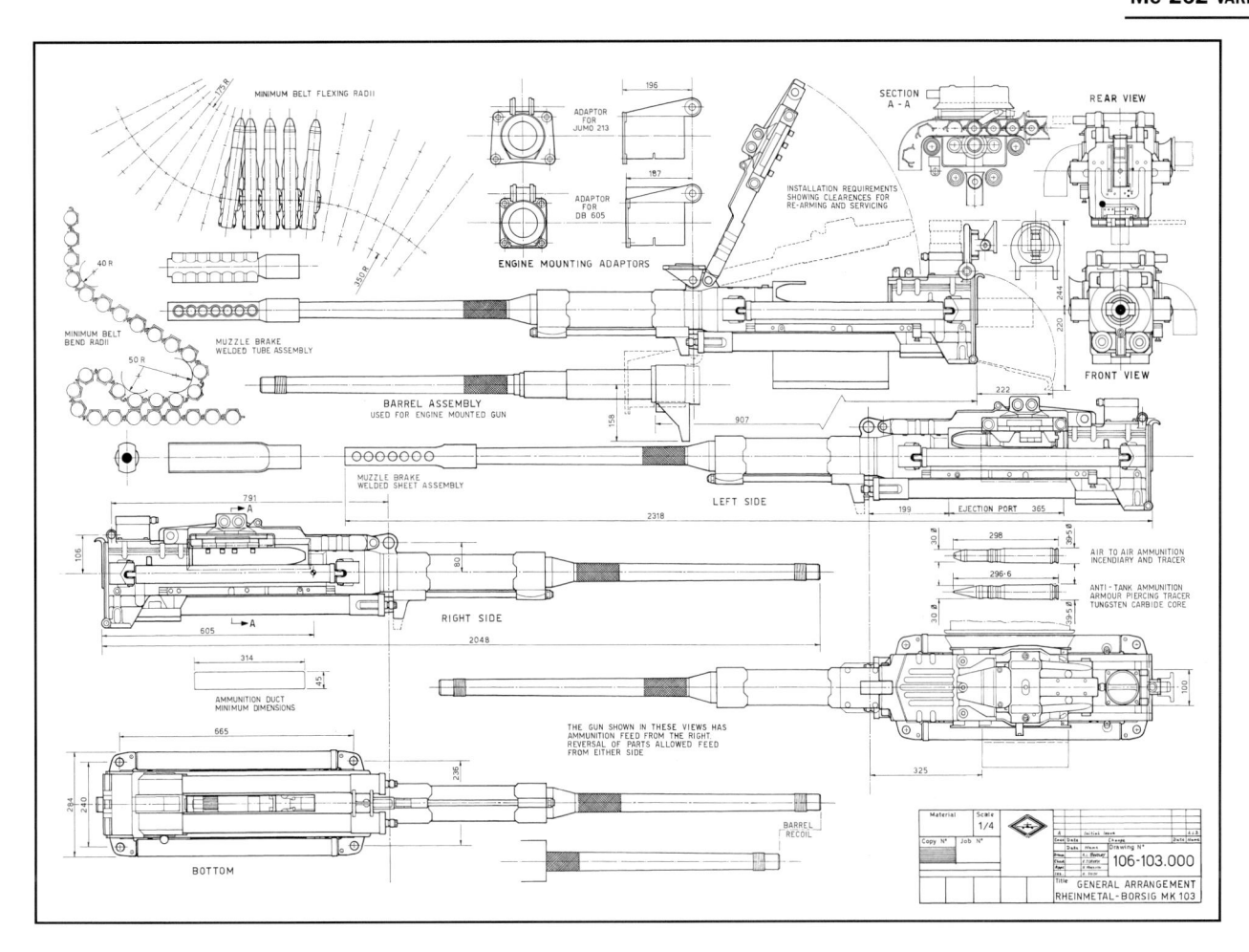

Above: The 30 mm Rheinmetall-Borsig MK 103 cannon was a long-range weapon, two were to be installed in the Me 262 A-1a/U1

Below: Four Mauser 30 mm MK 213 C revolver cannon were eventually to replace the MK 108s as the standard armament for the Me 262. This remarkable weapon has a rate of fire of over 1,000 rounds per minute.

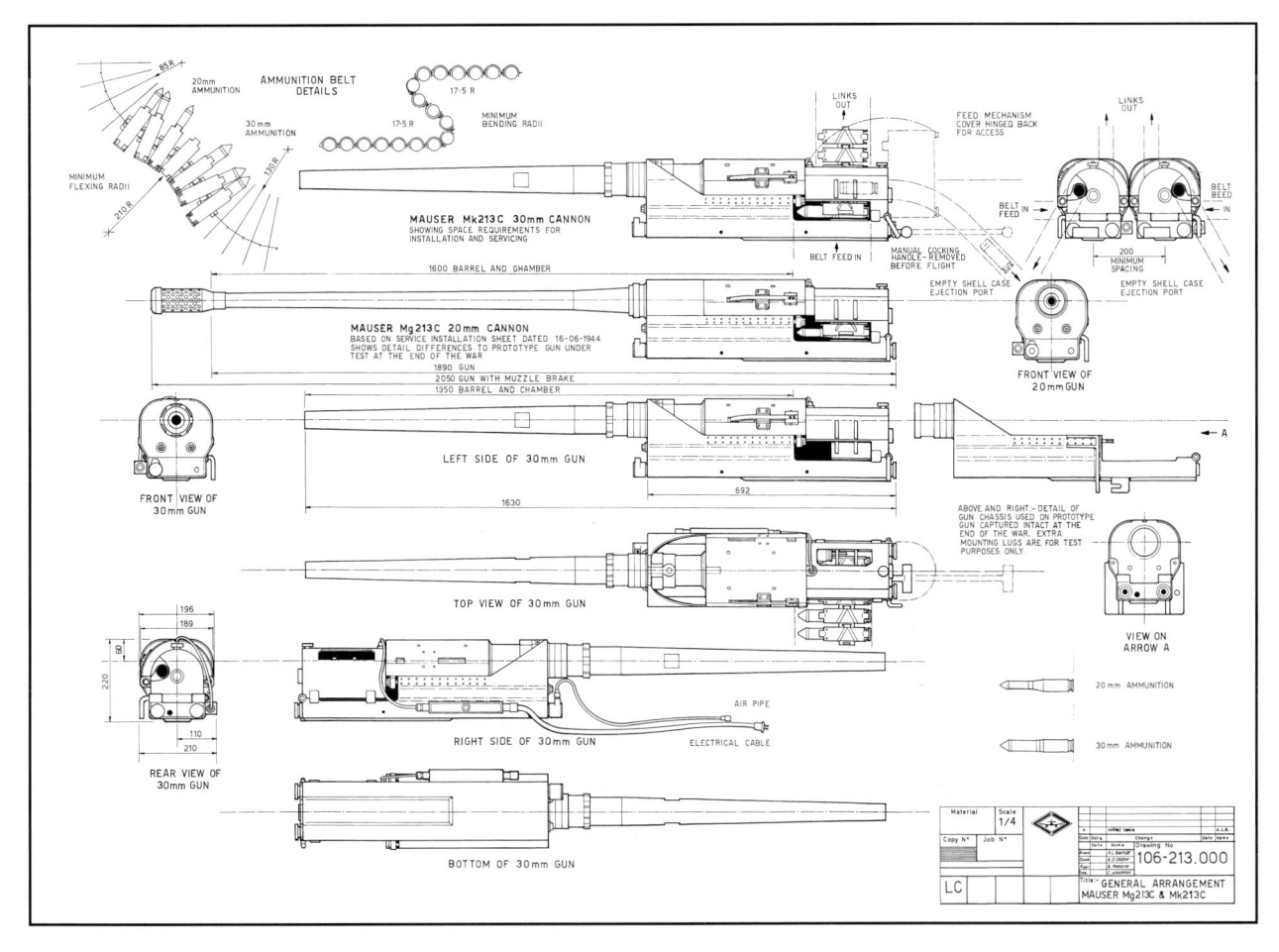

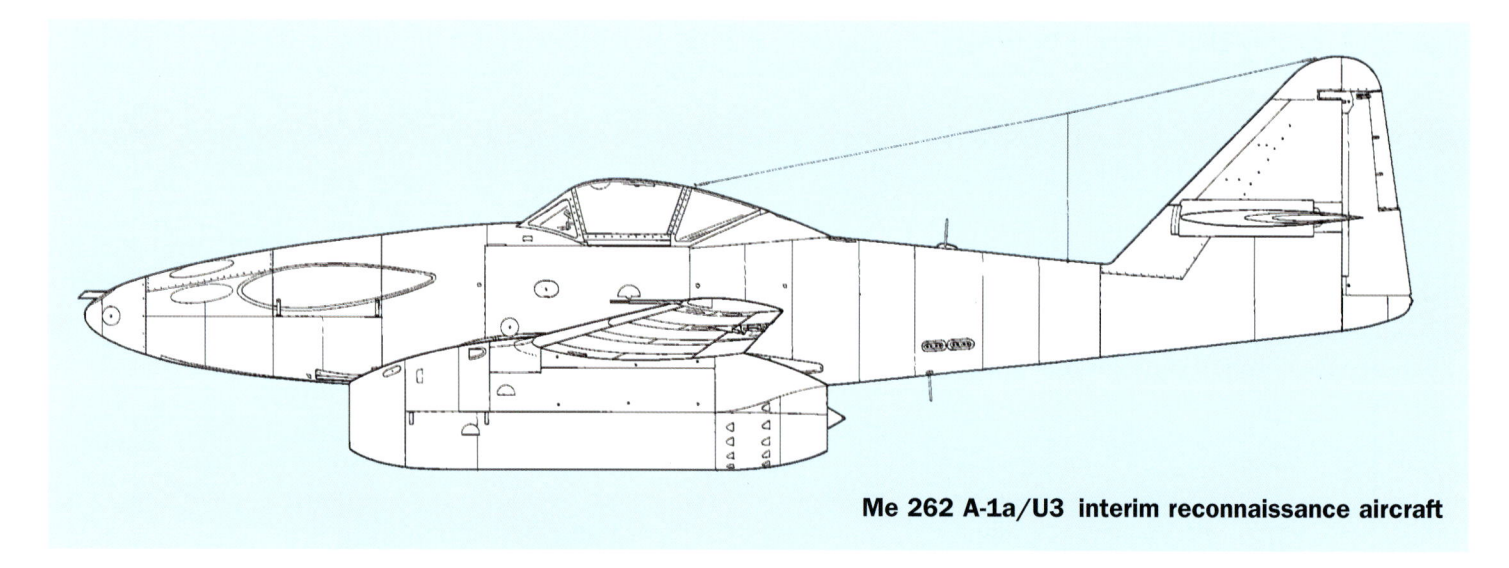

Me 262 A-1a/U3 interim reconnaissance aircraft

A Me 262 A-1a/U3 of NAGr 6 at Lechfeld 1945. Clearly visible in this photograph are the two Rb 50/30 cameras and the position of the single Mk 108 in the nose. For full details of this aircraft see Chapter 13.

Me 262 A-1a/U2
SCHLECHTWETTERJÄGER (ALL WEATHER FIGHTER)

This was an all weather fighter version of the A-1a. Besides the standard FuG 16 ZY and FuG 25a radio equipment, the variant also carried the FuG 125 *Hermine* VHF radio beacon signal receiver which operated on a frequency of 30-33.3 MHz and had a range of 200 km (125 miles). The variant was also to be fitted with the K 22 autopilot with the FuG 120 *Bernhardine* ground to air communications set being installed later. This operated in the same frequency band as FuG 125, but had a range of 400 km (250 miles). The information received (bearing of the ground station and running commentary on the air situation) was recorded on a strip of paper by the attached teleprinter unit. It was eventually intended that the -1a/U2 should supersede the A-1a in production during the middle of 1945.(see Appendix Seven)

Me 262 A-1a/U3
BEHELFSAUFKLÄRER (INTERIM RECONNAISSANCE)

As has been recorded in Volume One, Chapter 3, the first proposal for a reconnaissance version of the Me 262 was made on 26 September 1941. After the mock-up was inspected on 5 February 1942, it was proposed, on 26 March, to develop an improved version with FuG 16 Z or EZ 6 equipment and Rb 75/30 cameras. The General of the *Luftwaffe's* Reconnaissance Forces, *Oberst* Hans-Henning von Barsewisch, examined this design on 2 June 1943, it now being fitted with two Rb 50/30 cameras.

This version was eventually to be built as the Me 262 A-5a, but as an interim measure a modification of the A-1a *Jäger* was produced under the designation A-1a/U3. This had two Rb 50/30 cameras mounted in the nose, angled outwards at 11 degrees, which were controlled by an intervalometer with an attached drive motor. Because the cameras were too large to fit cleanly within the nose compartment, small horizontal tear-drop fairings were fitted to both left and right access doors to cover the protruding areas. Two small square glazed panels were provided for the camera lenses beneath the fuselage on either side of the nosewheel well. The variant also differed in having an FuG 16 ZS radio transceiver which operated on German army frequencies. The makeshift variant had a single MK 108 cannon mounted in the extreme nose, with its muzzle protruding level with the tip. On 18 July 1944, the proposed Bf 109 H-2/R2 reconnaissance aircraft was cancelled in favour of the Me 262 A-1a/U3.

Me 262 A-1a/U4 *Jäger* (Fighter)

Protokoll Nr.24 of 9 February 1944, proposed the fitting of a single large calibre cannon in the Me 262. Two weapons were suggested, the long range 50 mm MK 214 A and the shorter range but much faster firing 55 mm MK 112.

Development of the two heavily armed versions of the Me 262 proceeded very slowly until early 1945. On New Year's Day of that year Hitler and Göring held a discussion on air armament.

Hitler: "We must introduce an effective long-range weapon ... We must be able to get at them (the US bombers) with a weapon which is so effective at a distance so great that they can't reply. With his 12 mm he can't fire one and a half kilometers ... Now each hit with a 5 cm projectile will bring down a bomber without fail. Even the biggest would be shot down. As it is now, the American isn't suffering any losses, or very few. When I think the German planes must defend themselves against the fighters on one hand, and attack the bombers on the other ... The result is like shooting rabbits. And the effect on the population is deplorable. The bombers are our curse ... In my opinion the 5 cm cannon is the least we can use. I spoke with what's-his-name today.[2] He thinks he can build the 5 cm gun even into the Me 262."

Göring: "With the cannon the Me 262 will be able to retain its high speed completely."

Hitler: "He says it would be the same weight."

Göring: "That is immaterial. The armament is the main thing."

Hitler: "If they get up and shoot with a 5 cm cannon from a distance of say a thousand metres; say a swarm of forty Me 262s shooting from a distance of a thousand metres ... And we have no losses, and the others lose ten or more then that's all right."

Göring: "So far the matter's quite clear ... After all, we brought out the jet plane. We introduced it. And now we must have it in large numbers in order to retain our advantage."

Hitler: "Unfortunately the V1 can't end the war."

Göring: "This cannon is good. Just as a project which is doubtful at first will succeed in the end, so the bomber will come..."

Hitler: "That's a matter for the future."

Göring: "No, I don't think so."

Hitler: "Göring, the 5 cm cannon is here already: the other thing is a matter for the future."

Göring: "I think we shall have success with it, anyhow."

Hitler: "Very well then."

Me 262 A-1a/U4 W.Nr. 111899 was fitted with the MK 214 V2

Me 262 A-1a/U4

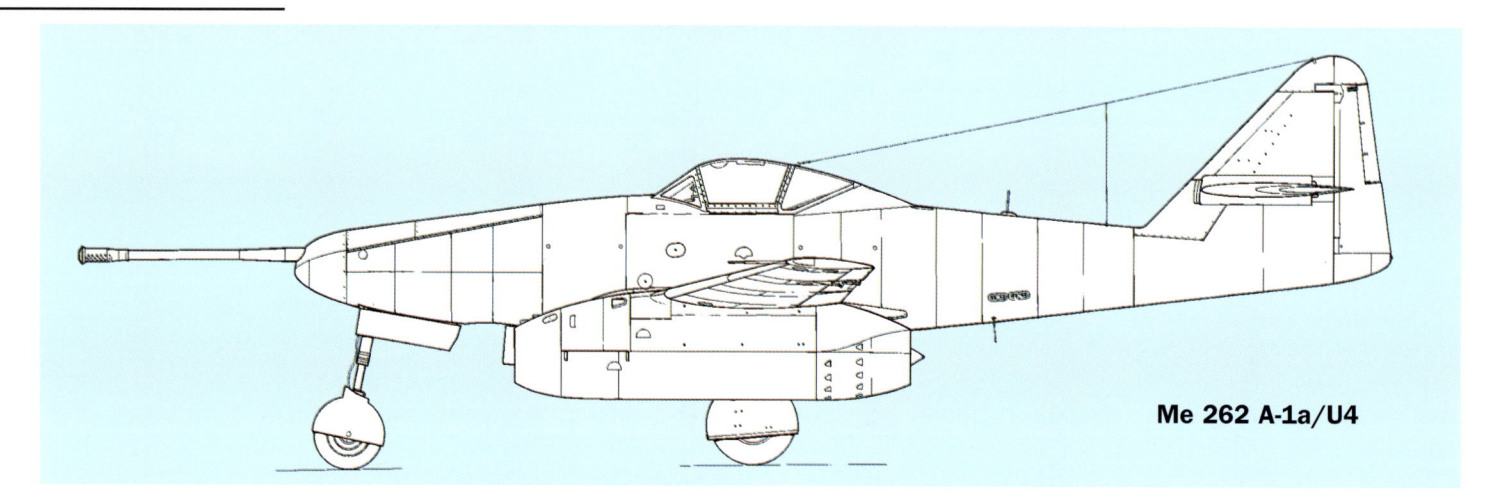

Only two prototypes of the Me 262 A-1a/U4 fitted with the 50 mm MK 214 A cannon in the nose were completed

At an armaments conference held between the 3rd and 5th, Hitler ordered immediate installation of the MK 214 in the Me 262. Between 11 and 17 February, a discussion took place between Messerschmitt and the Armaments Experimental Station at Tarnewitz regarding the installation of a MK 214, six MK 108, a MK 112 cannon and R4M rockets in the Me 262. For the former, it was proposed to remove the standard armament, and install the huge gun in the nose with its barrel projecting some 2 metres (6 feet 6 inches) forward. To make additional room for the gun, the nosegear was modified so that it swivelled to lie flat in the nose when retracted. The variant was designated Me 262 A-1a/U4.

Modification of the first prototype, W.Nr. 111899, was carried out very quickly, work beginning on installation of the MK 214 A V2 from 11 March. The aircraft made its first flight on 19 March with Messerschmitt chief test pilot Karl Baur at the controls. Baur made 19 flights in the aircraft, firing a total of 47 rounds on the ground and 81 in the air. It was then handed over to the night fighter ace, *Maj.* Wilhelm Herget on 5 April. After practicing against a ground target, Herget flew two operational missions against a US bomber formation on 16 April but, on both occasions, the gun jammed.

A second aircraft, W.Nr. 170083, which had already been used by Messerschmitt for tests with various undercarriage modifications, was fitted with the MK 214 A V3 in April, it also being known as the second V4. It is doubtful whether the aircraft was flown with the gun before it was captured by American troops at Lechfeld in May 1945. It was planned to produce the MK 214 armed variant under the designation Me 262 E-1, this being fitted with the EZ 42 gyroscopic gunsight.

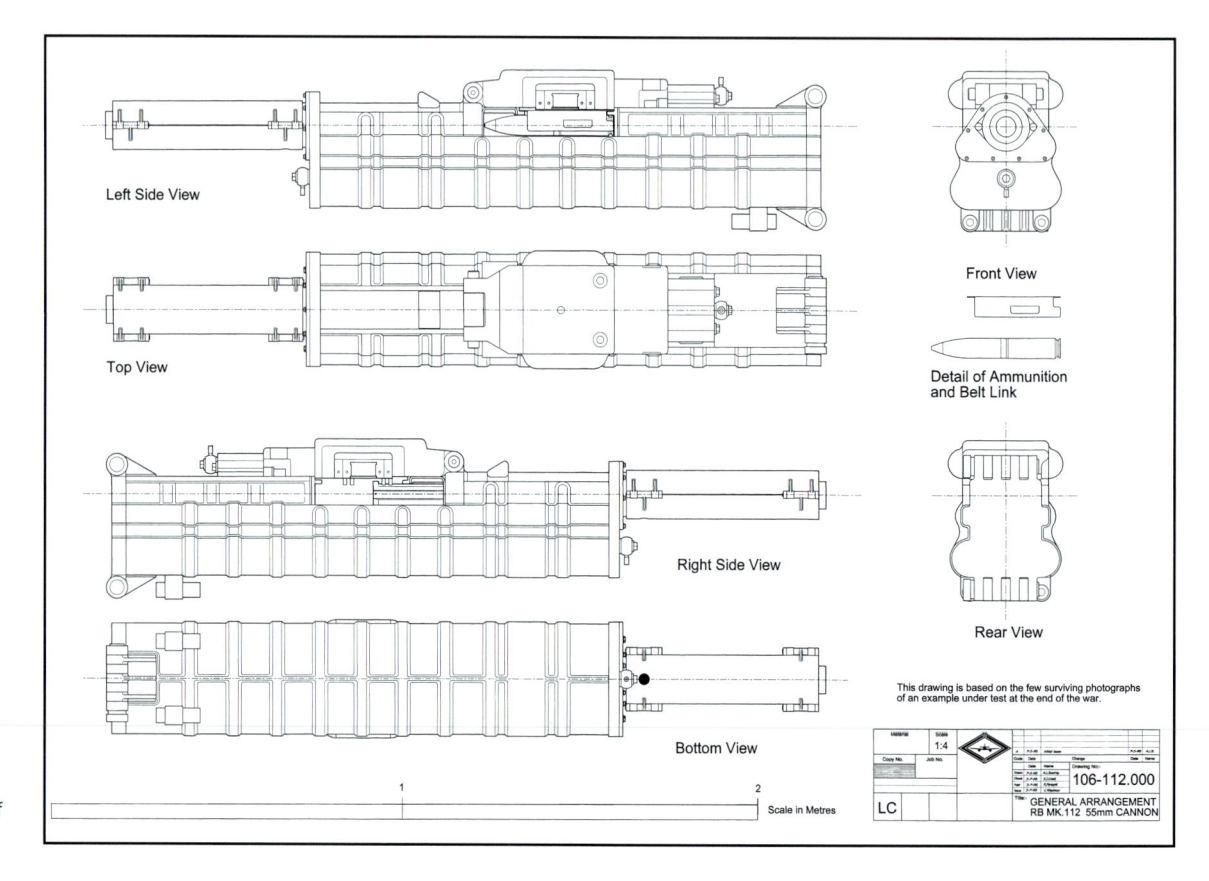

The 55 mm Rheinmetall-Borsig MK 112 had a much shorter range than the MK 214 cannon but had a much greater rate of fire.

MAUSER Mk 214A 50mm CANNON

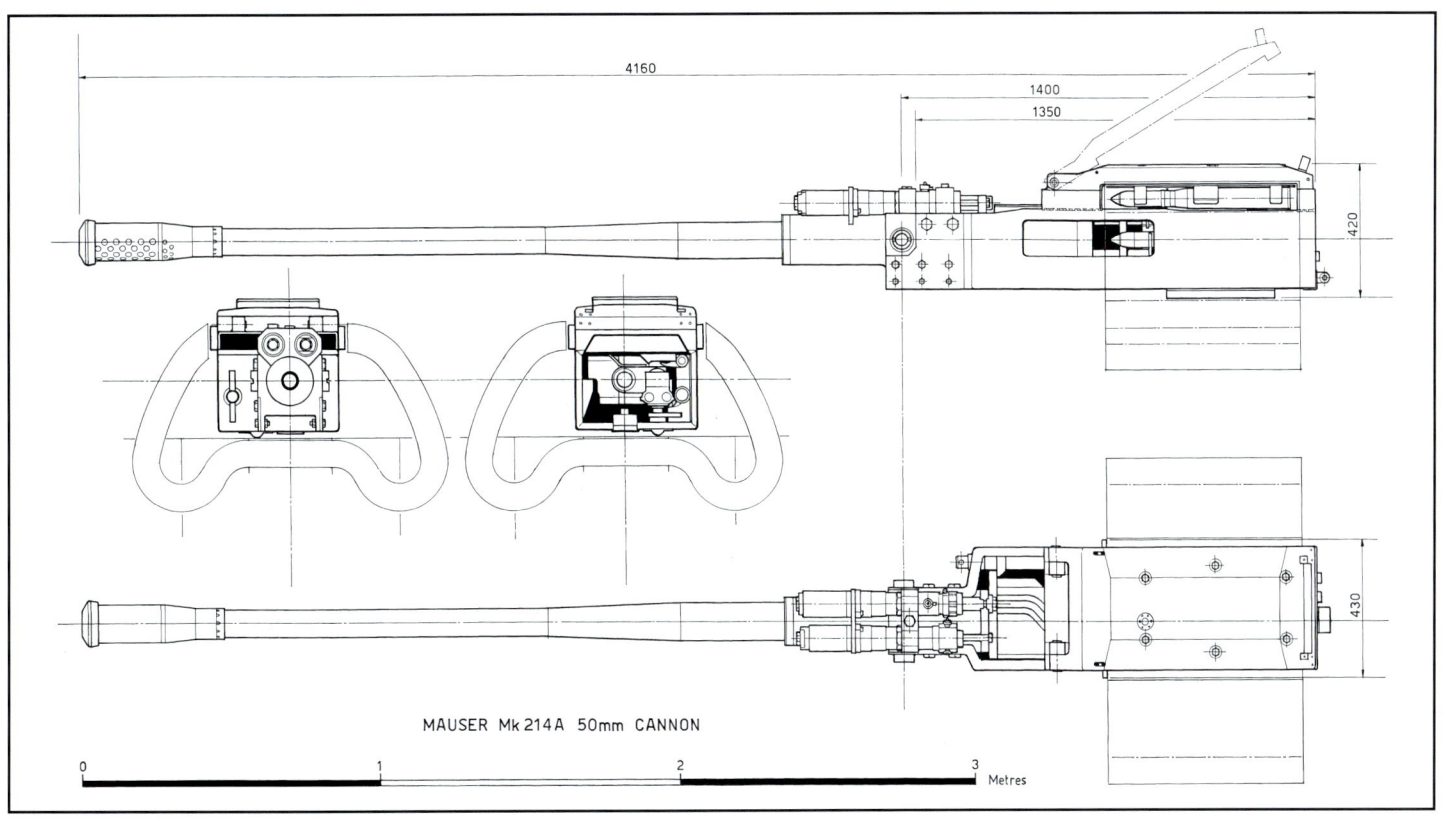

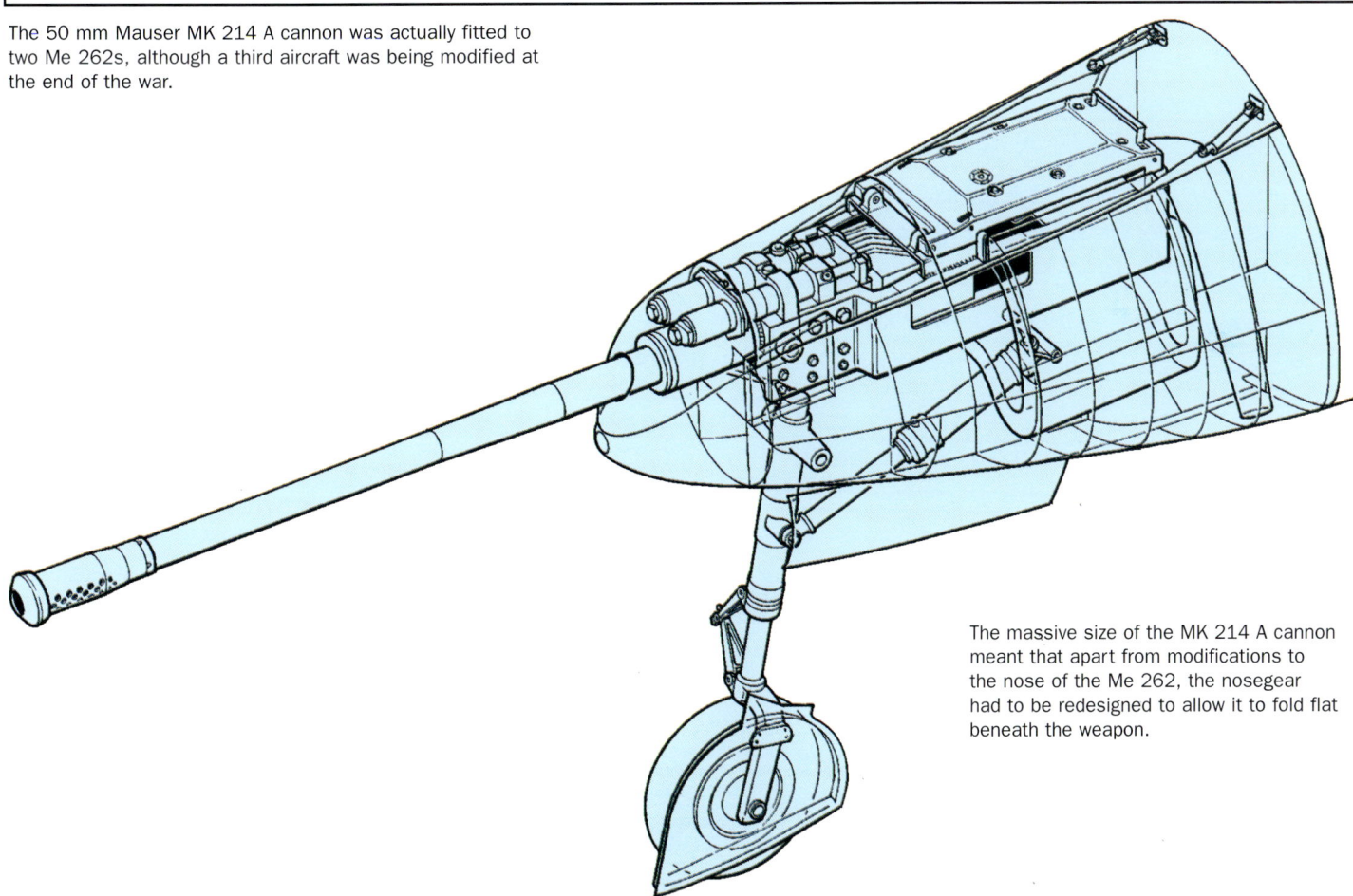

The 50 mm Mauser MK 214 A cannon was actually fitted to two Me 262s, although a third aircraft was being modified at the end of the war.

The massive size of the MK 214 A cannon meant that apart from modifications to the nose of the Me 262, the nosegear had to be redesigned to allow it to fold flat beneath the weapon.

Comparison figures between the MK 214 and MK 112

	Weight	Length	Rate of fire	Muzzle velocity
MK 214 A	490 kg (1,080 lbs)	4,160 mm (13 ft 8 ins)	150 rounds/minute	920 m/sec (3,018 ft/sec)
MK 112	275 kg (606 lbs)	2,000 mm (6 ft 6 ins)	300 rounds/minute	600 m/sec (1,969 ft/sec)

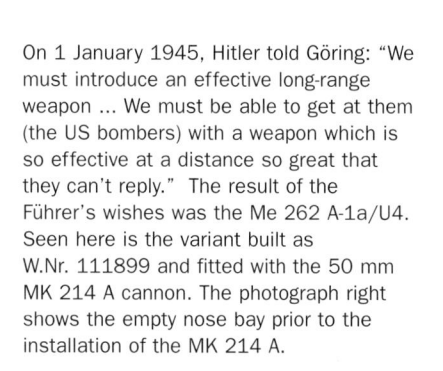

On 1 January 1945, Hitler told Göring: "We must introduce an effective long-range weapon ... We must be able to get at them (the US bombers) with a weapon which is so effective at a distance so great that they can't reply." The result of the Führer's wishes was the Me 262 A-1a/U4. Seen here is the variant built as W.Nr. 111899 and fitted with the 50 mm MK 214 A cannon. The photograph right shows the empty nose bay prior to the installation of the MK 214 A.

Below: The prototype MK 214 V1 50 mm cannon. As far as is known, this prototype was not fitted to an aircraft, but the V2 and V3 were mounted in two Me 262s, respectively W.Nr. 111899 and 170083.

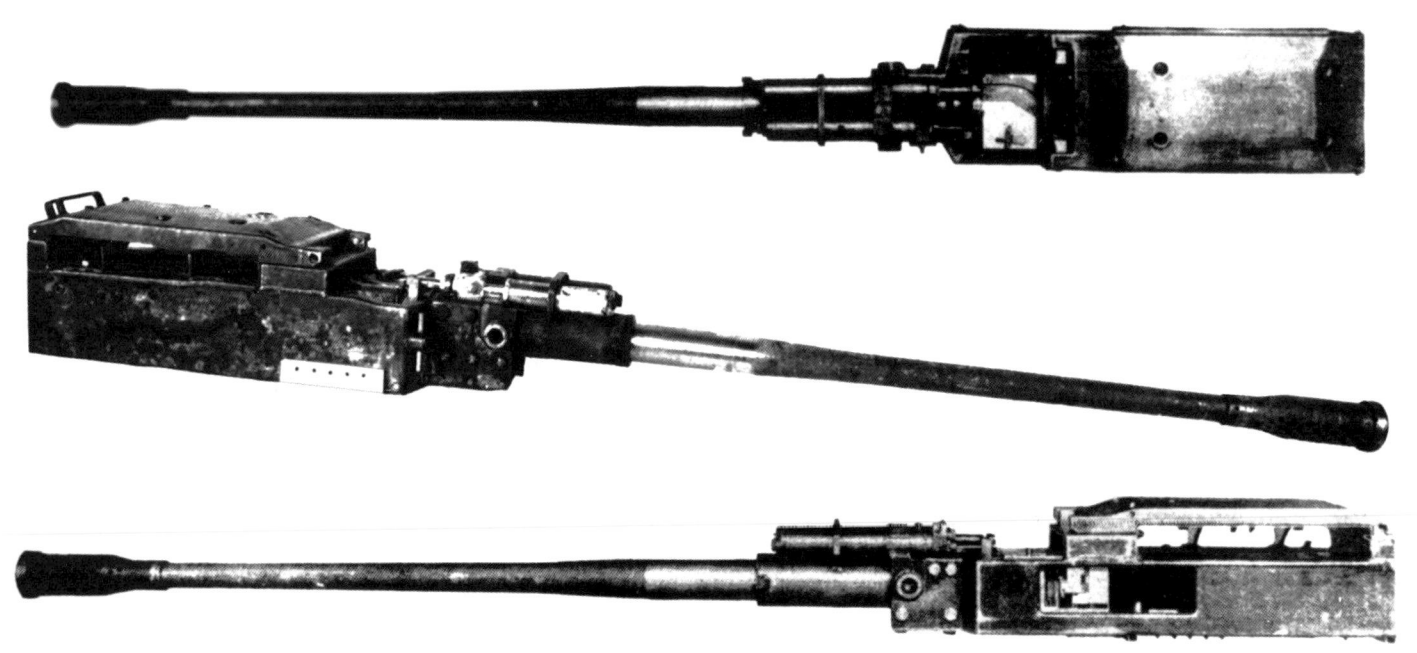

Me 262 A-1a/U4 W.Nr. 111899
This aircraft was fitted with the MK 214 V2 cannon. The aircraft made its first flight on 19 March 1945 with Karl Baur at the controls. After testing, the aircraft was handed over to JV 44 where it was flown by *Maj.* Wilhelm Herget.

Above: Karl Baur, Messerschmitt's chief test pilot, loads a 606 mm (2 ft) long shell into the breech of the 50 mm MK 214 A cannon as fitted into Me 262 A-1a/U4, W.Nr. 111899. Baur made 19 flights in the aircraft, firing a total of 47 rounds on the ground and 81 in the air. He scored 27 hits out of a possible 30 on a rectangular target 32 m (105 ft) long. The aircraft made its first flight on 19 March 1945.

Below: Messerschmitt personnel, including Karl Baur, gather around Me 262 A-1a/U4, W.Nr. 111899 to inspect the MK 214 A.

Above: The loaded weapon is ready for ground firing tests.

Me 262 VARIANTS • 279

Left: Following the successful completion of firing tests by the Messerschmitt chief test pilot, Karl Baur, the Me 262 A-1a/U4, W.Nr. 111899 was handed over to the Luftwaffe for operational evaluation. The pilot charged with assessment of the machine was the night-fighter ace, Major Wilhelm Herget. After practicing against a ground target, Herget flew two operational missions against a US bomber formation on 16 April but, on both occasions, the gun jammed. Herget, left, is seen here in June 1943 having been newly decorated with the Ritterkreuz along with two other leading night-fighter aces, Hptm. Helmut Lent, centre, (Gruppenkommandeur IV./NJG 1 who later died of injuries on 5.10.1944 having scored 102 night victories and gained the diamonds to his Ritterkreuz) and Hptm Hans-Dieter Frank of NJG 1 who shot down six enemy aircraft in one night in June 1943 (KIA 27.9.43)

Below: A photograph of another Me 262 A-1a/U4 as found by Allied forces at Augsburg 1945. The re-engineering of the nose section needed to be carried out prior to installation of the 50 mm MK 214 A cannon. A member of a BIOS (British Intelligence Objectives Sub-Committee) field team can be seen standing beside the aircraft.

Above: As found by US troops and prior to being re-painted, the considerable size of the MK 214 installed in Me 262 W.Nr 170083 necessitated a redesigned nose and undercarriage, resulting in the leg and wheel being rotated at right angles on retraction to allow the wheel to lie flat beneath the gun. The undercarriage door design differed from W.Nr. 111899.

Above and left: The second Me 262 A-1a/U4 W.Nr. 170083 which was fitted with the MK 214 V3. It is not known whether this aircraft actually flew prior to its capture by the Americans. The aircraft is seen here at Lechfeld in 1945 still carrying its original national markings although the Hakenkreuz appears to have been applied by the US troops. The aircraft was the subject of considerable interest and various parts were re-painted including the name "Wilma Jeanne" being applied on the port side nose. The full post war story of this aircraft appears in Volume Four.

Me 262 W.Nr. 170083

The aircraft carried dark green (81) upper surfaces with a pale blue grey (76) beneath. A large white "V" and also the last three figures of the Werk Nummer 083, were painted on both sides of the fuselage nose. Prior to being tested with the 50 mm gun, the aircraft was also used to test a curved nosegear fork to improve castering and prevent shimmy. W.Nr. 170083 was captured by US forces at the end of the war and named "Wilma Jeanne" and later "Happy Hunter II". It crashed in France during a transfer flight from Melun to Cherbourg, piloted by the German test pilot, Ludwig Hoffmann who managed to bail out unhurt. The aircraft is shown here fitted with the third prototype of the 50 mm MK 214 A cannon.

Me 262 A-1a/U5 JÄGER (FIGHTER)

Most of the projected developments of the Me 262, described in Volume One, Chapter 5, were to carry an armament of six MK 108 cannon. Only one prototype (W.Nr. 112355) was fitted with this installation under the designation Me 262 A-1a/U5. Two of the MK 108s were to have 100 rounds each, two 85 rounds each and two 65 rounds each. The prototype was flight tested in March 1945 and is thought to have flown operational sorties with JV 44 in April.

The nose of Me 262 A-1/U-5 W.Nr. 112355, specially adapted to carry six MK 108 cannon. The rearward four guns were installed as a standard arrangement, with the extra pair fitted further forward, their barrels projecting ahead of the nose.

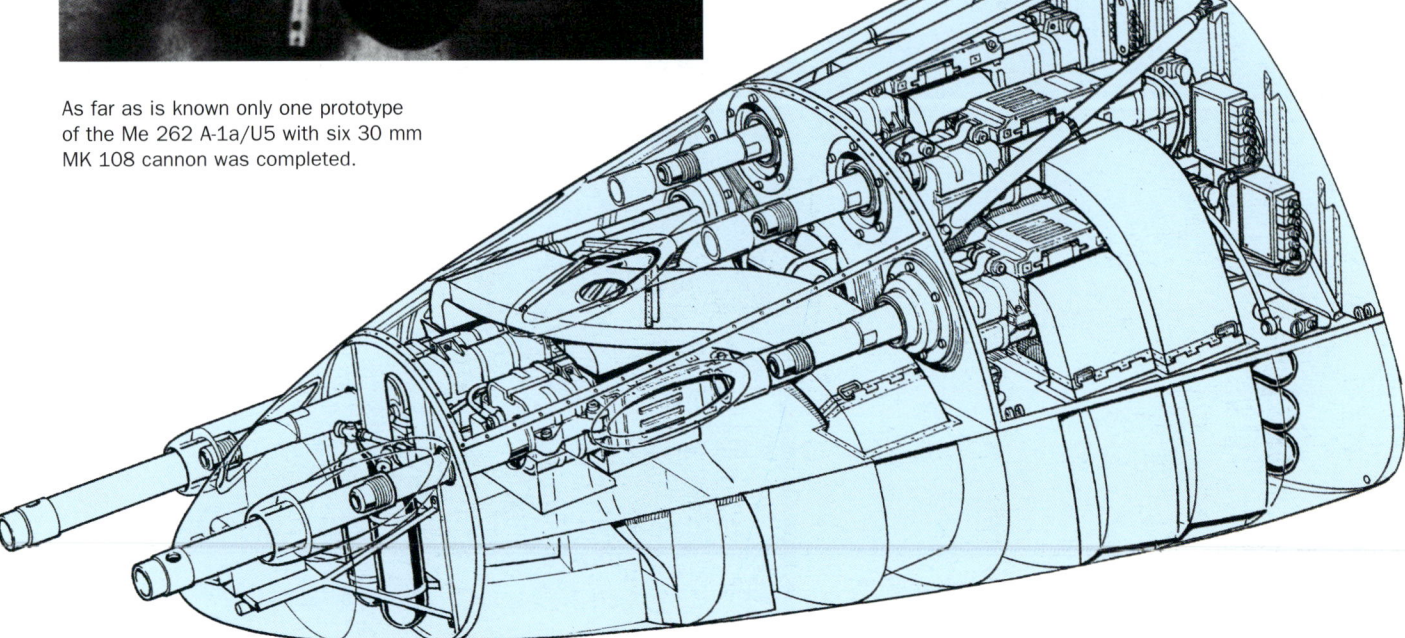

As far as is known only one prototype of the Me 262 A-1a/U5 with six 30 mm MK 108 cannon was completed.

Me 262 A-2a BLITZBOMBER (FAST BOMBER)

A high speed bomber version of the A-1a *Jabo* with the two upper MK 108 cannon removed. This aircraft could be fitted with either two ETC 503 or *Wikingerschiff* bomb racks, with a proposal to replace these later with an improved version of the ETC 504. The alternative bomb loads were detailed in a document dated 30 March 1945:

(with ETC 503)	two SC 250 blast bomb two SD 250 fragmentation bombs two AB 250-2 weapons containers one SC 500 blast bomb one SD 500 fragmentation bomb one AB 500-1 weapon container one AB 500-3 weapon container one BT 200 torpedo bomb
(with *Wikingerschiff*)	2 x SC 250 2 x SD 250 2 x AB 250-2 1 x SC 500 1 x SD 500 1 x AB 500-1
(with ETC 504)	as ETC 503 plus 1 x BT 400 (see *Me 262 Volume One* for details)

By March 1945, it was hoped to conduct operations using the Me 262 A-2a Blitzbomber fitted with a ETC 504 bomb rack carrying the massive BT 400 torpedo bomb. However, no evidence has been found that any such operations were undertaken. Readers should refer to *Me 262 Volume One*, pages 127-128.

Below: An early converted Blitzbomber or "fast bomber" was Me 262 A-1a W.Nr. 110813. Externally very similar to the Me 262 A-1a, the A-2a had the upper pair of MK 108 cannon removed and was fitted with either a pair of ETC 503 or Wikingerschiff bomb racks. This machine was used as an early test aircraft to evaluate the bomb carrying capacity of the Me 262. After completion of these trials this aircraft was converted back to a standard fighter and transferred to Kommando Nowotny where it was relegated to a training role, carrying both a green letter 'S' and number '3'. See Chapter 13.

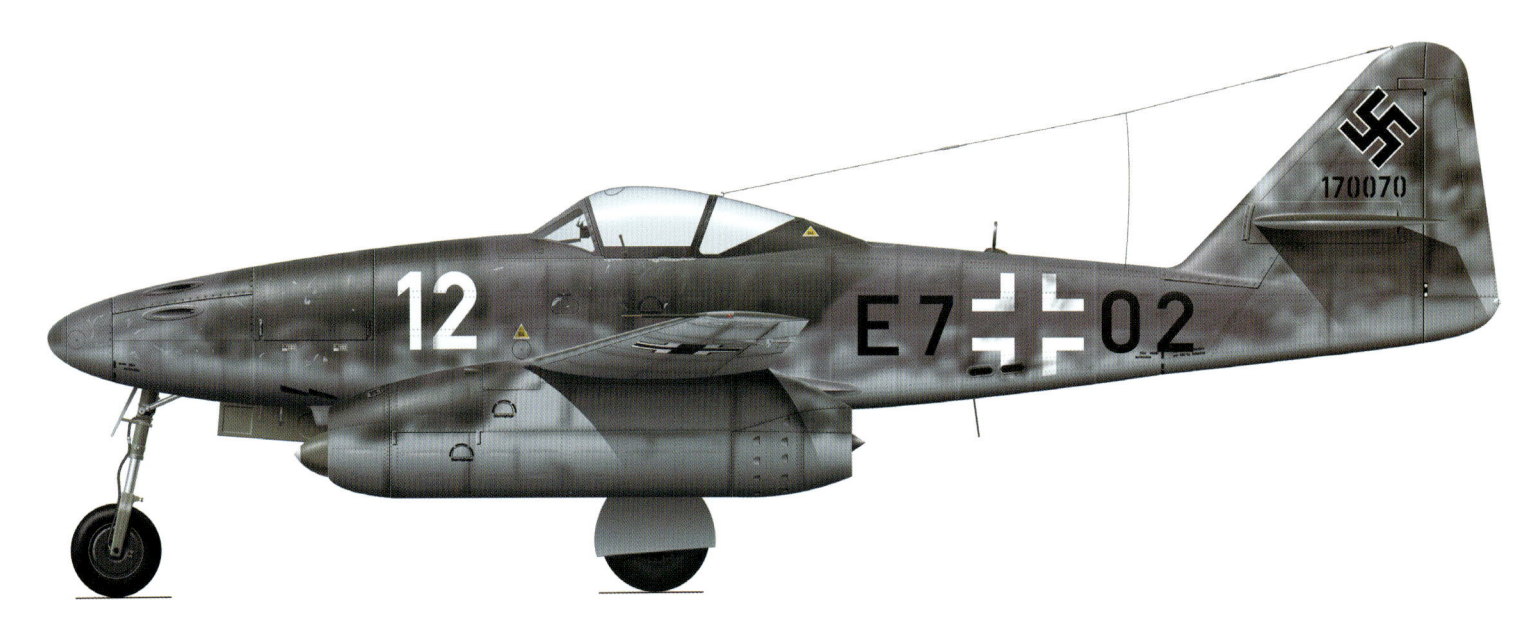

Me 262 A-1a W.Nr. 170070 "White 12" Erprobungstelle Rechlin

This aircraft was used for TSA bombsight trials by department E7 at the Rechlin test centre. The machine had the code "E7+02" painted on the fuselage sides in black, indicating the second Me 262 test aircraft of that department. The presence of the white number "12" on the nose was unusual for a Rechlin aircraft and this may have been retained from when the aircraft was previously in service with an operational unit prior to being transferred.

Left: Another view of Me 262 A-1a W.Nr. 110813. The aircraft is fitted with a pair of Wikingerschiff bomb racks each carrying two SC 250 blast bombs. Aircraft thus equipped were used by KG 51 over the Western Front during late 1944 harassing Allied troop concentrations, armour and airfields.

Opposite centre: Two views of the instrument panel of the Me 262 A-2a/U1 showing the target indicator lamp of the TSA 2D bomb-aiming device.
Opposite bottom: The installation of the Zeiss TSA (Tiefwurf– und Schleuderanlage) 2D low altitude bomb dropping and catapulting device in the cockpit of one of the three Me 262s which tested the apparatus at Rechlin. Used in conjunction with the Revi 16b gunsight, it permitted accurate bomb aiming even in bad visibility.

Me 262 A-2a/U1
BLITZBOMBER MIT TSA
(FAST BOMBER WITH TSA)

The TSA 2D bomb aiming device is described in *Me 262 Volume One*, Chapter 7 Three Me 262s were tested with the device at Rechlin, W.Nr. 130164, 130188 and 170070.

Right: Found abandoned off the Hamburg-Bremen Autobahn in 1945, this is Me 262 A-1a, W.Nr. 170070, E7+02, carrying the tactical marking "White 12", was with Erprobungsstelle Rechlin. The aircraft was used to test the TSA 2D bomb aiming device and various bomb-dropping trials.

Me 262 A-2a/U2
Schnellstbomber mit Lotfe (fast bomber with Lotfe)

This variant underwent several designation changes during its development. It was known initially as the A-2a/U1 but was renamed Me 262 A-3a in the 14 September 1944, *Protokoll Nr. 49*. Late in November 1944 it received its final designation Me 262 A-2a/U2.

Although generally similar to the standard A-2a, the variant was fitted with a special enlarged wooden nose with a glazed cone and upper panel. This was to accommodate a bomb aimer lying prone who was to operate a *Lotfe 7H3* bombsight. To compensate for the increased weight, fuel capacity was reduced to a total of 1,970 ltrs (520 Imp gals). Early aircraft were to be unarmed, but it was eventually intended to install two MK 108 cannon.

The first prototype, W.Nr. 110484 (otherwise known as the second Me 262 V8), flew for the first time in September 1944. It was then transferred to Lechfeld on 22 October and by the end of December had completed 22 test flights. Messerschmitt reported on two bombing trials with the aircraft fitted with two ETC 504 bomb racks in December. During the first, with Baur as pilot and Bayer as bomb aimer, on 5 December, one 250 kg bomb was dropped at a speed of 600 km/h (370 mph) from 2,000 m (6,600 ft) in the north-east corner of the Ammersee peninsula. For the second test five days later, Messerschmitt test pilot Lindner replaced Baur as pilot. This time two bombs were carried and were to be released at 620 km/h (385 mph). Only the first was dropped however because a rattling noise experienced after release led the crew to think that the locking device had worked loose. The report concluded that: "...the results may be considered satisfactory bearing in mind that the pilot and bomb aimer had little practice working together and that the latter was seeing the sight for the first time. Several modifications were carried out during the tests including the fitting of a wooden bulge to lessen noise when the *Lotfe* sight was extended and more padding and improved safety belt for the bomb aimer. It was also decided to move the bomb release button as it was found that this could be easily operated by mistake by the bomb aimer when setting the speed button! On 7 January 1945 the aircraft was transferred to Rechlin where it underwent detailed evaluation. Its eventual fate is unknown.

A second prototype, W.Nr. 110555, was converted in January 1945, being fitted with the modified *Lotfe Kanzel II*. As well as being less bulky the most noticeable feature of the new nose was the installation of a long probe on both sides. The aircraft, which received the alternative designation Me 262 V11, first flew in February, completing a total of six flights during that month and ten more in March. On 30 March it was flown to Schröck near Marburg on the Lahn by a defecting German pilot, but its undercarriage failed to extend and its engines were damaged in the ensuing belly landing. As far as is known, the aircraft was not flown by the Americans.

Me 262 A-2a/U2 prototype W.Nr. 110484 fitted with the Lotfe Kanzel I
After the loss of the W.Nr. 130003, this aircraft became the second Me 262 V8. Like the second V4, the aircraft had dark green (81) upper surfaces. Records indicate it made its first flight on 22 October 1944 and, by the end of December, had flown 22 times, accruing a total flying time of 8 hours 14 minutes. It was transported to E–stelle Rechilin on 7 January 1945 but its fate remains unknown.

Me 262 VARIANTS • 287

The second Me 262 V8 – a Me 262 A-2a/U2 variant, W.Nr. 110484, is towed across a mud-caked Rechlin airfield in early 1945. The aircraft is fitted with a wooden nose housing a prone bomb aimer and a Lotfe 7H gyro-stabilised bombsight. The second aircraft is believed to be W.Nr. 130015, the second Me 262 V1 (note the numerals applied to the nose, just visible beneath the camouflage drape). Both aircraft are seen here during experimentation with a multiple towing apparatus.

Above: As an interim measure, Messerschmitt designed a small "bulge" to cover the protruding lens of the Lotfe 7H bombsight.

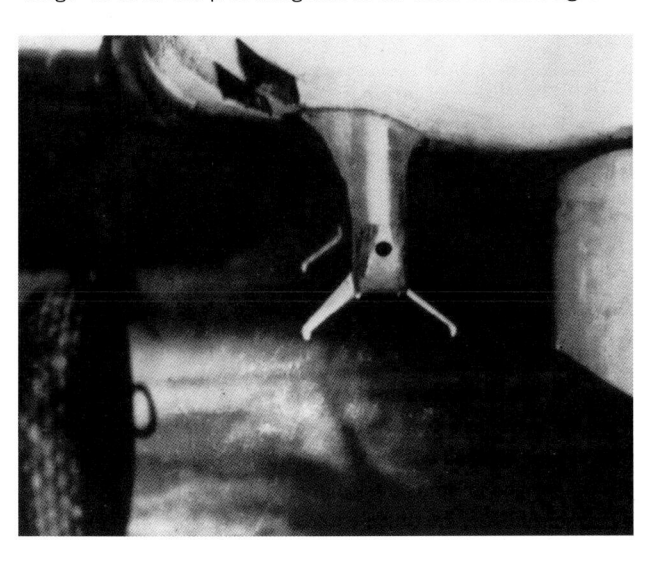

Right and above: Two views from early December 1944 showing the glazed Lotfe Kanzel I bomb aiming position as fitted to Me 262 A-2a/U2, W.Nr. 110484, and in which the bomb aimer would lie prone.

Left: Close-up of the slimmer ETC 504 bomb rack as fitted to the Me 262 A-2a/U2 with the Lotfe Kanzel. Note that this is a standard late production aircraft with treaded tyres.

The second aircraft to be built as a Me 262 A-2a/U2 was W.Nr. 110555, also known as the V11. The aircraft was converted in January 1945, being fitted with the modified Lotfe Kanzel II. Here, Messerschmitt chief test pilot, Karl Baur, lifts open the access panel to the Kanzel (bomb aimer's compartment).

Below: A rearrangement of the instrumentation as conducted at Rechlin.

Below: The original instrumentation arrangement of the Lotfe Kanzel in a Me 262 A-2a/U2, showing the LKS – the switching key – and supplementary bombsight.

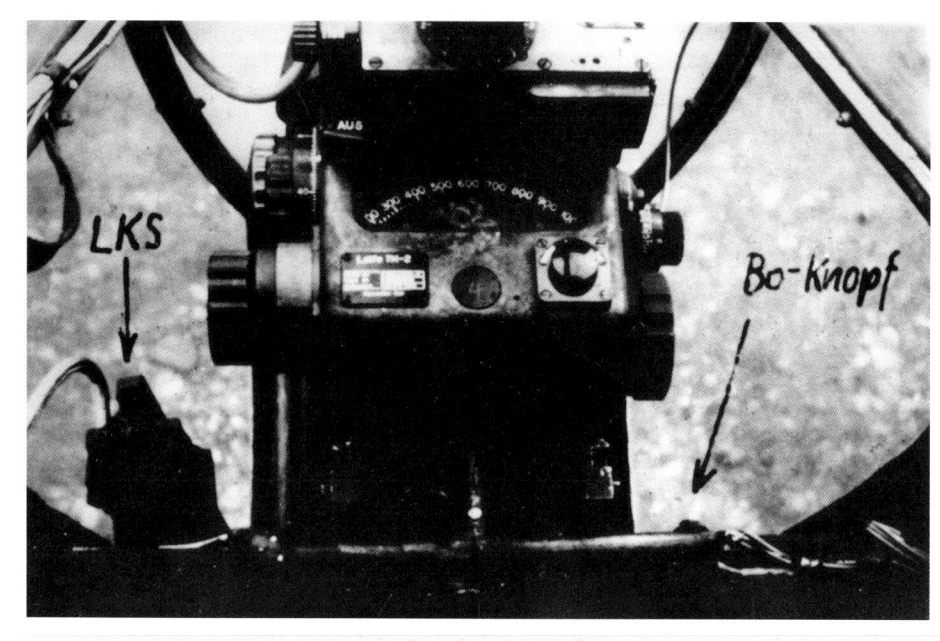

Me 262 VARIANTS • 289

Above: The Me 262 V11, W.Nr. 110555. By the end of March 1945 this aircraft had accumulated 22 flights totalling 5 hrs 5 mins.

Left: On 30 March 1945 Oblt. Benz of 1.(F)/100 based at Saaz flew the second Me 262 A-2a/U2 with two passengers on board to Weimar-Nohra. Because of the short runway there and problems with the undercarriage, Benz decided to make a belly landing which was much safer for his passengers. This photograph shows the aircraft just after capture by American troops on 8 May 1945. The prototype number V555 was painted in white on both sides of the nose.

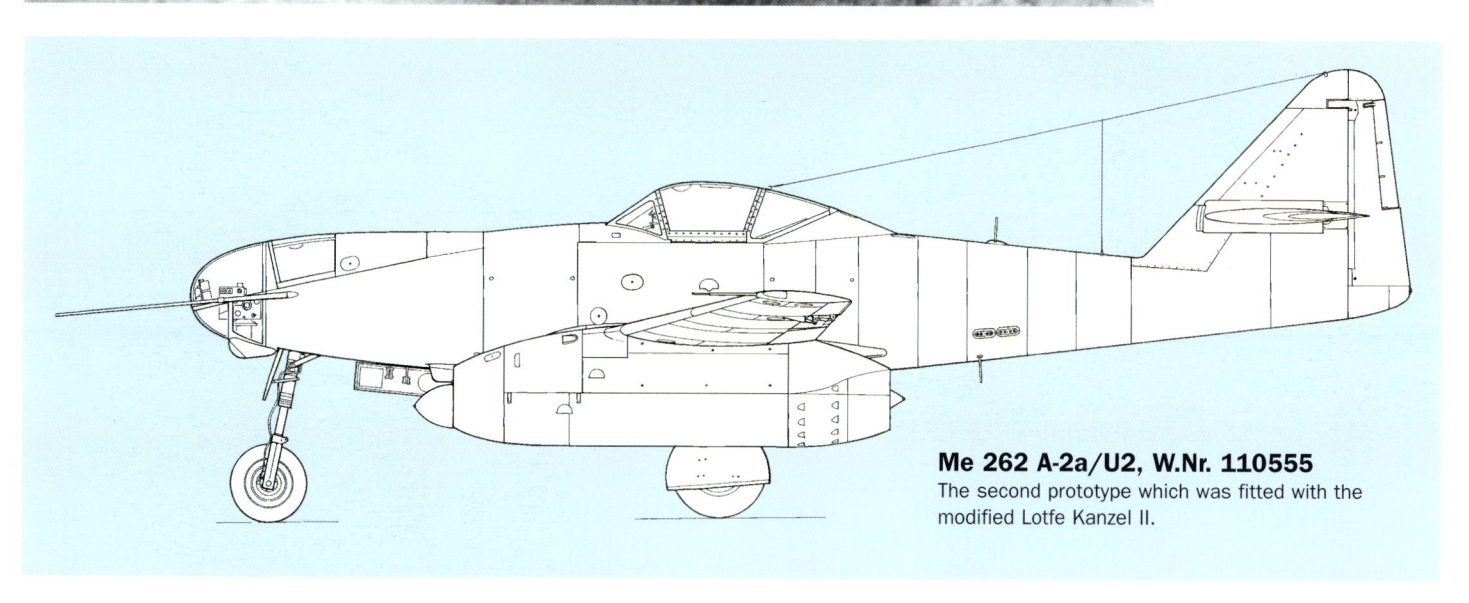

Me 262 A-2a/U2, W.Nr. 110555
The second prototype which was fitted with the modified Lotfe Kanzel II.

Me 262 A-2/U2, W.Nr. 110555

This aircraft, also designated as the Me 262 V11, was fitted with the wooden Lotfe Kanzel II. The nose accommodated a bomb aimer who lay prone using the Lotfe 7H bomb sight. The most noticable difference between the nose of this aircraft and W.Nr. 110484 was the installation of the long probes fitted on both sides of the nose, possibly to aid range finding. The aircraft first flew in February 1945, completing a total of six flights during that month and ten more in March. On 30 March, in the hands of a defecting pilot, it was flown to Schröck near Marburg and captured by US Forces.

Me 262 VARIANTS • 291

In this sequence of photographs, V555, W.Nr.110555, is seen being salvaged by a US recovery team. The probes mounted on either side of the Lotfe Kanzel were fitted in connection with tests of a special sonic range-finding device code-named 'Baldrian'.

With the aircraft hoisted and the mainwheels lowered, the starboard Jumo engine has been removed from the wing. As far as is known, the aircraft was not flown by the Americans.

Me 262 A-3a *Panzerflugzeug* (Armoured Aircraft)

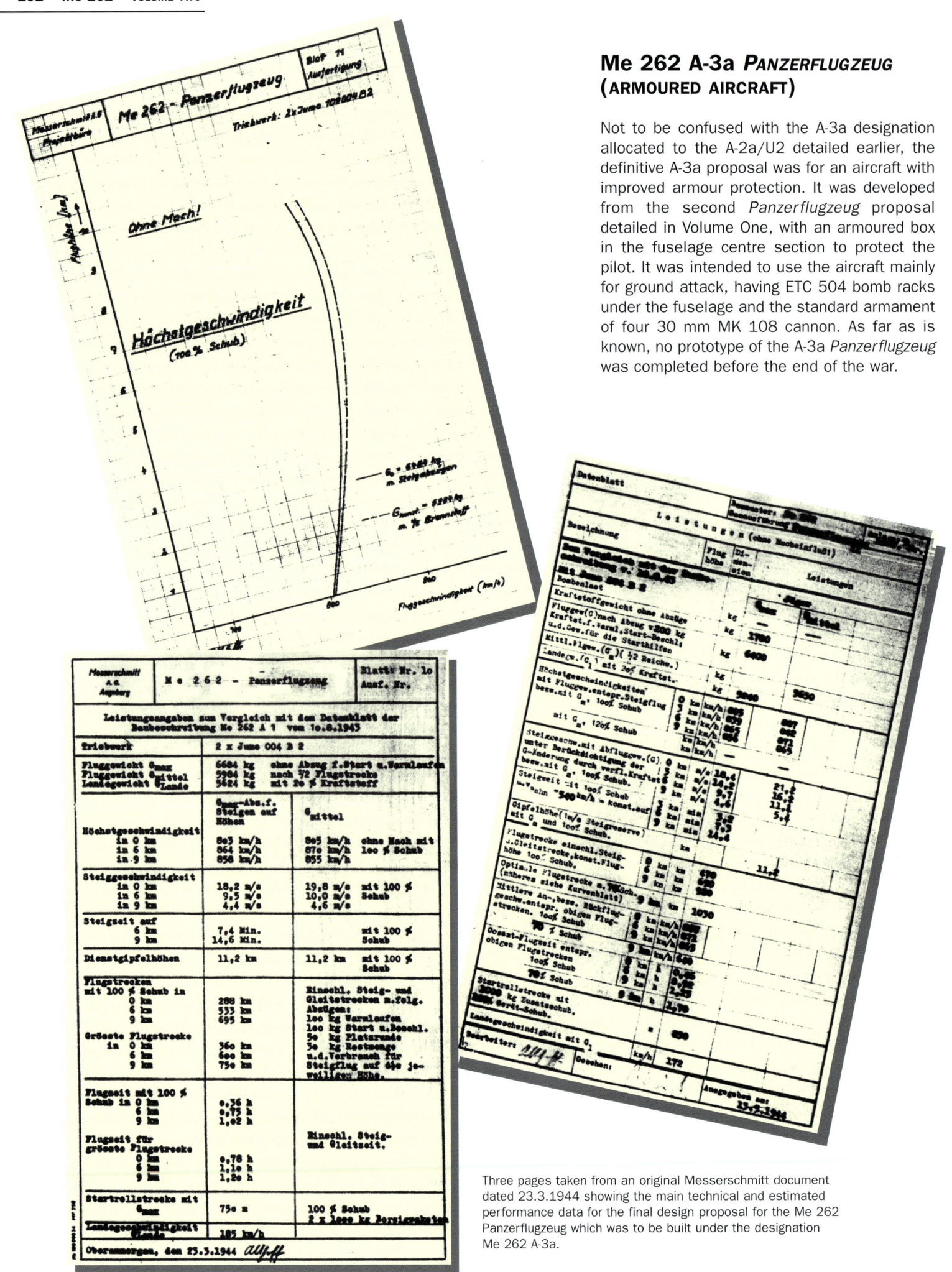

Not to be confused with the A-3a designation allocated to the A-2a/U2 detailed earlier, the definitive A-3a proposal was for an aircraft with improved armour protection. It was developed from the second *Panzerflugzeug* proposal detailed in Volume One, with an armoured box in the fuselage centre section to protect the pilot. It was intended to use the aircraft mainly for ground attack, having ETC 504 bomb racks under the fuselage and the standard armament of four 30 mm MK 108 cannon. As far as is known, no prototype of the A-3a *Panzerflugzeug* was completed before the end of the war.

Three pages taken from an original Messerschmitt document dated 23.3.1944 showing the main technical and estimated performance data for the final design proposal for the Me 262 Panzerflugzeug which was to be built under the designation Me 262 A-3a.

Me 262 A-4a BEHELFSAUFKLÄRER (INTERIM RECONNAISSANCE)

Some mystery surrounds the Me 262 A-4a designation. In a *Flugzeug-Baureihen-Blatt*[4] of 1 November 1944, the aircraft is described as a *Behelfsaufklärer*, unarmed but carrying two Rb 50/30 cameras. Production Programme 227/I (described in Chapter 12 and detailed in Appendix seven) indicates that the variant was fitted with a small SSK camera but armed with two MK 108 cannon. This source indicates that three aircraft had been completed by the end of November 1944, and that at least another one hundred were planned for assembly by the Eger factory. Certainly one A-4a (W.Nr. 500095) was reported damaged on 20 February 1945. It is unlikely that many aircraft were completed since a *Baureihen-Übersicht*[5] of 1 January 1945 records that the A-4a designation was "unallocated".

Me 262 A-5a AUFKLÄRER (RECONNAISSANCE)

In the *Flugzeug-Baureihen-Blatt* of 1 November 1944 mentioned previously, the designation Me 262 A-5 was allocated to an interim single-seat night fighter variant with FuG 353 and FuG 120 radio equipment. This was soon abandoned and the designation A-5a re-used for a production reconnaissance version with a purpose built nose housing the two Rb 50/30 cameras plus two 30 mm MK 108 cannon with 66 rounds. Like the A-1a/U3 the camera magazines were to be covered by bulges, but, although larger, these were slimmer and more streamlined than those fitted to the earlier provisional variant. Standard fuel tankage was carried with provision for two 300 ltr (79 Imp gal) drop tanks beneath the fuselage. As with the A-1a/U3, the aircraft was equipped with the FuG 16 ZS transceiver.

The Me 262 A-5a Aufklärer (reconnaissance)
This aircraft was to be fitted with two Rb 50/30 cameras and two 30 mm MK 108 cannon. The cannon blisters were to be much slimmer than those fitted to the earlier provisional variant.

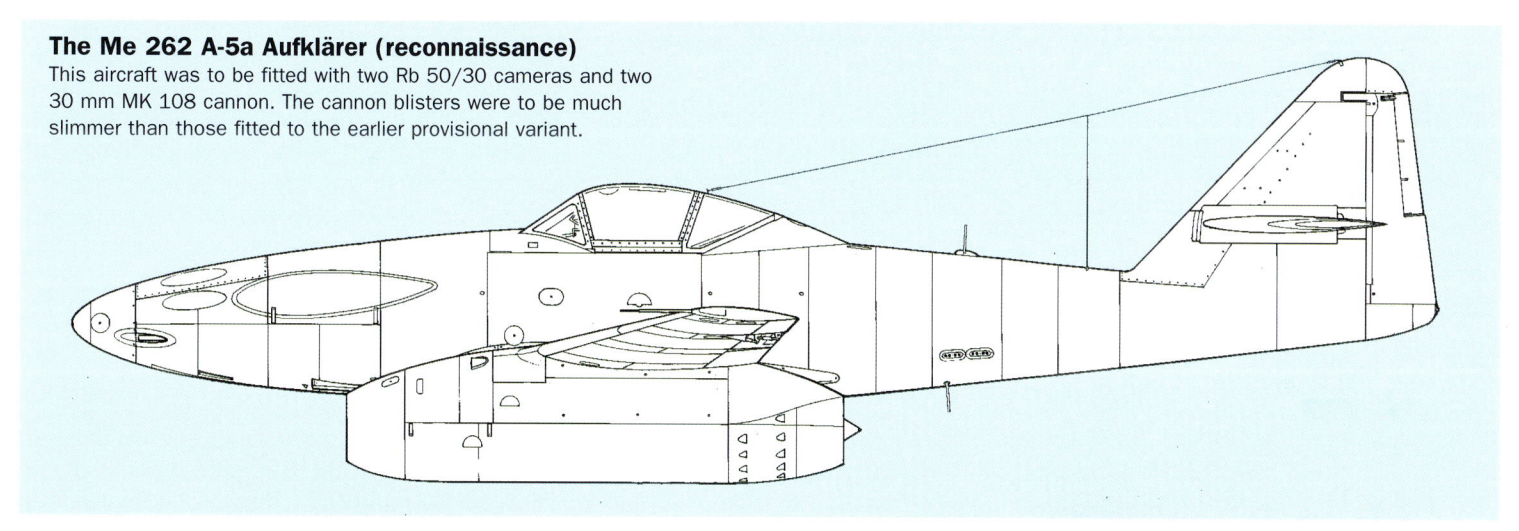

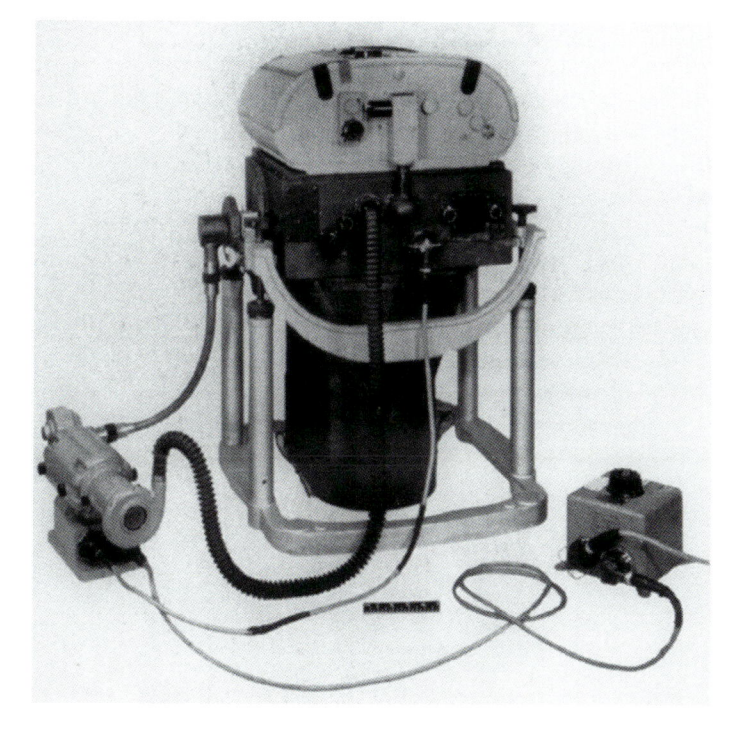

Left: An Rb50/30 camera installed in its mounting and servicing cradle. The upper pale box is the removable film magazine which, when fully loaded, could take 64 m of film (210 ft).

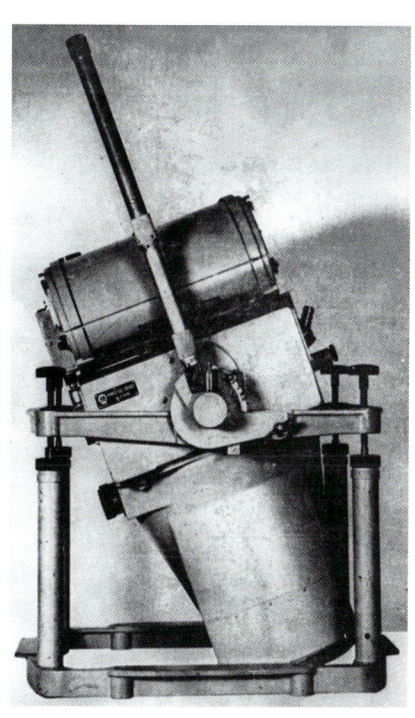

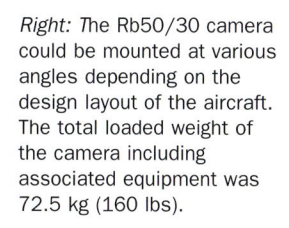

Right: The Rb50/30 camera could be mounted at various angles depending on the design layout of the aircraft. The total loaded weight of the camera including associated equipment was 72.5 kg (160 lbs).

Me 262 B-1a Schulflugzeug (Trainer)

Following the *Schulflugzeug* project issued in July 1943 (see *Me 262 Volume One*, Chapter 5), a proposal for modifying standard Me 262s to the two-seat training role was originated on 2 March 1944. These were to be converted from standard A-1as by the Blohm und Voss company at Wenzendorf, 30 km (20 mls) south-west of Hamburg. Blohm und Voss were already producing rear fuselages and tailplanes for the aircraft, completing 1,577 such components before the end of the war. On 18 March it was decided to place an order for a mock-up of a two-seat Me 262 to be produced when possible, with two prototypes to follow.

The two-seat prototype, the Me 262 S5 (W.Nr. 130010), flew for the first time on 28 April 1944, later being transferred to Blohm und Voss for conversion. It was similar to the original *Schulflugzeug* proposal, but had the two rear tanks replaced by two smaller containers housing 400 and 250 ltrs (110 and 65 Imp gals) respectively. The space created was filled by a second seat for the instructor and full dual controls were provided. A new elongated canopy was fitted, and the standard armament of four MK 108 cannon retained. Two 300 ltr (80 Imp gal) drop tanks were normally carried beneath the ETC 503 racks to supplement internal fuel capacity. The Blohm und Voss built prototype took 8,800 manhours to complete, of which approximately 5,500 hours were for the conversion work and the remainder for modifications and test flying.

On 30 August 1944 a delivery schedule of Me 262s for conversion to two-seaters was issued, *Deutsche Lufthansa* workshops at Berlin-Staaken being slated to join in conversion work in November (see Table 1).

The first four production Me 262 B-1as, as the variant was designated, were completed in September 1944. Two of these later went to KG 51, one to KG 54 and the other to *Erprobungskommando 262*. By 6 October nine aircraft had been converted at Wenzendorf but, on that day, the factory was heavily bombed. This resulted in the destruction of twelve aircraft that were being converted, and it was not until January that the next machine was produced by Blohm und Voss.

Fortunately for the programme, *Lufthansa* were able to carry on production, with Blohm und Voss completing another seven aircraft before the Wenzendorf factory was almost completely destroyed in another bombing raid on 7 January 1945. Five aircraft were destroyed this time and Blohm und Voss were only able to produce one further conversion before the end of the war. Nevertheless, Blohm und Voss and *Lufthansa* between them managed to build 67 aircraft by the end of March 1945. These were distributed in small numbers to various units (see Table 2).

III./KG 76 conducted bombing operations over the Western Front in late 1944-1945 using the Arado Ar 234. However, at least three Me 262 B-1a trainers were delivered to the unit for training purposes. One such aircraft is seen here having been refuelled at Burg in late 1944.

Table 1

Month	Blohm und Voss	Lufthansa
July 1944	1	–
August 1944	3	–
September 1944	6	–
October 1944	9	–
November 1944	11	1
December 1944	12	3
January 1945	10	5
February 1945	8	7
March 1945	5	10
April 1945	0	15
TOTALS	65	41

Table 2

Unit	Sep 44	Oct 44	Nov 44	Dec 44	Jan 45	Feb 45	Mar 45	Totals
EKdo 262	1	1	–	–	–	–	–	2
III./EJG 2	–	–	–	1	–	9	10	20
IV./EKG 1	–	–	–	–	4	3	4	11
II./EKG(J)	–	–	–	–	–	1	2	3
Fl.Üb.G 1	–	–	–	1	–	4	2	7
I./JG 7	–	–	–	2	1	–	–	3
II./JG 7	–	–	–	–	–	2	–	2
III./JG 7	–	–	–	–	–	–	1	1
JV 44	–	–	–	–	–	–	2	2
KG 51	2	–	–	–	–	–	–	2
III./KG 76	–	1	1	1	–	–	–	3
III./KG(J) 6	–	–	–	–	–	–	1	1
KG(J) 54	1	–	–	4	–	–	–	5
NAG 6	–	–	–	–	3	–	–	3
TLR	–	–	1	–	–	–	1	2
TOTALS	4	2	2	9	8	19	23	67

Hptm. Diether Lukesch commanded both the jet bomber training Gruppe, III./EKG 1 and the Ar 234 operational element – the Einsatzstaffel – of III./KG 76. Both units employed a limited number of Me 262 B-1a trainers, one of which can be seen behind Lukesch in this photograph.

Me 262 B-1a Schulflugzeug (two-seater trainer)

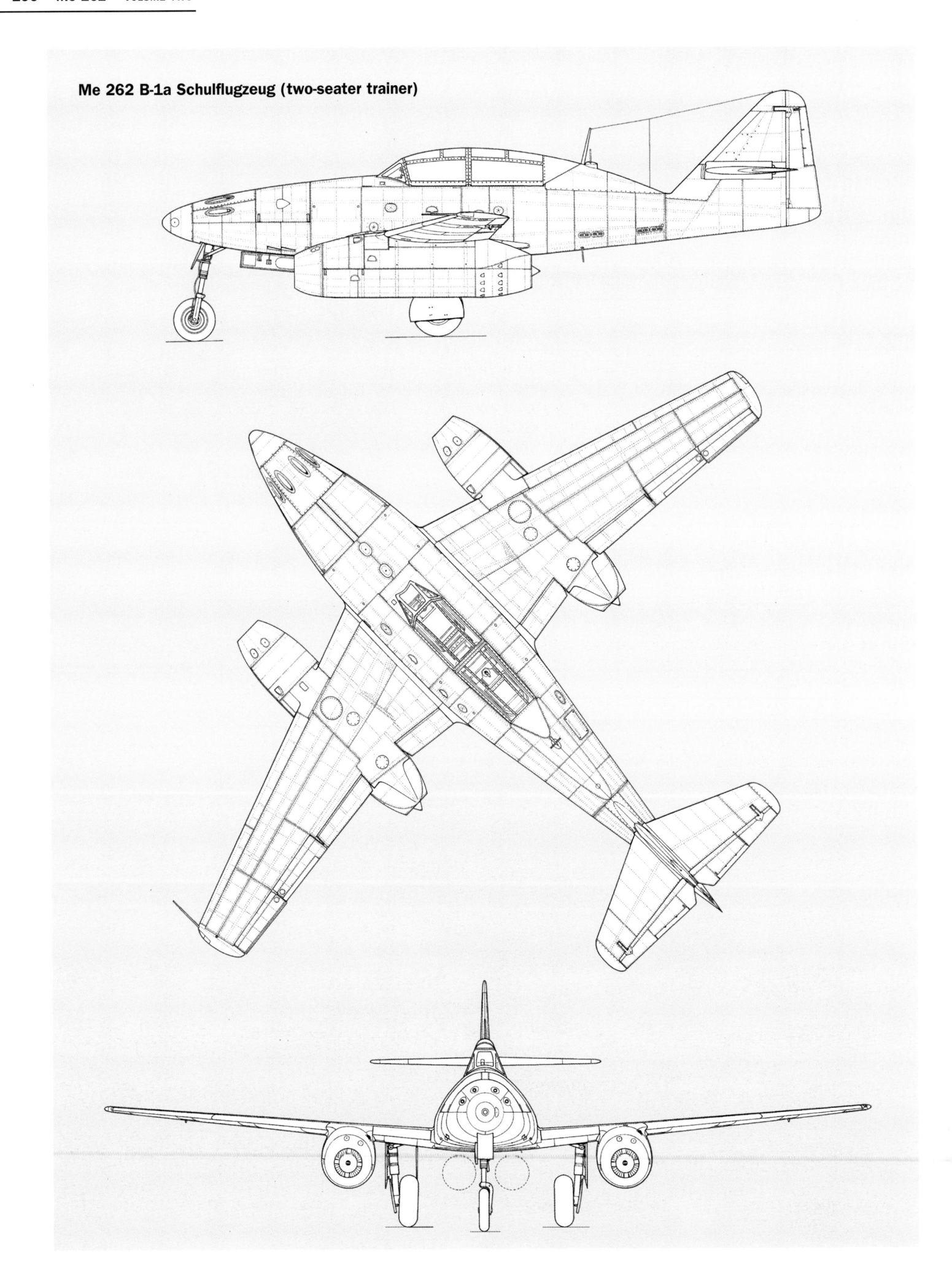

Me 262 B-1a/U1 Behelfsnachtjäger (interim night fighter)

See *Me 262 Volume Four*.

Me 262 B-2a Nachtjäger (night fighter)

See *Me 262 Volume Four*.

Me 262 C-1a Heimatschützer I (Home Defender I)

The development of the three fast climbing rocket boosted *Interzeptor* fighter proposals detailed in Chapter 5 at first proceeded very slowly. By the spring of 1944, they had been renamed as the *Heimatschützer I, II and III* respectively. Shortly after this, the third *Heimatschützer* (home defender) proposal, powered solely by two Walter rocket engines, was dropped, but work continued on the other two designs.

Work began on converting an early production Me 262, W.Nr. 130186, as the prototype *Heimatschützer I* during August 1944. This was basically a standard Me 262 A-1a with the rear fuselage and tail modified to house a Walter HWK RII/211 (109-509) rocket engine. The main external difference was that the rear fuselage and rudder were cut away to allow for the rocket exhaust. The standard 900 ltr (238 Imp gal) forward fuel tank was replaced by a special non corrosive container for *T-Stoff*, and *C-Stoff* was carried in the rear 600 ltr (159 Imp gal) fuselage tank. The remaining 900 and 170 ltr tanks were used for J2 jet fuel. Unlike the original *Interzeptor I* project, the prototype carried standard armament of four cannon. Although the prototype was known at one time as the Me 262 J-1, the official designation chosen for the *Heimatschützer I* was Me 262 C-1a.

The prototype made its first flight, with turbojets only, when it was transferred from Leipheim to Lechfeld on 2 September but ten days later it was slightly damaged in an air attack by the US Fifteenth Air Force. Following the change of the rocket engine and one of the Riedel starter motors, it made its second flight on 18 October. This flight was devoted to testing the *T-Stoff* jettisoning system, 900 ltrs of coloured liquid being ejected from the forward tank. The spread of stain over the entire bottom fuselage and undercarriage recesses showed that fuel dumping might result in fire from contact with waste oil.

On 21 October the aircraft carried out taxying trials with additional mainwheels and four days later the rocket engine was ground tested for the first time. Following modifications to the engine bearers a second test of the rocket was made, but this resulted in welding faults being discovered in the combustion chamber and the engine had to be changed. Several other modifications were made including relocating the radio equipment due to fumes seeping into that part of the fuselage and alterations to the pressurized cabin.

Following these changes, the rocket engine was ground tested twice on 23 November, but the fuel pump and *T-Stoff* tank had to be changed four days later. Another ground run was made on 2 December and 13 days later a third flight test

Below and next page: With its Walter rocket engine firing and test pilot Gerd Lindner at the controls, the Me 262 C-1a Heimatschützer I powers along the runway at Lechfeld in February 1945.

was conducted to further test the fuel jettisoning system. This confirmed the findings of the earlier trial and resulted in the design team moving the fuel dumping tube to below the rear fuselage, emptying behind the tail.

The rocket was fired on the ground again on 18 December but this time another fault in the welding of the combustion chamber resulted in a small fire. After this was changed, on 4 January, water was flushed through the complete system. Unfortunately surplus water froze in the pipes, leading Messerschmitt to complain that the Walter company had failed to advise them of what type of anti-freeze to use. Two further ground runs were made on 13 January without the rear fuselage fitted. After this was added, another test was made two days later, but this resulted in yet another fire. A third combustion chamber was then fitted, and the Flight Test Department was charged with developing a quick release system for the rear fuselage to minimize the time needed to remove and refit it.

Ground runs were made with the rocket on 29 January and 3 February, and three days later the new fuel jettisoning system was tested successfully. Further problems with faulty welding in rocket engine components were then experienced and it was not until 20 February that three successful ground tests were made. Three days later the turbojet and rocket engines were run together for the first time and on 27 February 1945, the first flight with all three engines running was made. Four further rocket boosted flights were made on 16 March, one by Gerd Lindner and three by Herr Kaiser. Three days later Lindner was forced to abort a flight

Above and far left: Photographs taken at Farnborough of the Me 262 C-1a's specially modified rear fuselage. In the picture to the left it is possible to see the strengthening band and the damaged rocket fuel dumping tube beneath.

Close-up of the rear fuselage of the Me 262 C-1a prototype. Carrying the experimental number 'V-186' (the last three digits of the Werk Nummer), the aircraft was also known as the second Me 262 V6 after the loss of W.Nr. 130001. The aircraft first flew on 2 September 1944, but was not flown with the rocket firing until 27 February 1945, its fifth flight.

Below and inset right: Two close ups of the Walter HWK 509 A-2 rocket engine mounted in the rear fuselage of the Me 262 Heimatschützer I. This photograph was taken whilst the fuselage was under examination at the Royal Aircraft Establishment at Farnborough, England after the war.

Above: This close-up of the rear fuselage of the Me 262C-1a showing the access panel for maintenance to the Walter HWK 509 A-2 rocket engine.

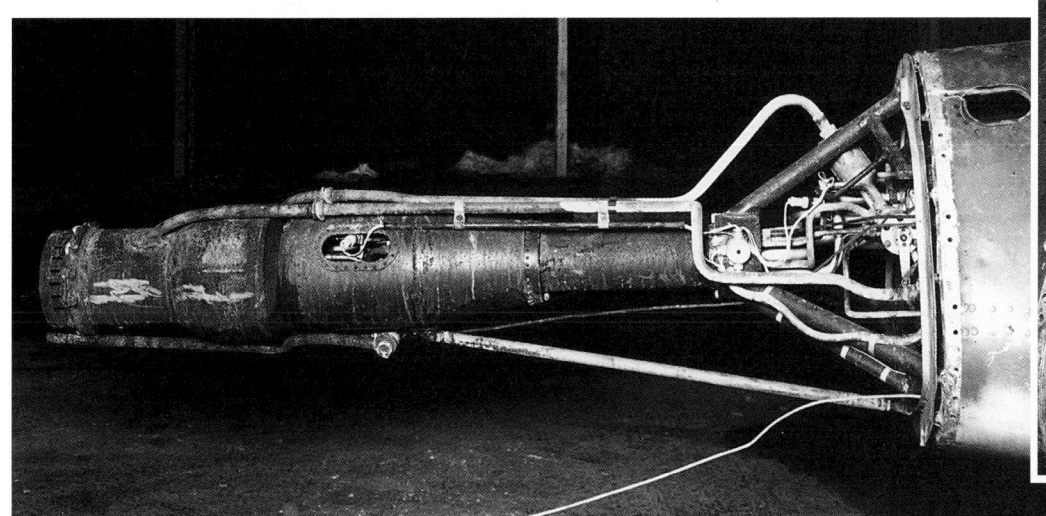

Me 262 C-1a Heimatschützer I rocket-boosted fighter

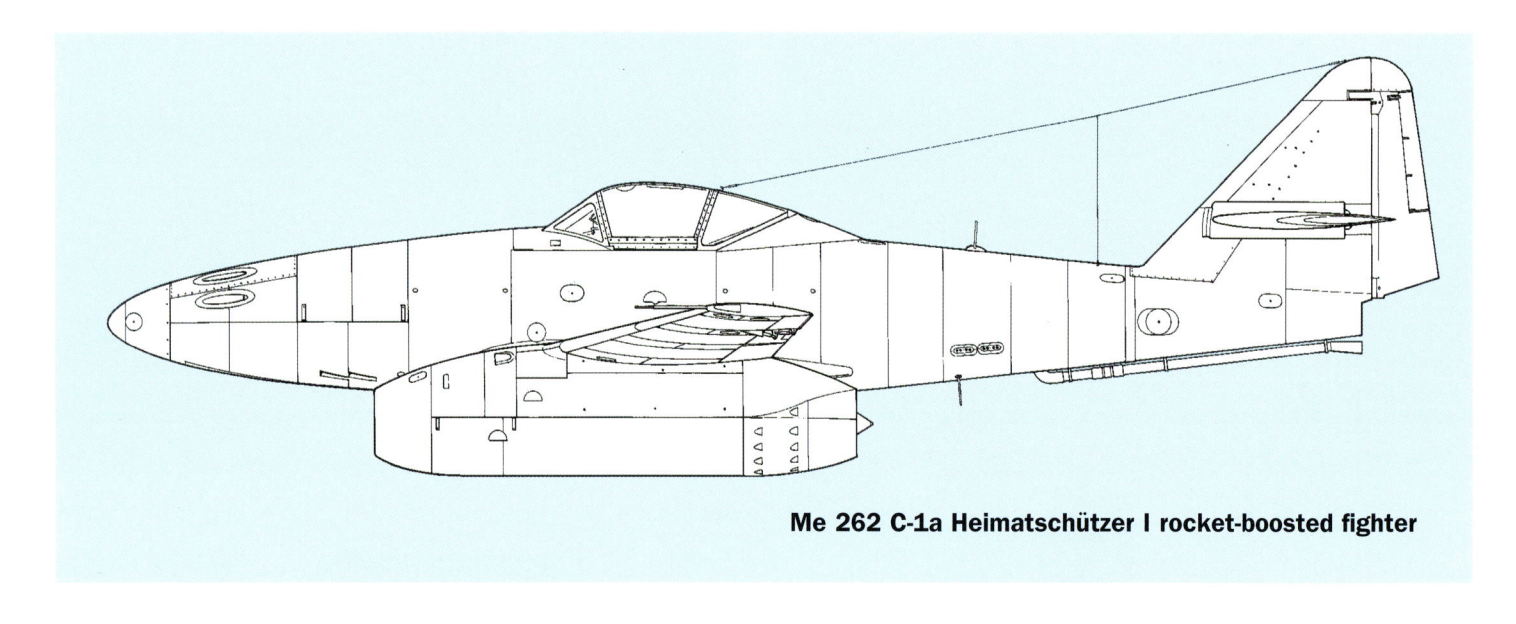

The starboard BMW 003 TLR composite jet and rocket engine of the Me 262 C-2b being examined by ground staff following the engine fire which took place on 25 January 1945.

when excessive nosewheel flutter was experienced. The aircraft was then 20% damaged in an Allied air attack on Lechfeld on 23 March and was probably never flown again. Its fuselage (which was also known as the second V6) was found at Lechfeld at the end of the war and shipped to the Royal Aircraft Establishment at Farnborough for examination.

The Walter HWK 509 A-2 rocket engine developed 1,700 kgs (3,750 lbs) of thrust for 3.5 minutes. Forty seconds of this time was used for takeoff, 60 seconds for acceleration and 110 seconds for climb up to 6,500 m (21,000 ft). Take-off weight was estimated as 7,800 kg (17,200 lbs). A proposal was also made to exchange the HWK 509 with the experimental BMW P 3390 C (109-510) engine.

Me 262 C-2b Heimatschützer II (Home Defender II)

The C-2b, which was based on the *Interzeptor II* project, was a standard Me 262 with the engines replaced by two BMW 003 TLR composite turbojet and rocket units. These comprised a standard BMW 003 A turbojet to which was attached a BMW P.3395 rocket engine which used a combination of *R-Stoff* (Tonka self igniting fuel) and *SV-Stoff* (concentrated nitric acid). The first prototype, W.Nr. 170074 (which received the alternative designation V12), was transported by road to Lechfeld on 20 December 1944 after being equipped with two BMW-TLR factory conversion sets. After modifications had been made to the electrical wiring and the ventilation system for the *SV-* and *R-Stoff* tanks, the aircraft made its first flight on the power of the turbojets alone on 8 January.

During January a series of checks were made with the rocket engines using water instead of the rocket fuels, but these revealed various problems with the pumps, ventilation pipes and seals. The Riedel starters for the turbojets also gave problems and had to be changed several times. It was not until 24 January that the first satisfactory water test was made with the rocket engines. Next day the rocket engines were ground run for the first time, but the starboard unit exploded immediately after

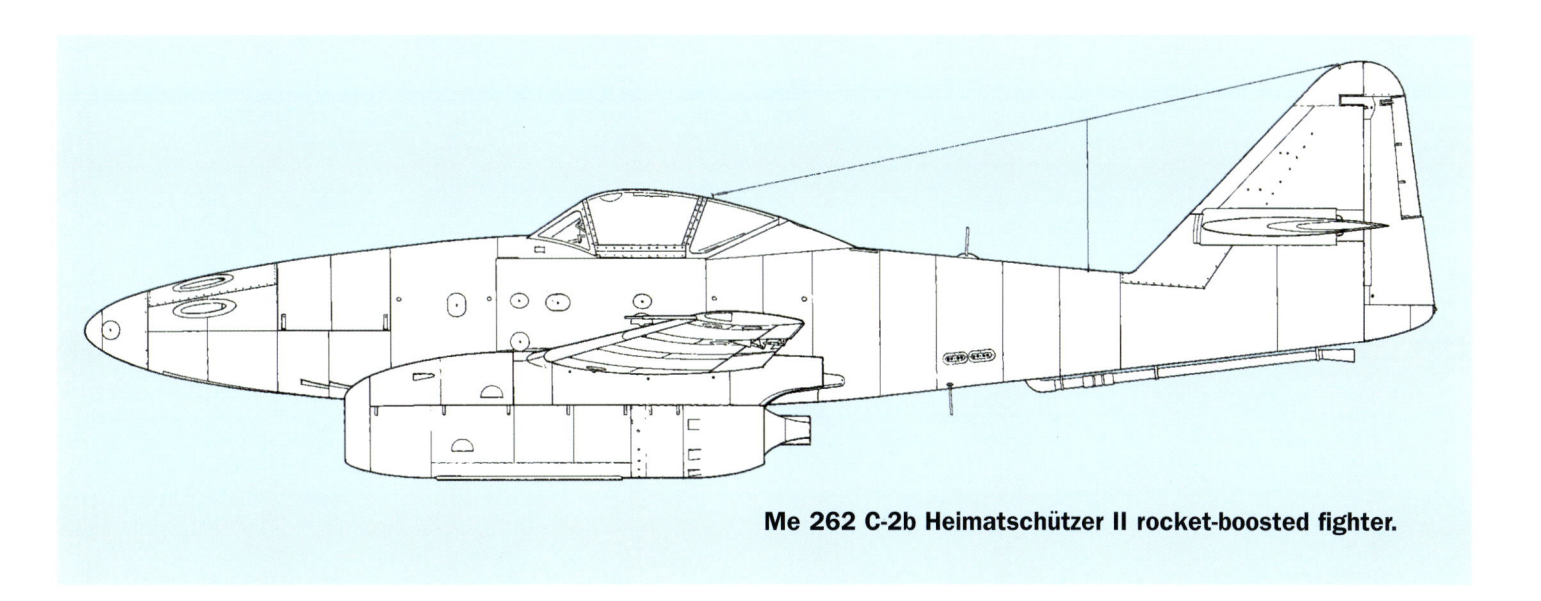

Me 262 C-2b Heimatschützer II rocket-boosted fighter.

ignition. The resulting sheet of flame severely damaged the turbojet and part of the wing and burnt all the paint off the fuselage side.

BMW held that the explosion was due to the *R-Stoff* being contaminated with water, but Messerschmitt investigations seemed to indicate an excess of *SV-Stoff* being injected into the engine. They pointed to the absolute necessity for the pilot to be able to close the fuel cocks of both tanks from the cockpit. *"If this is not provided,"* their report continued, *"there will be an extensive danger of fire should the rocket engines fail to light due to the discharge of R- and SV-Stoff during the machine's landing run."*

On 1 February a series of static tests were made with the new BMW 003 TLR engine, this being fitted to the aircraft on the 7th. Again problems were experienced with both the *SV-Stoff* tanks and seals, mainly due to the volatile nature of this fuel. After modifications were made, a series of 'sharp' or powered runs were made on 18 February with both rocket engines, but these were not entirely satisfactory. The port rocket engine was removed three days later followed by the turbojet itself the next day. Another water test, on the 23rd, revealed more pressure problems and faulty electrical wiring which BMW were asked to investigate.

After these problems were overcome, the aircraft made its second turbojet powered flight on 24 March 1945. This satisfactory test led to the rocket engines being fired for the first time in flight two days later. The rockets burned for 40 seconds during a climb, and at last proved the feasibility of the engine. Another flight was made on 29 March but this time the rockets failed to ignite. Next day, a shortage of the B4 fuel needed for the BMW 003s led to them being removed for conversion to more readily available J2. The aircraft never flew again, and it was found, minus its engines, by American troops when they entered Lechfeld at the end of the war.

Three photographs of the Me 262 C-2b Heimatschützer II, W.Nr. 170074 during further testing of its BMW 003 TLR composite turbojet/rocket engines at Lechfeld, 23 March 1945. This testing revealed pressure problems and faulty electrical wiring which BMW were asked to investigate.

The results of the January 1945 rocket unit fire can be seen from this picture of the rear fuselage of the Me 262 C-2b. The flames were so fierce that they seared the paint from the structure.

Below: The extensively damaged rear of the starboard BMW 003 engine of the Me 262 C-2b Heimatschützer II seen following the fire damage to the rocket unit.

A dramatic photograph taken at Lechfeld on 25 January 1945, showing the Me 262 C-2b Heimatschützer II, W.Nr. 170074 – also known as the Me 262 V12 – undergoing a ground run of its BMW rocket engines. Unfortunately, the starboard rocket engine exploded immediately after ignition and resulted in a spectacular engine fire (see also chapter opener photograph).

Me 262 C-1a W.Nr. 130186 Heimatschützer I
Fitted with two Jumo 004 B and one Walther HWK 509 A engines, the Heimatschützer I prototype made its first flight on 2 September 1944, but was not flown with the rocket firing until 27 February 1945, its fifth flight. It became the second V6 but on 22 March it was damaged in an Allied air attack. Following the war's end, the rear fuselage was examined by the RAE Farnborough.

On 30 March 1945, the Me 262 C-2b Heimatschützer II, W.Nr. 170074, was returned to the workshops for the conversion of its BMW 003 turbojets to the more readily available J2 fuel. This modification was never completed and the aircraft was found abandoned at Lechfeld after the war. Behind the C-2b in this photo is the Me 262 V10, W.Nr. 130005, which tested various forms of armour protection and took part in bomb-dropping and towing trials.

Me 262 C-2b W.Nr. 170074 Heimatschützer II

The Heimatschützer II prototype, "V074" was also known as the Me 262 V12. It made its first flight using turbojets only on 8 January 1945. The aircraft is shown here after repairs had begun to the damage caused to the fuselage when the port rocket engine exploded during a ground test on 25 January 1945. The first flight with both turbojet and rocket engines firing finally took place on 26 March 1945. Shortage of B4 fuel needed for the BMW 003 turbojets led to them being removed on 30 march 1945 for conversion to J2. The aircraft was found by US forces at Lechfeld at the end of the war.

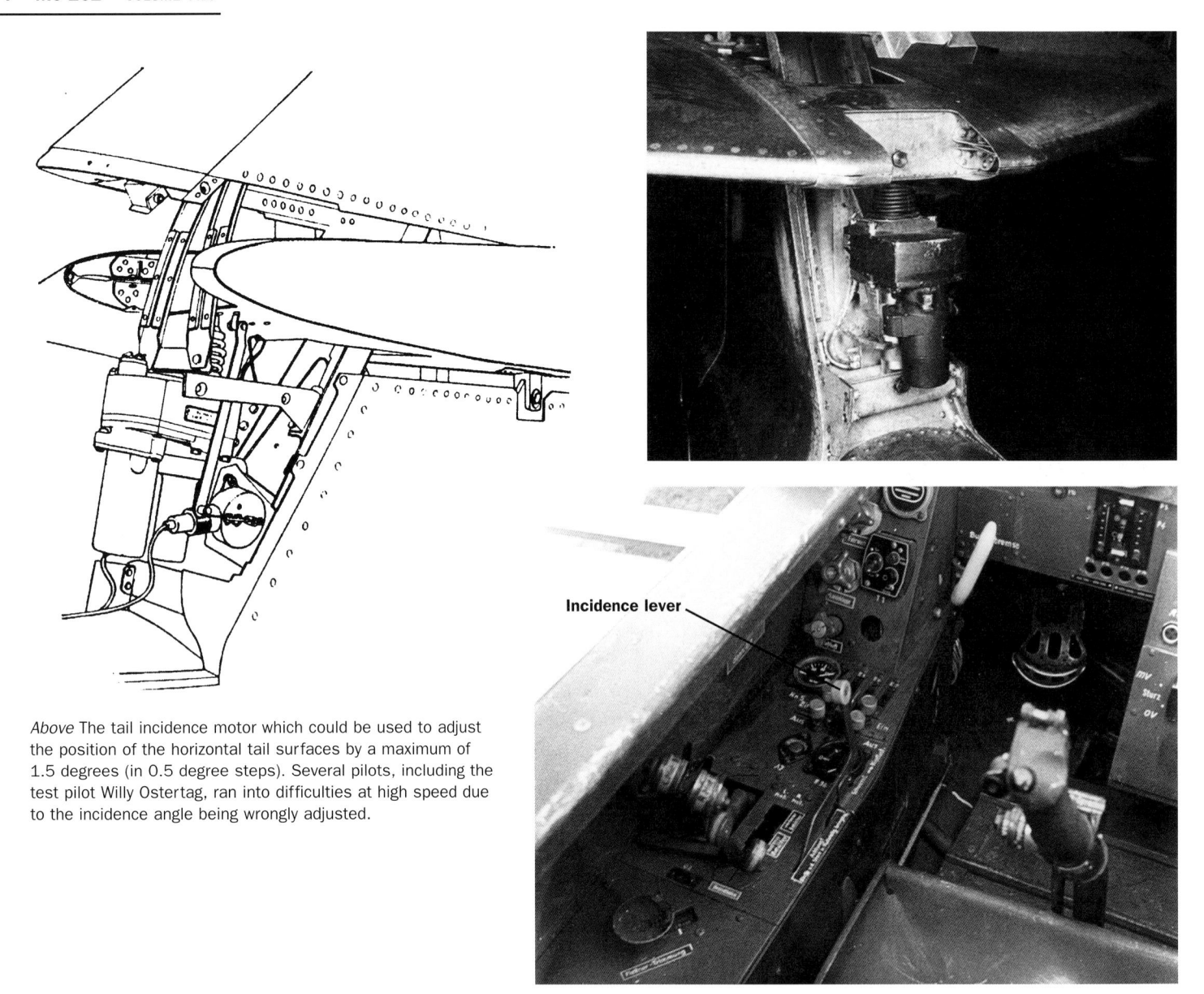

Above The tail incidence motor which could be used to adjust the position of the horizontal tail surfaces by a maximum of 1.5 degrees (in 0.5 degree steps). Several pilots, including the test pilot Willy Ostertag, ran into difficulties at high speed due to the incidence angle being wrongly adjusted.

Top: A close up of the tail incidence motor.
Above: Incidence adjustment could be carried out from inside the cockpit by moving the lever indicated backward or forward for downward or upward movement accordingly.

The rocket fuel jettisoning tube as fitted to the Me 262 C-2b Heimatschützer series. Note the fin fairings have been removed to expose the tail incidence motor.

Me 262 VARIANTS • 305

Left: An unusual view of the rocket fuel-dumping tube fitted to both the Me 262 C-1a and C-2b target defence fighters. The highly volatile nature of these fuels made the need for their quick release a necessity.

Below: The BMW 003 R combined turbojet and rocket engine which was fitted to the Me 262 C-2b. The BMW 718 (project designation P.3395) rocket unit can be seen mounted above and behind the turbojet.

Messerschmitt technicians assist a test pilot with his parachute harness on the wing of the Me 262 C-2b. Clearly visible is the outlet for the BMW rocket engine mounted above the main turbojet unit.

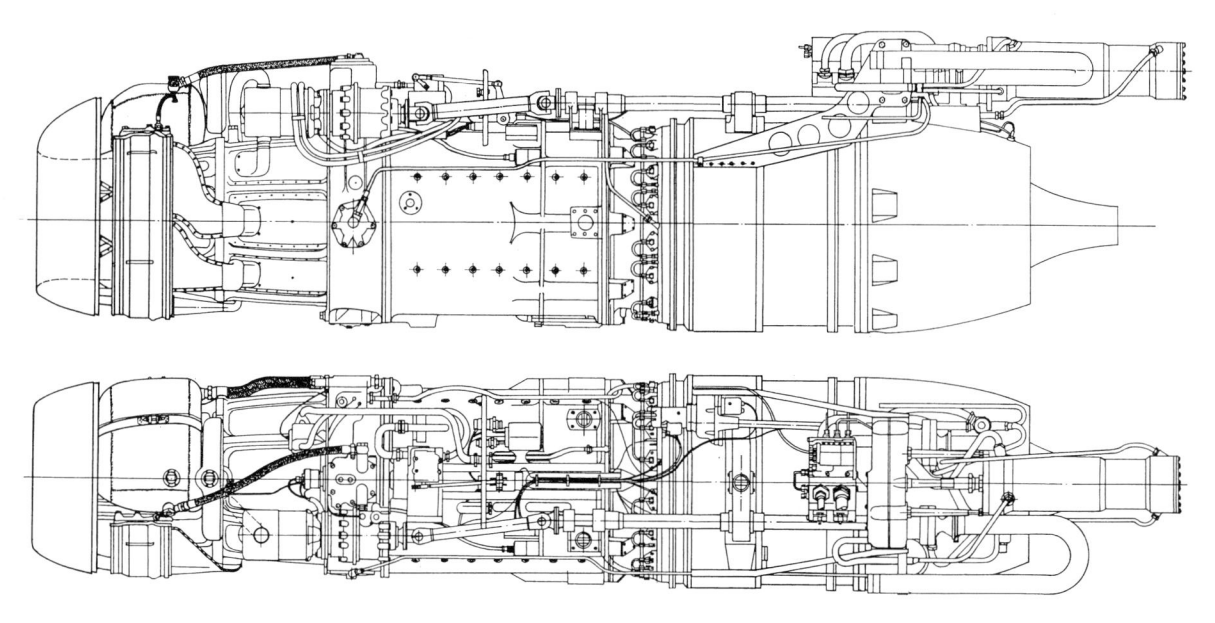

The BMW 003 TLR (Turbinen-Luftstrahltriebwerk mit Rakete) combined turbojet and rocket engine. This comprised a standard BMW 003 A turbojet to which was added a specially designed BMW P 3395 (109-718) rocket engine. This burned a mixture of SV-Stoff (concentrated nitric acid) and R-Stoff (Tonka self-igniting fuel) which gave the engine a thrust of 1,000 kg (2,200 lbs) for three minutes. The propellant pumps for the rocket engines were electro-hydraulically coupled via a 125hp extension shaft to the turbojets.

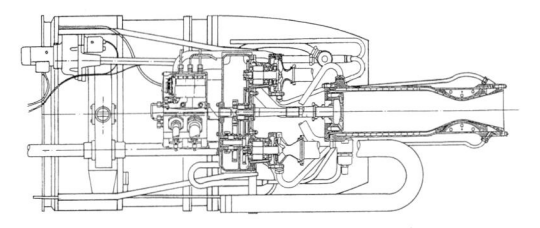

Me 262 Interzeptor III
(see Me 262 Volume One)

Me 262 C-3a Heimatschützer IV (Home Defender IV)

On 11 January 1944, Karl Althoff, a design engineer in the *Projektbüro*, put forward a proposal for a fourth rocket boosted version of the Me 262. This had the Walter HWK 509 A-2 rocket engine mounted in a jettisonable fairing beneath the fuselage. This proposal was further developed in a project description of 5 February 1945, the designation Me 262 C-3 being allocated. The proposal stated:

"Experience has shown that easy accessibility of the rocket engines is of major importance. With the Me 262 C-3, the R-equipment will be fitted under the fuselage in the form of a *Rüstsatz*. This has the following advantages:

1.) A standard Me 262 fighter can be employed as a *Heimatschützer*, since airframe modifications are minimal.
2.) Maintenance is greatly simplified by easy accessibility of the *R-Rüstsatz*.
3.) The dangerous caustic *T-Stoff* is kept entirely outside the aircraft and can be jettisoned in case of danger.
4.) As the need arises, the *R-Rüstsatz* can be used on other aircraft."

The modification consisted of a standard Me 163 rocket engine which produced 1,500 kg (3,300 lbs) thrust, two drop tanks for *T-Stoff* with the rear auxiliary fuselage tank replaced by one containing *C-Stoff*, and certain other fittings. The fully jettisonable *Rüstsatz* was fitted to a frame, which in turn was attached to the standard RATO unit brackets. The fairing for the engine was to be held by quick-release catches. It was anticipated that, during ground runs, with the fairings removed, the equipment would be accessible from all sides for checks and monitoring, greatly improving serviceability. Like the C-1 and C-2, two auxiliary mainwheels, size 660 x 190 mm (26 x 7.5 inches) could be fitted, but initial tests would be made at reduced take-off weights, eliminating the need for the auxiliary undercarriage.

The estimated weights and performance figures (shown opposite) were included in the report, comparing two versions of the C-3 (Version I with only 50% jet fuel, Version II with full fuel) with the C-1.

Three prototypes of the C-3 were to be built, but none of these was completed before the end of the war. The main problem delaying the development of the variant was that the tanks supplying the rockets were mounted slightly below it and this resulted in severe fuel supply difficulties.

Me 262 D-1

The original designation for the Me 262 C-2b *Heimatschützer II*.

Me 262 E-1

Proposed production version of the Me 262 A-1a/U4 with the 50 mm MK 214 cannon.

Me 262 E-2

This designation may have been allocated to a version of the Me 262 fitted with six RA 55 (*Raketen Automat* - automatic rocket dispenser)

Me 262 C-3a Heimatschützer IV rocket-boosted fighter

	Me 262 C-3		Me 262 C-1
	Version I	*Version II*	
Altitude to total fuel exhaustion	9,000 m 29,528 ft	7,000 m 22,966 ft	10,800 m 35,433 ft
Climbing time to the above mentioned altitude	4.5 mins	4.5 mins	4.5 mins
Endurance at the above mentioned height with full turbojet power	21 mins	42 mins	27 mins
Take-off weight	8,315 kg 18,331 lbs	9,020 kg 19,885 lbs	8,290 kg 18,276 lbs
Landing weight	4,900 kg 10,802 lbs	4,980 kg 10,979 lbs	5,054 kg 11,142 lbs

mountings each holding no fewer than 21 55 mm air-to-air R4M missiles. This was proposed in a report dated 13 April 1945. The RA 55 was an automatic device, built by LGW (*Luftfahrt Gerätewerke* - Aviation Equipment Works) in Berlin, designed to launch the R4M missile at a high rate of fire. Only 28 complete units had been built by the end of the war, although a large number of half completed devices were found by the Allies.

Me 262 *Rüstsätze* (Field Conversion Packs)

In an attempt to establish some kind of commonality for the *Rüstsätze* intended for *all* jet fighters for 1945-46, at least nine conversion packs were designated for use by these aircraft. Some of these *Rüstsätze* designations *may* have been applied to the Me 262. These were:

R1 A 500 ltr (132 Imp gal.) drop tank under the fuselage
R2 A pair of 500 kg (1,100 lbs) thrust Rheinmetall-Borsig rocket assisted take-off units mounted under the fuselage. See *Me 262 Volume One*.
R3 A non-jettisonable rocket engine for boosting thrust, especially to improve climbing performance. In the case of the Me 262, this may have been applied to both the Me 262 C-1a and C-2b *Heimatschützer I* and *II*.
R4 Radar equipment for night and all weather fighting. Two packs were proposed, the first comprising FuG 350 Zc *Naxos* with its EA 350 Zb receiving aerial in the forward fuselage, the second FuG 218 *Neptun V* with a Siemens *Geweih* aerial in the nose. Both radars are described elsewhere in this chapter. See *Me 262 Volume Four* for full details of night-fighter development.
R5 A fixed armament of four MK 108 cannon.
R6 ETC 503 A-1 bomb racks beneath the fuselage which could carry a total of 500 kg (1,100 lbs) of bombs. This could be made up of one SC 500, SD 500 or AB 500-1 or two SC 250, SD 250 or AB 500-2 weapons. To aim these weapons the TSA 2D bombsight (described above) was to be used.
R7 Twenty-four R4M unguided missiles.[6]
R8 Two R 100 BS unguided large calibre missiles.[7]
R9 Four Ruhrstahl X-4 guided missiles.[8]

Below: The 210 mm calibre R 100 BS unguided missile was to be aimed with the aid of the Oberon automatic firing system developed by Arado. When the missile was approximately 80 m (260 ft) from the target, a time fuse detonated the warhead which comprised of 460 incendiary pellets which blasted out in a conical pattern.

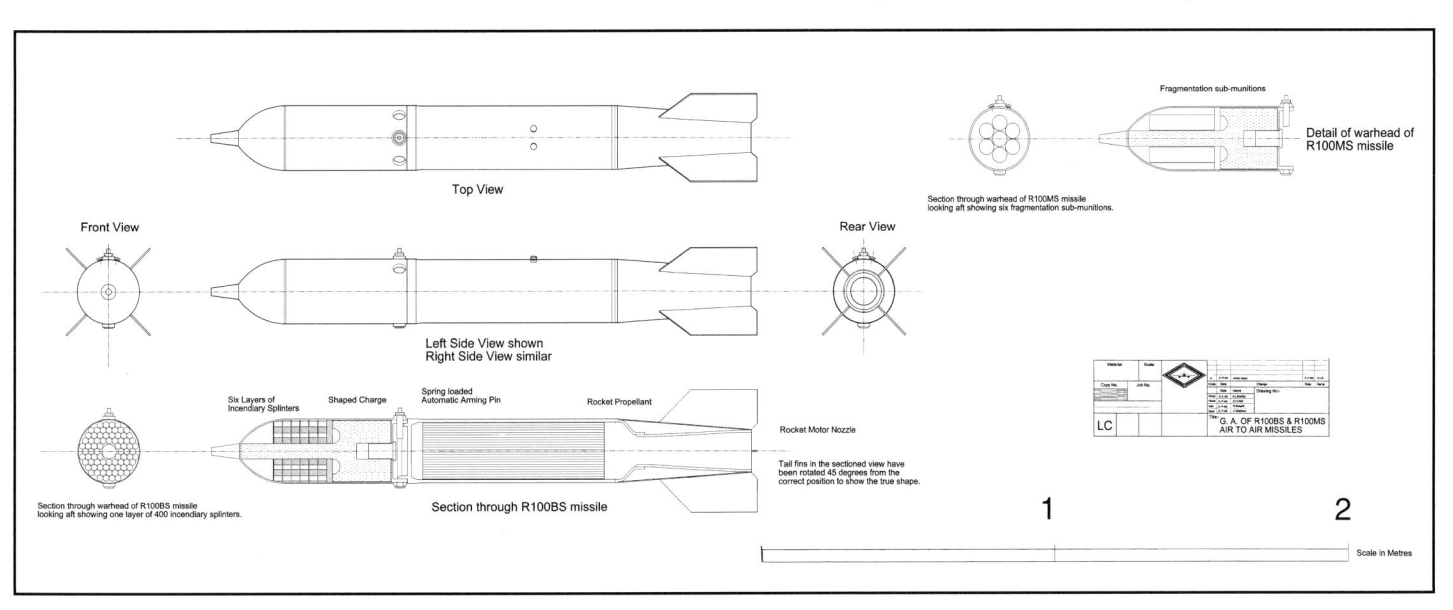

BMW 003 ENGINED Me 262s

As will be remembered, the original power plants proposed for the Me 262 were the Bramo 002 and BMW 003. The former was abandoned in 1942, but development of the latter continued although it encountered many problems. To help in its evolution, BMW set up a special *Erprobungsstelle* at Berlin-Adlershof, but it was not until its transfer to Oranienburg in January 1944 that it received its first test beds. These comprised two Ju 88 A-5s and a Ju 88 S-1, all of which could carry the turbojet beneath the wing centre section. Following continuous testing by two civilian test pilots, *Herren* Clauss and Karner, the BMW 003 was at last pronounced suitable for installation in the Ar 234 V15. This aircraft made its first flight on 20 July 1944, being transferred from Alt Lönnewitz to Oranienburg on 8 August.

Successful tests with various prototype Ar 234s[9] and the acceptance of the controversial *Volksjäger* programme led to the engine being again considered for the Me 262. The first prototype to be fitted with the unit was W.Nr. 170078 which made its first flight on 21 October 1944, piloted by Karl Baur. Essentially similar to the standard fighter, the Me 262 A-1b, as the variant was designated, could be distinguished by its completely redesigned cowlings.

A second test flight was made by Baur on 5 November and, four days later, Gerd Lindner flew the aircraft for the first time. His report was somewhat critical:

"Take-off. While the rpm of the Junkers engines moves to 2,000 automatically with the help of the Riedel starter and fuel injection and the throttle can be left in the 'stop' position - the BMW's throttle has to be set to full once the Riedel motor has accelerated the engine to 800 rpm. This simultaneously ignites the Kärcher jets which results in fuel being injected into the circular combustion chamber. In contrast to the Jumo engines, temperature rises rapidly and, bearing in mind that the engine has to accelerate further, it must be ensured that it does not go above 750°C (1,300°F). This can only be done by manipulating the throttle which, I think, requires considerable dexterity and knowledge of the engine that cannot be demanded of the average pilot. The starting method adopted for the BMW forms a considerable danger to the engine from overheating during starting. A better method requires much rethinking and cannot be proposed by me at this stage.

"Acceleration from idling (3,000 rpm) to full power (9,600 rpm) is considerably faster than with the Jumo engine. In this respect the BMW is much better since the

Below: As well as testing the BMW 003 under Ju 88s, in June 1943, E-Stelle Rechlin also employed a Ju 88 as a test bed for the Jumo 004 jet engine. The engine was mounted beneath the Ju 88's port wing centre section. Seen here is Ju 88 A-5, GH+FQ testing the Jumo 004 V11.

Me 262 A-1b powered by two BMW 003 A turbojets

danger of overheating during acceleration, particularly at lower revs., is not as great.

"Jet adjustment. The Jumo engine works automatically but the BMW has a separate switch for each engine. This has four positions for starting, take-off, climb and horizontal flight and combat at altitude.

"Take-off, landing and combat require the pilot's full attention to correct the jet position in relation to the speed and altitude, attention that could be better directed toward enemy aircraft if an automatic system was provided. Take-off and landing requires complete concentration because the switches on the engines have to be changed several times. This problem could be eased if only three positions were available, one for take-off, one for idling and one for all flying conditions.

"During normal flying the engines give a very good impression with their quiet and smooth running. They were properly synchronised. Synchronisation by ear is much easier than with the Jumo engines. Speed changes, quickly following one another, have no influence on performance, but I cannot explain the very noticeable changes in engine noise.

"Performance. Nothing can be said yet about the flight performance, particularly regarding stability about the vertical axis, as weather conditions during the flight were very unfavourable. Trim changes during the lowering of the undercarriage (at around 350 km/h or 220 mph) were not so marked about the lateral axis as with with the Jumo engines. The BMW engined aircraft has a much better 'kurvenwillig' (willing to turn) impression than the Jumo powered aircraft.

"Switching off is easier than with the Jumo engines. Additional injection to get fuel into the main fuel lines for renewed starting is not

Karl Baur (centre) and Gerd Lindner (left), the two Messerschmitt test pilots who flew Me 262 W.Nr. 170078 in late 1944, fitted with BMW 003 turbojets. Seen on the right is Oberleutnant Ernst Tesch who was seconded to the Me 262 testing programme and who conducted bomb-carrying tests in the Me 262 V10 in June 1944.

An early production BMW 003 A-0 turbojet (W.Nr. 029) which was test flown beneath a Ju 88 test bed (VK+DD) at Rechlin in early May 1944. The cowling of this engine differed considerably from that adopted for the series production units.

A BMW 003 turbojet found by British troops at a depot in Schleswig-Holstein, 1945. This engine had been taken from a He 162 Volksjäger. An Fw 190 D-9 can be seen behind the engine.

5 December, the second, W.Nr.130164, E3+32, on 1 January and the third, W.Nr.130174, E3+35, on 25 January 1945. Actual first flight dates were 15 and 20 January and 17 February respectively. They were used for general tests, experiments with governors, turbine wheel strength, high altitude operation, thrust nozzle control, automatic fuel injection and trials with different fuels. Most of this testing was carried out at Rechlin and by Kappus's Sonderkommando Burg, the latter facility also having a Ju 88 engine test bed, RG+RW, fitted with a BMW 003, and three similarly powered Ar 234 prototypes, the V14, V15 and V17.

necessary. After acceleration to about 5,000 rpm the pumps are shut off, the fuel cocks closed and the throttles simply put on 'stop'. Afterburning of engines, which occurs frequently with the Jumos, has not been noticed so far."

By the end of October 1944 it was proposed that all variants of the Me 262 should employ BMW 003 engines as alternative power plants. On 31 October 1944, Peter Kappus, heading the BMW test facility at Oranienburg (which later moved to Burg), reported that three Me 262s were to be converted to BMW 003 engines for experiments at Rechlin's Department E3 engine test division. The first of these, W.Nr.130188, E3+31, was to be ready for flight testing on

Initially the BMW powered Me 262s were to be distinguished by the number '3', the Jumo 004 engined variants retrospectively receiving the number '4'. Thus the Me 262 A-1 4/U1 would have been Jumo powered, the A-1 3/U1 BMW powered. By early 1945 this system had been changed, a lower case 'b' being used to identify the BMW engined aircraft. Thus the Me 262 A-5a would be powered by Jumo 004 B-1 or B-3 engines, the A-5b by BMW 003 A-1 engines. Between 600 and 700 BMW 003s were built in total, but apart from those already mentioned, only one other Me 262, W.Nr.130170, E3+36, was definitely fitted with these engines. Of these five aircraft, four survived the war, only W.Nr.130188 being destroyed. This crashed on 2 February 1945 following an engine failure near Rechlin. The pilot, Major Hans Furchner of the OKL, was killed. Two further machines, W.Nr.170094 and 170272 may also have been BMW powered.

Me 262 A-1b W.Nr. 170078 with two BMW 003 A-1 engines
This was the first BMW engined prototype which made its first flight on 21 October 1944 and had the last three figures painted in white on both sides of the nose. The engine nose ring and rear part of the cowling were painted black. Only four such aircraft were built plus the TLR engined C-2b. This aircraft was found wrecked, minus its engines and tail unit, at Lechfeld at the end of the war.

A post-war photograph of former test-pilot and prize-winning sports pilot, Dipl.Ing Peter Kappus who, as head of the BMW test facility at Oranienburg, played a major role in the development and eventual acceptance of the BMW 003 turbojet.

The only known photographs of one of the BMW 003 engined Me 262 A-1b prototypes (possibly W.Nr. 170078). This aircraft made its first flight on 21 October 1944, and was found wrecked at the end of the war at Lechfeld. The engines were not as long as the Jumo 004s, and their cowlings were considerably different in shape. W.Nr.170078 completed at least 22 flights totalling six hours duration before it was discovered by US troops at Lechfeld in a badly damaged condition.

---

1   As has been seen in Volume One Chapter 7, the ETC 503 rack did not prove satisfactory when fitted to the Me 262.
2   Unfortunately the identity of "what's-his-name" remains a mystery.
3   For a description of this sight, see Volume One, Chapter 7.
4   Aircraft model listing.
5   Literally, "Construction Overview", a description of the aircraft variants then under consideration.
6   For a description of this weapon, see Chapter 10.
7   For a description of this weapon, see Chapter 10.
8   For a description of this weapon, see Chapter 10.
9   See Monarch Series No.1 on the Ar 234 by J Richard Smith and Eddie J Creek published by Monogram Aviation Publications.

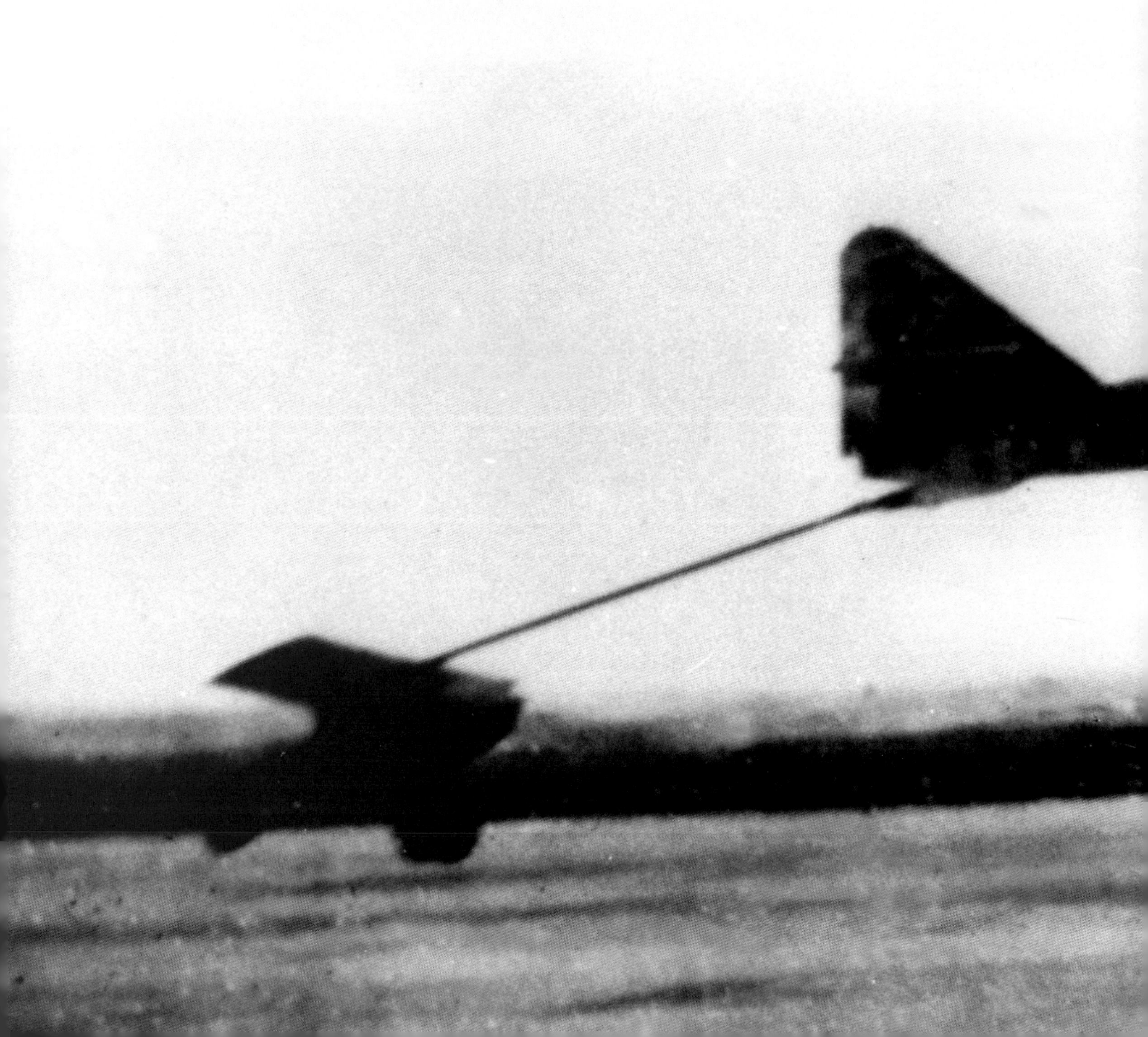

CHAPTER TEN
"THE CRUCIAL FACTOR"

On 1 August 1944 the duties of the *Jägerstab*, the "Fighter Staff" committee established to rejuvenate and manage German's fighter production industry, were taken over by the *Rüstungsstab* or Armaments Staff under the overall control of Albert Speer, Hitler's Armaments Minister. This dealt not only with the manufacture of aircraft but with production for the army and navy as well. On the day of its disbandment, the head of the *Jägerstab*, *Hauptdienstleiter* Karl-Otto Saur reflected on the achievements of his staff:

"Now for the crucial factor - the aircraft. For a whole week we have been making the greatest efforts with regard to aircraft sponsored by the *Jägerstab*, and this applies in particular to those who have worked at this task unremittingly and with fanatical devotion. Until yesterday morning we did not believe it possible that fighter output would reach 3,000 aircraft a month and we saw absolutely no prospect of a total output of 4,000 aircraft. We still hoped to manage the 3,000 but there was really no question of 4,000. However, yesterday our final output reached 3,145 aircraft sponsored by the *Jägerstab*, a total of 3,678 operational aircraft and a total of 4,675 military aircraft of all types. This enormous increase is 500 above the output in June and 600 above that in May. Thus production has increased by 100 per cent in two months; fighter production alone has increased from 2,300 to 3,100, that is by 800 aircraft in two months.

"It is gratifying that deliveries of single-engined day fighters have been made in full. There is no deficit here, but there is an appreciable deficiency with regard to night fighters, twin-engined fighters and tactical reconnaissance aircraft. I request that this be dealt with immediately."

Protokoll Nr. 43, the minutes of a meeting on Me 262 progress held on 10 August 1944, reviewed the production of the aircraft up to that time. Only ten V-series prototypes and 112 production aircraft had been completed. Of the latter, 32 had been destroyed or badly damaged, as follows:

Nine destroyed on the ground on 24 April 1944, in a US Eighth Air Force bombing attack on Leipheim.

One aircraft crashed into the Ammersee on 14 July during a practice bombing attack. (*Stabsfw.* Mosbacher of *Kommando Schenk* was killed).

One lost in combat on 18 July. (This was Thierfelder's aircraft details of which are given in Chapter 8).

Ten destroyed and two damaged on the ground on 19 July, seven at Leipheim and five at Lechfeld, in US Eighth Air Force raids.

One aircraft lost on 29 July during a test flight.

In addition three aircraft were destroyed due to fires on transfer flights and another five suffered engine failures which resulted in their destruction. Two pilots were killed in these actions, the others bailed out.

Of the remaining eighty aircraft, 33 had been delivered to KG 51, 15 to *Erprobungskommando 262*, seven to Messerschmitt (with four others converted), one to the Junkers Motorenwerke, ten to Blohm und Voss for conversion to dual controls and 14 to the *E-Stelle* at Rechlin.

The Aviation Research Establishment at Rechlin on the Müritz Lake north of Berlin, which was commanded by *Maj.* Otto Behrens, was to play an important part in the testing and development of the Me 262. The establishment first became heavily involved with the Me 262 after Hitler's order that the aircraft should be converted as a bomber in May 1944. Six of facility's departments were to undertake development work on the Me 262. These, and the work they did, were:

Department E 2 – Aircraft (*Obstabsing.* Harry Böttcher)

Performance at various altitudes (speed and climb), permissible

American bombs rain down on Lechfeld on 19 July 1944. Nearly 100 B-17s of the US Eighth Air Force's 1st Bomb Division raided the important German development and testing centre destroying ten Me 262s and damaging a further two.

Left: Lying apparently and miraculously unscathed amidst the smoking debris of the Messerschmitt hangar at Lechfeld on 19 July 1944 and visible at the far left of this photograph is the Me 262 V3. The prototype was badly damaged in another Allied air attack on 12 September 1944.

Above: Fire fighters dampen down the last smouldering remains of the fire in the Messerschmitt company's hangar at Lechfeld following the American raid on 19 July 1944.

Below: A USAAF post-strike reconnaissance photograph taken of Lechfeld following the 19 July attack. The area around the Messerschmitt Hangar 5 bore the brunt of the raid and several He 177s visible on the taxiway were damaged.

Below: With the debris from the raid cleared away, there was relief at confirmation that the Me 262 V3 had just about survived intact. However, the necessary repairs were never carried out and the aircraft did not fly again.

Top left: An aerial view of the Erprobungsstelle Rechlin, north of Berlin.
Top right: The main control buildings and tower at Rechlin. Note the camouflage netting on the roof of the building has been made to give the appearance of tree tops.
Left: Hangar facilities at Rechlin – like many other German airfields – were camouflaged so that from the air they took on the appearance of non-military buildings.

Me 262 A-1a W.Nr. 170038 fitted with two Jumo 004 B engines, Erprobungsstelle Rechlin.
This aircraft was delivered to the Engine Development Department E3 at E-Stelle Rechlin and was used for Jumo 004 testing. Coded 'E3+03', it crashed on 5 September 1944 killing the pilot, Fl. Stabsing. Johann Ruther.

Left: Oberstleutnant Edgar Petersen, former Kommodore of KG 40, was appointed controller of all the Luftwaffe test centres. As such, Rechlin fell under his jurisdiction and Behrens would have reported to him.

Right: A crowd gathers to view the Me 262 A-1a, W.Nr. 130170, E2+02, another aircraft used by the E2 section of the Erprobungsstelle Rechlin in this case to test improved power and performance. These tests were carried out by Heinrich Beauvais, one of Rechlin's fighter aircraft specialists, during July-August 1944.

Above: This photograph shows E2+02 being towed by nose wheel. Towing directly on the nose wheel was to become strictly forbidden

Above: Me 262 A-1, W.Nr.170041, 'White 10' photographed at E-Stelle Rechlin-Lärz on 1 December 1944 during a display of the latest German aircraft arranged for Karl-Otto Saur. The aircraft in the foreground is the Do 335 V5, the only known photograph of this prototype. This type was potentially one of the fastest propeller-driven aircraft ever built with a top speed in the area of 765 km/h (475 mph), but it could not match the performance of the Me 262.

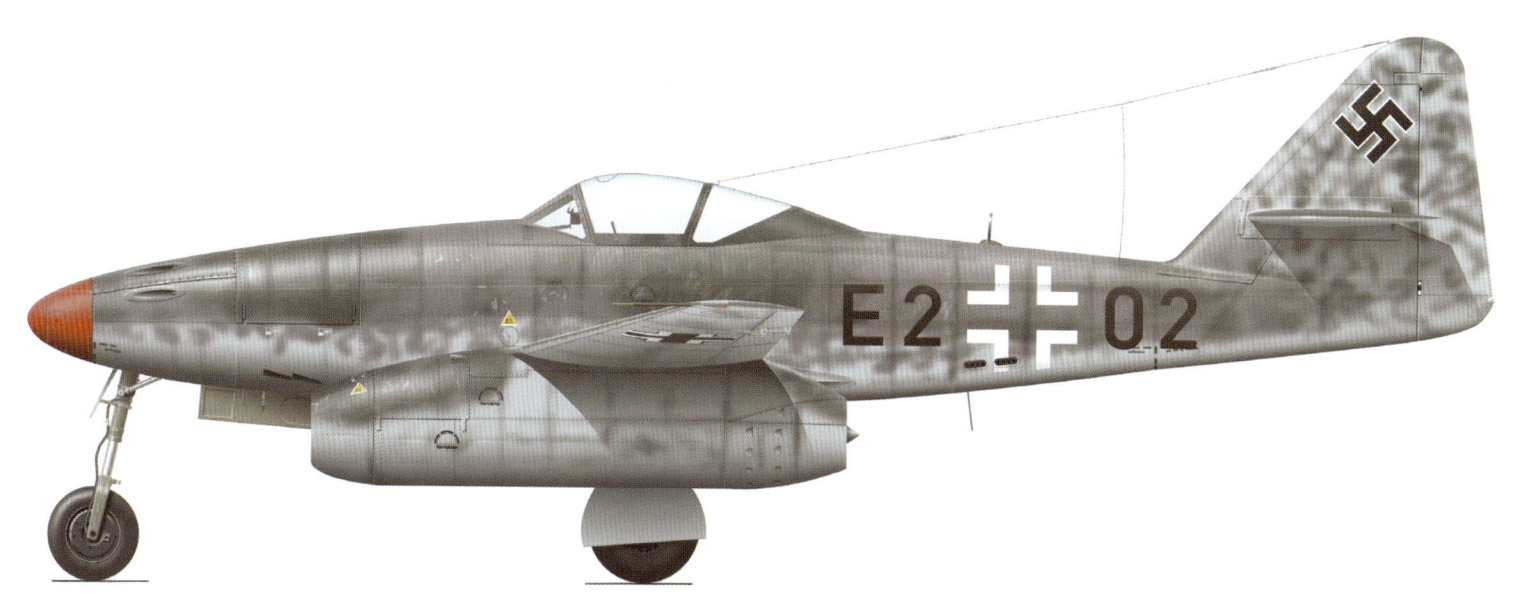

Me 262 A-1a W.Nr. 130170, Erprobungsstelle Rechlin.
This aircraft was delivered to E-Stelle Rechlin fitted with two Jumo 004 B engines. It was used for general performance analysis. It was coded 'E2+02' with the upper surfaces painted dark grey (74) and medium grey (75) with pale blue grey (76) underneath. An unusual feature of this aircraft was the red nose cone.

Three views of Me 262, W.Nr. 170095, KD+EA. This aircraft was used by the Erprobungsstelle Rechlin to test landing gear and hydraulics, as well as auxiliary tanks, aerobatics and nightfighter deployment potential. Note the unusual single arm towing apparatus attached to the nose wheel. This method of towing was later strictly forbidden.
Above right: In the background can be seen the first Me 262 V8, W.Nr.130008, one of the few known photographs of this prototype. It was the first aircraft to be fitted with four MK 108 cannon and was used for gun firing trials.

Me 262 A-1a W.Nr. 170095, Erprobungsstelle Rechlin.
Another aircraft delivered to E-Stelle Rechlin, this machine was used in a large number of undercarriage and hydraulic tests, and was fitted with two 18 litre pumps with pressure relief valves. Most Me 262s only had one engine driven pump and, if this failed, the aircraft lost all hydraulic pressure. The aircraft retained its factory radio call sign "KD+EA and later in the war flew a number of operational night fighting trials (see Volume Four for more details).

Left: Generalmajor Martin Harlinghausen, second from right, was one of many senior officers who regularly visited the Rechlin test centre and he is seen here on one such visit. Harlinghausen was an anti-shipping specialist. As Fliegerführer Atlantik he had waged an air campaign against Allied shipping in the Atlantic, the Bay of Biscay and parts of the Mediterranean. He had also led Luftwaffe formations in North Africa and took a keen interest in anti-shipping weapons which would probably explain his visits to Rechlin.

Below: This extract (with translation) is taken from document B.Nr.22140/45 dated 15 January 1945 and lists the Me 262s then under test at Erprobungstelle Rechlin.

Appendix 2

Arrangement of Me 262 trials aircraft

Serial No.	Call sign	Test purpose
130 163	E2 + 01	Undercarriage load trials, pre-spinning of wheels via air scoops.
130 170	E2 + 02	Performance analysis
130 018	E3 + 01	Engine tests.
130 168	E3 + 02	High altitude engine tests.
170 038	E3 + 03	Junkers engine tests.
130 165	E4 + E5	Hydraulic tests, 2 x 18 liter pumps and pressure relief valves, FuG 16 ZY Jägerkurssteuerung 2 x 300 Watt generators.
130 188	E7 + 01	Stuvi, BZA, TSA (bomb sights)
170 070	E7 + 02	TSA installation, dropping trials.
130 164	WA + TA	Gun firing tests, TSA installation (continuation of tests with W.Nr. 130 188).
170 057	WA + 02	Gun firing trials.
170 095	KD + EA	Undercarriage and hydraulic tests C of G trials Additional fuel tanks 2 x 18 liter pumps and pressure relief valves Aerobatic and tactical manouvres Operational night fighting tests.
130 172	EK + L1	Fuel consumption trials, long term undercarriage and tyre trials.
130 174	EK + L2	Long term trials
170 039	EK + L3	Long term trials Engine tests (needle control and acceleration control unit)
130 010	VI + AJ	Two-seat trainer trials Throttle brake Needle control test engines Auto-pilot 850 km/h verification flights

Reduction in performance with *Wikingerschiff* bomb racks fitted			
Engine rpm	1 x SC 250 bomb 1 *Wikingerschiff*	2 x SC 250 bombs 2 *Wikingerschiff*	1 x SC 500 bomb 1 *Wikingerschiff*
8700	40 km/h (25 mph)	75 km/h (47 mph)	55 km/h (34 mph)
8400	35 km/h (22 mph)	65 km/h (40 mph)	45 km/h (28 mph)

centre of gravity limits, take-off distances with bombs and rocket assistance (two RI 502 engines), range with two 250 kg or one 500 kg bomb (as compared with no bomb load).

Department E 3 – Engines (*Obstabsing*. Otto Cuno)

Rapid throttle movement at altitude with new double jet regulator, engine thrust measurements, engine acceleration behaviour and duration tests. Much of this work was to be done in co-operation with the Junkers company.

Department E 4 – Radio and Signals (*Obstabsing*. von Hauteville)

General test flights with radio equipment, in particular with reliability, target seeking equipment.

Department E 5 – Controls, instruments etc. (*Obstabsing*. Helmut Roloff)

Examination of hydraulic system, on-board controls, instrumentation, development of mountings, tests with automatic pilot (for fighter and bomber operations).

Department E 7 - Bombs, fuses and sights (*Stabsing*. Othmar Schürfeld)

Bomb aiming procedures with Revi and TSA sights, glide angle calculations and procedures, BZA equipment and measurements using the PV 1 and supplemental calculator, gun cameras, loading and handling problems with two 250 kg bombs, one 500 kg bomb and the BT 200 C and BT 400 torpedo bombs, general tests with bombs and drop tanks.

Department E 8 Ground equipment (*Oberstabsing*. Lauschke)

Tests with various towing vehicles (the *Fiat-Schlepper*, *Kettenkrad* and *Scheuch-Schlepper*), standardisation of towing by the nosegear, trials with jet engine transport vehicles.

Much of the early work performed at Rechlin was concerned with calculating the loss of performance that various bomb loads would have on the Me 262. Using the *Wikingerschiff* (Viking Ship) rack[1] each of which reduced the aircraft's maximum speed by some 5 km/h (3 mph), a reduction in performance figures was obtained (all at 4,000 m or 13,000 ft altitude) and is detailed in the above chart.

Climbing time to 8,000 m (26,000 ft) without bombs was 14.3 minutes, with two SC 250 bombs this was increased to 20.5 minutes. Rechlin also carried out experiments with many other types of bombs including the ER 4 supplementary rack to carry four SC 50 bombs.

Other trials carried out by Rechlin were with the pre-spinning vanes mentioned later in this Chapter. It was hoped that these would help to reduce the tremendous stress on the tyres when the aircraft landed with heavy weights still attached. Because of its strategic position, Germany had to make considerable use of

Right: The tyres of a Siebel Si 204 fitted with pre-spinning vanes designed to prevent bursting. Experiments with such devices – which were later used on a Me 262 – were carried out at the Erprobungsstelle Rechlin.

Below: Drawing showing detail of spinning vanes as fitted to the main undercarriage wheels of a Me 262.

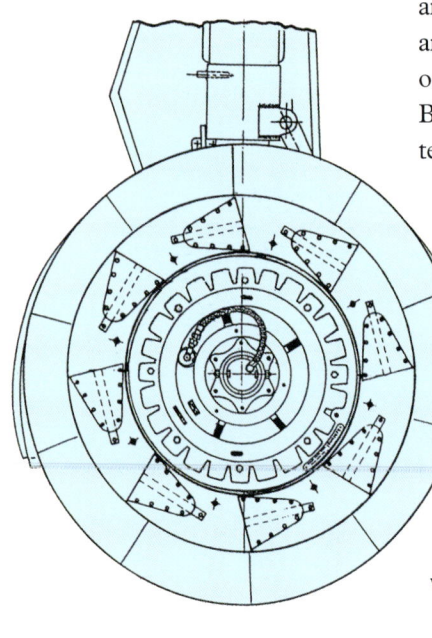

synthetic rubber, the quality of which was such that it often resulted in tyres bursting on landing. Rechlin carried out experiments with these vanes using both a Si 204 and a Ju 88, and the device was later fitted to a Me 262.

By the end of June 1944, no fewer than six of the original ten Me 262 prototypes, the V1, V2, V4, V5, V6 and V7 had been destroyed or badly damaged. To replace these, Messerschmitt decided to take aircraft from the production line and give them the then defunct *Versuchs* numbers. The earliest of these was Me 262 S10, W.Nr. 130015, which made its first flight on 30 June, becoming the second Me 262 V1.

By the end of 1944, the new V1 had completed 117 flights totalling over 40 hours in the air. It was used to test a large variety of equipment including brakes, wooden tail surfaces, ailerons, wing slats and the adjustable control stick. It also carried out a large number of performance trials, but perhaps the most interesting tests were of the lengthened engine intake duct designed for the Messerschmitt P 1101 project and a new windshield with a 25 degree slant. This was found to give better visibility in the rain and improved aerodynamics over the standard canopy. It was proposed that a number of test aircraft be fitted with this type of canopy for use as all weather fighters.

The second Me 262 V2, W.Nr. 170056, made six flights before being assigned to the test programme on 6 August 1944. By the end of March 1945 it had completed 176 flights totalling 49 hours 45 mins flying time. Tests were carried out with brakes, Hecker brake linings, Flettner tabs, ailerons, external fuel tankage and bomb release equipment, assisted take-off, window washing, and various radio sets. In connection with the last item, the aircraft was fitted with various night fighter antennae. Special pre-spinning vanes were also attached to the mainwheels in an attempt to reduce tyre wear. As has been recorded earlier, these had been tested on a Ju 88 and Si 204 at Rechlin, and wind tunnel experiments were also carried out by Junkers in connection with the Ju 287 programme. As far as is known, the device was not adopted for operational use.

The second Me 262 V4, W.Nr. 170083, was fitted with the MK 214 cannon and has already been described in Chapter 9, but the V5 was W.Nr. 130167 coded SQ+WF. This aircraft first flew on 31 May 1944, completing 303 flights by March 1945, by which time it had completed 50 hours 25 mins flying. Among other things the new V5 was used to test brakes, an offset nosewheel fork, pre-spinning vanes, extension of the undercarriage at high speed, stability with a 500 kg bomb, *Wikingerschiff* and ETC 503 bomb racks, FuG 125 radio equipment, window washing and heating and jet engine guards. Perhaps the most interesting piece of equipment tested by the aircraft was the EZ 42 gyroscopic gunsight (see page 7) which was later used operationally by JV 44.

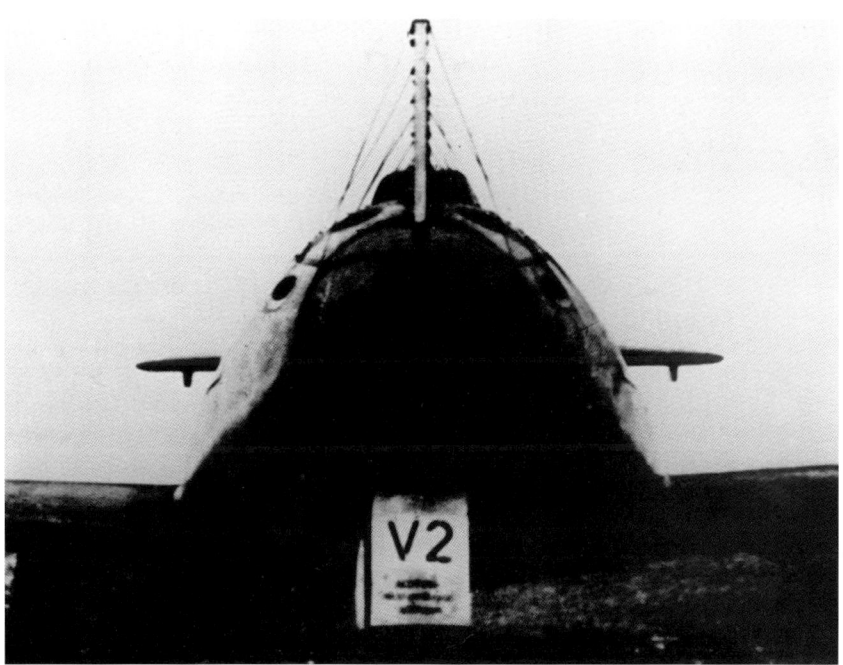

The second Me 262 V6 was the alternative designation for the Me 262 C-1a prototype, while W.Nr. 170303 became the second V7. This aircraft made its first flight on 22 September 1944, completing 67 tests totalling 18 hours 38 mins by the end of February 1945.

The second Me 262 V2, W.Nr. 170056, first flew in the summer of 1944, conducting experiments with brakes, RATO units and stability, during which the aircraft was flown with reduced vertical tail surfaces. It is seen here in November 1944 fitted with a large vertical fin above the nose to improve its performance as a gun platform.

Erprobungsbericht Nr. 53
30.11.1944 – 31.12.1944.

The following document is a facsimile of original Messerschmitt Test Report No. 53 dated 2 January 1945. The document shows the testing and research programme carried out during the period 30 November to 31 December 1944. Various prototypes are listed together with the flights carried out and hours flown. It also shows, for the first time, the proof of the re-numbering of the prototypes as well as the status of each in the test programme. Space in this book precludes a complete translation but it is felt that by publishing the original document complete nothing will have been lost in the translation.

Messerschmitt A.G. Augsburg — Erprobungsbericht Nr. 53 vom 30.11. – 31.12.1944. — Bl. -1-

Geh. Kommandosache

I. **Allgemeines:**

Von den 15 zeitweise vorhandenen Erprobungsträgern waren nicht im Flugbetrieb :

- V-9 — Einbau der Änderungen für Hochgeschwindigkeit Stufe I, zzt. abgestellt.
- 083 — Triebwerke ausgebaut, Messeinbauten für Fahrwerksuntersuchungen.
- 555 — Einbau der 2. Lotfekanzel, eingetroffen am 10.12.1944

Ausserdem

- 170 055 — Doppelsitzer, leihweise am 11.12. von der Truppe für Lamellenbremsenversuche. Bruchlandung am 22.12. mit stehendem Triebwerk. (Beschädigung 70 %)
- 056 — 12.12. Bruchlandung bei Einmotorenlandung mit verkleinertem Seitenleitwerk, seither abgestellt, ohne Triebwerke.
- 186 — 1. Flug (Schnellablassprobung) dann Jumo-Triebwerk ausgebaut, R-Triebwerk unklar.
- 499 — am 10.12. an Truppe leihweise gegen 055 abgegeben.
- 773 — 17.12. nach Rechlin als Mustermaschine überführt.

Im ganzen wurden 159 Flüge mit insgesamt 27 h Flugdauer in der Berichtszeit durchgeführt.

Alarm, bzw. Voralarm 36 h.

Die Wetterlage liess zu 37,5 % keine Versuchsflüge zu.

Aus Mangel an TL-Triebwerken wurden an einigen Versuchsträgern (welche stillgelegt wurden) die Triebwerke ausgebaut.

Lechfeld, den 2.1.1945.
Stu.

Abteilungsleiter :   Sachbearbeiter
        Erprobungsleiter :

Messerschmitt A.G. Augsburg — Erprobungsbericht Nr.53 30.11. – 31.12.1944. — Bl. -2-

II. Aufstellung der durchgeführten Flüge

Werk-Nr.	Flug zahl	Flug dauer	Gesamt flugzahl	Gesamt flugdauer	Bemerkungen
130 015	3	48'	88	29 h 39'	Druckverteilung an den Vorflügeln
170 056	8	3h 45'	110	34 h 26'	Hochachsenstabilität
170 078	8	2h 16'	14	3 h 44'	Triebwerks- und Leistungsmessungen mit BWM-Triebwerken.
130 083	keine Flüge 1 (siehe Erprobungsbericht Nr. 52)				
130 167	75	5h 47'	229	39h 16'	Lamellen- und Backenbremsenproben, Innenausgeglichenes Seitenruder
130 186	1	10'	3	29'	Heimatschützer I, Schnellablass
130 303	14	3h 48'	37	13h 43'	Abfangen, 2 x 1000 kg-Startraketen, 1000 kg Bomben, Hydraulik
110 484	11	5h 04'	22	8h 14'	Lotfe-Erprobung, Hochachsenstabilität, Kursteuerung.
V-9	keine Flüge (siehe Erprobungsbericht Nr. 52)				
V-10	20	2h 50'	94	29h 40'	Einfliegen (Mustermaschine)
110 773	4	46'	10	2h 15'	Vereinfachte Waffenschaltung, der Truppe zur weiteren Erprobung leihweise überlassen.
110 499	3	43'	7	1h 49'	2x18 Ltr.-Pumpe
170 055	10	1h 02'	—	—	Von der Truppe geliehen, Bruch wegen Triebwerksausfall (70 %)

Messerschmitt A.G. Augsburg — Erprobungsbericht Nr. 53 vom 30.11. – 31.12.1944 — Bl. -3-

III. **Eigenschaften** (Bearb. T i l c h)

Innenausgeglichenes Seitenruder

Mit der jetzigen Nasenform wurde die Drehachse durch Abschneiden der Ruderhinterkante bis auf ~31 % verschoben. Bei grösseren Staudrücken sind die Kräfte immer noch zu hoch, bei Ruderausschlägen > 12,5° tritt jedoch Kraftabnahme ein. Weitere Versuche werden mit einer spitzeren Nasenform durchgeführt. Siehe VB 262 10 E 44.

1000 Kg - Bombenwurf.

Die Versuche sind noch nicht abgeschlossen. Bis jetzt werden max. n = 4,5 g erreicht, bei einer Ausgangs-S-Lage von 15 %.

Mustermaschine K D E

Die Werk-Nr. 110 77 3 wurde nach Behebung von einigen Beanstandungen (eigenschaftsmässig, unsymmetrischer Kraftverlauf im Querruder, Hängen bei ausgefahrenen Landeklappen) nach Rechlin überführt.

Hochgeschwindigkeit Stufe I (V 9)

Wegen Fehlens der Kabine (O'gau) ist die Maschine abgestellt.

Vorflügeldurchbiegung

Die Durchbiegung des Vorflügels im Schnellflug wurde bis v_a = 900 km/h, q = 3910 kg/m² durchgeführt.

Richtungsstabilität (Bearb. Hörstke)

a) **Verkleinerung des normalen Seitenleitwerkes**

Mit der 4. Verkleinerung des Seitenleitwerkes (F = 2,36 m² statt normal 2,96 m²) wurden weitere Versuche durchgeführt. Beim Flug am 3.12. mit Pilot Baur wurden in Bezug auf Dämpfung ein hervorragendes Ergebnis erzielt

$$\left(\frac{T_y}{y} = 0,6 \div 0,8\right)$$

Dabei sehr grosse Rollbewegung.

Dieses gute Ergebnis liess sich bei Wiederholung nicht wieder darstellen, ausser durch Entgegensteuern der Rollbewegung durch Querruderbetätigung.

| Messerschmitt A. G. Augsburg | Erprobungsbericht Nr. 53 vom 30.11. - 31.12.1944. | Bl.-4- |

Versuche wegen Bruchlandung des Versuchsflugzeuges am 12.12. nicht weitergeführt.

b) **Innenausgeglichenes Seitenleitwerk**
Bisher noch Versuche, um den Kräfteverlauf in Ordnung zu bringen.

c) **Lotfe-Bomber**
Kleine Schwingungszeiten
Mit 2 x 250 kg Bomben sehr schlechte Dämpfung über 25 % l_{aer} S-Lage, bei S-Lage ~ 22 % mit Bomben Restschwingungen bei allen Staudrücken, bei $q = 1000 kg/m^2$ kaum noch Dämpfung.
Ohne Bomben im höheren Fahrtbereich ($v_w = 850$ km/h andauernde Restschwingungen bei allen S-Lagen-
Starke Schieberollmomente.

IV. **Triebwerk:** (Bearbeiter Kaiser)
BMW-Triebwerk
Inzwischen 5 weitere Flüge, 2 weitere Triebwerke gewechselt.
(Punkt 1 - 4 siehe Erprobungsbericht Nr. 52)
5.) Turbinenschaufelbruch (vielleicht durch Überhitzen beim Rollen)
6.) Späne im Ölfilter
Die Leistungsmessung im Ist-Zustand ist fertig.
Siehe VB 262 34 L 44

Heimatschützer I
Ein Wasserversuch im Flug mit dem neuen Schnellablass zeigt, dass immer noch Wasser in den Rumpf gesaugt wird. Der Austritt des Schnellablasses wird zzt. unter das Seitenruder verlegt. Beim Standlauf ist wieder eine Schweissnaht am Ofen des Walthergerätes gerissen.
Ursache: Herstellungsfehler.
Zzt. wird ein neuer Ofen besorgt.

Heimatschützer II
Eingetroffen am 20.12. bei FAV-L. Die Maschine wird zzt. aufgerüstet

Standschub
Für ein Neuprojekt wurde der Einfluss eines 3 m langen Einlaufs auf den Standschub untersucht. VB 262 28 L 44 lag schon dem Erprobungsber. Nr. 52 bei
Öltemperatur.
Zur Beurteilung der Temperaturabhängigkeit des Drehzahlreglers wurde die Öltemperatur im Fluge ge-

---

| Messerschmitt A. G. Augsburg | Erprobungsbericht Nr. 53 vom 30.11. - 31.12.1944. | Bl. -5- |

messen. Siehe VB. 262 33 L 44.

V. **Leistungen.** (Bearb. Reichel)
Schutzrohre
Am Flugzeug, Werk-Nr. 303 wurde der Geschwindigkeitseinfluss von 4 verlängerten MK 108 Schutzrohren vermessen.
VB 262 31 L 44.

Beschleunigung bei Start und Landung
Mit Werk-Nr. 303 wurden Messungen des Geschwindigkeitsverlaufes vom Flugweg bei Start und Landung bis zum Schnellflug durchgeführt. Vers.Ber. 262 32 L 44.

Leistungen Werk-Nr. 773 (Bearb. Kaiser)
Vor der Abgabe an KDE wurde die Leistung obiger Maschine kurz überprüft.
Vers.Ber. 262 30 L 44.

VI. **Zelle** (Bearb. Krauss Gregor)
Vereinfachte Wanne im Triebwerk ohne Längsprofile.
Durch Bauchlandung des Erprobungsträgers wurde die vereinfachte Wanne so stark beschädigt, dass die Wiederinstandsetzung nicht lohnt. Die Betriebszeit der Dauer-Erprobung beträgt 32½ Flugstunden ohne Beanstandung. Die Erprobung gilt somit als abgeschlossen.

Holzseitenleitwerk
Das zweite Holzseitenleitwerk wurde an der Werk-Nr. 170 303 eingebaut. Die Betriebszeit beträgt für beide Holzseitenleitwerke 3 Std.
Durch Aufquellen infolge langen Stehens im Regen kam die Seitenrudernase zum Blockieren, sodass die Spalteinlage in der Seitenflosse nachgearbeitet werden musste.

Vereinfachung der Leitwerksverkleidung
Zur Vereinfachung der Leitwerksverkleidung zwecks Montageerleichterung auf Vorschlag der Fa. Blohm & Voss wurden an mehreren Flugzeugen die Führungszapfen vorne ausgebohrt, sodass die Verkleidung nunmehr durch das vorne aufgesetzte und das hintere Führungsblech geführt und durch die Schraube in der Nähe des Drehpunktes gehalten wird. Bei ca. 2½ Flugstunden trat noch keine Beanstandung auf. Ergebnisse der Breitenerprobung müssen noch abgewartet werden.

Verölen der FT-Anlage
Durch austretenden Kraftstoff verölt die FT-Anlage, wodurch sie nicht mehr funktionsklar bleibt. An eigenen Versuchsträgern und an Truppenflugzeugen wurde eine Breitenuntersuchung an Stand und an einem Erprobungsträger

---

| Messerschmitt A. G. Augsburg | Erprobungsbericht Nr. 53 vom 30.11. - 31.12.1944. | Bl. -6- |

Versuche im Fluge vorgenommen. Das Ergebnis wurde im Versuchsbericht 262 005 Z 44 bekanntgegeben.

Entwässerungsleiste für Kabine A 1354.262 Z
Ein Standversuch mit den eingebauten Entwässerungsleisten zeigte, dass die Ausführung nach Zeichnung noch nicht entspricht und eine Änderung der Dichtdecken mit weiteren Versuchen erforderlich macht.

Beurteilung der Brandhahnkulisse mit Druckpunkt für H_v und H_h ohne Rasten für die Schalthebel
Dem Wegfall der Rastbleche für die Schalthebel der Ventilhalterungen kann nicht zugestimmt werden.
Beurteilung durch die Flugzeugführer siehe Flugbericht Nr. 131/134 vom 27.12.1944.

Holzflügelrandkappen 262507/508-101 Behrteil 219a/b
Ein neuer Satz o.a. Randkappen wurde am 30.12. von AVS angeliefert, sodass mit dem Anbau und der Erprobung begonnen werden kann.

Deichselschlepp
Der Rumpfanschluss wurde in verstärkter Ausführung angeliefert und ist im Einbau fertig.

Technische Beanstandungen
Holzleitwerk
Durch langes Stehen im Regen ist das Leitwerk angequollen, sodass das Seitenruder am Füllstück im Ruderspalt nicht mehr frei ging und nachgearbeitet werden musste.

Einheitsverstellscheit
An einem Einheitsverstellscheit brachen die Graugusslagerbuchsen am Pedalhalter. Nach Mitteilung KL sind Graugussbuchsen nur in wenigen Verstellscheiten eingebaut. Normal werden KWJ-Buchsen verwendet. Die Buchsen müssen jedoch zum Bund mit Übergangsradius versehen werden, da Kerbwirkung eintritt.

Obere Federbeinabdeckung am Hauptfahrwerk
Bei Rollen im nassen Schnee wird derselbe hochgeschleudert und setzt sich zwischen die Gleitbahn und den Rollenbock fest. Beim Einfahren des Fahrwerks presst sich der Schnee zusammen und beschädigt die Beinabdeckung und verursacht den Bruch des Schellenbandes vom Rollenbock. Ferner packt sich die Radnische voll Schnee, wodurch das Einziehen des Fahrwerkes verhindert wird.

| Messerschmitt A. G. Augsburg | Erprobungsbericht Nr. 53 vom 30.11. - 31.12.1944. | Bl. -7- |

Tragwerk, lose Nietung
An Werk-Nr. 170 303 lösten sich im Bereich des hinteren Hilfsholmes von R. 0 bis R. 1 und entlang der Rippe 1 eine grosse Anzahl Nieten. Dies dürfte auf grosse Beanspruchung durch Bremsenerprobung zurückzuführen sein.

Truppenbetreuung

Rumpfspitze
An Werk-Nr. 110 526 brach der Rumpfspitzenanschlussbeschlag am rechten unteren Anschluss an der Schweissstelle der Tüte mit dem Flanschstück. Der angebohrte Beschlag wurde dem Stabü in Augsburg zu Bearbeitung übergeben.

Antrieb für Restabdeckung
Mit Änderungsmeldung 5/500 Zeichng. 262.500-001 wurde der Lagerbolzen für den Umlenkhebel des Antriebes für die Restabdeckung dahingehend geändert, dass dieser Bolzen zwecks leichterer Auswechselbarkeit des Arbeitszylinders nur mit einem Splint in seiner Lage gehalten wird. Durch den T.A. wird die Änderung bereits bei Truppenmaschinen durchgeführt. Der geänderte Lagerbolzen ist lt. Beanstandungsmeldung des III.E.J.G. 2 vom 28.12.44 an Werk-Nr. 110 306 aus der Lagerung herausgerissen und die Lagerrippe ausgeknickt und gerissen.
Die Truppe ändert diesen Lagerbolzen nun dahingehend, dass auf der Holmseite eine Annietmutter eingesetzt und eine durchgehende Lagerschraube kopfseitig mit Draht gesichert wird.
Es ist unverständlich, weshalb solche grundsätzlichen Änderungen nicht vor dem serienmässigen Einlauf der Flugabteilung zur Erprobung übergeben werden. Aus diesem Grunde wurden 30 Flugzeuge unklar und mussten gesperrt werden.

Änderungen

V-1, Werk-Nr. 130 015
Triebwerkseinlaufhaube im rechten Triebwerk austauschen gegen Mess-Einlaufhaube.
Schutzkorb am linken Triebwerkseinlauf anbringen.

V-2, Werk-Nr. 170 056
Einbau der verstellbaren Querruderlager 262$^{500}_{501}$-093/094/095. Einbau der Regenabweisprofile an den Rumpfgurten.

| Messerschmitt A.G. Augsburg | Erprobungsbericht Nr. 53 vom 30.11. - 31.12.1944. | Bl. -8- |

Einbau der von O'gau gelieferten Musterausführung des Serien-Seitenruders.
Ausbau des verkleinerten Seitenleitwerkes - Einbau des normalen Seitenleitwerkes.

V-4, Werk-Nr. 170 083
Einbau der Hauptfahrwerksfederbeine mit Doppellenker;
Bugrad mit gekröpfter Gabel.
Messeinbauten für Fahrwerksdruck - und Wegmessung

V-5, Werk-Nr. 130 167
Einbau der Abdeckschieber am Gleitführungsausschnitt der oberen Federbeinabdeckung n.Skizze von BmL.
Einbau der 2-ten 18-Ltr.-Pumpe für Hydraulikanlage.
Einbau der neuen Bremsbeläge am Hauptfahrwerk.
Einbau der gekröpften Bugradgabel.

V-6, Werk-Nr. 130 186 (Heimatschützer)
Verstärkung des Trennspantes am Rumpfende f. Hecktriebwerk.
Verlegung des Schnellablasses von vorne nach hinten.
Neue Gashebel im Führerraum.
Schutzblech für Seitenruder gegen Verschmoren durch das Hecktriebwerk anbringen.
Rumpfobergurt und Stirnrahmen aufgefüttert, damit der Dichtschlauch nicht überzogen wird und platzt. Abstand zu gross.

V-7, Werk-Nr. 170 303
Einbau des Holzseitenleitwerkes (2. im Erprobungsbetrieb).
Einbau der gekröpften Bugradgabel.
Ausbau des Seitenruders in Holzkonstruktion, Einbau eines S-Ruders mit Spreizkante.
Einbau 2 x 18 Ltr. Pumpe für Hydraulikerprobung.
An der Leitwerksverkleidung vorderer Führungszapfen entfernt.

V-8, Werk-Nr. 110 484 (Lotfe-Kanzel)
An der Leitwerksverkleidung vorderer Führungszapfen entfernt.
Änderung zur Fertigablieferung an E-Stelle; wie Anfertigung der Kinnstütze, Verbesserung der Polsterung, Verbesserung der Gurthalterung, Änderung des Kabinennotabwurfes, Anbringen einer Hutze vor den Lotfe-Klappen, Neue Lagerung des Ei-V-Gerätes.

V-9, Werk-Nr. 130 004
Einbau der Kabinenklappe in O'gau.

| Messerschmitt A.G. Augsburg | Erprobungsbericht Nr. 53 vom 30.11. - 31.12.1944. | Bl. -9- |

V-10, Werk-Nr. 130 005
Verstärkung des Anschlusskastens f. Deichselschlepp.
Einbau der Endstücke am TL-Triebwerksauslauf f.Versuchszwecke.
Einbau 2 x 18 Ltr. Pumpe für Hydraulikerprobung.

V-11, Werk-Nr. 110 555, (Lotfe-Kanzel II)
Einbau der Lotfe-Kanzel.
Änderungen in der Kanzel, wie Kinnstütze, Polsterung Gurthalterung, Änderung des Notabwurfes, Abweishutze vor Lotfe-Klappen.
Anbauten für Zwiebelerprobung.

V-12, Werk-Nr. 170 074 (Heimatschützer II)
Einbau der Triebwerksentlüftung.
Änderung der Leitungen zu den Sonderkraftstoffbehältern mit Abzapfung aus der 7. Stufe statt wie bisher aus der 4. Stufe.

VII. Elt. Erprobung (Bearbeiter: Bosch, Richter)

a) <u>Doppelbeheizte Panzerscheiben ohne Temperaturregler.</u>
Die Scheibe ohne Regler in 8-262, Werk-Nr. 167 wurde bei weiteren 77 Flügen mit einer Flugzeit von 5 Std. 48 Min. im Berichtszeitraum in Betrieb gesetzt und hat sich gut bewährt.

b) <u>Panzerscheibe mit Regler</u>
Die in Werk-Nr. 303 eingebaute Heizscheibe hat sich bei 13. Flügen mit einer Flugzeit von 3 Std. 22 Min. im Berichtszeitraum wiederum gut bewährt.

c) <u>Generatorbelüftung</u>
Neues Belüftungsrohr bzw. Entlüftungsrohr für die Generatoren wurden eingebaut. Die Messgruppe konnte wegen Arbeitsanhäufung den Messeinbau noch nicht durchführen.

d) <u>Strom- und Spannungsmessungen am elt. Bordnetz</u>
Die Vermessung des elt. Bordnetzes wird zzt. durchgeführt.

e) <u>Isolationswert des elt. Bordnetzes</u>
Über schlechten Isolationswert des elt. Bordnetzes sind im Berichtszeitraum keine Klagen eingelaufen.

| Messerschmitt A.G. Augsburg | Erprobungsbericht Nr. 53 vom 30.11. - 31.12.1944. | Bl. -11- |

2. <u>Pressluftnotausfahren</u>
An einer Maschine wurde bei Geschwindigkeiten von 280 - 570 km/h das Fahrwerk und Bugrad mit Pressluft ausgefahren. Die Ausfahrzeit lag bei diesen Geschwindigkeiten bei rd. 10 sec. Nach Pressluftnotausfahren und Landung der Maschine wurde Pressluft nachgefüllt und wieder gestartet. Das Einfahren ging einwandfrei vor sich. Bei dieser Maschine brauchte kein Hydrauliköl nachgefüllt werden. Der Druck in der Pressluftflasche sank von 130 auf 70 atü. Es wäre also in diesem Fall noch möglich gewesen ein 2. Mal mit Pressluft auszufahren.

3. <u>Anlage mit 1 x 18 Ltr. Pumpe</u>
Es wurden noch in 2 Maschinen Winkelhebel eingebaut um die Empfindlichkeit der Einstellung der Steuerventile herabzusetzen bzw. um die Wanderung des Fahrwerks auszugleichen.
Die Hebel bewährten sich und es wäre ein Einlauf in die Serie zu empfehlen.

<u>Kabinenheizung</u>

1. <u>Heimatschützer I</u>
Die Maschine ist mit Kesselanlagen für Druckkabine versehen, kam aber bis jetzt noch zu keinem Höhenflug, da einmal die Kabine noch gedichtet wird und andererseits Triebwerk und Triebwerksanlagen noch nicht in Ordnung sind.
Es ist daher bis heute noch nicht möglich zu entscheiden, ob ein Verdichter für Flüge über 12 km Höhe notwendig wird.

2. <u>Heimatschützer II</u>
Für die Kabinen-Luftversorgung ist neuerdings das linke Triebwerk vorgesehen, während das rechte für die Triebwerkskraftstoffversorgung benötigt wird.
Da die Luftförderleistung der BMW-Triebwerke wesentlich geringer, als die der Jumo-Triebwerke ist, muss noch geklärt werden, ob ein Triebwerk für den Luft- und Heizungsbedarf ausreicht.
Es werden Besprechungen mit BMW geführt, um evtl. eine Erhöhung des Luftdurchsatzes zu erreichen.

IX. <u>Bewaffnung</u>
1. 4 MK 108
a) <u>Gurteinziehband</u>
Dieses, welches bisher von der 8-109 übernommen wurde,

| Messerschmitt A.G. Augsburg | Erprobungsbericht Nr. 53 vom 30.11. - 31.12.1944. | Bl. -12- |

wurde auf Anforderung O'gau-Probü von uns für die 8-262 vereinfacht. Geänderte Unterlagen wurden am 21.12. nach O'gau gebracht. (s.Mitteil. 22.12.)

<u>b)Gurtzerleger</u>
Bei der Truppe, sowie bei einigen in Lechfeld von uns eingeschossenen Flugzeugen traten wiederholt Brüche der Blattfedern für die beiden rechten Waffen auf. Es kann sich nur um Material-bzw. Härtefehler handeln, da Federn aus der 1. Lieferung der gleichen Lieferfirma (Augsburg,Federnfabrik) bei uns und in Rechlin ohne Beanstandung erprobt wurden. BmL 262 wurde durch Mitteilg. vom 21.12. unterrichtet und um Nachforschung bei der Lieferfirma gebeten.

<u>c) E P D 101</u>
Eine neue Baureihe der E P D 101, die zzt. angeliefert wird, unterscheidet sich von der bisherigen Ausführung durch seitliches Versetzen des Eingangsstutzens um 18 mm. Ein Austausch bei den insgesamt 8 Geräten pro Maschine ist nur in 2 Fällen ohne Änderung der Pressluftanlage bzw. der Lagerung der EPD's möglich. In 2 weiteren Fällen (Abfeuerventile der oberen Waffen) ist Versetzen der EPD's mittels neuer Bohrungen ohne grösseren Aufwand möglich. Für die restlichen Fälle ist Änderung notwendig.

<u>d) Leergurtableitschächte der beiden oberen Waffen</u>
Nachdem die von uns in langwieriger Kleinarbeit ermittelte Form der Leergurtableitung der beiden oberen Waffen ohne Ausbeulung der oberen Waffenverkleidungen funktionsklar ging, stellte sich heraus, dass die serienmässigen Schächte eine Beule links und rechts in der Rumpfspitzenabdeckung notwendig machen. Als Ursache wird uns von der Kontrolle ein Zeichnungsfehler mitgeteilt, aufgrund dessen die Schächte rein zeichnerisch 9mm in den Straak eindringen.
Bei der Nacherprobung der 1. Serienschächte in der V-9 musste zwar auf der linken Seite eine leichte Ausbeulung durchgeführt werden, dies wurde jedoch auf die Einbauungenauigkeiten zurückgeführt, weil auf der rechten Seite umsomehr Luft war.
Wir sind nun soweit, wie wir schon vor 1/2 Jahr hätten sein können, wenn wir uns nicht mit allen Mitteln gegen die von Herrn Amtmann Krause vom E-Kdo 262 verlangte Waffenbeule gesträubt hätten!

| Messerschmitt A. G. Augsburg | Erprobungsbericht Nr. 53 vom 30.11. – 31.12.1944. | Bl. -13- |

2. **Vereinfachte Waffenschaltung 4 MK 108** (VB 262 16 A 44)

Am 5.12. erfolgte die Abnahme durch die E-Stelle Tarnewitz in Lechfeld ohne grundsätzliche Beanstandungen.
Die Einführung der vereinfachten Waffenschaltung war infrage gestellt, nachdem nun endlich die Schaltschiene wider Erwarten schon im Februar 45 in Fertigung gehen sollte.
Endgültige Freigabe für den Einlauf in die Serienfertigung erfolgte am 16.12. mit FS Nr. 83 nachdem, wie wir von Herrn Stach Probtü erfuhren, die Schaltschiene wieder einmal nicht funktioniert.

3. **BSK 16 Einbau**

Die Arbeiten am Versuchseinbau unterm Rumpf wurden eingestellt, da lt. tel. Unterrichtung durch Herrn Bruders der Einbau der Rumpfspitze den Anforderungen genügt. Diese Feststellung entspricht auch unserer Stellungnahme vom 28.7.44.
Trotzdem wird voraussichtlich von Seiten General der Jagdflieger eine Änderung des Einbaues noch einmal verlangt werden.

4. **1000-kg-Startraketen**

Stand und Flugversuche mit 1000 kg Raketen bei 8° Abwinklung des Schubstrahles nach unten bewiesen die einwandfreie Anwendbarkeit dieser Geräte. Für die Aufnahme der Schubkomponente gegen den Rumpf ist eine Abstützung erforderlich.

5. **Aufhängebeschläge für Startraketen.**

Bei den zzt. neu eingebauten für 1000 kg Schub verstärkten rumpfseitigen Aufhängebeschlägen und bei den Aufhängeschellen der Startraketen sind in der Serienausführung die zulässigen Toleranzen weit überschritten. Abhilfe ist dringend erforderlich. Nähere Einzelheiten wurden mit Herrn Penning, BmL 262 am 14.12.1944 besprochen.
Abwurfversuche mit Startraketen müssen solange zurückgestellt werden, bis uns einwandfreie Beschläge übergeben werden. Die Neuausführung des Raketenaufhängeschlosses mit der Möglichkeit die Verriegelung einwandfrei zu kontrollieren (s. Mustereinbau V-10) ist trotz höchster Dringlichkeit noch nicht in die Serie eingelaufen.

6. **Lotfe-Bomber** (s. Bericht Nr. 262 17 A 44)

Ausser den im Bericht aufgeführten 2 Bombenwürfen wurde am 27.12. ein 3. Abwurfversuch mit 2 X 250 kg Bomben mit gutem Erfolg durchgeführt (Pilot: Lindner, Bombenschütze Bayer).

| Messerschmitt A. G. Augsburg | Erprobungsbericht Nr. 53 vom 30.11. – 31.12.1944. | Bl. -14- |

An der 2. Lotfespitze wurden versuchsweise Verbesserungen bezüglich Notwurf für Haubendach, Verstellbarkeit des Anschnallgurtes und Kopfstütze eingebracht, welche zzt. in die 1. Lotfespitze Werk-Nr. 484 übertragen werden. Eine weitere Verbesserung für das Liegen des Schützen in der Wanne wird durch eine besser gepolsterte Liegematte mit Ausschnitt für das Fallschirmschloss eingebracht. Anfertigung wird verabredungsgemäss durch Herrn Kempter, Probtü O'gau zum Termin 30.12. veranlasst.
Der letzte Bombenflug am 27.12. ergab die Beschädigung des rechten hinteren Federpuffers der Lotfe-Aufhängung (Geräteteil) beim Rollen über gefrorene Bodenfurchen (Radspuren). Dies zeigt, dass der Einbauort unmittelbar vor der Bugradlagerung eine Vergrösserung der Federwege in den Federpuffern oder eine zusätzliche Federung der zellenseitigen Aufhängung notwendig macht, da die normale geräteseitige Federung bis zum Anschlag ausgenützt wird. Eine Ausnützung des Federweges bis zum Anschlag ist für das Gerät nicht zulässig.

X. **Fahrwerk**

Drei weitere gekröpfte Bugradgabeln von O'gau angeliefert und eingebaut sind in Erprobung.

Lamellenbremsenerprobung
Entsprechend Mitteilung vom 15.12. wurden 100 Landungen mit nur einer Nachstellung nach 40 Landungen durchgeführt. Eine stark abgenützte Scheibe wurde gegen eine neue ausgewechselt. Diese bisher günstig verlaufene Dauererprobung wird im Rahmen des sonstigen Flugprogrammes fortgesetzt.

Bremsschild und Radfelge wurden auch nach 9 hintereinander günstig stark gebremsten Landungen nur handwarm, sodass eine erhebliche Bremsleistungsreserve vorhanden ist.

Die Ansprechzeit bei fremdhydraulischer Betätigung, sowie bei Betätigung mit Fusspumpe ist noch zu gross. Nach mündlicher Mitteilung sollen Anfang Januar Bremsen mit 50 % mehr Lamellen geliefert werden (12 statt 8 Innenscheiben). Es wird angenommen, dass damit der durch Fusskraft aufgebrachte Druck ausreichend ist.

Grundsätzliche Fahrwerkuntersuchungen als Unterlagen für Lastannahmen mit geändertem Federbein müssen wegen Triebwerksmangel verschoben werden.

85 und 70 mm breite Bremsen

Der Entscheid der E-Stelle, die mit Heckerbelag ausgerüsteten Bremsen nur 70 mm breit zu machen, um das Bremsmoment von 280 mkg nicht zu überschreiten, ist abwegig. Seitens Mtt.AG. und Ringführer Bremsen und Räder, Herrn Dr. Eisbein wird gefordert, dass 85 mm beibehalten wird, da die Bremswirkung sich bereits an der unteren Grenze der

---

| Messerschmitt A. G. Augsburg | Erprobungsbericht Nr. 53 vom 30.11. – 31.12.1944. | Bl. -15- |

erforderlichen Leistung befindet. Selbst auf der 2 km langen Rollbahn unseres Platzes wird häufig ein Weiterrollen beobachtet, das oft zu erheblichem Bruch des Flugzeuges führt.
Mit 70 und 85 mm breitem Heckerbelag werden an zwei Versuchsträgern Landungen mit kleiner Ausrollstrecke durchgeführt.

Zulassung von Fahrwerk und Landeklappen

Entsprechend Mitteilung vom 8.12. wurde das Fahrwerk bis zu 550 km/h ausgefahren, ohne Bruch, bleibende Deformationen, oder Verfahrschwierigkeiten.
Landeklappen bei 400 km/h und bis zu 10° Schiebewinkel.

Die Geschwindigkeiten für diese Nachweisflüge wurden aus zwei Mitteilung des Stabü's Anfang Dezember entnommen.
Eine am 28.12.44 eingegangene Mitteilung der E-Stelle verlangt 450 km/h und 10° Schiebewinkel und zwar 20 Mal mit derselben Fahrwerksausführung.
Der Verfahrvorgang wird daraufhin wiederholt und 20 Mal bei der mehrfach erreichten Geschwindigkeit von 550 km/h durchgeführt.

This series of photos show the Me 262, W.Nr. 170056, after its two upper cannon were removed for experiments with the development of the Me 262 A-2a bomber variant. The nose wheel door has the last three digits of its Werk Nummer applied in black together with the legend "*Nicht am Bugrad schleppen*" ("Do Not Tow by the Nosewheel"). The first flight of the Me 262 V-056 took place during the middle of July 1944, the aircraft being assigned to the test programme on 6 August. One of the most widely tested prototypes it survived until the end of the war.

Below and right: Later in its test programme, W.Nr. 170056 was fitted with FuG 218 Neptun search radar for night fighting experiments. Siemens FuG 218 operated on frequencies in the 158 to 187 MHz range, had a search angle of 120º and a range of 5 km down to 120 m (3 miles to 400 ft). A distinctive feature of this equipment was the four-pronged antenna array mounted in the nose.

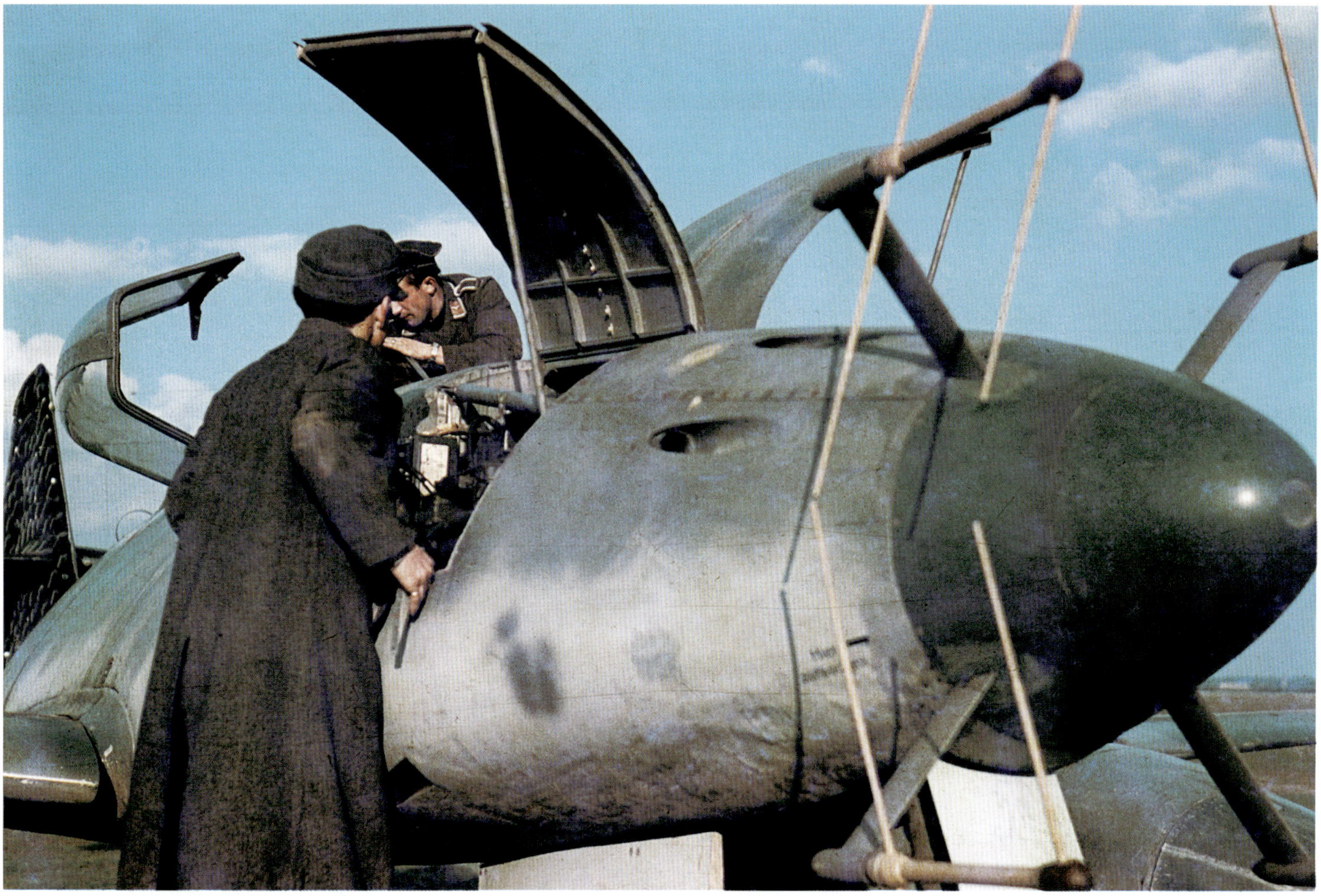

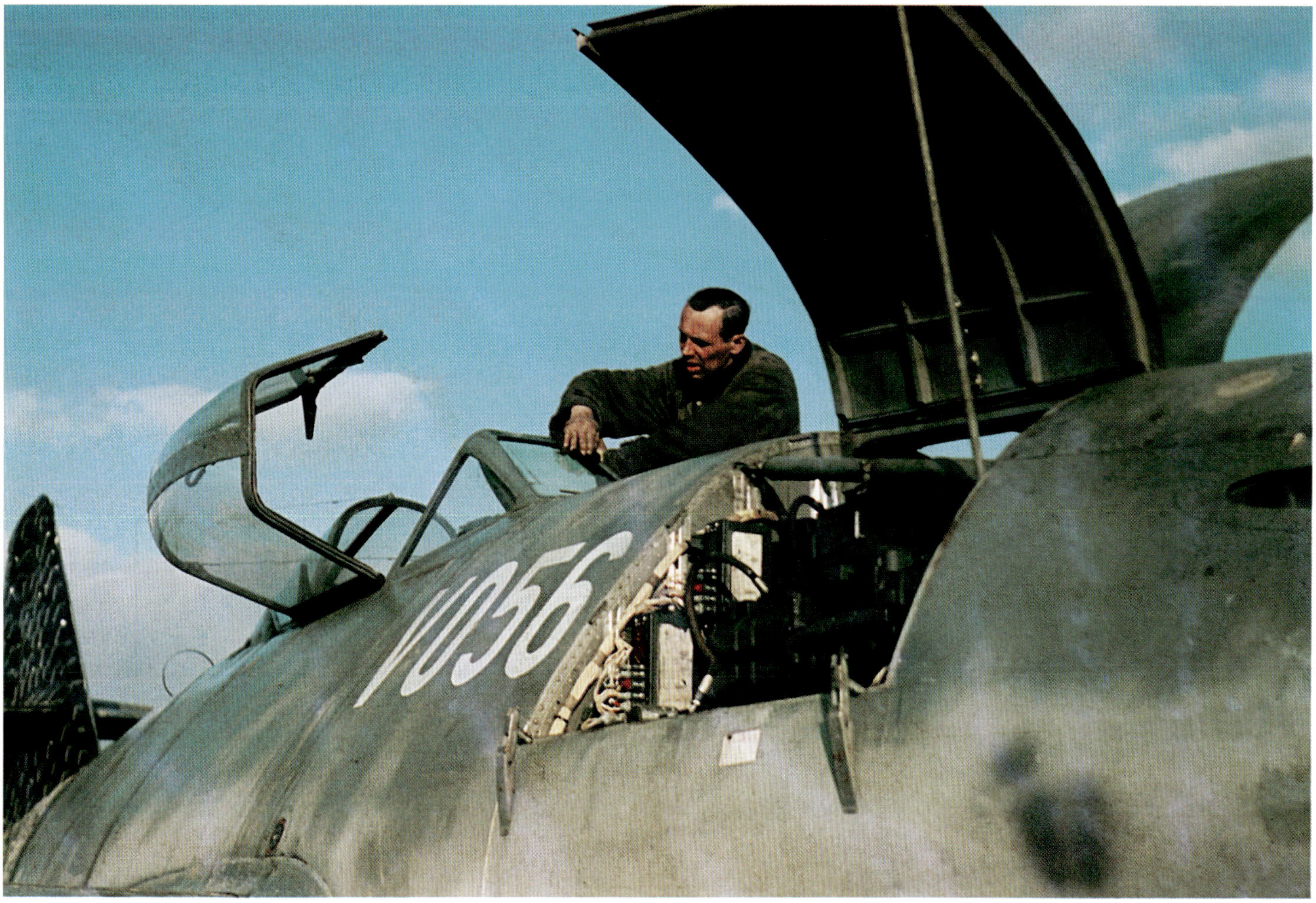
V056

Above and left: Two views of the Me 262 V2, W.Nr. 170056 showing its cut down tail.

Me 262 W.Nr. 170056
Fitted with two Jumo 004 B engines this aircraft was used in a wide variety of experiments. It had completed 176 flights by the end of March 1945, which totalled 49 hours 45 minutes flying time. The vertical tail area was reduced in various stages in connection with experiments to investigate improving control around the vertical axis. During later night fighting experiments, the aircraft became the second Me 262 V2 and had "V056" applied in large white characters on both sides of the front fuselage.

MESSERSCHMITT
Me 262 (second V2)
W.Nr. 170056

In one experiment, the second Me 262 V2, W.Nr. 170056 had a cut down fin and rudder fitted in an attempt to provide a pilot with more control about the vertical axis. Investigations into this problem were conducted in January 1945 by Messerschmitt test pilots Baur, Lindner and Herlitzius. However, these experiments did not prove successful and were probably abandoned before the end of the war.

Above: To investigate directional instability Me 262 W.Nr. 170056 is seen here, before being re-designated the second V2, fitted with an experimental large rudder trim and a vertical fillet above the fuselage and rear cockpit canopy. Note that the rear of the fuselage is painted black to which white woolen tufts were applied in order to observe the effects of airflow over the tail area.

Left: Two photos showing a device fitted to W.Nr. 170056 to measure the rudder forces which the pilot would have to exert when changing direction. The device, which was mounted on top of the forward fuselage, is shown in close-up in the photo to right.

It tested brakes, hydraulics, the adjustable control column, elevators, bad weather visibility equipment, improved cabin ventilation and assisted take-off units. It was also used for high speed and high altitude performance measurements and single engine flight tests. On 4 January it took off with two 500 kg bombs and two 500 kg thrust Borsig rocket assisted take-off units. The pilot, Heinz Herlitzius, reported that the aircraft reared up 50 to 60 degrees after the take-off units were released at 800 m (2,500 ft). The aircraft was damaged on 28 February when a 1,000 kg thrust rocket assisted take-off unit ripped off and it did not fly again before the end of the war. It, like the original V9 and V10, C-1a, C-2b and several A-1a/U3s were found at Lechfeld at the end of the war.

Following the severe damage to the Me 262 V8 on 18 October 1944, the two Me 262 A-2a/U2 prototypes (W.Nr.110484 and 110555) were given the alternative designations V8 and V11, and the designation V12 was used to identify the C-2b *Heimatschützer II* prototype. All three aircraft are described in Chapter 9.

On 30 August *General der Flieger* Werner Kreipe, the new *Luftwaffe* Chief of Staff, attempted to get Hitler to reverse his decision concerning the employment of the Me 262 as a fighter-bomber. He failed, but managed to obtain one minor concession - that every twentieth Me 262 would be equipped as a fighter. As a sidelight on this, a circular was intercepted by Allied intelligence on 2 September which stated that Hitler: "had *again* forbidden any discussions, suggestions or proposals concerning the purpose of employment and operational possibilities of the Me 262 which is still in its experimental stage and for the moment only available in small quantities". Three days later Kreipe's diary recorded a meeting at the Wolf's Lair which included Göring: "The *Führer* made a tirade against the *Luftwaffe*. Again the question of Me 262 operations was aired. The same arguments as to why only 'high speed bomber' versions can be considered. In milder form, Hitler again developed his idea of manufacturing only Me 262s in future, abandoning all conventionally powered fighters and tripling the flak."

On 14 September, Albert Speer telephoned General Kreipe to inform him that he intended to write to Hitler on the question of jet aircraft. Speer remembered: "...he strongly advised me not even to allude to the matter. At the very mention of the Me 262, Hitler was likely to fly off the handle, he said. And I would only be making trouble for him, since Hitler would assume that the *Luftwaffe* chief of staff had put me up to it. In spite of this warning I still felt that I had to tell Hitler once more that trying to make fighter aircraft serve as bombers would be pointless and, given our present military situation, a grave error. I emphasized that this opinion was shared by pilots and all army officers. But Hitler did not even discuss my recommendations, and after so many vain

The Me 262, W.Nr. 130167, 'V-167'.

Messerschmitt Me 262 (second V5) W.Nr. 130167

Below: Shown here after yet another engine change the aircraft was at this time being used to test the EZ 42 Adler (Eagle) gyroscopic gunsight.

Above and top: These photographs show V 167 after being fitted with a new nose cone and a replacement port engine. Note the unusual treaded nosewheel tyre fitted at this time.

Left and below: These two photographs show the Me 262, W.Nr. 130167, "V-167", sporting its first camouflage scheme. The aircraft first flew on 31 May 1944, becoming the second V5 after the loss of W.Nr. 000 0005. By the end of March 1945 it had completed 303 flights totalling 50 hours 25 minutes. Among other things the prototype was used to test various undercarriage modifications, window washing and heating equipment, was fitted with the BSK 16 gun camera, 500 kg bomb, RATO equipment, external fuel tanks, Wikingerschiff and ETC 503 bomb racks, EZ 42 gunsight and FuG 125 radio apparatus. As far as is known this aircraft always carried the white versuchs number 'V167' and not as far as is known the final designation, 'V5'. Note also, this was the only prototype to be fitted with a rudder without the counter balance horn.

Above and above right: The second Me 262 V5, W.Nr. 130167, SQ+WF, starts on another of its 303 test flights. One of the most widely flown of all prototypes. Apart from its test programme, the aircraft was also demonstrated to a Japanese commission.

Right: The fin and rudder of 'V167' was of a unique in not having the counter balance horn design. The design was not adopted as standard for the Me 262.

Left: Karl Baur in the cockpit of Me 262, W.Nr. 130167, clearly showing the prominent extent of the EZ 42 Adler (Eagle) gunsight behind the windscreen. This type of sight automatically computed the deflection angle required to hit a target when both aircraft were manoeuvering. Although very promising, faulty installation often made the sight useless and it was locked so as to function like a conventional fixed reflector sight.

The second Me 262 V5 W.Nr. 130167

Originally fitted with two Jumo 004 B engines the aircraft first flew on 31 March 1944, later becoming the second V5 after the loss of W.Nr. 000 0005. The aircraft was used in a wide variety of experiments, including a re-designed rudder, without the counter balance horn, and was also used to test the EZ 42 gyroscopic gunsight. Although potentially a very useful addition to the Me 262's armoury, the sight was never perfected. V167 completed at least 303 flights totalling 50 hours 25 minutes by the end of March 1945. The aircraft carried a camouflage pattern of dark greens (81) and (82) with pale blue grey (76) beneath.

MESSERSCHMITT Me 262 (second V7) W.Nr. 170303

This page and overleaf: A selection of photographs showing the second Me 262 V7, W.Nr. 170303 which first flew on 22 September 1944. Below the fuselage can be seen the Wikingerschiff bomb racks and 1,000 kp Rheinmettall-Borsig R-109-503 solid fuel rocket assisted take-off units tested by the prototype. Trials were also flown with various types of brakes and generators, and the aircraft took part in high speed single-engine and general performance flights, bomb release tests and experiments with improving visibility and cabin ventilation. The bomb in the foreground is in fact a concrete dummy practice weapon. Note in the centre photograph the V167 can be seen in the background.

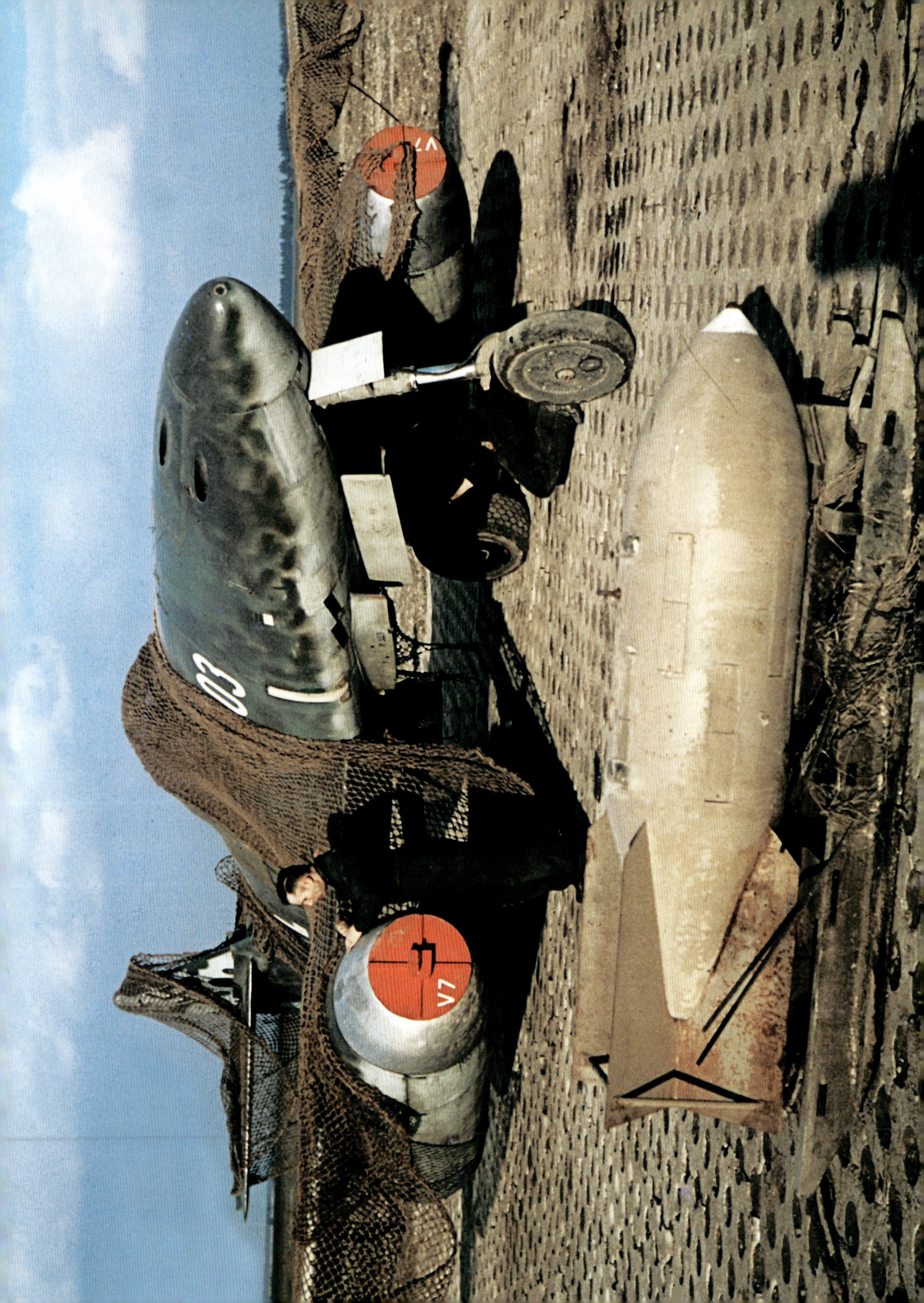
03
V7
V7

The second Me 262 V7 W.Nr. 130303
By the end of February 1945 when it was damaged this aircraft had completed 18 hours 38 minutes flying time. The aircraft was repaired and fitted with the tail taken from the BMW 003 powered W.Nr. 170078 although it is not known whether it ever flew again. It is seen here with two Jumo 004 B engines.

The second Me 262 V7, W.Nr. 170303, after it had been equipped with wooden elevators and two 550 kg bombs in December 1944. Special flash suppression tubes for the four MK 108 cannon were also fitted. The aircraft was powered at this time by two Jumo 004 B-1 engines, W.Nr. 146 (port) and W.Nr. 735 (starboard). It was in this form that former Erprobungskommando 262 pilot, Heinz Herlitzius *(inset)* flew the aircraft from Lechfeld on 22 December. The V7 completed 67 flights before before the end of February 1945 when a 1,000 kg take-off rocket was ripped from the aircraft causing severe damage. Repairs were started but is not known whether it ever flew again.

efforts I simply withdrew from the fray and confined myself to worrying over my own work."

Meanwhile an attack on 12 September by between 250 and 300 bombers from the US Fifteenth Air Force based in Italy damaged the Me 262 V3 and V10, and the second V1, V5 and V6 at Leipheim. The V3, although not that seriously damaged, never flew again, but several jigs for the Me 262 were destroyed in an attack on the Messerschmitt factory at Wasserburg.

By the end of September, Me 262 production was beginning to increase rapidly. A total of 265 aircraft had been completed, of which 32 had been destroyed as mentioned previously. Of the 74 Me 262 A-1s and A-2s produced in September, 17 went to the fighter units and 57 to the bombers. Of the latter, 46 were delivered to KG 51, six to KG 54, four to the Chief of Technical Air Armament (TLR) under *Oberst* Ulrich Diesing, and one to the *General der Aufklärer*, *Generalmajor* Hans-Henning von Barsewisch.

Much of the advanced development work carried out on the Me 262 was designed to improve the aircraft's already formidable fire power. One of the most remarkable guns proposed for the aircraft was the Mauser MG 213 C and MK 213 C cannon fitted with revolving magazines which gave the weapon an incredible rate of fire.

	MG 213 C	**MK 213 C**
Calibre	20 mm	30 mm
Weight	75 kg	75 kg
	(165 lbs)	(165 lbs)
Length	1,930 mm	1,630 mm
	(6 ft 4 ins)	(5 ft 4 ins)
Rate of fire	1,300 rounds/min	1,180 rounds/min
Muzzle velocity	1,065 m/sec	540 m/sec
	(3,494 ft/sec)	(1,772 ft/sec)

Four of the heavier calibre weapons were to replace the MK 108s as the Me 262's main armament, a prototype gun, the V/6-4 being found at the Messerschmitt Design Office at Oberammergau at the end of the war. It had been planned to produce no fewer than 4,000 of these weapons per month by the end of 1945. The concept of the revolver cannon was developed in several countries after the conflict in forms such as the American M-39 and British ADEN guns.

Apart from the 50 mm MK 214 and 55 mm MK 112 guns described in Chapter 9, it was also planned to fit the 55 mm Krupp MK 412 to the Me 262. A prototype of this gun, which was designed to compete with the MK 112, was completed early in April 1945 but no production was undertaken.

Another promising weapon proposed for the Me 262 was the SG 116 *Zellendusche* (literally Airframe Shower). This comprised three upward-firing 30 mm MK 103 cannon barrels mounted behind the cockpit of the aircraft, triggered by a photo electric cell. The idea was for the carrying aircraft to fly beneath a bomber formation, with the guns being fired automatically. As far as is known, the SG 116 was never tested by the Me 262, but both the Experimental Station at Tarnewitz and JGr 10 flew experiments with the weapon using the Fw 190.

A three-barrelled upward-firing SG 116 Zellendusche installed in the fuselage of a Fw 190 belonging to the air-to-air weapons testing unit, Erprobungskommando 25 at Parchim in July 1944. It was also proposed to install such a weapon in the Me 262.

A number of air-to-air missiles were also to be carried by the Me 262. The first such weapon to be installed in the aircraft was the 21 cm (8.5 inch) WGr 21 rocket mortar. This was a spin stabilised missile which was mounted inside a tube. Adapted from an army weapon it had a length of 1,260 mm (4 ft 15 ins) and a weight of 110 kg (250 lbs), the warhead being detonated at a pre-set distance of between 600 and 1,200 m (1950 and 3,900 ft). The missile had already been used operationally in some numbers by several types of piston-engined fighters. Its panic effect proved very successful in breaking up tight bomber formations, but it was not particularly accurate. Its main shortcoming was that its lack of speed (a maximum of 320 m/sec or 1,050 ft/sec) made it extremely difficult to aim, and it usually exploded harmlessly either short of the target or past it. As a makeshift measure, two of these weapons were mounted on the bomb racks of the Me 262 and tested operationally by the *Geschwader Stab* of JG 7.

A much more promising weapon was the 55 mm R4M *Orkan* (Tornado) folding fin missile.

A Fw 190 test fires a 21 cm WGr mortar during ground trials conducted at the Erprobungsstelle Tarnewitz. *Centre right*: Armourers secure and fuse a 21 cm WGr mortar shell in its launch tube as fixed beneath the wing of a Fw 190. Throughout the second half of 1943 and into 1944, this primitive and not very effective weapon was used by conventional fighter units operating against USAAF heavy bombers in the defence of the Reich. Later, the Geschwader Stab of JG 7 fitted a pair of such tubes to some of their Me 262s.

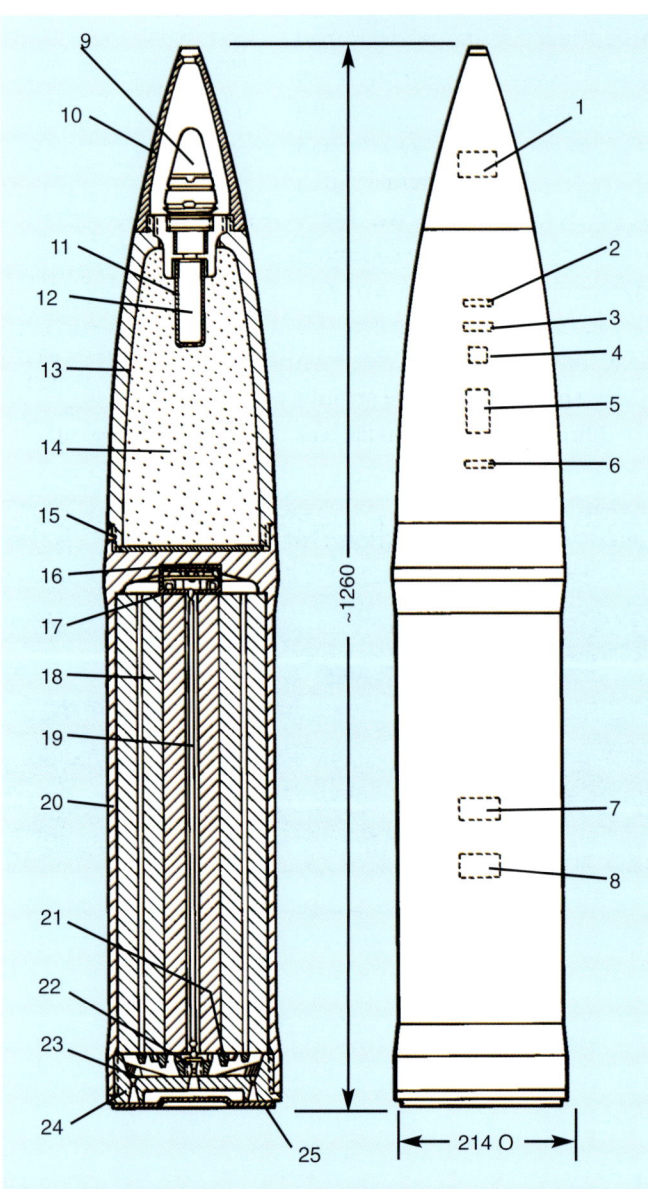

Key to 21 cm WGr air-to-air mortar shell
1. Fuse designation
2. Identification number for explosive. Month and year of loading stamped on.
3. Place, day, month, year of assembly and code mark of responsible agency (a)
4. Identification number for type of explosive.
5. Weight class in Roman numerals (a)(b) of assembled round.
6. Place, day, month, year of assembly of round (a).
7. Manufacturer's code, Lot No., year of loading propellant.
8. Place, day, month and year of assembly of propellant.
9. Time fuse S/30 and rocket combination fuse S/60.
10. Nose cone.
11. Adapter.
12. Booster 36F.
13. Explosive body.
14. Explosive charge.
15. Stake.
16. Igniter 65.
17. Base support.
18. Propellant (7 hole).
19. Ignition cord.
20. Casing.
21. Powder support.
22. Aluminium.
23. Igniter ring.
24. Turbine.
25. Closing plate

Note: Colour of mortar RLM 02 (Grey) all over.
(a) Superimposed in black (b) In two places opposite each other

The 55 mm diameter R4M Orkan air-to-air missile. This weapon was used to considerable effect by Me 262 fighter units in 1945 in their operations against heavy bombers. This weapon and details of its employment are covered in Volume Three.

This was 812 mm (2 ft 8 ins) long, weighed nearly 4 kg (8.8 lbs) but with a maximum speed of 525 m/sec (1,700 ft/sec) was much easier to aim. In its operational form, twelve R4Ms were mounted on a wooden rack positioned beneath each wing of the Me 262. They were normally fired in four salvoes of six missiles each at intervals of 0.07 seconds from a range of 600 m. The missiles diverged slightly after launch to produce a circular pattern with a diameter roughly equal to that of a four-engined bomber. The half kilo (1.1 lb) warhead which was impact fused, was sufficient to give an excellent chance of bringing down a bomber. Towards the end of the war, work was also being conducted on developing racks to enable 48 R4Ms to be carried by one Me 262, together with multiple honeycomb launchers and the RA 55 automatic launching device. It was also proposed to produce a modified version of the missile under the designation R4Hl - "Hl" indicating that it was fitted with a hollow charge warhead. This was to have a range of between 300 and 500 m (984 and 1,640 ft) and be used against tanks and armoured vehicles.

One other unguided missile was projected for the Me 262, the Rheinmetall-Borsig R 100 BS. This was designed to hit a bomber formation from outside the range of its escorting fighters. The R 100 BS was a large weapon with a calibre of 210 mm, a length of 1,840 mm (6 ft 5 ins) and a weight of 110 kg (240 lbs). It had a maximum speed of 450 m/sec (1,500 ft/sec) and a range of 2,000 m (6,600 ft). To overcome the problem of accurate aiming which had afflicted the WGr 21, the *Oberon* automatic firing system was developed by Arado under the direction of *Dipl.-Ing.* Kurt Bornemann, the company's chief engineer for aircraft armament. This was a FuG 218 *Neptun* radar set mounted in the launching aircraft with a fixed beam pointing forwards. Prior to the attack the pilot set the flying time for the missile on both the sighting computer and time fuse. Once he had done this he only had to hold the target in his gunsight, the radar measuring its range, the computer its closing speed. When the fighter reached the estimated firing range, the missile was

Two photographs showing the BT 400 aerial torpedo bomb; its advantage lay in its relatively short manufacturing time and the reasonable availability of its ferrous metal components. The torpedo bomb was designed to replace bombs used by fighter-bombers against shipping. The bomb was 2946 mm (9 feet 8 inches) long with a maximum diameter of 378 mm (14.9 inches). It weighed a total of 435 kg (959 lbs), 200 kg (441 lbs) of which made up the warhead.

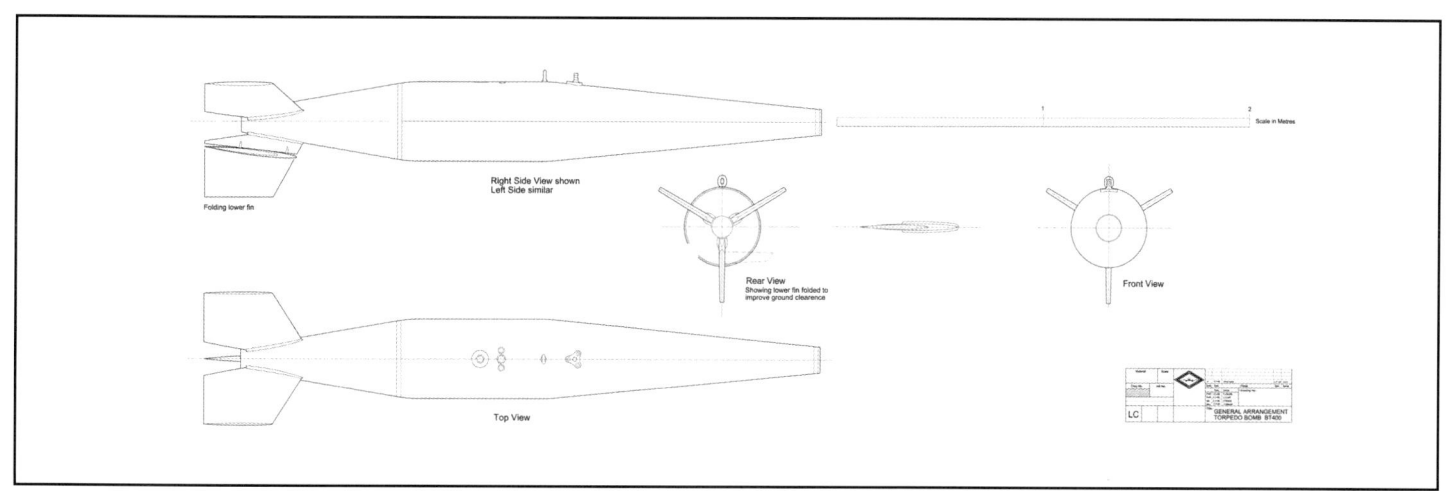

launched automatically. Then, when it was about 80 m (260 ft) from the target, the time fuse detonated the warhead. This comprised 460 *Brand Splitter* or incendiary pellets which were blasted out in a conical pattern in front of the missile. These were designed to slice through the tanks of the target aircraft and ignite its fuel. It was planned that the Me 262 would carry two of these potent weapons, mounted on the fuselage racks, but it failed to see service before the end of the war. Although very advanced in concept, the *Oberon* system would have been susceptible to jamming from Allied electronic counter-measures.

Yet another weapon proposed for the Me 262 was the BT 400 torpedo bomb. This was designed to replace the torpedo for use by fast fighter-bombers against shipping, but could also be used against land targets. The bomb consisted of a long truncated nose cone with a cylindrical centre section and a tail unit which tapered towards the rear on which were positioned three fins. It was designed to enter the water on a flat trajectory and continue beneath without deviation at as fast a speed and for as great a distance as possible. When compared with the LT F5 torpedo, the BT 400 had the advantage of being built mainly of more readily available ferrous metals, and taking merely 60 manhours to produce rather than 2,000. The bomb weighed a total of 400 kg (880 lbs), half of which comprised the high explosive warhead. It was planned that the BT 400 would be aimed with the aid of the TSA 2D bombsight.

In addition to the above, two air-to-air guided missiles were proposed for installation in the Me 262, the Ruhrstahl X-4 and the Henschel Hs 298. The X-4 was 2 m (6 ft 6.5 ins) long, had a small cigar-shaped body with four centrally-mounted swept back fins and four small tail fins. Two of the opposing fins held streamlined pods for the wire-control bobbins and a spoiler was fitted in each of the four tail fins, these giving pitch and yaw control. The missile was to be powered by the specially designed BMW 109-548 liquid fuel rocket engine which developed

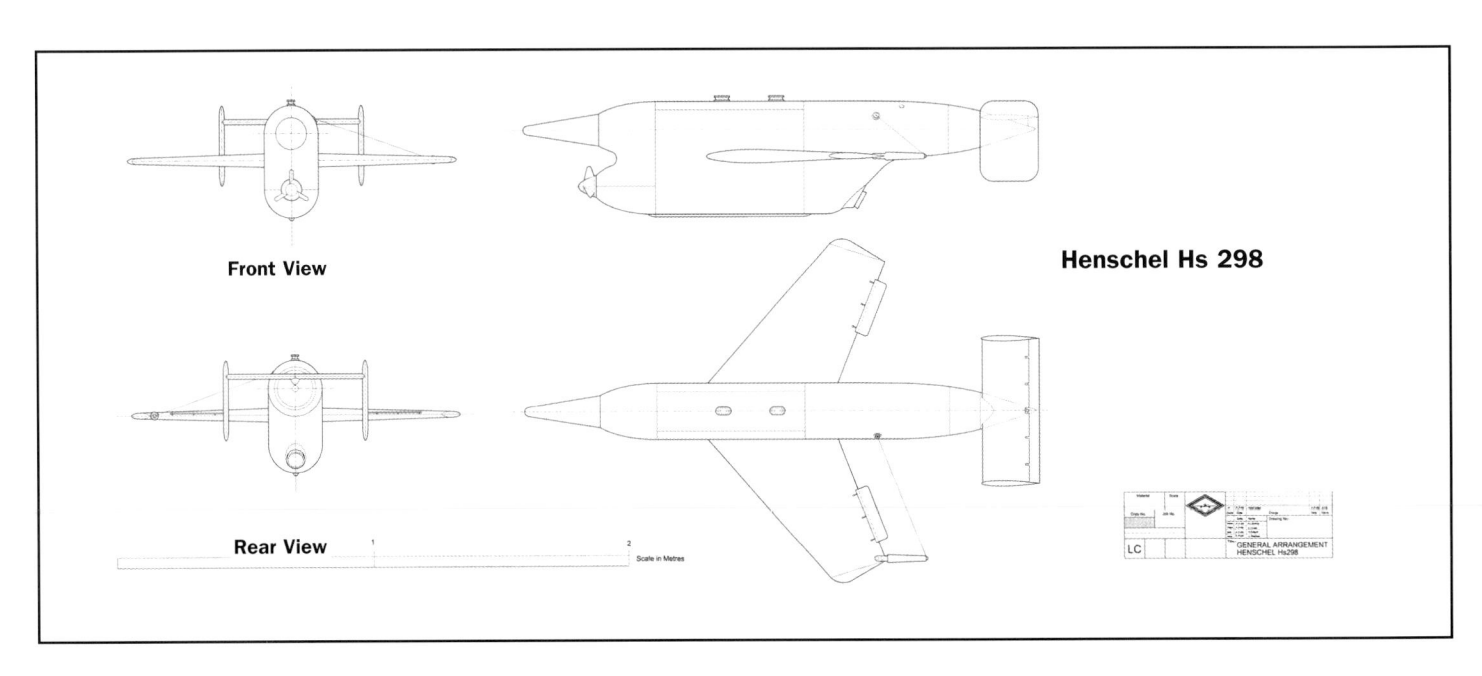

Right: The Henschel Hs 298 air-to-air guided missile. Two versions were built; the Hs 298 V1 with a 30 degree swept-back wing and the larger Hs 298 V2 with a 38 degree sweep.

Below: The Hs 298 fitted for trials under the wing of a Do 217N. It was proposed to fit three of the missiles to the Me 262.

Henschel Hs 298

an initial thrust of 140 kg (310 lbs). The simple direct-current wire guidance system comprised two 5.5 km (3.4 mile) transmission lines which unwound from the bobbins in the fins. The launching aircraft was equipped with the FuG 510 *Düsseldorf* transmitter with a simple joystick control for the pilot. The missile itself used the FuG 238 *Detmold* receiver.

The first trial launchings of the X-4 (8-344) from a Ju 88 took place in August 1944 from the *Erprobungsstelle* at Karlshagen (Peenemünde), it being intended that four of these missiles would be carried beneath the wings of the Me 262 on ETC 70/C-1 racks. The destruction of virtually all the BMW 548 engines at the company's Stargard factory by Allied bombing prevented the missiles being used operationally. This reverse led the propulsion specialist Professor Gladenbeck to attempt to design a solid fuel engine for the missile, a Me 262 being delivered to him for trials in January 1945. Gerd Lindner made a few test flights in a Me 262 (W.Nr. 111994) with two X-4s under the wings but no firing trials were undertaken.

The Hs 298 was developed by Dr. Max Kramer of the DVL late in 1942. It was similar in concept to the X-4, but possessed a lower performance. Two configurations were proposed, the Hs 298 V-1 with a 30 degree swept-back wing and the V-2 with 38 degree sweep. The missile was powered by the Schmidding 109-543 solid fuel rocket and employed a radio guidance system. The first experimental model was launched in May 1944 but, although over 300 were manufactured, the missile was cancelled in favor of the X-4. It was planned that three Hs 298s would be carried by the Me 262, two under the wings and one beneath the fuselage. Special racks were to be developed by the MWH company for this purpose.

During the middle of October 1944, proposals were made for towing both a 900 ltr (238 Imp gal) fuel tank or a 500 (1,102 lb) or 1,000 kg (2,200 lb) bomb behind the Me 262 in the *Deichselschlepp* rigid tow arrangement. In this the bomb or drop tank had an auxiliary wing mounted above it and was fitted with a two-wheeled take-off trolley. It was attached to the tail of the Me 262 by a 6 m (19 ft 8° in) hollow pole, this having a double joint to allow both vertical and horizontal motion. After take-off the wheels were jettisoned by igniting an explosive bolt and, on reaching the target, the aircraft was put into a dive where, using the normal *Revi* sight, the bomb was released by the detonation of another explosive bolt. When the towed bomb was replaced by a fuel tank the main fuel line passed through the hollow pole to feed the main fuel tanks.

Following the repair of the Me 262 V10, which had been damaged by an air attack on Leipheim on 12 September, the aircraft flew the first test with a towed 500 kg bomb on 22 October. It later tested a 1,000 kg weapon but this caused many problems. Messerschmitt test pilot Gerd Lindner, who conducted trials with the *Deichselschlepp* arrangement, found that the larger bomb tended to "porpoise" disconcertingly. On one occasion the explosive bolts failed to jettison the bomb and Lindner was forced to land with it still attached. During another test, putting the aircraft into too tight a turn caused the towing swivel to break away and

Because the X-4 was much lighter than the Hs 298 it was proposed to mount four of these missiles beneath the Me 262. One aircraft W.Nr. 111994, was fitted with two of these weapons and flown by Gerd Lindner before the end of the war, but it was too late to see operational service.

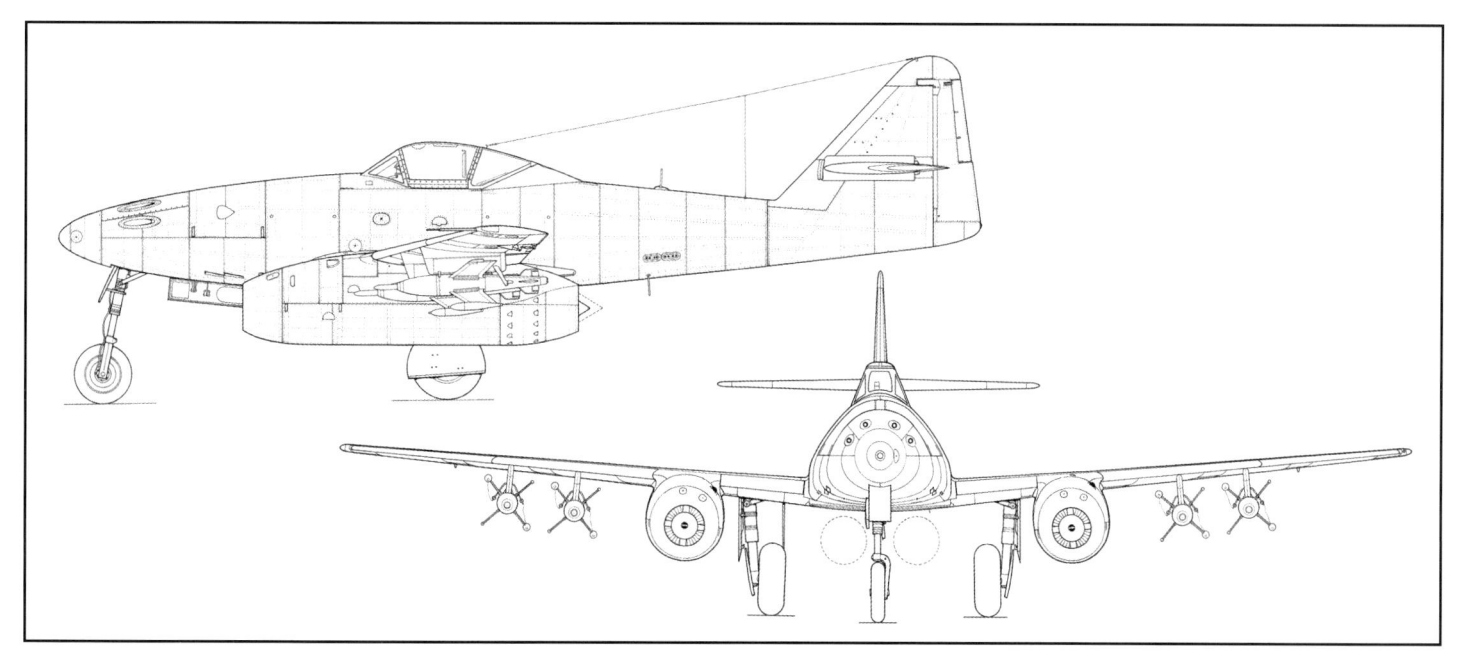

342 • Me 262 • VOLUME TWO

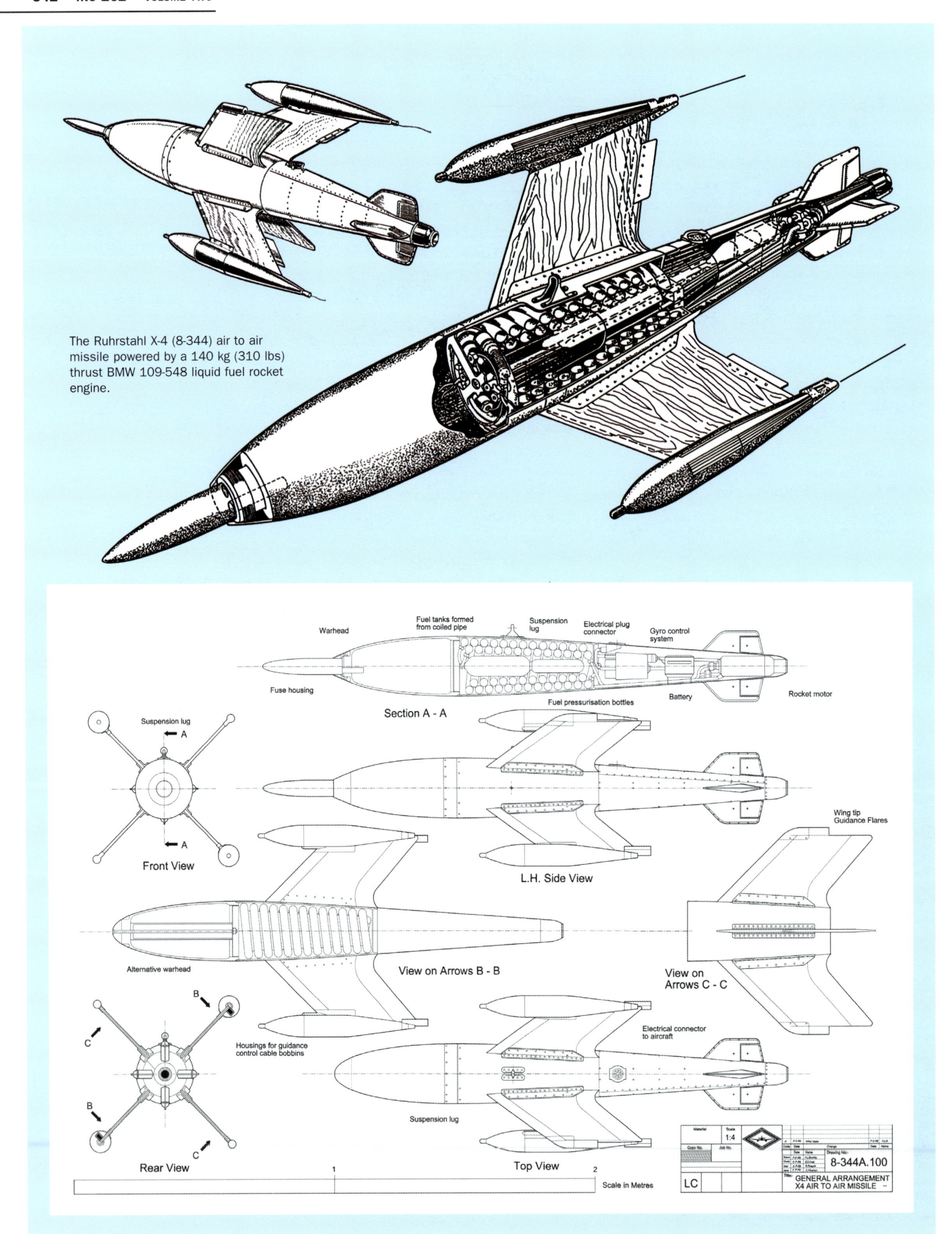

The Ruhrstahl X-4 (8-344) air to air missile powered by a 140 kg (310 lbs) thrust BMW 109-548 liquid fuel rocket engine.

Section A - A
- Warhead
- Fuse housing
- Fuel tanks formed from coiled pipe
- Suspension lug
- Electrical plug connector
- Gyro control system
- Fuel pressurisation bottles
- Battery
- Rocket motor

Front View
- Suspension lug

L.H. Side View

View on Arrows B - B
- Alternative warhead

View on Arrows C - C
- Wing tip Guidance Flares

Rear View
- Housings for guidance control cable bobbins

Top View
- Suspension lug
- Electrical connector to aircraft

Scale in Metres

Scale 1:4
Drawing No. 8-344A.100
Title: GENERAL ARRANGEMENT X4 AIR TO AIR MISSILE

A Fw 190 A-8 of the Erprobungsstelle Karlshagen taken in November 1944. The aircraft had been fitted with two ETC 71-C1 underwing racks, each carrying a Ruhrstahl X-4 air-to-air missile. Gerd Lindner flew a number of test flights in Me 262 W.Nr. 111994 which had also been fitted with X-4s. *Inset*: The X-4 missile fitted to its ETC 71-C1 underwing rack on a Fw 190 at the Erprobungsstelle Karlshagen in November 1944. A lag switch was built into the ETC 71-C1 which tripped after the missile had fallen a short distance following release. This switch also provided current for fusing the warhead and initiating the rocket motor. *Left*: A view of the X-4 directional control panel as built into the instrument panel of a Fw 190. The pilot was also provided with an elbow rest on the starboard side of the cockpit to allow comfortable operation of the unit. The missile release switch was located on the top left of the control column.

MESSERSCHMITT Me 262 V10 W.Nr. 130005

Above. The coupling located beneath the rudder of the Me 262 V10 which served to hold the 4 m (13 ft) rigid towline.

A 1,000 kg (2,205 lb.) bomb attached to the tail of the Me 262 V10 using the rigid tow pole method. This photograph shows the auxiliary wing mounted above the bomb and the jettisonable wheeled trolley below. This photo was taken just before the damage caused on the third flight.

Right and far right: Gerd Lindner takes off in Me 262 V10, W.Nr. 130005, at the start of another test with a towed 1,000 kg (2,205 lb.) bomb. These tests were eventually postponed when it was found that that the bomb possessed a tendency to porpoise. During one flight, this became so bad that Lindner was forced to bail out. A new aircraft was allocated to the test programme, but the problems associated with the arrangement were never fully resolved.

"THE CRUCIAL FACTOR" • 345

Apart from testing towed bombs, it was also intended that the Me 262 should be used to tow an unpowered version of the V-1 under the designation SG (Sondergerät) 5041. This was built by a DFS research group at Neuburg on the Danube and was fitted with a large bulge beneath the fuselage housing the towing equipment and a fixed spatted undercarriage. Towing trials, which did not prove very satisfactory, were carried out using the Ar 234 V8, but the SG 5041 was also intended to be towed by the Me 262. In the background of this photo can be seen the Me 262 V10.

The Me 262 V10, W.Nr. 130005, climbs above Lechfeld in October/November 1944 with Gerd Lindner at the controls towing a 500 kg (1,102 lb.) bomb attached by a rigid tow line or Deichselschlepp.

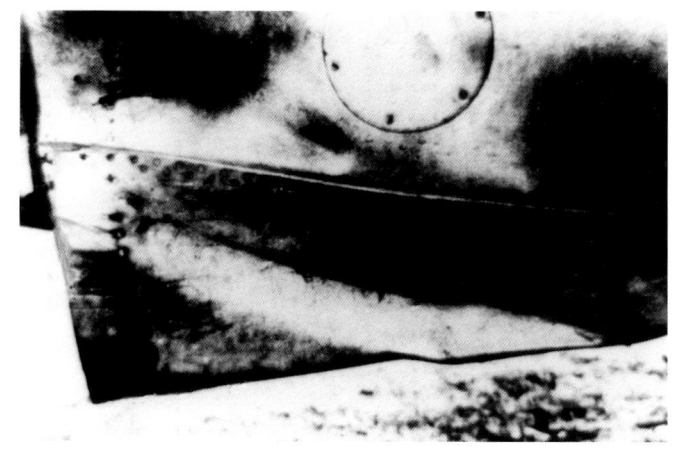

Above: Close-up of the rear fuselage of the Me 262 V10 showing the fairing of the bomb towing mechanism, which was damaged during the third flight on 21 November 1943.

The Me 262 V10, W.Nr. 130005, was used to perform various tests including the fitting of two experimental wooden drop tanks. However, trials were to show that these tanks leaked profusely and they were quickly abandoned.

damage the rear fuselage. Despite this Lindner considered that with an improved wing and the addition of a vertical fin, good results could have been obtained with towed bombs.

Another extremely promising aid to the Me 262 fighter pilot was the EZ 42 *Adler* (Eagle) gyroscopic gunsight developed by Askania. This type of sight automatically computed the deflection angle required to hit a target when both aircraft were manoeuvring. It thus gave to every fighter pilot the ability which up to that time had only been possessed by a few *Experten*. Although it was planned to fit 150 Me 262s with the EZ 42 in January 1945, only a few aircraft from JV 44 were ever equipped with the sight, but faulty installation often made the sight useless and it was locked so as to function like a conventional fixed reflector sight. The Zeiss-Ikon factory at Dresden-Striesen produced optical parts for the EZ 42, but the factory was seriously damaged in an air raid on the night of 13/14 February 1945 and deliveries of the device suffered accordingly.

Other items of equipment being developed for installation in the Me 262 included a pressurized cabin, an ejector seat, a braking parachute, and the carrying of two 600 ltr drop tanks. In common with many other German aircraft of the period it was also intended to replace the FuG 16 ZY transceiver with the more advanced FuG 15. Several aircraft were also to be fitted with the TSA 2 bombsight and the K 22 autopilot. It was also planned to introduce the SMK 16 (a 16 mm power-driven still camera) for gunnery control.

In January 1945 the DFS at Ainring issued a report suggesting the mounting of two ramjets over the top of the Me 262's turbojets above the wings. The ramjets, which were designed by Dr. Eugen Sänger, were to be 1.13 m (3 ft 8.5 inches) in diameter and no less than 5.9 m (19 ft 4 ins) in length and use normal J2 fuel. The following increase in the performance of the Me 262 was estimated:

1. Decrease in climbing time to 10,000 m (33,000 ft) from 26 minutes to 6 minutes.
2. An increase of up to 200 km/h (125 mph) in maximum horizontal speed.
3. An increase of nearly 4,000 m (13,000 ft) in service ceiling.

On the debit side, a decrease in range and flying time for a given fuel load was expected. For example, at an altitude of 10,000 m (33,000 ft), range was decreased from 1,400 km (870 miles) to 470 km (290 miles) and flying time from 145 minutes to 50 minutes. Ramjets had been tested above Do 17 and Do 217 test beds, but the engine was not fitted to a Me 262 before the end of the war.

One of the criticisms of many early jet aircraft was their tendency for directional snaking. To quote the Royal Aircraft Establishment's post-war assessment by Lt. Cmdr. Eric Brown: *"We experienced severe snaking trouble with the Meteor I and Lindner revealed an almost identical story of a lengthy trial-and-error process in attempting to eliminate the Me 262's tendency to snake. It had been ascertained that rough air snaking was due to a lack of effective fin area which was inherent in the design."*[2]

This directional oscillation lasted for between 1.3 and 1.9 seconds at 700 km/h (435 mph) and was accentuated in rough air. It was not accompanied by noticeable rudder movements and the snaking was less annoying at low speeds owing to the oscillation period lengthening as speed decreased. A surprising feature of this problem was that it worsened markedly with the rearward movement of the centre of gravity. In an attempt to artificially lengthen the oscillation period a prototype Me 262 was flown with the top one-sixth of its fin and rudder removed. Another prototype had no less than one-third of its fin and rudder removed. These modifications considerably relieved the snaking problem, but the reduced rudder area was inadequate to counter the asymmetric effects of an engine failure. With the standard fin and rudder the speed for minimum control on one engine was 260 km/h (160 mph), with the cut-down tail this was increased to an unacceptable 320 km/h (200 mph)

Further experiments to improve the aircraft's

Designed and manufactured by Askania and Carl Zeiss, the EZ 42 gyroscopic gunsight proved unpopular and ineffective. It was used operationally by at least one pilot of JG 7 and several with JV 44, but was soon abandoned.

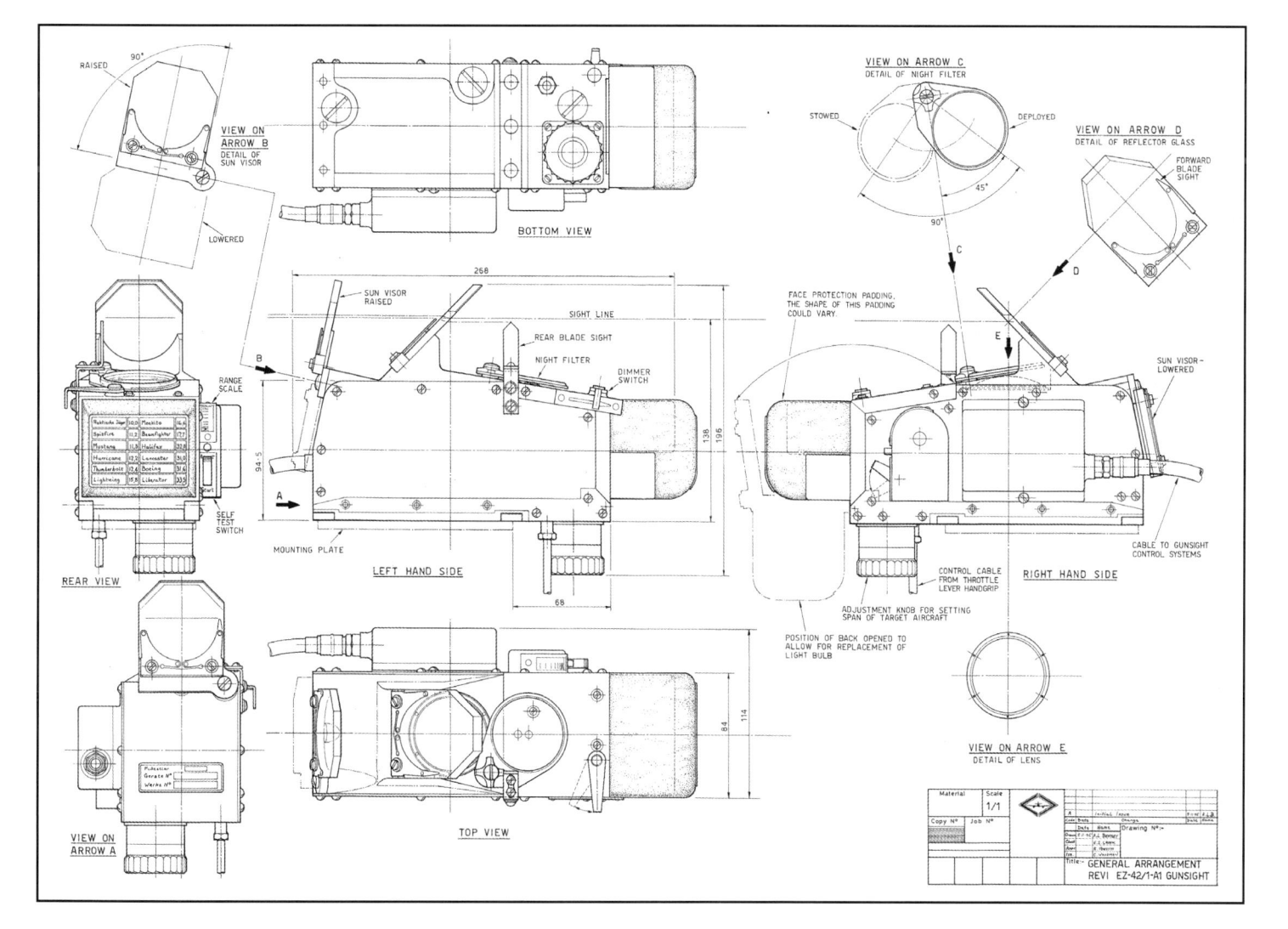

In January 1945 the DFS at Ainring issued a report suggesting the mounting of two ramjets on top of the Me 262's turbojets above the wings. The ramjets, which were designed by Dr. Eugen Sänger, were tested a Do 217 test bed, but no engine was fitted to the Me 262 before the end of the war.

snaking characteristics included the fitting of a narrow fin above the forward fuselage with a proposal to enlarge this to no less than 0.88 m² (9.5 sq ft). The former was tested, but, as far as is known, the latter remained a project only. The two prototypes used to test these features were the Me 262 V-056 (W.Nr. 170056) and V-167 (W.Nr. 130167).

After these experiments were carried out in November and December 1944, three much less radical modifications were instituted which did go some way to improving matters. These were:

To thicken the rudder trailing edge, finishing it with a U section instead of bringing the panels to a point.

Adding two strips of sheet metal along the trailing edge of the rudder bent outwards.

Bending in the shrouds covering the fin/rudder gap when the rudder was too thick and bending them out when it was too thin.

At an Armaments Conference held on 20 January, Hitler demanded improved armament for the fighter units, and in particular the Me 262. This included accelerated series production of the EZ 42 gunsight, rapid introduction of the R4M missile, the MK 213 and MK 214 cannon, improvement in the rate of fire of the MK 108 (to 800 rounds/min), and the early debut of the Me 262 A-1a/U5 with six MK 108s. On 14 February it was proposed to mount a total of no fewer than 48 R4Ms beneath the Me 262 on re-usable launchers. With the exception of the Me 262, all R4Ms were to be reserved for the Ar 234 and He 162. At a later Armaments Conference held on 22 March 1945, Hitler said that he wanted the Me 262 fighter-bomber rearmed as soon as possible as a fighter. In this he publicly admitted the error he had made a year and a half earlier when he had persistently refused the advice of the experts. He again talked of introducing heavier armament for the aircraft including the 50 mm or two 37 mm cannon and R4M rockets.

As will be seen in Chapter 12, two of the Me 262s delivered in December 1944 were for conversion to the *Mistel* combination aircraft. The idea of mounting a fighter above a war-weary Ju 88 bomber and launching the unpiloted lower component, fitted with a hollow charge warhead, against a heavily armoured target had been put forward by *Flugkapitän* Siegfried Holzbaur, the Junkers test pilot, early in 1943. The upper component could then make good its escape at high speed in the manner of a conventional fighter.

In July 1943, the RLM had placed an order for 15 of these combination aircraft under the code name *Mistel* (Mistletoe). Three different versions were proposed, the *Mistel 1* which comprised a Bf 109 F-4 and Ju 88 A-4, the *Mistel 2*, a Fw 190 A-6 and Ju 88 G-1, and the *Mistel 3*, a Fw 190 A-8 or F-8 and either a Ju 88 A-4, H-4 or G-10. The first *Mistel* operation was flown on 24 June 1944, by 2./KG 101, but this proved abortive. The unit's remaining five aircraft then attacked shipping in the Seine Bay, German reconnaissance asserting that four ships had been sunk. One of the other lower components somehow went off course and crashed near Andover in England. Following this, plans were made to carry out an attack on an important strategic target such as the Royal Navy's base at Scapa Flow or hydro-electric generating stations in the Soviet Union using the *Mistel*. Many problems surrounded these plans and eventually most *Mistel* were expended in

Me 262 project fitted with two Sänger ramjets
This project powered by two Sänger ramjet engines in addition to its Jumo 004 B turbojets was intended to dramatically increase the Me 262's maximum speed, service ceiling and climbing time. The ramjet engines were to use the same fuel as the turbojets and one can only speculate as to the effect of the handling characteristics. This remarkable project was proposed by the DFS at Ainring in January 1945.

Me 262 Lorin
two Jumo 004 B turbojets and ramjet

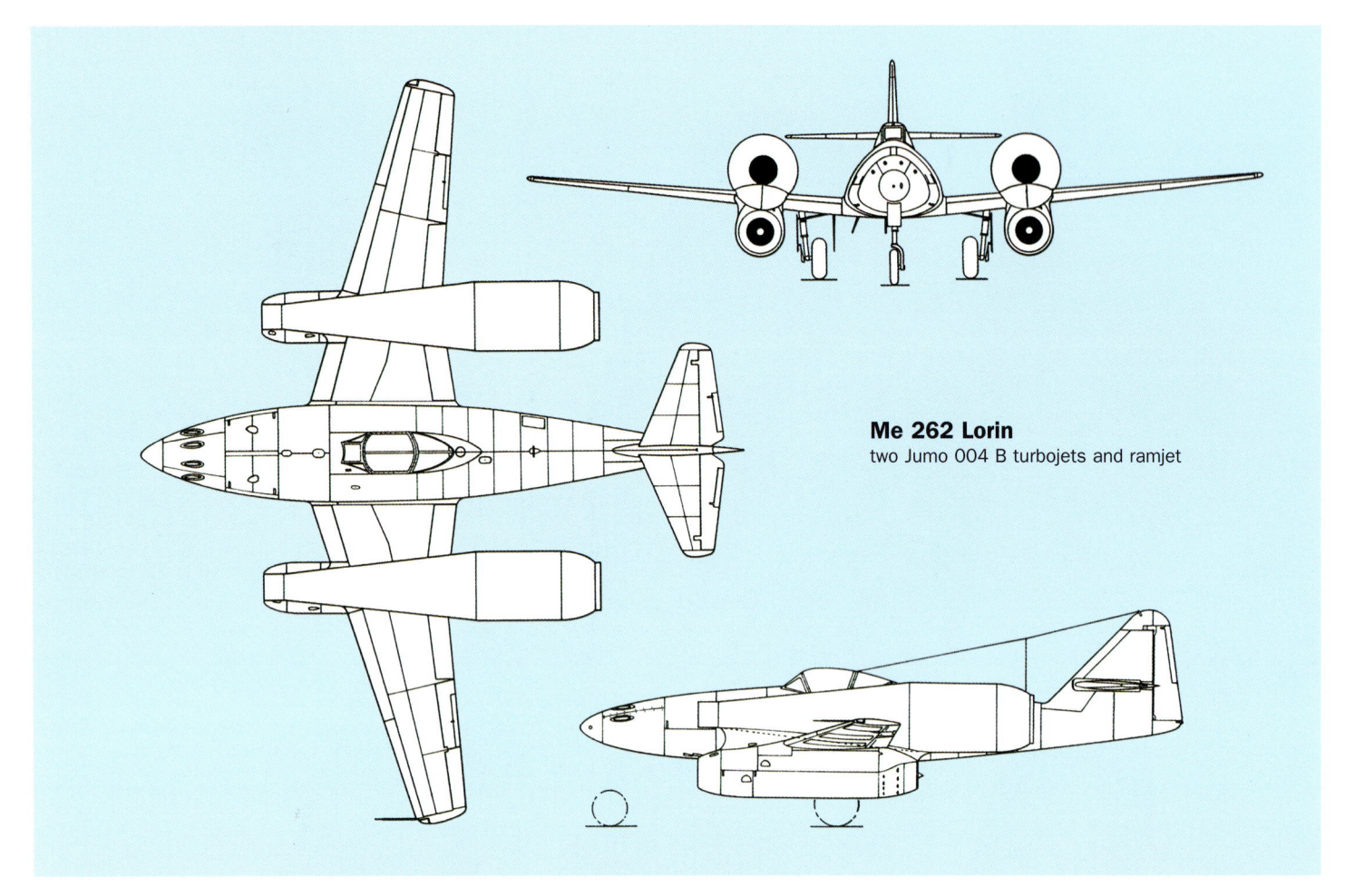

The ramjet boosted version of the Me 262 was expected to decrease the aircraft's climbing time to 10,000 m (32,800 ft) from 26 minutes to 6 minutes, increase its maximum speed by up to 200 km/h (125 mph) and boost altitude by 4,000 m (13,000 ft). On the debit side, the aircraft's already short range would have been reduced by about four-fifths.

desperate attempts to destroy river bridges in Poland and eastern Germany in an attempt to stem the advance of Soviet ground forces.

By 1944, the problem with the conventionally powered *Mistel* was its vulnerability to enemy fighters before the lower component could be released on its target. Therefore, in November 1944, a proposal was put forward to use two Me 262s as the upper and lower components of a new *Mistel 4*. The upper component was to be a Me 262 A-2a/U2[3] with the *Bomberkanzel* (bomber nose) housing a second crew member who would help to aim the lower component at its target. It was estimated that this upper component would have a take-off weight of 6,985 kg (15,400 lbs) with a fuel load of 2,570 ltrs (680 Imp gals).

The combination was mounted on a special five-wheeled trolley weighing 20 tons, developed by Rheinmetall-Borsig. The lower Me 262 was mounted on the trolley, after which the mother aircraft would be lifted on top and connected to it by struts fitted with explosive bolts. Take-off was accomplished with the aid of four Walter 501 rocket units, the five-wheeled trolley being jettisoned shortly afterward in the manner of the early Ar 234 prototypes.

Three different versions of the lower component were proposed, known as the *Ausführung A, B* and *C*. Version A was to have an armoured fuselage nose with liquid explosive, Version B was to have the forward fuselage formed of solid explosive with similar material in other fuselage areas, and Version C was to have the forward fuselage of Version B but with liquid explosive in the other areas. The following weights were proposed as per chart above left.

The first combination would have a total take-off weight of 16,900 kg (37,250 lbs), the second of 18,635 kg (41,080 lbs) and the third 17,110 kg (37,720 lbs).

Two Me 262s were delivered for conversion as *Mistel* during December 1944 but, as far as is known, the composite never flew before the end of the war. Two further *Mistel* (designated *Mistel 5* and *6* respectively) were proposed before the end of the war, one using the Ar 234 C-3 as its upper component, the other the He 162. There was also a proposal to use the Me 262 with a Ju 88 lower component (possibly jet powered) and some authors have claimed (although this has yet to be confirmed by documentary evidence) that there was a project to combine the Me 262 with a Ju 287 as the explosive carrier [4].

Photographed at Stassfurt in April 1945, a Mistel S-3c composite comprising a Fw 190 A-8 upper component and a Ju 88 H lower component. In November 1944, a proposal was made to build a Me 262 Mistel comprising a Me 262 A-2a/U2 atop a standard Me 262 mounted on a trolley.

PROPOSED Me 262 MISTEL VARIANTS

	Take-off weight	Fuel Reserve	Explosive weight
Carrier Aircraft	6,985 kg 15,399 lbs	2,133 kg 4,702 lbs	none
Ausführung A	9,917 kg 21,863 lbs	1,454 kg 3,205 lbs	4,460 kg 9,832 lbs
Ausführung B	11,650 kg 25,683 lbs	1,494 kg 3,294 lbs	6,030 kg 13,294 lbs
Ausführung C	10,125 kg 22,321 lbs	1,494 kg 3,294 lbs	5,210 kg 11,486 lbs

Me 262 Mistel
with four Jumo 004 turbojets. Details taken from a document dated 28 November 1944.

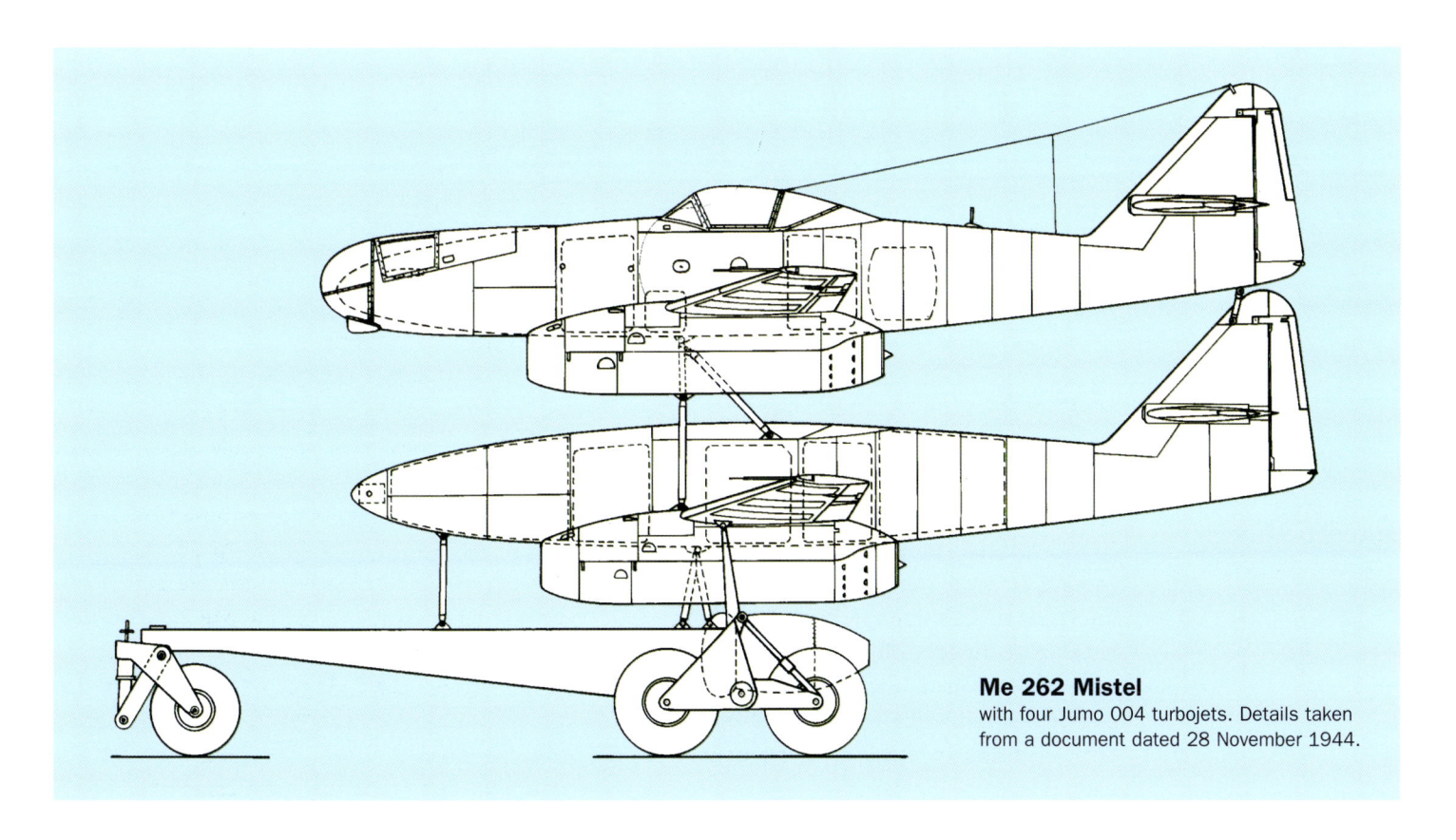

On 23 March 1944, Messerschmitt's *Projektbüro* at Oberammergau, put forward a series of *Baubeschreibungen* (Project Descriptions) for two developments of the Me 262 with enlarged fuselages designated P 1099 and P 1100.

MESSERSCHMITT P 1099

The P 1099 was a multi-seat heavy fighter and destroyer with the wings of the Me 262 and a completely new fuselage, but powered by two Jumo 004 C engines. Two main proposals were issued, known as *Lösung* (solution) *A* and *B*. The *Lösung A* was a two-seat fighter with fixed forward-firing offensive armament, with several variations (identified by drawing numbers) proposed:

Drawing No.XVIII/79
Jäger I - Ausführung (version) *A*
    Four 30 mm MK 108 cannon
Jäger I - Ausführung B
    Two 30 mm MK 103 cannon
Jäger I - Ausführung C
    Two 30 mm MK 108 and two MK 103 cannon

Drawing No.XVIII/87
Jäger II - Ausführung A
    One 30 mm MK 108 and
    one 55 mm MK 112 cannon
Jäger II - Ausführung B
    One 50 mm MK 214 A cannon

The *Lösung B* introduced remotely-controlled defensive armament. Again several variations were proposed:

Drawing No.XVIII/85
Three-seat fighter with a twin MK 103Z installation in the rear cockpit, one FPL 151 remotely-controlled gun barbette on either side of the rear fuselage and one flexible FHL 151 gun in the fuselage nose.

Drawing No.XVIII/83
Ausführung A
    Heavy fighter with four fixed 30 mm MK 108 cannon and an FPL 151 remotely-controlled gun barbette on either side of the rear fuselage each housing a 20 mm MG 151 cannon.
Ausführung B Destroyer with a fixed forward-firing armament of two MK 103 and one 50 mm MK 214 cannon plus two FPL 151 gun barbettes.

Drawing No.XVIII/84
Ausführung A
    Night fighter with a fixed forward-firing armament of four 30 mm MK 108 cannon and two further MK 108s in a *Schräge Musik* installation.

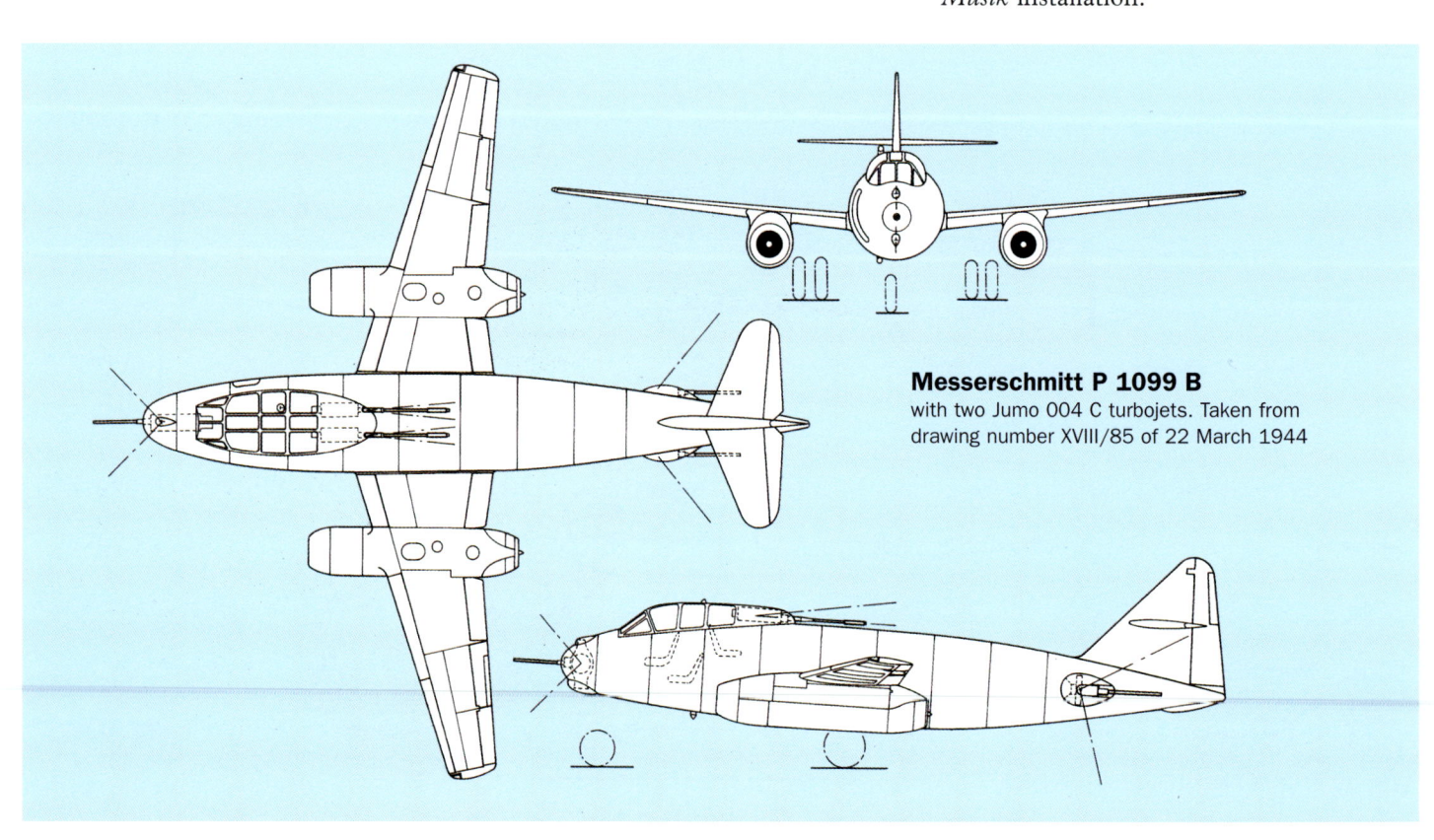

Messerschmitt P 1099 B
with two Jumo 004 C turbojets. Taken from drawing number XVIII/85 of 22 March 1944

Messerschmitt P 1100 Schnellbomber II

The proposed aircraft was to be powered by two Jumo 004 C turbojets. This project, from drawing number XVIII/78 dated 22 March 1944, was to be fitted with a remotely-controlled FHL 108 barbette in the nose housing a single MK 108 cannon, with one FHL 151 turret on either side of the fuselage each housing a single MG 151/20 gun.

MESSERSCHMITT P 1100

The Messerschmitt P 1100 had a similar enlarged fuselage to the P 1099 but was designed as a high-speed bomber. Again, several variations were proposed, all identified by drawing numbers.

Drawing No. XVIII/70

Two versions of this unarmed bomber were produced, the /1 having a small single-seat cabin offset to port and the /2 a larger two-seat cabin. Both variants were to have three 900 ltr (238 Imp gal) and two 600 ltr (158 Imp gal) tanks in the fuselage and carry their 2,000 kg (4,410 lbs) bomb load internally. This could comprise any combination of one 1,000 kg or two 500 kg weapons mounted in separate compartments one behind the other. To support the project's extra weight, a double wheel main undercarriage was to be fitted.

Drawing No. XVIII/77

Schnellbomber I with fixed 30 mm MK 108 cannon firing forward and aft

Drawing No. XVIII/78

Schnellbomber II with one remotely-controlled FHL 108 barbette in the nose, and one FPL 151 turret on either side of the rear fuselage.

Drawing No. XVIII/87

Fitted with an enlarged wing with 35 degree sweep back and HeS 011 engines buried in the wing roots.

Drawing No. XVIII/88

Later project (dated 7 May 1944) with wing span increased to 12.74 m (41 ft 9.5 ins), small canopy offset to port but with no defensive armament. Two versions were proposed, the first unarmed, the second with two FHL 151 barbettes fore and aft.

	P 1099		P 1100	
	Lösung A - Jäger I		*Bomber II*	
Take-off weight	8,562 kg	18,876 lbs	9,992 kg	22,028 lbs
Landing weight	6,110 kg	13,470 lbs	6,040 kg	13,316 lbs
Maximum speed				
at sea level	769 km/h	478 mph	722 km/h	449 mph
at 6,000 m (19,685 ft)	810 km/h	503 mph	746 km/h	464 mph
at 9,000 m (29,528 ft)	776 km/h	482 mph	——	——
Climbing speed				
at sea level	13.4 m/sec	44.0 ft/sec	10.1 m/sec	33.1 ft/sec
at 6,000 m (19,685 ft)	5.6 m/sec	18.4 ft/sec	3.3 m/sec	10.8 ft/sec
at 9,000 m (29,528 ft)	1.1 m/sec	3.6 ft/sec	——	——
Climbing time				
to 6,000 m (19,685 ft)	11.1 mins	11.1 mins	15.9 mins	15.9 mins
to 7,000 m (22,966 ft)	14.2 mins	14.2 mins	——	——
Service Ceiling	9,800 m	32,152 ft	9,200 m	30,183 ft
Normal range				
at sea level	610 km	379 mls	638 km	396 mls
at 3,000 m (9,483 ft)	910 km	565 mls	863 km	536 mls
at 7,000 m (19,966 ft)	1,310 km	814 mls	1,248 km	775 mls
Landing speed	184 km/h	114 mph	183 km/h	114 mph

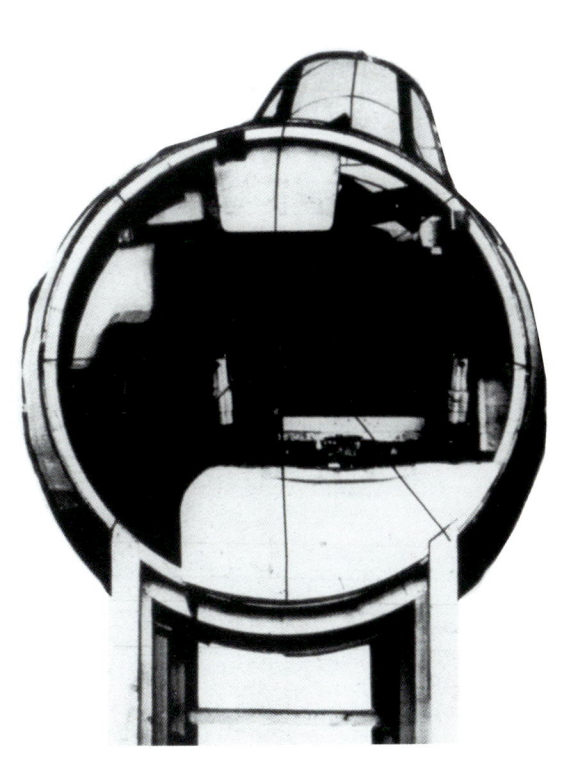

"The Crucial Factor" • 355

Provisional instrument layout for the Messerschmitt P 1100 Schnellbomber project as built in to the wooden mock-up.

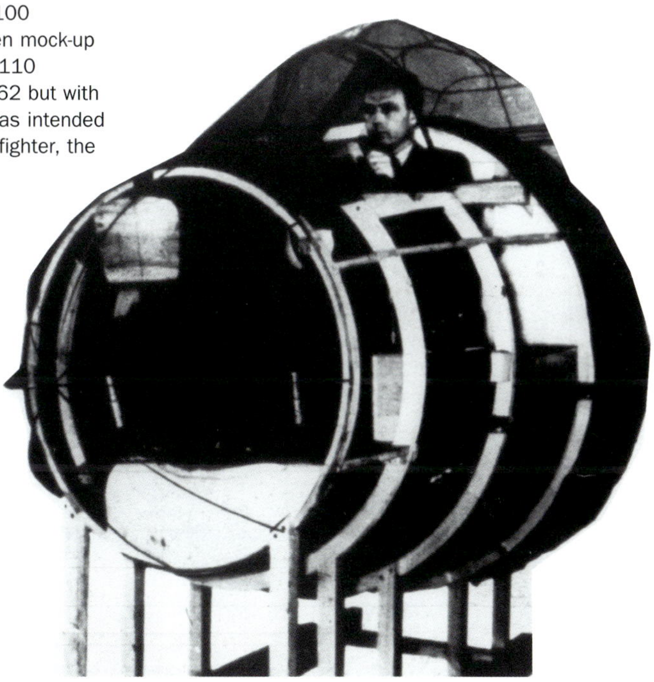

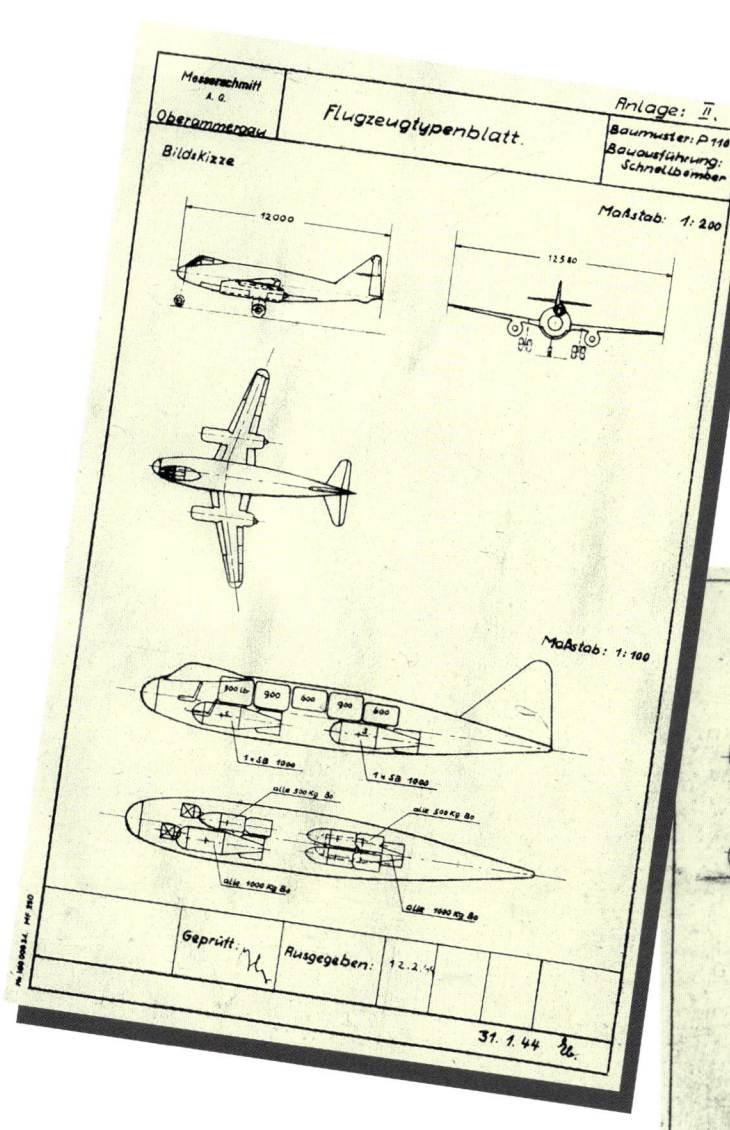

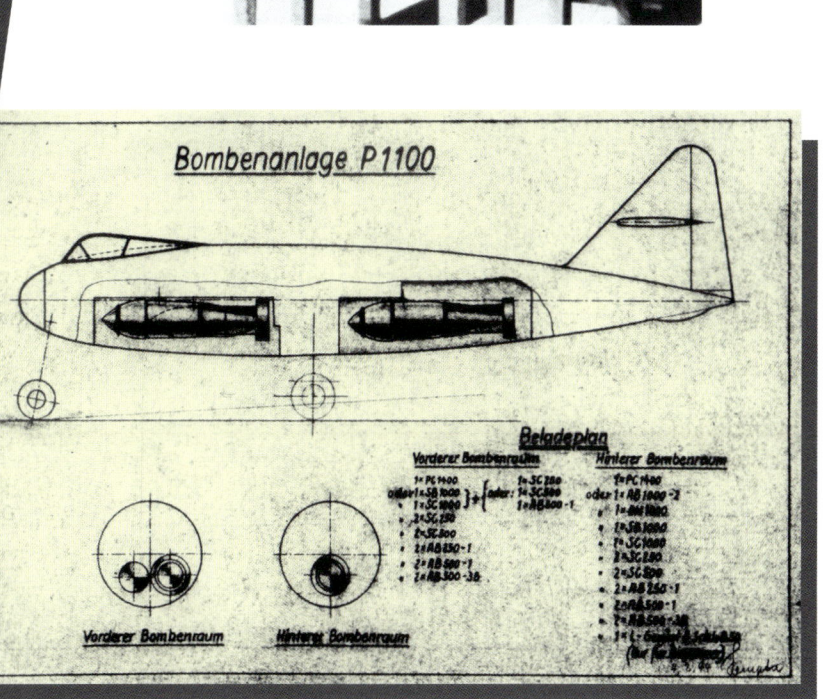

In order to determine the best instrument layout for the Messerschmitt P 1100 Schnellbomber, a project a wooden mock-up was built. Both the P 1099 and P110 projects were based on the Me 262 but with enlarged fuselages. The former was intended for the role of destroyer or heavy fighter, the latter as a fast bomber.

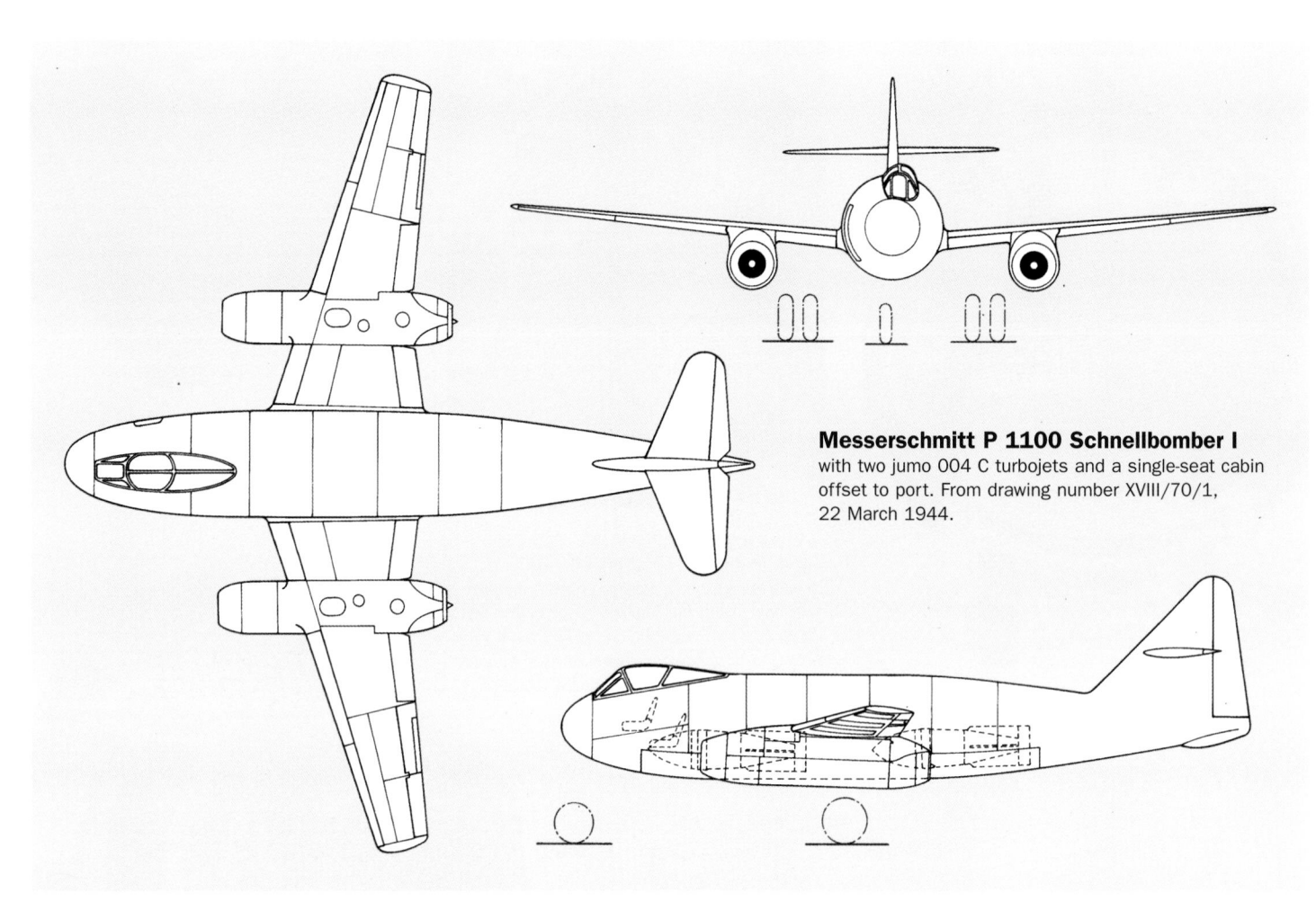

356 • Me 262 • VOLUME TWO

Messerschmitt P 1100 Schnellbomber I
with two jumo 004 C turbojets and a single-seat cabin offset to port. From drawing number XVIII/70/1, 22 March 1944.

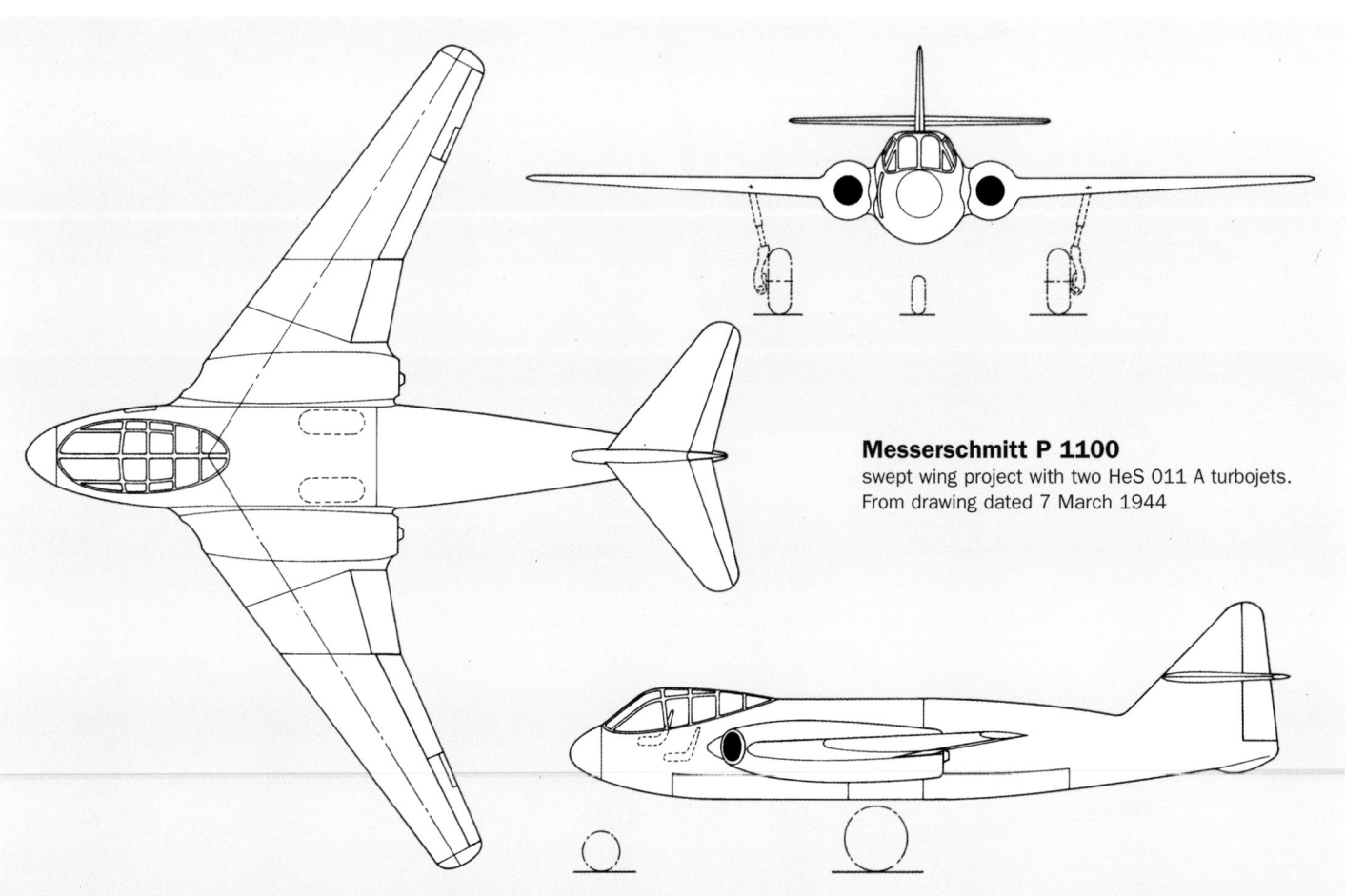

Messerschmitt P 1100
swept wing project with two HeS 011 A turbojets. From drawing dated 7 March 1944

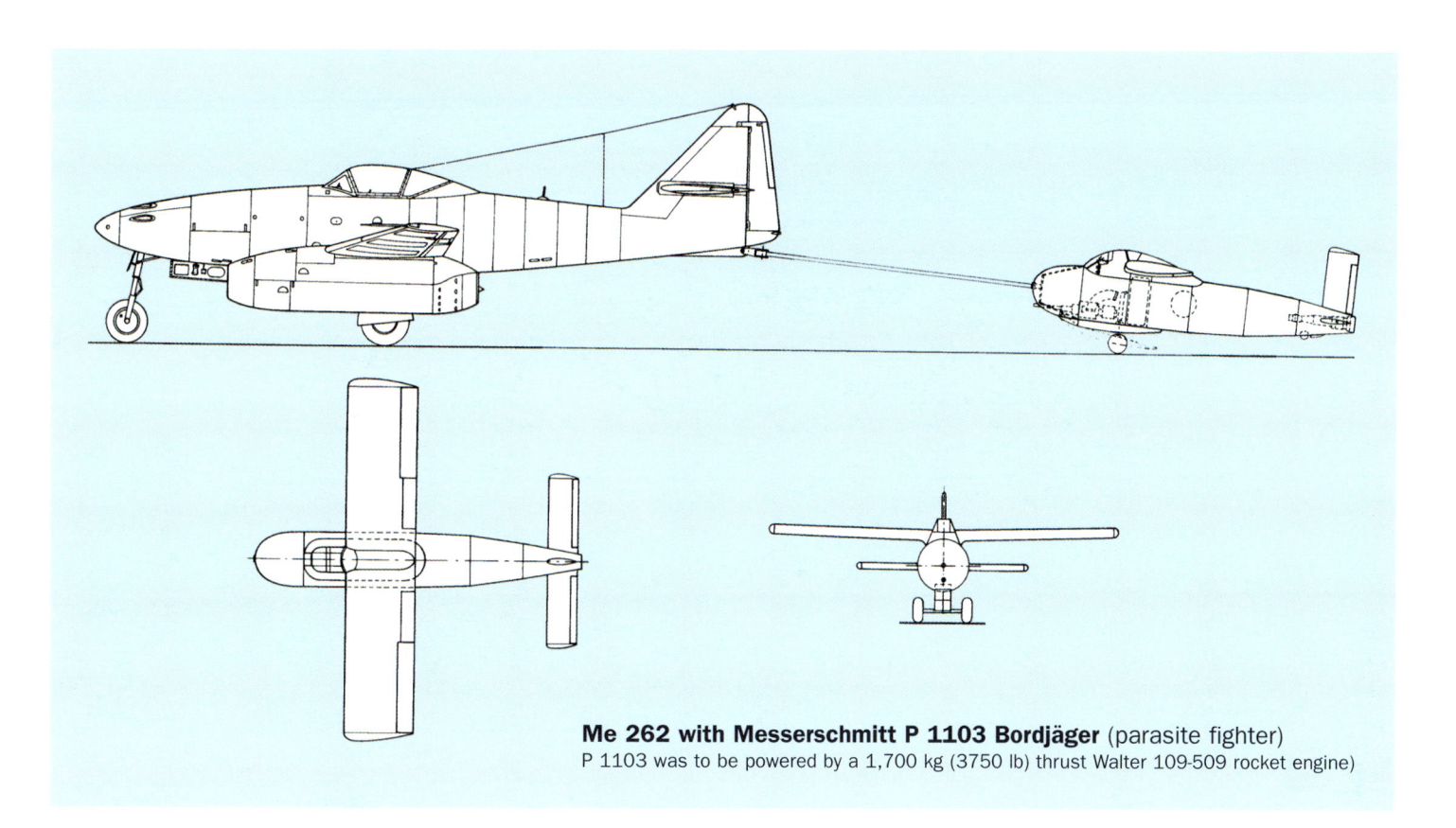

Me 262 with Messerschmitt P 1103 Bordjäger (parasite fighter)
P 1103 was to be powered by a 1,700 kg (3750 lb) thrust Walter 109-509 rocket engine)

MESSERSCHMITT P 1103

The P 1103 was a project for a small parasite fighter to be towed behind the Me 262. Little is known about the P 1103, but it was intended to be towed behind a fighter and released when in range of a bomber formation. The idea was that its small frontal area would present enemy gunners with an almost impossible target until it opened fire with its cannon. The P 1103 was a simple shoulder-wing monoplane with a jettisonable undercarriage powered by a Walter 109-509 rocket engine. Armament was limited to a single 30 mm MK 108 cannon. The estimated weights for the type are shown in the following table:

Fuselage and armour	355.1 kg	782.8 lbs
Wing	120.0 kg	264.5 lbs
Tail	35.0 kg	77.2 lbs
Controls	10.0 kg	22.0 lbs
Undercarriage	14.0 kg	30.9 lbs
Total Equipped weight	**534.1 kg**	**1177.4 lbs**
Engine	60.0 kg	132.3 lbs
Equipment	48.4 kg	106.7 lbs
Armament (one MK 108)	61.0 kg	134.5 lbs
100 rounds ammunition	60.0 kg	132.3 lbs
Crew	80.0 kg	176.4 lbs
Fuel *(C-Stoff)*	150.0 kg	330.7 lbs
Fuel *(T-Stoff)*	54.0 kg	119.0 lbs
Take-off weight	**1047.5 kg**	**2309.3 lbs**
Landing weight	**985.5 kg**	**2172.6 lbs**

---

1 The *Wikingerschiff* rack is described in Volume One, Chapter 7.
2 Eric "Winkle" Brown was the first naval officer to command the Aerodynamics Flight at the Royal Aircraft Establishment in Farnborough. He flew no fewer than 55 different types of German aircraft during and after the war and also interrogated many leading German aviation personalities including Willy Messerschmitt.
3 See Chapter 9.
4 The first description of the Me 262/Ju 287 Mistel appeared in the July 1949 issue of "Interavia" magazine, but no confirmation of the combination has been found in wartime German documents.

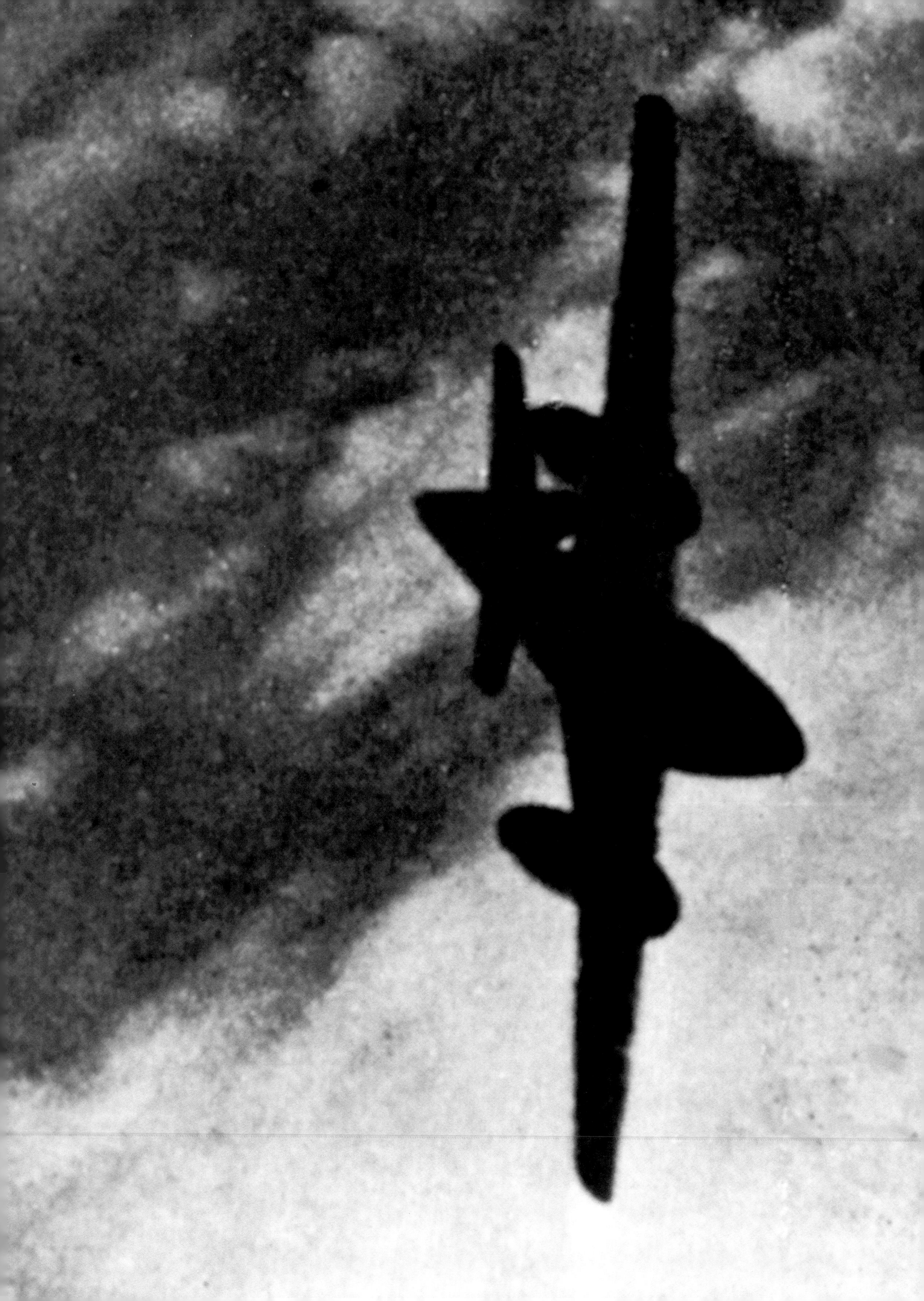

CHAPTER ELEVEN
"MY GOD, WHAT WAS THAT?"

Following Hitler's order of May 1944 that the Me 262 was to be transferred to bomber operations, it was decided that the *Edelweiss Geschwader*, KG 51, would be the first wing to operate the type. Named after the well-known Alpine flower which it used as its emblem, the Geschwader had been formed in 1937 under the designation KG 255. It had taken part in the invasion of France and Battle of Britain in 1940, the attack on the Soviet Union in 1941 and 1942 and also in some operations in the Middle Eastern theatre early in 1943. During May of that year its first *Gruppe* returned to Germany where its Ju 88s were replaced by Me 410 high-speed bombers. By the spring of 1944 its other remaining operational component, II./KG 51, was also re-equipped with the Me 410.

Junkers Ju 88A-4s of III./KG 51 in formation over the Russian front, 1942.

During the middle of May, the first *Gruppe* of KG 51 was withdrawn from operations on the Western Front to begin retraining on the Me 262. To develop operational tactics for use by the Me 262 bomber, it was decided to set up a special *Einsatzkommando* (operational detachment) under the leadership of *Maj.* Wolfgang Schenck. On 20 June the unit, designated *Kommando Schenck*, began training at Lechfeld. The first of twelve pilots arrived by 10 July, six Me 262s being delivered to the unit on this day. It suffered its first loss four days later when *Stabsfw.* Mosbacher was killed when his aircraft, W.Nr. 130177, crashed into the Ammersee while making a practice bombing run.

Meanwhile, ground personnel from the *3. Staffel* of KG 51 under *Oblt.* Eberhard Winkel transferred to Memmingen and fourteen days later to Leipheim for training on the maintenance procedures needed for the Me 262 and its radical new engines. At the end of June the *Staffel* moved to Lechfeld where it joined 1./KG 51. A few days later the first Me 262s were delivered, six of these going to 3./KG 51. Around 10 July the first pilots began to arrive at Lechfeld, but on the 17th of the month between one and two hundred ground personnel were loaded into lorries for transfer to Châteaudun in France.

On 6 July 1944, *Hauptdienstleiter* Karl-Otto Saur[1] addressed the *Jägerstab* on aircraft production, giving details of priorities. When it

WOLFGANG SCHENCK

Wolfgang "Bombo" Schenck was born on 7 February 1913 in Windhoek in South West Africa (now Namibia). He joined the Luftwaffe in 1936, serving first with I./JG Richthofen, but transferring to I./ZG 1 for the campaign against Poland, Norway and France. He was shot down and badly injured on 16 May 1940 by an RAF Hurricane but, after recuperation, became Staffelkapitän of 1./Erprobungsgruppe 210 in September 1940. This unit was renamed 1./SKG 210 in April 1941 and later took part in the invasion of Russia. On 16 August 1941 he was awarded the Knight's Cross, and during the next month he took over Erprobungsstaffel 210 at Rechlin whose task was to introduce the Me 210 into operational service. He became Kommandeur of I./ZG 1 on 1 January 1942 and was awarded the Eichenlaub (Oak Leaves) on 30 October 1942 while serving with the Luftwaffe Führungsstab. On 3 January 1943 he was appointed Kommodore of the newly-created Sch.G.2 on the Mediterranean front flying ground attack Fw 190s. He was injured again in December 1943 but was appointed as an Inspector at the Reisestab Dr. Gustav (involved with air defence planning for the anticipated Allied invasion). In March 1944 he was made Taktischer Berater (Technical Adviser) in the Luftwaffe's Technisches Amt (Technical Department), becoming responsible for Me 262 bombing trials in June 1944. He was to fly a total of 300 combat missions and achieve 18 victories.

came to the Me 262, he commented:

"The aircraft is being produced as a *'Blitz-Bomber'*, its output last month being 22, then increasing to 60, 150 in September, 225 in October, 325 in November, and 500 in December. When output reaches 500 bombers, production above this level and up to 1,000 will be switched to fighters. This programme for the 262, which should reach an output of 500 in the next few months means that, although we have so far fallen far short of it, the programme until now in force for the type has been doubled. We are lagging badly behind in the fourth month of production of this type. Nevertheless, we have attempted not only to carry out the old programme, but also will we have to push through this doubled programme at all costs."

Saur was referring to Programme 226, initiated on 9 July, which called for a total output of 6,400 aircraft by September 1945 of which 80 per cent were to be fighters as compared with only 40 per cent proposed by the previous Programme 225. As mentioned by Saur, a total of 1,000 Me 262s were to be built in July 1945 instead of the 670 previously requested.

On 16 July *Protokoll Nr.36*[2] listed various items of equipment for the aircraft. ETC 504 bomb racks (built by *Mechanische Werkstätten Neubrandenburg*) were to replace the Focke-Wulf designed ETC 503s which had proved far from satisfactory when fitted to the Me 262, RATO equipment was requested for fifty aircraft, the first to be delivered to KG 51. A 600 ltr (159 Imp gal) drop tank was to be tested by W.Nr. 170283 and 200 ltr (59 Imp gal) tanks were proposed for series aircraft beginning with W.Nr. 170094 from Leipheim and W.Nr. 170074 from Schwäbisch Hall. Simultaneously, the two-seat trainer was given the official designation Me 262 B-1.

On 19 July the US Eighth Air Force mounted a series of attacks on various targets in Western and South-Western Germany. These included the Messerschmitt airfields at Lechfeld and Leipheim where a total of ten Me 262s were destroyed and two others damaged. Three of these (the S2, S4 and W.Nr. 170057) were being used by Messerschmitt for various tests, the remaining nine (the S8, W.Nr. 170007, 170009, 170012, 170050, 170064, 170062, 170065 and 170066) having been delivered to *Kommando Schenck*.

By this time each pilot from *Kommando Schenck* had made about four flights in the Me 262, and on 20 July they transferred to Châteaudun with nine aircraft for operations against the Allied invasion. Messerschmitt's trouble shooter, Fritz Wendel, later reported to the Directors of the Messerschmitt company on the situation:

"At the time when Major Schenck received his orders, operational employment as a fighter would

In the summer of 1944, the Messerschmitt test pilot, Fritz Wendel (seen here, centre, during a demonstration for the Wehrmacht), who had test flown the Me 262 V1, V2 and V3 prototypes, was ordered by the company to travel to France to report on the operational progress and efficiency of the Me 262 in service with Kommando Schenck. His reports were often concise but critical.

A typically busy scene as British infantry and armour prepare to move out of a village in Normandy, early August 1944. Enemy concentrations such as these were the intended targets for the Me 262 jet bombers of Kommando Schenck.

have been possible, not so, however, as a bomber. There were many problems:

a. The range was insufficient for bomber missions, since the operational base had to be located more than 100 km (60 miles) from the front due to strong enemy fighter activity over the front.

b. For the increased take-off weight with bombs, the undercarriage and tyres had to be strengthened.

c. After the fitting of extra fuel tanks, when dropping bombs in a shallow dive, there were stability problems due to the centre of gravity shifting towards the rear. To keep take-off weight down, two of the nose guns had been eliminated. As a result the centre of gravity had moved further rearwards. Following flight tests, the rear tank was limited to 400 litres (instead of 600) to circumvent these problems, and rather complicated instructions on the method of drawing fuel from the rear tank issued. The 400 litre (106 Imp gal) maximum was also introduced in order to keep the weight below 7,000 kg (15,500 lbs). Since the tank had no fuel gauge and its fuel pump was prone to failure, the exact contents could not be checked before take-off. Moreover, it happened frequently that there was still too much fuel in the tank after the bombs had been dropped[3] with resulting considerable stability problems, i.e. the aircraft pulled out from the dive on its own.

Two Me 262s of Kommando Schenck take-off at dusk from Juvincourt on another mission to harass Allied troops in Normandy, July 1944.
Inset: Major Wolfgang Schenck (centre, wearing forage cap) in discussion with pilots of KG 51 at Juvincourt, late August 1944. To the far left is Oblt. Horst Götz of Kommando Sperling which shared Juvincourt at this time with Kommando Schenck. Götz had been flying an Ar 234 jet reconnaissance aircraft on missions to photograph Allied positions along the Invasion front.

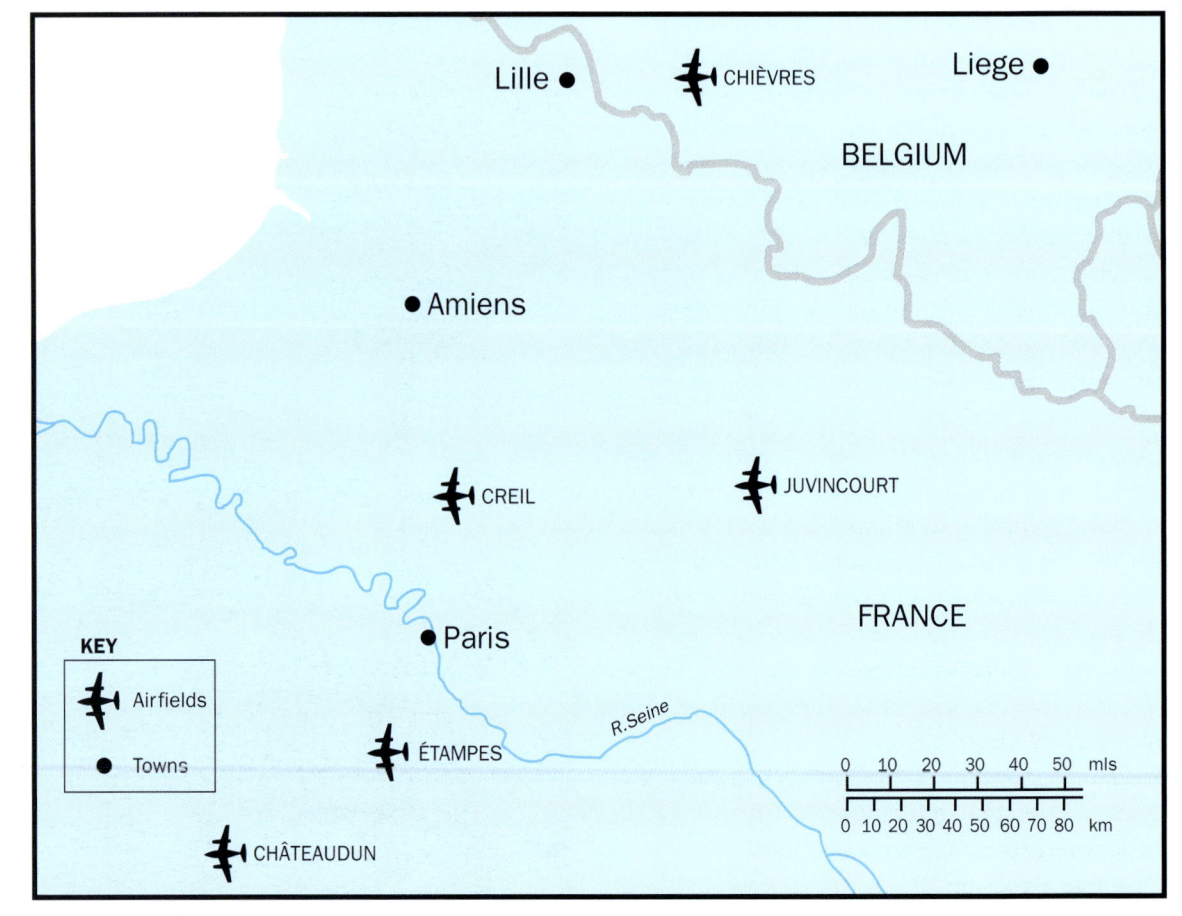

d. There was no bomb sight suitable for the single-seater. As a result the fighter Revi sight was used in shallow dive bombing. This method had still to be tested and operational pilots instructed in its use.
e. It was then found that the maximum speed of 850 km/h (530 mph) for aircraft fitted with fabric-covered control surfaces was being exceeded. Introduction of metal control surfaces had to be accelerated, tested and retro-fitted.
f. The airframe had to be variously strengthened not only in order to permit speeds in excess of 850 km/h, but also for the fitting of extra fuel tanks and take-off rockets required for take-offs with bomb load."

In addition, Hitler had ordered that the aircraft should not operate at altitudes below 4,000 metres (13,000 ft). By late July 1944, German forces in the west were in full retreat, and conditions at Châteaudun were so chaotic that no operations were flown by *Kommando Schenck* before it transferred to Étampes on 12 August. On 26 July the unit had reported a strength of four pilots, with only two active, and five Me 262 A-1s of which four were serviceable.

Three days after arriving at Étampes the Allied advance forced the unit to move to Creil and then to Juvincourt near Reims on 22 August. The *Kommando* was then reinforced by elements of 3./KG 51 which were sent to reinforce Schenck's unit at Juvincourt on 23 August, but of the nine aircraft that took off from Lechfeld, only five arrived. Two crashed on take-off due to pilot error, the third crashed on take-off from the intermediate stop at Schwäbisch Hall and the fourth could not find Juvincourt and made a forced landing. The surviving aircraft then flew almost continuous attacks against Allied troops near the Seine, north-west of Paris and in the Mélun area, but with little success. To quote Wendel again: "*In level flight, the Revi was useless for accurate bombing. Pinpoint targets could not be hit. Kommando Schenck was therefore unable to claim any tactical successes.*"

Two aircraft were written-off during this period, one in a crash landing and one when the nosewheel tyre burst on touchdown.

Undeterred, on 28 August, the unit managed to get seven Me 262s into the air to mount attacks against Allied troop assembly points using AB 500 weapon containers loaded with SD 10 anti-personnel bombs. Following this operation, the threat of street fighting in the town of Juvincourt forced the *Kommando* to leave for Chiévres in Belgium. Near Termond, *Ofw.* Hieronymous Lauer's Me 262 was intercepted by two P-47s from the US 78th Fighter Group. Spotting the Me 262 way below, the American pilots put their fighters into a 45 degree dive and after reaching a speed of 475

British Royal Engineers work at dusk to assemble one of several pontoon bridges intended to carry Allied troops and vehicles across the Seine in late August 1944.

Exposed to air attack, troops of the British 43rd Wessex Division cross the pontoon bridge at Vernonnet, late August 1944. Me 262s of Kommando Schenck flew almost continuous attacks against such targets near the Seine at this time.

Me 262 A-1a
W.Nr. 130179
Kommando Schenck,
July 1944

"MY GOD, WHAT WAS THAT?" • 365

A walk-around sequence of photographs showing Me 262 A, W.Nr. 130179, "Black F" of Kommando Schenck on the compass swinging table at Lechfeld before the unit's transfer to Châteaudun in July 1944. Note the unusual positioning of the Werk Nummer which has been applied below the horizontal tail surfaces. Note also the two painted diagonal lines just visible on the Plexiglas canopy to assist the pilot in lining up his aircraft for a dive bombing attack. "Black F" is seen here with "Wikingerschiff" bomb racks, although several of Kommando Schenck's other aircraft had the alternative ETC 503s fitted. Note the extended position of the leading edge slots. The aircraft was completely destroyed by fire on 19 July 1944 during an American bombing attack.

Me 262 A-a W.Nr. 170179 "Black F" Kommando Schenck, July 1944

The Me 262s of the first jet bomber unit, Kommando Schenck, carried black letters outlined in white on their fuselage noses. Camouflage was dark grey (74) and medium grey (75) on the uppersurfaces and pale blue grey (76) beneath. An unusual feature of this aircraft was the red tip to the nose.

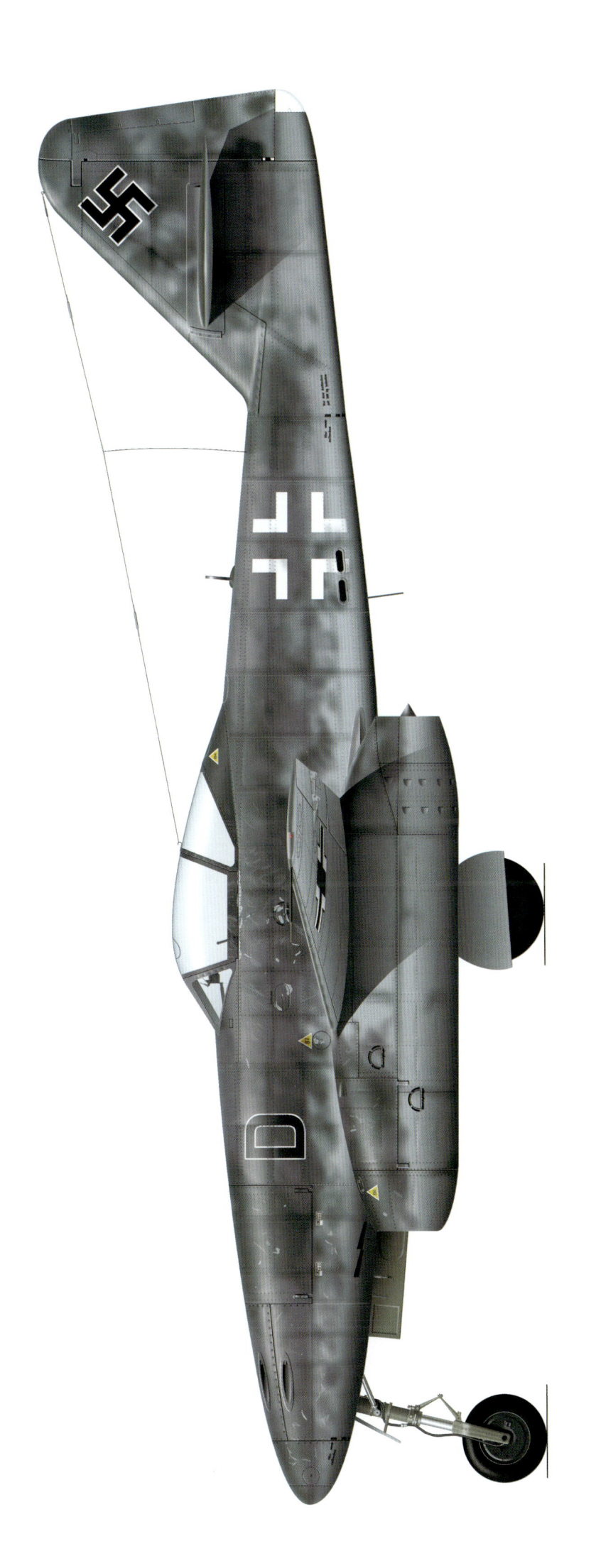

Me 262 A-1a "Black D" Kommando Schenck, Rheine, September 1944.
The Me 262s of the first jet bomber unit, Kommando Schenck, carried black letters outlined in white on the fuselage noses. Camouflage was dark grey (74) and medium grey (75) on the upper surfaces with pale blue grey (76) underneath.

Me 262 A-1a, "Black D" of Kommando Schenck undergoing an undercarriage test, summer 1944. This sequence shows that the hydraulically operated mainwheels extended before the nosewheel. If the port turbojet failed, hydraulic pressure was lost, but the undercarriage could still be lowered using an emergency compressed air system.

Below: The port side of a Jumo 004 turbojet showing the hydraulic pump which was used to extend the undercariage. One of the problems with the Me 262 was that this pump was only fitted to the port engine so that if this failed the pilot was unable to extend the undercarriage. It was eventually intended to fit a second pump to the starboard engine, but this was not done on production aircraft before the end of the war.

Pump

mph (765 km/h) began to overhaul it. Lauer began a series of evasive turns before Maj. Joseph Myers in the leading P-47 opened fire. At almost the same time the Me 262 ploughed into a field before the P-47s' bullets struck. Lauer escaped injury. This was the first Me 262 to be claimed by Allied fighters, shared by Myers and his No.4, Lt. Manford O. Croy Jr. Wendel's report on the action was somewhat different:

"A total of nine aircraft have so far been employed operationally. Of these, one was badly damaged while still in France following an emergency landing near its base due to pilot disorientation and subsequent fuel shortage. The pilot was unhurt but the aircraft had to be blown up when the area was evacuated. Another aircraft had to make the transfer flight to Belgium with its undercarriage extended. The pilot had made an emergency landing on a French airfield due to disorientation. During the final approach, the port engine stopped due to fuel shortage. The undercarriage had therefore to be lowered by compressed air.[4] Since the wheel covers do not lock in the down position when compressed air is used, the undercarriage switch has to be set to 'off' before the gear is retracted again. In this case the pilot neglected to do so (there are no instructions covering this at the moment) and, in consequence, the undercarriage could not be retracted. Due to its low speed with extended undercarriage, the aircraft was repeatedly attacked by several Spitfires (sic), coming under heavy fire. The two starter fuel tanks caught fire and the pilot made a forced landing on the main undercarriage with the nosewheel retracted. The pilot was unhurt. The badly damaged aircraft was later blown up."

Meanwhile, 3./KG 51 continued to train on the Me 262, losing two pilots, *Lt.* Rottmann and *Fw.* Helber, killed in accidents on 3 and 6 August respectively. On 28 August, an Ultra decrypt of a *Fliegerkorps IX* message to *Luftflotte 3* recorded that the *Einsatzkommando* of KG 51 (*Kommando Schenck*) should receive five more aircraft and crews by 1 September. "I./KG 51", it continued, "is to be trained uniformly. The remainder of I./KG 51 will not be ready before 1 October. The *Einsatzkommando* has crews with emergency training only, not really enough for operations. It seems that reinforcing of the *Einsatzkommando* is necessary to prevent a breakdown in testing of the type."

On 30 August, due to continuing Allied advances, *Kommando Schenck* moved to Volkel in Holland, spending two days at Ath-Chièvres in Belgium en route. Despite heavy Allied aerial bombardment the unit managed to fly sorties against targets near Louvain and Antwerp and on the Albert Canal. Early in the afternoon of 3 September approximately 130 RAF Lancasters bombed Volkel, destroying two of *Kommando Schenck's* remaining Me 262s. This included Schenck's own aircraft, W.Nr. 170016. The British attack rendered the airfield unusable for operations and, next day, the *Kommando*, with its one remaining aircraft, left for Rheine near Osnabrück.

On arrival at Rheine on 5 September, *Kommando Schenck*, and the experimental Ar 234 jet reconnaissance unit, *Kommando Sperling*, did not receive the reception they might have been expected. *Oblt.* Erich Sommer, flying the Ar 234, remembers: "During the night we were disarmed by an infantry unit (Inf.Bat. 60) who showed me an order from Himmler which said that all *Luftwaffe* units retreating from the west were to be considered unreliable and had to be disarmed. It was useless, wearing our night attire, to argue. Next day we came to grips with the infantry commander who apologised for the previous night's action and made good."

On 8 September, *Lt.* Rolf Weidemann of *Kommando Schenck*, flying an Me 262 A-1a, W.Nr. 170040, coded '9K+OL', was shot down and killed by flak north-east of Diest in Belgium. The remains of the aircraft were the first to be examined by Allied intelligence. The two damaged turbojets were later sent to England for examination. The next day of four aircraft that bombed Diest one was lost, but the results of the strike were not observed.

During these two missions, the *Kommando* was plagued with radio communication problems when the installations in virtually

Above: Leutnant Erich Sommer of the Ar 234 unit remembered a hostile reception when the jets arrived.
Below: Ground crew fit a Walter "Kraft-Ei" (powered egg) RATO unit to an Ar 234 of Kommando Sperling at Rheine, autumn 1944. The unit transferred to Rheine with the Me 262s of Kommando Schenck on 5 September 1944.

every aircraft broke down. The malfunction occurred as the aircraft approached the target area. The *Kommando* urgently requested the OKL *Führungsstab* and the OKL *Generalquartiermeister* to send an experienced radio specialist acquainted with the Me 262 to try and rectify the problem. A specialist technician from a night-fighter unit based at Rheine endeavoured to effect repairs but but was unable diagnose the cause of the problem.

The report made by Fritz Wendel[5] three days later, was more favourable than that quoted in the first part of this Chapter and makes interesting reading:

"At the time of writing, the Kommando, based on an airfield in north-west Germany, flies bombing missions. The field has three runways between 1,400 and 1,800 m long. Operations are mounted as if flown according to a timetable. There have been hardly any problems with engines or airframes. The pilots are enthusiastic about the operations. They have often had to fly through formations of enemy fighters but none of these have been able to get into a firing position. The Kommando has so far not tried to shoot down any enemy aircraft but concentrated on completing its bombing missions. During my visit, attacks were flown repeatedly against Liège. The target was normally approached at 4,000 m, the bombs being dropped in a steep dive. The distance from the airbase to the target is 230 km. On return, also made at 4,000 m, the aircraft's main fuel tanks still contained an average of 350 litres each. The normal flight time was exactly 50 minutes. According to the pilots, all bombs hit targets somewhere within the town. In one case a road was hit. I am not in a position to judge the military value of these operations.

"Two further losses occurred during my visit, the pilots failing to return from an attack on Liège. No news about the fate of the aircraft had been received before I departed. It can be assumed that the two pilots flew off in the wrong direction and came down behind the enemy lines.

"These losses were all due to faulty navigation, an opinion unanimously shared by the pilots. Apart from these losses, several emergency landings without damage had been made on other airfields for the same reason. The slow reaction of the compass and malfunctioning radio equipment coupled with the unfamiliar high air speeds and short flight duration are mainly to blame. After each shallow dive the compass rotates for several minutes. I believe that the compass is over-compensated and therefore unreliable in its directional capacity. The FuG 16 ZY and FuG 25a only function properly during about 5% of all flights. It is therefore impossible to guide the aircraft by Y-Führung or Tornado-Peilung.[6] Herr Tovar of the Technical Department has just gone to the airfield to check the electronic equipment.

"Apart from the above difficulties, there are only the following minor problems:

1. In two cases the extra fuel tank transfer pump failed. Bomb release was therefore made with the centre of gravity too far aft, and dive recovery was violent. In several cases the pilots failed to properly transfer the fuel. Here too, acceleration during recovery after bomb release was too violent. In one case this led to buckling of the wing skin over the engines. The area had already been strengthened on some aircraft. Subsequently, the aircraft concerned was also modified.

2. The yawing tendency has not yet been fully eliminated. This is highly irritating at high speeds during bombing attacks. However this is of minor importance at the moment as precision attacks are not being made.

3. One aircraft was delivered with smooth tyres. Four days later, tyre damage occurred. All other aircraft have treaded tyres, and from the start of operations until now there were no damaged tyres.

4. The short circuits which occurred regularly were in 80% of the cases due to faulty undercarriage cylinder switches for the position indicators.

5. There was one case of the nosewheel bearing seizing. Similar reports have been made by the Lechfeld flight test department.

6. Attention has again been drawn to the lack of an air vent, particularly when fuel is transferred wrongly, leading to fuel overflow. The smell in the cockpit is unbearable, causing nausea.

7. Production aircraft arrive with the wrong camouflage scheme. Major Schenck insists that the correct camouflage is applied retrospectively at Lechfeld.

8. The force needed to operate the emergency bomb release handle is too great, only resulting in a bent handle. Therefore emergency bomb release has so far been impossible

9. A small hand towing device is needed. This could be carried on board during transfer flights enabling the ground crews to move the aircraft after landing.

Fifty missions were flown in three weeks of operations. The navigational problems in addition to the well known Führerbefehl forbidding attacks below 4,000m, make successful completion of missions entirely dependent on weather conditions.

Sufficient J-2 fuel has so far been available on all operational airfields."

On the night of 9/10 September, 18 Fw 190 mounted a nuisance raid against the western district of Liége and on 10 September, 15 aircraft of *Kommando Schenck* bombed the same district and the road to Huy. *Oblt.* Werner Gärtner from 3./KG 51 was reported missing near Liège when his Me 262, W.Nr. 170013, was destroyed by flak. Next day *Kommando Schenck* reported a strength of six aircraft and nine crews and was detailed again to attack Liége and canal crossing points at Beeringen. One aircraft was lost when *Uffz.* Herbert Schauder was killed near Arnhem, this time falling victim to *German* flak! On the 13th five of the Kommando's aircraft attacked Lommel whilst another two machines struck at Allied positions in the Hechtel area and the Maas-Scheldt canal. The same day, the commander of I./KG 51 ordered that Kommando Schenck's activities should be directed exclusively at enemy troops in the Beverlo area " ...until further notice." One pilot was lost on the 17th when *Fw.* Bernhard Bertelsbeck was killed in an accident near Leipheim.

On 17 September the Allies launched 'Operation Market Garden', an attempt by paratroops to capture the bridges over the Maas at Grave, the Waal at Nijmegen and the Rhine at Arnhem. It was hoped that this would assist the main advance and affect the German ability to launch V-2 missiles against London.

On 18 September 3 Me 262s from I./KG 51 and 12 from III./KG 51 attacked targets in the Neerpelt area. The next day 14 aircraft from I./KG 51 attacked gliders: 4 at Nijmegen-Groosbeek and 10 at Deelen-Arnhem-Bennekom. Bombs fell amongst equipment and gliders, several of which were left burning.

After troops from the US 82nd Airborne Division took Nijmegen on 20 September *Kommando Schenck* flew regular operations against both the bridge and airfield until 7 October. As with earlier operations, most of the attacks were made with a single AB 500 container mounted on each aircraft holding SD 10 anti-personnel bombs, although the aircraft sometimes carried two SD 250 fragmentation bombs. During these attacks, an Me 262 was damaged by a Spitfire of 416 Squadron RCAF on 28 September and another by Spitfires of 441 Squadron RCAF on the 30th. At this time the *Kommando* reported an operational strength of eleven aircraft and twelve crews.

During the first days of October 1944 *Kommando Schenck*, which had been assimilated into I./KG 51 in all but name, continued to strike at Allied airfields and troop concentrations in the Nijmegen area. However, with few aircraft and no effective bombsights, and the fact that the Me 262s still had to operate at heights of over 4,000 m (13,00 ft), the effect of 3./KG 51 was little more than derisory.

Some of these KG 51's attacks were later co-ordinated by *Gefechtsverband Hallensleben* which had been formed in the Autumn of 1944 from the *Stab* of KG 2 under *Obstlt.* Rudolf von

Above and below: Tanks of the British XXX Corps roll across the Nijmegen bridges following its capture by paratroops of the US 82nd Airborne Division on 20 September 1944. For the next 17 days, the Me 262s of Kommando Schenck flew regular sorties against the bridges using anti-personnel and armour-piercing bombs, during which the unit suffered at least two damaged aircraft. By the end of the month, the bridges had been damaged by German action, though attempts by Kommando Schenck to stem the flow of Allied troops and armour were not successful.

Wearing the Ritterkreuz around their necks, Obstlt. Rudolf von Hallensleben (left) shares a joke with Oberst Joachim Helbig. Both pilots were to lead a Gefechtsverband - an ad hoc command usually formed to co-ordinate operations by a small number of autonomous units. Hallensleben's command controlled operations by a number of night ground attack formations, including, at one time 3./KG 51. Helbig was later to lead a Gefechsverband which attempted to to destroy bridges in the face of the Soviet advance into Germany in March 1945.

Right: Looking resplendent in its virtually all metal finish, this is a P-47D Thunderbolt of the 388th Fighter Squadron, 365th Fighter Group, Ninth Air Force seen at either Lignerolles, Bretigny or Juvincourt in France in 1944. Production of the aircraft was financed by war bonds raised by the employees of the Republic Aviation Corporation in the USA. It was an aircraft from this Group, piloted by Capt. Valmore J. Beaudrault, which brought down the Ninth's first Me 262 on 2 October 1944.

Hallensleben. The command's main task was to control night operations by a variety of *Luftwaffe* units against advancing Allied troops. At the time of its formation Hallensleben's unit was based at Hennef, east of Bonn, and controlled only *Nachtschlachtgruppen* 1 and 2, both having three *Staffeln* of Ju 87s adapted for night operations.

Both Ju 87 units had begun life as ad hoc harrasing units on the Eastern Front, operating a variety of light aircraft before being re-equipped with *Stukas* as these were supplanted on daylight missions by ground attack variants of the Fw 190. In the case of NSGr 1 this conversion, from Arado Ar 66, had taken place at Kaunas in Latvia in April 1944. After a period of blind flying and weapons training the *Gruppe* returned to operations on the Latvian Front in June, being withdrawn to Wormditt in East Prussia during Sept-ember for its aircraft to be fitted with FuG 16Z radio and FuG 25a IFF. The *Kommandeur* of NSGr 1, *Hptm.* Hilberg, was ordered to report to Hallensleben on 16 October 1944.

Later in the year two other units were attached to the *Gefechtsverband*, I./KG 51 equipped with the Me 262 and III./KG 51 (later renamed NSGr 20) with the Fw 190 G-8 *Schlachtflugzeug*. These two units often operated against the same targets with varying degrees of success.

On 1 and 2 October the unit bombed Grave airfield, inflicting about 35 casualties on 421 Squadron RCAF during the second series of attacks. Some revenge was extracted when P-47s of the US 365th Fighter Group spotted four Me 262s south-west of Münster. One of the American pilots,

Capt. Valmore J. Beaudrault, was alerted by his number three, Lt. Robert Teeter shouting *"My God, what was that?"* as an Me 262 shot into the clouds after attempting to bounce the fighters. Beaudrault and his wingman chased after the jet, only to find it turning to attack them several times. Then suddenly the Me 262 ran out of fuel and crashed into the ground, cartwheeled and exploded. The pilot of the aircraft, W.Nr. 170069, was *Ofw.* Hieronymous Lauer of 3./KG 51 who was badly injured in the crash. This was the Ninth Air Force's first claim against a jet.

Next day, 3./KG 51, reported a strength of ten aircraft and twelve crews. On 4 October the unit conducted operations against targets in the Nijmegen bridge area and against Volkel and Grave airfields using armour-piercing and anti-personnel bombs, but operations were seriously handicapped by mist during the late morning and then an electrical storm and heavy cloud during the afternoon. Bombs were dropped only through gaps in the clouds. On the 5th the unit lost two pilots killed. The first of these was *Hptm.* Hans-Christoff Buttmann, flying W.Nr. 170093, which was shot down in flames by Spitfires of 401 Squadron RCAF in the Nijmegen area. Its destruction was shared by five pilots[7] - the first jet to fall to British Commonwealth Air Forces. The other 3./KG 51 Me 262 to be lost was W.Nr. 170082 piloted by *Uffz.* Gerhard Francke, who was killed at Engden near Nordhorn. On 6 October Lt. C.W. Mueller of the US 353rd Fighter Group claimed the destruction of an "He 280" short of Rheine runway. It is probable that his victim was *Fw.* Joachim Fingerloos of 3./KG 51 who was seriously injured in this area flying W.Nr. 170117. That day, at least two Me 262s dropped "canisters" in the area south-east of Nijmegen, but it is not certain whether these were a form of ordnance.

Bad weather and an ill-timed air raid warning impeded operations on 7 October when 3./KG 51 mounted three separate operations using seven aircraft all equipped with fragmentation bombs against the same targets as those attacked on the 3rd. One of the AB 500 containers loaded with SD 1 bombs was seen to explode some 100 metres beneath one aircraft and it was decided to abandon this type of ordnance load.

Meanwhile, the 12. *Ergänzungs* (operational conversion) *Staffel* of KG 51 had begun retraining pilots from the first *Gruppe* on the Me 262. The unit suffered its first jet loss on 11 October when W.Nr. 170036 crashed at Lechfeld airfield. Also on the 11th, 3. Staffel once again attacked Nijmegen, Volkel and Grave using SD 250 bombs and AB 500 containers loaded with SD 4s. Results at Grave and Nijmegen could not be ascertained, but Volkel, hits were seen on the airfield perimeter, just beyond parked aircraft.

At 15.38 hours on the next day an Me 262 dropped two 250 kg bombs on Grave airfield, killing five airmen and destroying a Spitfire of 416 Squadron and damaging another nine. Attacks were also made on Volkel, Eindhoven, Nijmegen and Helmond using some 7 aircraft, each machine making two sorties. For the first time *Kommando Schenck* operated under the Benito ground control interception station at Rheinberg. On 13 October Pilot Officer Bob Cole flying a Tempest V of 3 Squadron RAF encountered an Me 262 at 14,000 ft (4,300 m) near Volkel.

An Allied report described the subsequent operation as follows. *"The Me 262 climbed rapidly, slightly above him, and was engaged with two long bursts as it passed 100 feet (30 m) above the Tempest. The latter became caught in the slipstream but recovered, turned through 180º and gave chase at about 480 mph (770 km/h) in a*

Royal Engineers pump out water from a crater so that RAF technical intelligence experts can study the wreckage of Me 262, W.Nr. 170093, piloted by Hptm. Hans-Christoff Buttmann of 3./KG 51 near Nijmegen on 5 October 1944. Buttmann had been attacked by RCAF Spitfires and was the first jet pilot to be shot down by British Commonwealth Air Forces. The aircraft dived into the ground and exploded among gliders being used by Allied airborne troops during their operations in Holland and these can be seen in the background of the above photograph.

Throughout October 1944, the Hawker Tempest Mk V air superiority fighters of 3 Squadron, RAF, frequently encountered the Me 262s of Kommando Schenck and KG 51 – though pursuing the jet bombers proved to be a difficult task. Here, two of the squadron's Tempests are seen dispersed amongst the wrecked hangars of Volkel airfield, a former home to Kommando Schenck.

Pilot Officer (shown here as Flight Sergeant) R.W. Cole of 3 Squadron, RAF. On 13 October 1944, Cole pursued the Me 262 of Uffz. Edmund Delatowski of 3./KG 51 near Volkel. Cole's Tempest was able to close in on the German jet, and, according to an Allied report, Delatowski's Me 262 " ... appeared to explode like a flying bomb" before going down in a spin.

shallow dive. At this speed the Me 262 pulled away slightly. It continued to dive for some miles and then suddenly climbed vertically for about 800 feet (250 m) and levelled out again. The climb did not appear to affect its speed. The Tempest began to turn right and, as the enemy also turned right, it managed to close up a little. The pursuit continued straight and level for about 40 miles (65 km), but losing height slightly. After then the jet pilot slowed a little, probably believing that he had shaken off the Tempest, allowing the latter to overtake. At about 10,000 feet (3,000 m) the Tempest fired a short burst at about 500 yards (450 m) dead astern which missed, and closing to 150 yards (140 m) fired another short burst. The Messerschmitt then appeared to explode like a flying bomb and threw off a number of pieces, including the pilot on his parachute. The aircraft went down in a spin and exploded on the ground where the remains burnt out. The RAF pilot reported that the jet aircraft was painted light grey without any special markings."

The Me 262 was W.Nr. 170064 piloted by *Uffz.* Edmund Delatowski of 3./KG 51 who, surprisingly, escaped with slight injuries. The German unit attempted to take revenge when three Me 262s bombed Volkel on the 14th. Next day two Me 262s from KG 51 flew separate operations each against Chiévres and Nijmegen. *Fj.Fw.* Edgar Junghans of 3./KG 51 was severely injured when his aircraft was shot down by a P-51 piloted by Lt. Huie H Lamb of the US 78th Fighter Group over Rheine airfield. Lt. Hugh O. Foster from the same unit also damaged another Me 262 near Bohmte.

DIETRICH PELTZ

Born on 9 June 1914 at Gera in Thüringia. After training as an engineer, Peltz joined the German army in April 1934, transferring to the Luftwaffe in 1935. By 1937 the young officer had been appointed Adjutant of I./St.G 162, and at the outbreak of war was a Staffelkapitän in I./St.G 76 equipped with Ju 87s. Following the defeat of France, he served with the Geschwader Stab of KG 77, flying Ju 88s during the Battle of Britain. He was awarded the Knight's Cross in October 1940 and in March 1941 he took over command of II./KG 77. During the invasion of the Soviet Union he led low level sorties against the Russian rail network, being awarded the Oak Leaves in December 1941. During the summer of 1942 he led the experimental torpedo bomber unit, I./KG 60 in Norway and the Mediterranean and in December of that year he was appointed Inspekteur der Kampfflieger (Inspector of the Bomber Units).

On 20 October 1944, Me 262s of *Kommando Schenck* flew three separate operations, one against Eindhoven airfield, one against Nijmegen airfield and one over the Nijmegen area. Next day Me 262s bombed Grave airfield, killing one airman and damaging 18 Spitfires from 127 Wing. Two jets were claimed damaged by 3 Squadron RAF near Rheine, one by Flt.Lt. Umbers and one shared by Flt.Lts. Duff and Dryland.

Towards the end of October 1944, *Kommando Schenck* was officially re-incorporated into KG 51. By this time it had received approximately 25 aircraft and had flown a total of 400 individual missions. Some pilots had flown up to six missions on a single day. A larger number of sorties was impossible due to the recurrence of extremely bad weather over the target area. The penultimate missions flown by the unit were meteorological reconnaissance sorties over the Maas on 25 October. Next day the unit suffered its last loss when one Me 262 was destroyed and another damaged on the ground at Rheine by 3 Squadron RAF. Eleven months earlier, in November 1943, Hilter had appointed *Generalmajor* Dietrich Peltz *"Angriffsführer England"*, (Attack Leader England). Still retaining his position as Inspector of Bombers, Peltz took over command of the *IX. Fliegerkorps* equipped with a motley collection of Ju 88s, Ju 188s, Do 217s, Me 410s, a few He 177s and Fw 190s, these aircraft being charged with the task of launching a new bombing offensive against the British Isles. Because of the relative inexperience of many of the crews and the much improved British night defences, the offensive proved ineffectual and, by May 1944, the total number of aircraft available had dwindled from 550 to 144. After suffering this disastrous attrition rate, the *IX. Fliegerkorps* was withdrawn from operations, leaving the *Luftwaffe* with around 200 relatively well-trained bomber pilots for whom there was no role.

Peltz, supported by *Generalmajors* Diesing and Storp, then proposed to Göring that these men be retrained on the Me 262, reasoning that they already possessed the skills needed for all weather operation. Certainly they were trained in blind and bad weather flying, and were used to multi-engined aircraft, while the fighter pilots had few of these abilities. Göring was immediately enthused by the idea, and thus

Generalmajor Dietrich Peltz (second left), the "Angriffsführer England", addresses bomber pilots from a unit of the IX. Fliegerkorps on a rain swept airfield somewhere in France during the spring of 1944.

Me. 262 Operations on Western Front
4th – 12th October, 1944

TOP SECRET U

Date	2nd T.A.F. Reports		
4/10	Volkel	2 bombs (250 kilo?) dropped on S.E. of a/f. N.D.C.	
	Nijmegen	5 Me.262 at 16,000' jettisoned bombs.	
5/10		Nil on bombing 1 Me.262 shot down North of Nijmegen 1 jet seen near Rheine by 24 Typhoons attacking A/f.	
6/10		S.E. OF Nijmegen 2 Me.262 at 14,000' dropped 2 cannisters.	
7/10	Grave	One of 4 Me.262 seen dived out of cloud at 20,000 and released one cannister of 1 kilo A/P bombs at 17,000. Opened at 14,000 and exploded on impact.	
	Grave	One Me.262 at 1,000 seen to dive and drop bomb 15 miles E. of airfield.	
11/10	S. of Nijmegen.	Bombs. A/c not identified.) Comment:	
	Volkel.	Bombs. " " ") Almost certainly Me.262	
12/10	Volkel	Antipersonnel bombs. (Almost certainly a/c not identified. Me.262)	
	Volkel	1 Me.262 bombs.	
	Grave	1 Me.262 2 bombs.	

ULTRA

Date		
4/10	Operations Report:	5 operations with 12 a/c of which 8 against Nijmegen, 1 against Volkel, and 3 against Grave. Bombs: 2 SC 250, 18 SD 250, and 2 AD 500, SD10. Ops. very seriously handicapped by mist in forenoon and electrical storm in afternoon as well as heavy cloud at target. Bombs dropped only through gaps in clouds.
5/10	Operations Report:	Bombs jettisoned, 1 a/c lost, 1 overdue. Latter later reported to have crashed while jettisoning bombs at Nordhorn.
6/10	Operations Report:	Intentions 4 a/c to take off 1045 against Nijmegen.
7/10	Operations Report:	3 ops. with 7 a/c. 3 a/c Nijmegen area: 1 AB 500, SD10, 2AB500 SD1 2 a/c Grave A/f : 2 AB 500, SD10 2 a/c Volkel A/f : 2 AB 500, SD1 Operation impeded by bad visibility and airraid warning. An AB500 SD1 observed to explode 100 m. under the a/c. Issue stopped.
11/10	Operations Report: 1700	1 Volkel a/f. 2SD 250 3 Grave a/f. 6SD 250 4 Nijmegen 4AB500 SD4. Results at Grave and Nijmegen not observed. At Volkel hits on perimeter, outside parked aircraft.
	Special Ops. Report 2200:	Benito control being used.
12/10	Operations Report:	7 Volkel A/d. 4 SD250, 5 AB 500, SD4 3 Grave 4 SD250, 1 AB 500, SD4 1 Eindhoven 1 AB 500, SD4 4 Nijmegen 8 SD 250 1 Helmond) 1 Eindhoven town) not known 17 (Comment: Approx. 2 sorties per serviceable aircraft).

AI 2G.
16.10.44

Above: Dated 16 October 1944, this reproduction of a contemporary British document compares Me 262 operations reported by fighters of the RAF's Second Tactical Air Force with signals decoded by the "Ultra" code-breaking system. Note the "TOP SECRET U" legend in the top right-hand corner.

began a feud between the fighter and bomber leaders which did nothing to help the success of the Me 262.

Galland, supporting the fighter cause, wrote in his diary: "During a decisive meeting, I tried to prove that only the most experienced fighter pilots would be able to fly the Me 262 successfully, and that bomber pilots could not successfully convert to the jet without (training on) a conventional fighter and that they lacked the proper judgement of fighter pilots. I recommended that IX. *Fliegerkorps* be disbanded while Peltz demanded that his *Fliegerkorps* should remain intact at all costs. He made rash promises that they could operate in bad weather. I countered this by saying that was irrelevant and thereby aroused the anger of the 'fat gentleman' and was given a frightful ticking off, and was told that I was to make no mention of it again."

Oberst Hajo Herrmann, who took over the 9. *Fliegerdivision* (which operated under Peltz), countered these arguments in his autobiography. "One precondition only had to be met, one which persuaded the *Reichsmarschall* to give the jet fighters to the bomber men: independence from the weather. That could guarantee that sufficiently large formations would be able to climb through the clouds in good order and navigate accurately to intercept the enemy."

At the end of September, one of Peltz's bomber units, KG 54, the *Totenkopf* (Death's head) *Geschwader*, began preparations to receive the Me 262. The unit had a long and distinguished history. The first *Gruppe* had been formed from III./KG 254 at Fritzlar on 1 May 1939. It was equipped originally with the Ju 52/3m bomber-transport but by the outbreak of the Second World War had converted to the He 111. It then took part in the invasions of Poland, Holland, Belgium and France where it was joined by II./KG 54 (formed from the second *Gruppe* of KG 28) and the newly established III./KG 54. The latter unit was quickly disbanded, but the remaining *Gruppen* flew operations against the British Isles, then re-equipped with the Ju 88. It then transferred to Polish bases for the invasion of the Soviet Union, with I./KG 54 moving to Sicily in January 1942. In September 1942 a new III./KG 54 was formed from KGr 806, this unit and I./KG 54 moving to Italy in 1943. These two groups transferred to French bases in 1944 for operations against the British Isles but, in April, II./KG 54 was disbanded.

Following the severe mauling that the unit received during the Allied invasion of France, I. and III./KG 54 were withdrawn respectively to Giebelstadt and Neuburg an der Donau. On 1 October 1944, the unit was given the new designation KG(J) 54 ("bomber wing on fighter operations") a designation chosen for all bomber units converted to the interceptor role. Because of a shortage of jet aircraft, I./KG(J) 54 received at first only one Me 262, a B-1a two-seater (thought to be W.Nr. 170075). To help familiarize its crews with small fast fighters, six Fw 190 F-8s were also delivered to the unit. A bombing attack on Giebelstadt resulted in the loss of much material and the death of an *Unteroffizier* on 3 October and eleven days later KG(J) 54 suffered its first aircraft loss when *Ofw.* Kurt Schwarz was killed flying in a Fw 190 A-8 (W.Nr. 172698) coded B3+TH.

KG(J) 54 had received ten Fw 190 F-8s for training by 20 October and, on the same day, IV.(Erg)/KG 54 was disbanded, its personnel going to form II./KG(J) 54 in January. On the 23rd *Oberst* Walter Marienfeld, the *General der Kampfflieger* and an ex-*Kommodore* of KG 54, was killed in an accident while inspecting I./KG(J) 54 at Giebelstadt. In the same accident, *Hptm.* von Oppel, *Adjutant* of KG(J) 54 was injured.

At this time the unit commanders were:

KOMMODORE	*Obstlt.* Volprecht Riedesel Freiherr zu Eisenbach
ADJUTANT	*Hptm.* Karl-Friedrich von Oppel
I. GRUPPE KOMMANDEUR	*Hptm.* Ottfried Sehrt
I. GRUPPE ADJUTANT	*Oblt.* Walter Draht
1. STAFFELKAPITÄN	*Hptm.* Werner Tronicke
2. STAFFELKAPITÄN	*Oblt.* Dr. Heinz Oberweg
3. STAFFELKAPITÄN	*Oblt.* Christian Wunder
III. GRUPPE KOMMANDEUR	*Hptm.* Eduard Brogsitter
III. GRUPPE ADJUTANT	*Oblt.* Axel Studt
7. STAFFELKAPITÄN	*Hptm.* Helmut Kornagel
8. STAFFELKAPITÄN	*Oblt.* Heinz Rall

Left: A Junkers Ju 88 A-4 of 1./KG 54 runs up its engines prior to another bombing mission against the British Isles during the summer of 1940. The 'Death's Head' Geschwader emblem was carried on many of the unit's aircraft throughout the war including the Me 262.
Above: A later photograph showing a KG 54 Ju 88 A-4 belonging to the Geschwader's Ergänzungs Staffel taken at Gardelegen in 1944. note the variation in the unit badge. The unit would convert to the Me 262 within months.

Me 262 B-1a W.Nr. 170075 "B3+SH", 1./KG 54 November 1944
This was the first two-seat trainer delivered to KG(J) 54 and had a spectacular white lightning flash painted on the nose.

An Me 262 B-1a two seat trainer, W.Nr. 170075, of I./KG(J) 54 probably photographed at Giebelstadt in late 1944 and bearing an unusual lightning flash marking across its nose.

---

1 Born in 1902, Karl-Otto Saur attended Freiburg and Karlsruhe Universities and graduated as a Diplom-Ingenieur. He worked for Thyssen in the steel industry until 1937, when he joined the Büro Todt under Dr. Fritz Todt which had responsibility for all state construction work under Göring's Four Year Economic Plan. In 1940, when Dr. Todt was appointed Minister of Armaments and Munitions, Saur moved to that Ministry as Todt's principal assistant. In February 1942, Todt was killed in an aircraft accident and was succeeded by Albert Speer, whose office was renamed the Ministry of Armaments and War Production in 1943. Because of his Nazi Party connections, Saur was appointed Chief of the Technical Office in the Armaments Ministry in 1942, and rose to the rank of Hauptdienstleiter (Chief Party Leader) - the second highest in the Party hierarchy. Saur had no knowledge of aircraft design or production methods, but he did possess great drive and was given dictatorial powers when he was appointed Head of the Jägerstab in March 1944. On 1 August 1944 the Jägerstab was replaced by the Rüstungsstab (Armaments Staff), and Saur's authority was extended to include tank, submarine, V-Weapons, and all aircraft production. His phenomenal memory for dates and figures made Saur a favourite of Hitler, with whom he held regular Armaments Conferences in the war's closing stages. In Hitler's last testament, dated 29 April 1945, Saur was named as Speer's successor as Armaments Minister, but he never took up the post. Although Saur remains one of the lesser-known personalities of the Third Reich, he nevertheless exercised considerable power over the entire German armaments industry, and, under Speer's direction, he did much to maintain the fighting capabilities of the Wehrmacht during the last year of the war by increased production output. He died in 1966.
2 The Messerschmitt company held a series of meetings to discuss future development of the Me 262. The minutes or Protokoll of these meetings were given progressive numbers.
3 Management of fuel was quite a tricky problem for the pilot of the Me 262 bomber. Fuel should have been drawn from the rear tank first, otherwise the aircraft would be tail heavy after the bombs were released.
4 One problem that was to manifest itself was that the Me 262 only had one hydraulic pump which was driven by the port engine. If this engine failed the aircraft also lost hydraulic power. It was planned to fit a second pump to the starboard engine, but this was never employed operationally.
5 Leading Messerschmitt's Technical Field Team or Technischer Außendienst.
6 Radio navigation beams.
7 The pilots were Sqd/Ldr. R.I.A. Smith, Flt/Lts. Everard and Davenport and F/Os. Sinclair and J. MacKay.

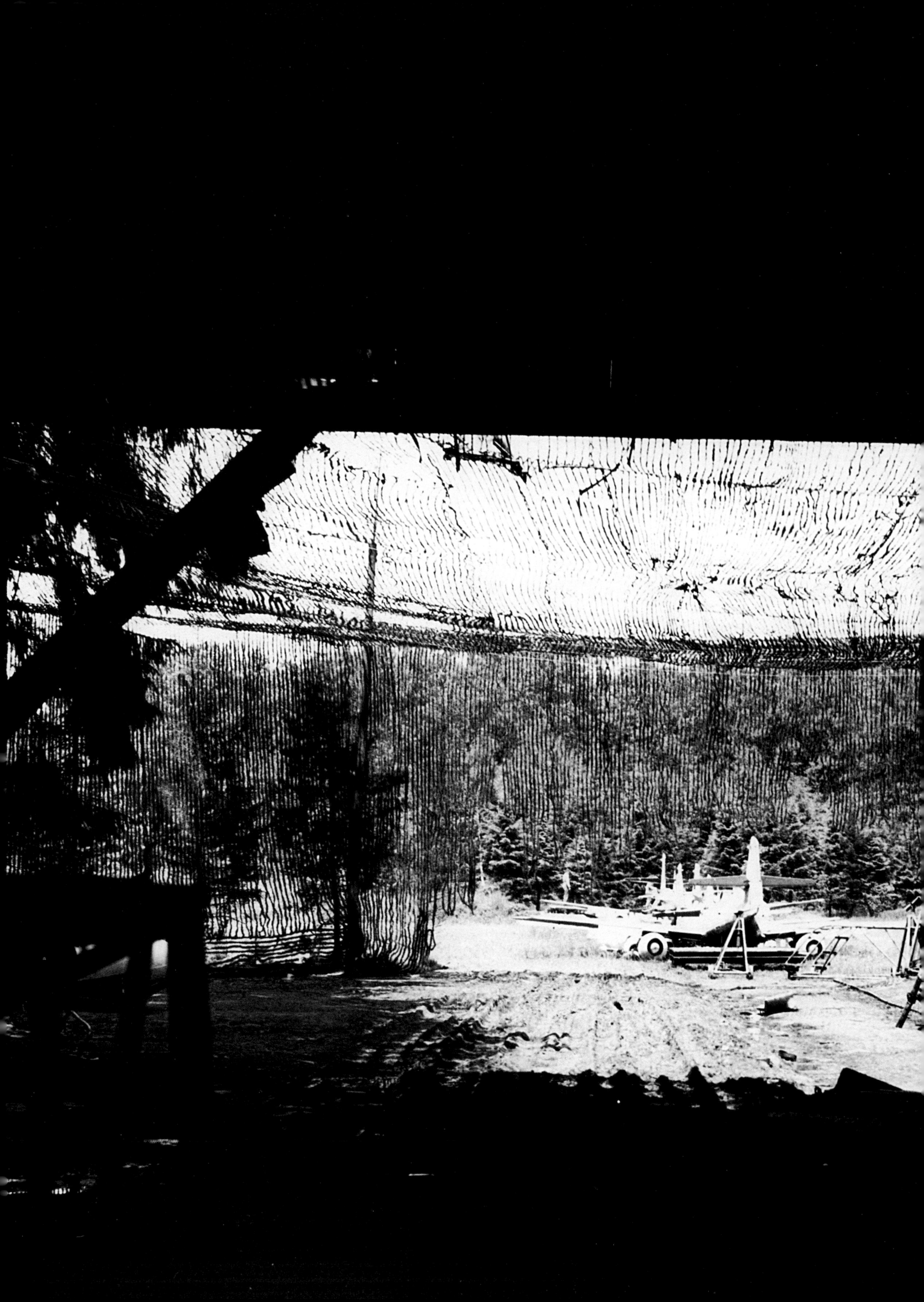

CHAPTER TWELVE
"IN ACCORDANCE WITH THE FÜHRER'S ORDERS"

Willy Messerschmitt's revolutionary masterpiece: the Me 262A-1a jet fighter. The factory-fresh example shown here, W.Nr. 110371 is a standard production variant and illustrates the 18.5 degree swept back wing with the automatic leading edge slats in the open position. This aircraft served briefly with Kommando Nowotny and 10./EJG 2. It suffered an engine failure on 31 January 1945 and was completely destroyed, the pilot, Ofw. Helmut Klante, being injured.

During October 1944, and in spite of Hitler's edict to the contrary, a total of 52 Me 262 fighters had been delivered, all except one (which was transferred to the TLR) going to *Kommando Nowotny*. During the same month 65 Me 262 bombers had been delivered, 52 going to KG 51, five to KG 54, five for conversion to two-seaters, two to the ferrying unit, *Flieger Überführungs Geschwader* and one to the *General der Aufklärungsflieger*. Two Me 262 trainers were also converted, one going to the *General der Jagdflieger* the other to KG 76. Total output up to this date was 265 Me 262s, with 30 destroyed at Messerschmitt, leaving 235. Estimated production for November and December 1944 was 130 and 200 aircraft respectively.

By this time it was becoming increasingly obvious, even to Hitler that the Me 262 was wasted as a bomber and, at an armaments conference held between 1 and 4 November, he finally gave permission to begin series production of the Me 262 as a *fighter*. Even then the *Führer* stipulated that each aircraft "must be able to carry at least one 250 kg (550 lb) bomb in case of emergency". As late as 8 January 1945, Hitler again insisted on equipping the Me 262 with 500 kg bombs to disrupt the enemy's railways and dockyards behind the Western Front.

A strafing attack on 18 November by between 60 and 80 P-47s and P-51s from the U.S. Eighth Air Force on Leipheim destroyed 17 Me 262s and damaged a further 19. This reverse meant that only 78 Me 262s were built in November and three repaired. Of this total of 81, 18 went to I./KG 51, 25 to II./KG 51, four to IV./KG 51, five for night fighter conversion, two for two-seat conversion, two to the TLR, five to III./JG 7, twelve to the *General der Jagdflieger* (for weapons development), three to EJG 2, two to NAG 6 and three to the *Flieger Überführungs Geschwader*.

On 15 December 1944, production Programme 227 was issued to replace Programme 226[1] which had been amended on 23 September 1944. It was designed to take into account the reduced productive capacity resulting from air raids on the German aircraft industry since the middle of the year. It provided for a peak of 6,400 aircraft to be produced monthly by October 1945, but with a subsequent decline to a level of 6,020 from February 1946 onwards. Production of such types as the Ju 88, Ju 388, He 219, Do 335, Me 163 and Sk 257 trainer was to be dropped or severely curtailed,

(Left) Final assembly of an Me 262 at one of the main production plants in Southern Germany, 1944-45. There were five of these; at Leipheim, Schwäbisch Hall, Obertraubling, Neuburg an der Donau and Kuno, the latter a code name for a Waldwerk (forest factory). *(Below)* Prior to being delivered to their allocated operational units, each Me 262 underwent stringent manufacturers proving tests. Following successful completion of these tests, many aircraft were then handed over to the Flieger Überführungs Geschwader who would then deliver them to their assigned units. Seen here a newly manufactured Me 262 W.Nr. 110604 undergoes tests at Lechfeld and, later (*Inset taken from a movie film*), ready to be delivered to 11./EJG 2 and assigned its tactical number, "Red 1".

with considerable increases in construction of the Me 262 and He 162 jet fighters.

Soon after the goals for Programme 227 were finalised it became obvious that they were impossible to attain. Over and above the difficulties arising from the bombing of the factories, the dislocation of transport, the calling up of workers and the loss of territory began to be felt. Accordingly, on 1 March 1945, Programme 228 was instituted which planned for a peak figure of 4,200 aircraft to be built in July 1945. The Bf 109 and Fw 190 piston-engined fighters were to be phased out in favour of the Ta 152, Me 262 and He 162. To paraphrase Goebbels' diary for 16 March 1945:

> "According to a Führer decision, production is to be concentrated on the Me 262. This can stay in the air for 70 minutes and uses a sort of Diesel fuel of which 44,000 tons are available and this level of stock can be maintained. To meet the programme, Reichsminister Speer has ordered concentration of all resources, transport capacity and labour, on the Me 262. Sorties so far flown justify the assumption that the casualty rate will be 5 to 1

Reichsminister Albert Speer points out a detail to Hermann Göring. In the final year of the war, Goebbels wrote: "Speer has ordered concentration of all resources, transport capacity and labour, on the Me 262..." In his own post-war memoirs, Speer wrote that the Me 262 was "... the most valuable of our "secret weapons.'"

in our favour. A Mosquito will be simply torn apart by a hit from the Me 262 and four hits will finish off a bomber. After one month of fighting on these terms Anglo-Saxon losses in the air will inevitably become so grievous that they will reduce their air raids."

Although the ten Me 262 prototypes and first five production aircraft were built at Augsburg-Haunstetten, most subsequent aircraft were produced by five final assembly plants, all dispersed in forest locations, known as *"Waldwerk"*. Three of these operated under the control of Messerschmitt's parent plant at Augsburg, two under the 'shadow' factory at Regensburg. They were:

AUGSBURG

Leipheim Situated near Leipheim airfield with a production area of 4,200 m² (5,023 sq yds). Following Allied attacks on the airfield, the complex used the nearby Autobahn for flight testing and delivery.

Schwäbisch Hall Situated near Schwäbisch Hall airfield with a production area of 3,800 m² (4,545 sq yds).

Kuno I Situated at Burgau some 35 km (21 miles) west of Augsburg on the Augsburg-Ulm Autobahn. This complex initially used Leipheim airfield and then the Autobahn itself for test flying. It had a production area of 4,700 m² (5,621 sq yds). A similar complex, Kuno II, was built near Leipheim.

REGENSBURG

Obertraubling Situated near Obertraubling airfield. Began final assembly of the Me 262 in November 1944. Production area of 4,400 m² (5,263 sq yds).

Neuburg an der Donau Situated near Neuburg airfield with a production area of 4,400 m² (5,263 sq yds).

Kuno I was a typical example of the *"Waldwerk"* with 21 temporary-style wooden buildings including seven barracks to house workers. The roofs of the buildings were painted green to help camouflage them against possible Allied aerial

Purportedly, a photograph showing the ceremony to commemorate the handing-over by Messerschmitt of an early production Me 262 to the Luftwaffe in April 1944. On the far left of the picture is Gerhard Caroli who headed Messerschmitt's flight test department. Adorning the lectern is the traditional fir wreath used on such occasions.

Above: Gauleiter Fritz Sauckel, Reichs Plenipotentiary-General for Labour Mobilisation and originator of the REIMAHG aircraft production facility at Kahla.
Left: A US technical intelligence official examines an Me 262 airframe at the Kahla factory, south of Jena in Thüringia. The aircraft is virtually completed save for the nose section which has not been fitted to the main fuselage. Note the bare metal surfaces with the brown coloured filler.

reconnaissance. Kuno I employed a total of 845 people, working on a two shift rota. The wing assembly area was about 100 m (320 feet) long by about 15 m (50 feet) wide.

In addition to the *"Waldwerk"*, six gigantic semi-underground factories, known as 'Bunkerwerke' were to be constructed, but only one of these, codenamed Weingut 2 (Vineyard 2) was nearing completion as the war ended. This plant was to be built near Landsberg with slave labour drawn from 11 specially established facilities (offshoots of the nearby Dachau concentration camp). Weingut 2 was a semi-subterranean vault, 400 m (1,300 ft) long by 30 m (100 ft) high built in a valley. A total of six pre-cast floors totalling 95,000 m2 (approximately 1,000,000 sq.ft.) were to be installed beneath the semi-circular concrete roof of the carapace type, which was to be constructed of 5 m (16 ft) thick reinforced concrete. Well over two-thirds of the area thus created was to be used to build 300 aircraft a month, Me 262s, Do 335s and Ta 152s. By the end of the war machine tools and jigs had been moved in, although excavations under the concrete roof were far from finished. The site was captured by American troops at the end of the war who were staggered at the vastness of the enterprise. It was later used by American forces who, with additional work, considered it to be virtually nuclear bomb proof.

Other Me 262 production plants were completed at Erding near München and at Kahla/Thüringen. On 28 July 1943, the AGO aircraft company factory at Oschersleben, which produced Fw 190s, was bombed by the U.S. Eighth Air Force. Further attacks in January and February 1944, forced the company to relocate production, using the facilities of ARWA, a hosiery manufacturer. On 8 March, Fritz Sauckel[3], the *Reichs* Plenipotentiary-General for Labour Mobilisation, suggested to Göring that a massive complex of bomb-proof factories be built in the Kahla-Pössneck area, south of Jena, to be named REIMAHG after *Reichsmarschall Hermann Göring*. This was to take over production of the Fw 190 and Ta 152 formally assigned to Oschersleben, it being intended that monthly production would increase from around 100 aircraft to 500.

Leipheim airfield where several of the Me 262 prototypes performed flight tests. The airfield was bombed on several occasions by the USAAF Eighth and Fifteenth Air Forces resulting in damage to the Me 262 V3 and V10 and the second V1, V5 and V6. This photograph was taken on 18 November 1944 following a raid by the US Eighth Air Force during which 29 Me 262s were destroyed

A scene from one of the hangars at Leipheim. Partially completed Me 262s are lined up on the taxiway. Behind them is a Me 321 "Gigant" transport.

Busy scenes in the workshop/hangar at Leipheim; (*Above right*) an Me 262's underside wing surface is checked by an engineer, whilst (*Left*), work is carried out on a newly fitted Jumo 004 turbojet. (*Above left*) Crates containing parts line the walls of the hangar. On the floor can be seen a gun-port hatch.

Following repeated Allied air attacks on Leiphem, a decision was taken to use the nearby Autobahn (Stuttgart-München) for flight testing and delivery. Seen here discussing the various technical problems that would enable the Me 262 to take-off from the road are, from left, Ing. Jaudt, manager of the Kuno I production facility, and Ing. Delang, project manager. The Luftwaffe officer visible only by his cap is believed to be Hptm. Thierfelder of Erprobungskommando 262.

Construction of the first factory began in a former china clay mine on 11 April 1944 and by 6 May the workforce comprised 75 skilled German workmen, 187 Italian and 390 Polish or Russian slave workers including 153 women. It had been planned that final assembly of the Fw 190 should begin on 1 August, but this proved unrealistic because relocation had only just begun. Göring and Saur visited Kahla on 10 October 1944, by which time 10 million *Reichsmarks* had been spent on the complex, it being estimated that this would eventually rise to 50 million.

Two days after the visit of the two leaders, a *Führer-Erlass* (decree) was issued, stating that production was to switch from the Fw 190 and Ta 152 to the Me 262. On 18 October, Sauckel ordered Dr. Roloff to assume full responsibility for Me 262 production at Kahla, stressing the importance of beginning mass production despite the difficult conditions. Towards the end of the month, Messerschmitt made one aircraft and some sub-assemblies available, and three more semi-finished Me 262s arrived in November. A complete set of components and parts also arrived to serve as demonstration models for jigs and tools. It was also planned to switch production of wings from *Arbeitgemeinschaft Gutbrod* at Leonburg and of Jumo 004 engine fairings from *Gläser Karosserie* at Dresden to REIMAHG. It was anticipated that the total cost of one Me 262, minus armament, would be 135,598 RM.

By January 1945, building had progressed far enough for final assembly of the Me 262 to begin. The complex now comprised 75 tunnels, totalling 32 km (20 miles) in length offering 10,000 m² (108,000 sq ft) of production space. Four bomb-proof buildings or bunkers had also been completed. Bunker 0, constructed of 2 m (6 ft 6ins) reinforced concrete, housing the design and administration offices together with a dining hall seating 3,000. Bunkers 1, 2 and 4, also made of 2 m thick concrete, were for final assembly and five cantilever wooden assembly hangars with a floor space measuring 100m (330 ft) by 20 m (65 ft) were also available. The assembly tunnels had a cog railway which was capable of transporting one fully assembled Me 262 to the specially constructed runway built on the crest of a hill. This runway was 1,300 m (4,300 ft) long by 50 m (165 ft) wide and was to be used for ferrying a completed aircraft to its destination. At this time, over 15,000 labourers were employed at Kahla of whom about two-thirds were slave workers or foreign prisoners.

This page and opposite: Taken by US Fifteenth Air Force personnel, these photographs illustrate the rudimentary and primitive component storage conditions at the Obertraubling plant. In the photograph to opposite left, Me 262 nose sections with 30 mm MK 108 cannon installed, lie on wooden supports on the floor. Note that the MK 108s have been test fired in these sub-assemblies. The photograph at bottom right shows four tail sections, probably unloaded from a railway wagon, and above, turbojet frames and fuel tanks lie stacked from floor to ceiling.

Looking out from the assembly line at the Messerschmitt final assembly plant at Obertraubling, south of Regensburg. This facility covered 4,400 m² (5,263 sq. yds).

Below: Overgrown railway tracks lead into a camouflaged assembly line built between the trees at Obertraubling. Assembly trolleys lie abandoned in the foreground and a Me 262 can be seen in the trees to the left.

The Messerschmitt final assembly plant at Obertraubling, as American forces found it at the war's end in 1945. Partially completed Me 262 airframes lie in the open air in a forest clearing, hastily and ineffectively camouflaged with tree branches. A single track railway – the line running to Straubing and Landshut – passes close by, which would have provided a connection to other Messerschmitt plants and suppliers.

The massive concrete aircraft production bunker known as Weingut 2 was still under construction near Landsberg in southern Germany at the end of the war. It was built by constructing a square section concrete tunnel in the base of the valley with trap doors in the roof. An enormous quantity of gravel was then poured on top of this tunnel and smoothed off to form a semi-circular former. Reinforced concrete was then poured on top and after the first layer was set, the trap doors were opened and the gravel allowed to run out where it was transported along to begin the construction of the second section of the complex. Several further layers of concrete were then poured on to the roof until the desired thickness was obtained. It was then planned to furnish the huge bunker with six stories of prefabricated concrete flooring sections. An extensive rail network was built to import raw materials and transport completed aircraft to the nearby airstrip. These photographs show the various stages of the construction process.

It was anticipated by the time Kahla was in full production it could assemble forty aircraft simultaneously. Despite this, only about 15 Me 262s had been completed by March 1945, most of these from parts supplied by other Messerschmitt factories. When U.S. troops entered Kahla on 12 April 1945, they found parts for 200 aircraft including 10 complete Me 262 fuselages plus many other parts scattered around the area. Thus, despite all the money, effort and misery expended in building the complex, actual total production was probably not much more than 40 aircraft.

Actual Me 262 production increased a little in December 1944, a total of 114 fighters being delivered with a further 17 repaired. Of this total of 131, 45 were at the factory and 17 with *Luftflotte Reich*. Of the remaining 69, 41 were delivered to III./JG 7, 15 to I./KG(J) 54, two to the *Ergänzungs-Jagdgruppe*, two for night fighter conversion, one for two-seat conversion, two for *Mistel* conversion, one for weapons conversion, four to *Kommando Welter* and one to *Kommando Braunegg*, these latter two units engaged in night-fighter and reconnaissance operations respectively. During the same month one Me 262 trainer was built and a further eight converted, four going to KG 54, two to I./JG 7, one to KG 76, one to the *Flieger Überführungs Geschwader* and one to III./EJG 2.

An interesting insight into the production difficulties suffered with the Me 262 is given in a report written post war for the Allies by Otto Lange of the Messerschmitt office at Oberammergau:

"*It was unfortunately typical of methods of work at Messerschmitt that the aircraft manufacturing side still lagged behind, necessitating extra work and further loss of time. Further, during flight testing, unpredictable instability cropped up when flying at speeds exceeding 800 km/h (500 mph). The cause was not recognisable immediately, and led to many alterations. Moreover, the plant was burdened with additional measures for strengthening the undercarriage, wings, tail unit, nose etc. It was also necessary to introduce changes to the production of accessories such as the fuel pumps. In other words, technical alterations were still being made while the aircraft was being mass produced.*

"*Bottlenecks had varying effects on production. For example, during the last three months, production depended on the supply of power units. Previously however, between August and December 1944, it had depended on the production of wings and/or noses. For a short time there was also a bottleneck in the production of tail units. Apart from this, problems also manifested themselves with test flights during the winter months, December 1944 to April 1945. The exceptionally high speed of the aircraft placed demands on the length of the runway and visibility at high altitudes. Difficulties were also caused by snow softening up the airfields, destruction of runways by enemy action and loss of time through air raid warnings. On many airfields, during the winter months, only 40 hours test flying could be carried out. As a result of enforced concentration of production, there were insufficient test airfields in the vicinity of the assembly shops. The increasing unreliability of rail transport, due to enemy bombing, which from December 1944 increased noticeably every month, made it impossible to ensure delivery according to schedule. Loss of territory to the Allies also increased the difficulties."*

In an attempt to relieve the bottlenecks in test flying mentioned by Lange, and ensure delivery of newly manufactured aircraft, a group under *Generalleutnant* Kurt Kleinrath, the former head of the *Luftwaffe* Quarter Master General's *Abteilung* (Department) 6, was attached to Speer's Armaments Ministry in December 1944. Kleinrath had the imposing title of *Bevollmächtigter des Reichsmarschalls für Überwachung des Einflugbetriebes* (Reichsmarschall's Plenipotentiary for the Control of Flight Testing Acceptance). His mission, which was designated *Sonderkommission Kleinrath*, included at least four travelling staffs which were charged with investigating conditions at the flight testing centres throughout Germany.

On 2 January 1945, *Maj.* Wilhelm Herget, was made head of the mission dealing with Me 262 flight-testing. His staff included *Oberstabsing. Dr.* Engelmann, the head of the BAL[4] organisation attached to Messerschmitt, his old *Gruppe* signals officer and *Jägerleitoffizier*. After being told that at least 100 Me 262s were standing on airfields awaiting testing, he set out on a tour of the flight test centres including Schwäbisch Hall, Leipheim, Memmingen, München-Riem and Lechfeld.

During his tour Herget was able to slightly increase the rate of testing by making adjustments to meal times and hours of work. It was also arranged that test flying should take place in weather conditions which had formerly been considered unsuitable, and special

An early production Me 262 A-1a, W.Nr.130170, carrying the four letter code SQ+WI. This aircraft carried out a large number of varied tests at E-Stelle Rechlin, coded E2+02 between June and December 1944. It may have been modified to test the TSA bomb aiming device in connection with the development of the Me 262 A-2a/U1. It was returned to Messerschmitt at the end of December and fitted with BMW 003 engines as an A-1b prototype. It was then test flown by Dipl.-Ing. Heinz Borsdorff at Rechlin as 'E3+36'.

A newly completed Me 262 being tested at Messerschmitt's Lechfeld facility.

Above: A newly completed Me 262 A-2a awaits delivery to an operational unit. The single rectangular white patch under the gun access hatch would indicate that this aircraft is fitted with two MK 108 cannon and therefore probably destined for a bomber unit.

Below : Completed Me 262 A-2as await collection from the satellite production facility at Eger in the Czech Protectorate, late 1944. The aircraft in the foreground has been left with bare metal surfaces and with its brown coloured filler visible.

Below: Civilian technicians and engineers prepare a Me 262 for a test run at an unidentified production plant. The picture to the right shows a "wet start"; occasionally a small amount of fuel leaked into the base of the Me 262's engine cowling causing a sheet of flame to pour from the turbojet when ignited. Such an event, although spectacular, rarely resulted in damage to the aircraft.

WILLI HERGET

Born on 30 June 1910 at Stuttgart, Herget flew as a "sports" pilot during the mid-1930s. Already serving in the Luftwaffe reserve, he was promoted to Leutnant and transferred to 6./ZG 76 on 25 August 1939. Flying during the campaign against France and during the Battle of Britain, Herget had gained 14 victories by the end of 1940. During May and June 1941 he was a member of the special "Juner" task force which operated in Iraq and, in November of that year, he took over command of 7./NJG 3. At the beginning of May 1942 he became Kommandeur of II./NJG 4 and was awarded the Knight's Cross on 20 June 1943 after gaining 30 victories. By the time of the award of the Oak Leaves in April 1944, he had scored 63 victories, destroying eight RAF bombers in one night on 20 December 1944. He later flew the Me 262 A-1a/U4 as is recorded in Chapter 9. In total he flew 700 operational sorties, claiming a total of 73 victories. He died on 27 March 1974 in Stuttgart.

arrangements were made for flying to continue even during air raid alerts. This latter procedure was made possible by the establishment of a special warning service operated by a signals organisation set up for the purpose by Herget's signals officer and *Jägerleitoffizier*, which continuously kept the test pilots informed of the movements of hostile aircraft.

Although this slightly improved matters, further investigations proved that the main problem with Me 262 production lay with the factories and not with the testing. He therefore interviewed *Dr.* Engelmann who finally admitted that flight testing difficulties had been exaggerated in order to hide factory deficiencies. The real bottleneck was the unsatisfactory Me 262 wing output from Leonberg, which amounted to 150 sets per month as opposed to the scheduled output of 750 sets. A new wing factory was under construction at Plochingen near Stuttgart, but this was not yet in production and, in any case, its capacity was to be inferior to that at Leonberg.

Following this discovery Herget decided to exceed his orders and investigate the position at Leonberg for himself. On arrival at the factory he was horrified to find that a large proportion of the staff consisted of workers from concentration camps who had the appearance of walking ghosts and were so weak that many of them fainted at their work. Under these circumstances it was hardly surprising that the output was not all that it should have been. Herget then remonstrated with the SS official in charge of slave labour who stated that he himself had attempted to secure adequate food supplies for his workers, but that the authorities on higher levels refused to co-operate and that, in any case, even if provisions had been made available, he would not have had the necessary motor transport with which to collect them.

Professor Wilhelm Messerschmitt (right), designer of the Me 262, was horrified to learn of the concentration camp conditions which prevailed in the Leonberg wing factory and promptly dismissed the factory manager. Messerschmitt is seen here with test pilot Hermann Wurster.

Three views – taken covertly by a member of Lehrgeschwader 1 – show the only known Me 262 belonging to the so-called "Schnellaktion Prof. Gladenbeck" outside Hangar 4 at Brandis in March 1945. Note the aircraft appears to have no code or unit markings, but is fitted with a Wikingerschiff bomb rack. This small unit – which had its own office, workshops and hangar – was involved in testing high-frequency radio equipment and acoustics. At the end of January 1945, and in addition to the Me 262 shown in these pictures, "Schnellaktion Prof. Gladenbeck" had on strength 3 Me 163s, 1 He 111, 1 Ju 88 and a single high performance glider of a type unknown. The unit had transferred to Brandis from Sagan in the east under the command of Hptm. Baumgart and worked alongside Erprobungskommando 16, the Me 163 test unit based there. At least twenty ground personnel were known to have been assigned to the unit, with a further twenty technical personnel seconded from the firms of Telefunken, Patin, Lorenz and AEG as well as from a scientific institute – the Physikalischtechnische-Reichsanstalt – and from the Technical College in Braunschweig.

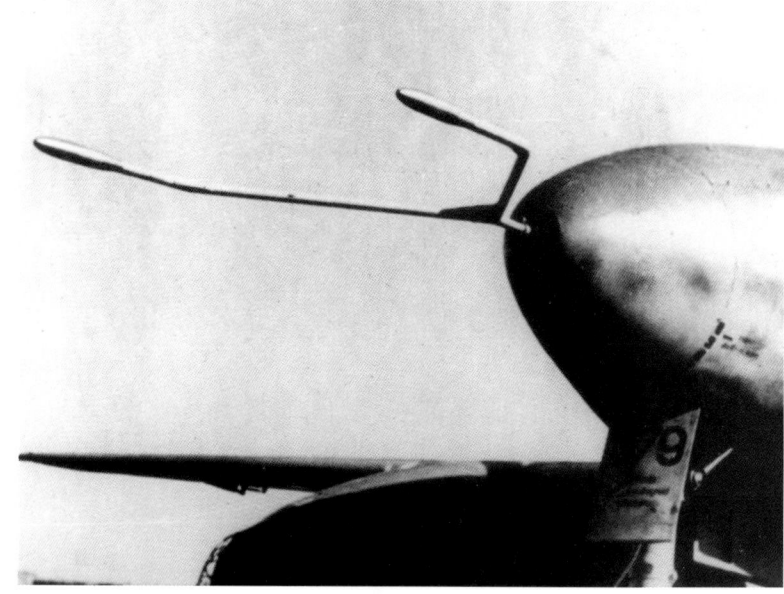

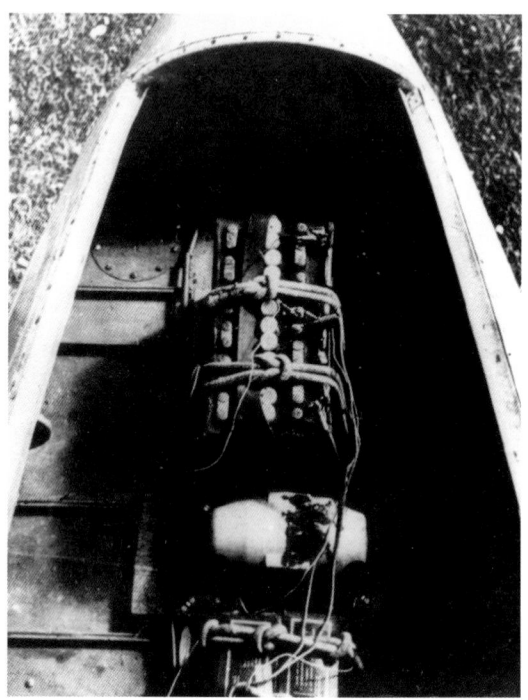

Four photographs dating from September 1944 showing the experimental electro-acoustical radar code-named Baldrian designed by the Elektrophysik company. This equipment was fitted to three Me 262s, the S10, W.Nr. 110555 and W.Nr. 170079 (seen here). Tests by Schnellaktion Prof. Gladenbeck were to reveal that sound waves emanating from an aircraft could be picked up over a distance of 750 m by an electro-acoustical direction finding apparatus with a favourable degree of accuracy being obtained over a range of 350 m. These experiments revealed that sound waves emanating from an aircraft could be picked up over a distance of 750 m by an electro-acoustic direction finding apparatus, with a favourable degre of accuracy being obtained over a range of 350 m. These experiments showed for the first time that acoustic direction signals could be picked up by an aircraft whose frequency spectrum differed from that of the source. The intention was to extend the range by three or four times by increasing the sensitivity through evaluation of perfect frequency spectra.

Herget reported these facts to *General* Kleinrath who then went to Oberammergau for a personal interview with *Prof.* Messerschmitt and Friedrich Seiler, the Chairman of Messerschmitt AG. According to Herget, both these men, who had hitherto been ignorant of the state of affairs at Leonberg, were horrified at his revelations and had the factory manager, a *Herr* Kittelmann, dismissed on the spot. It was learnt however, that this step had no effect because the responsible authorities made no extra allocation of provisions and showed themselves to be completely uninterested in conditions at the factory.[5] Kleinrath, appreciating the importance of stepping up Me 262 production, then took the Leonberg matter directly to Göring, who in turn consulted Speer's Ministry. The only result of this intervention was that Herget was severely reprimanded for interfering in matters in which he had no concern, and was forbidden henceforward to set foot in *any* Messerschmitt factory, with the implication that he would be far better employed on operational duties! Shortly afterwards, in fact, he was transferred to JV 44.

During January, 148 Me 262 fighters were delivered and 14 repaired, a total of 162. Of these, 30 were delivered to I./KG(J) 54, 15 to I./JG 7, eleven to III./JG 7, eight to the *Industriesselbstschutzschwarm*, six to III./KG(J) 54, four to the TLR, three to *Kommando Welter*, two to III./KG(J) 6, two to the *Flieger Überführungs Geschwader*, one to Prof Gladenbeck,[6] one for conversion and one to IV./EKG 1. In addition seven trainers were built and one converted. Of these four went to IV./EKG 1, three to NAG 6, and one to I./JG 7.

On 10 February 1945, the OKL war diary recorded:

"In order to speed up the production and issue of the Me 262 so that this type can be put into operational service in some strength as soon as possible in accordance with the Führer's orders, the following have or will be appointed by the Reichmarschall *or* Hauptdienstleiter *Saur:*

a Plenipotentiary for production,
(Gerhard Degenkolb)
a Plenipotentiary for testing at factories,
    (Kleinrath)a
a Plenipotentiary for ferrying
aircraft to squadrons
an Inspector for Jet Aircraft
(Obstlt. Wolfgang Schenk)
The Inspector will be directly subordinated to the Luftwaffe Operations Staff."

The draconian measures instituted by the Plenipotentiaries did help to increase production in February, 212 Me 262 fighters being delivered and twelve repaired. Of this total of 224, 93 were at the factory, 20 were being converted, with 44 returned. A further 42 had been delivered to *Luftwaffen Kommando West*. Of the remaining 113, 28 were delivered to III./KG(J) 54, 25 to I./JG 7, 19 to II./KG(J) 54, 13 to I./KG(J) 54, ten to II./JG 7, seven to III./JG 7, six to III./KG(J) 6, three to 10./NJG 11, one to the *Flieger Überführungs Geschwader* and one to JV 44. Apart from the fighters, 19 trainers were produced and 13 Me 262 short-range reconnaissance aircraft converted. All the latter went to NAG 6, with nine trainers going to III./EJG 2, four to the *Flieger Überführungs Geschwader*, three to IV./EKG 1, two to II./JG 7 and one to II./EKG(J).

Apart from problems with production of the Me 262, the Allied air offensive had badly hit German fuel supplies. The OKL war diary entry for 12 February 1945, reported that: *"...at present the fuel supply for jet aircraft (J2) is still adequate, but should be closely watched in view of the increasing numbers of aircraft. Experiments are now in progress to convert reject gasoline (approximately 200,000 tons available) for use by jet aircraft. Prospects of success are described as good."*

Nine days later, Göring informed the *Führer* that about two thirds of the *Luftwaffe* fuel quota had been used for training and industrial

Gerhard Degenkolb, a former director of the infamous Camp Dora slave labour factory in the Harz Mountains, was also Chairman of Albert Speer's V-2 rocket production committee. As a result of his strenuous and ruthless efforts in this area, he oversaw a substantial increase in production of the rocket. In February 1945, on orders from Hitler, he was appointed special Plenipotentiary for Me 262 Production. Degenkolb's goal was "... to speed up the production and issue of the Me 262 so that this type can be put into operational service in some strength as soon as possible in accordance with the Führer's orders..."

The draconian measures adopted by Gerhard Degenkolb to increase Me 262 production resulted in February 1945 in a total of 19 badly needed trainers being delivered to the operational units. These photographs show some of the Me 262 B-1a trainers delivered to III./EJG 2 at Lechfeld.

Bottom: Major Erich Hohagen, (left, in woolen skull cap) a 56-victory Ritterkreuzträger who underwent conversion on to the jet fighter and who would later fly with JG 7 and JV 44, walks along the taxiway at Lechfeld in November 1944 with another unidentified pilot. To the far right of the picture, parked next to Me 262 A-1a "White 7" can be seen Me 262 B-1a trainer, W.Nr. 170014, "White 17". *Below*: In November 1943, Adolf Galland appointed Oberst Hannes Trautloft, former Kommodore of JG 54, as Inspector of Day Fighters. Awarded the Ritterkreuz in July 1941, Trautloft's operational career went back to the Spanish Civil War where he scored five of his eventual 58 victories. Here, Erich Hohagen, in woollen skullcap, looks up at the tall figure of Trautloft on the wing of an Me 262 B-1a during the latter's inspection tour of III./EJG 2 at Lechfeld in late 1944. *Right*: A pilot of III./EJG 2 checks the cockpit of Me 262 B-1a "White 17" at Lechfeld in late 1944, as members of the ground crew refuel the machine in readiness for flight.

purposes and only one third for operations. Hitler ordered that in future operational flying should receive 60% of the allocation. By the end of the month, stocks of the Me 262's J2 fuel totalled 44,455 tonnes, but heavy air attacks on the Böhlen and Merseburg synthetic fuel plants early in March[7] severely disrupted production for over a month. On 15 March *Reichsminister* Speer issued a discussion document suggesting how this problem would affect aircraft production under the modified Programme 228 (*see below and overleaf*).

Also during March 1945 a letter from the *Führer's* HQ gave the Me 262 programme priority over all other production in Germany and, in a further attempt to speed Me 262 construction, Hitler appointed *SS Obergruppenführer* Hans Kammler *Bevöllmachtigter der Führer für Strahlflugzeuge* (The *Führer's* Plenipotentiary for Jet Aircraft) on 27 March. His order stated that: "All powers previously held by the Reichsminister for Armament and War Production for jet aircraft are transferred to *SS-Obergruppenführer und General der Waffen-SS Dr.Ing.* Kammler." In many ways, Hitler's choice

---

Anticipated production of aviation fuel and resulting requirement of Aircraft.

J 2

J 2 production March 6,000 t
Increasing in June up to 35,000 t
October   50,000 t

Compared to this, consumption is the following :

March approx 20,000 t
June approx 40,000 t
from October increasing to 50,000 t

The current stock of 44,000 tonnes of J 2 has been taken into consideration in the above calculations.

The following aircraft programme would thus be possible:
a)   Me 262   March   300 t[8]
              gradually increasing to   500 t
              by June and then remaining at this level

Ar 234 C   March   10 t
             gradually increasing to   50 t
             by June and then remaining at this level

He 162   March   100 t
             June   200 t
             remaining at this level

b) In the case where the above calculations should refer to the Me 262 only stock and production of J 2 would permit manufacture of new aircraft as follows:

              March   300 t
              increasing until June   700 t
              rising until October to   800 t
              and remaining at this level

(continued overleaf)

> **Programme**
>
> The present fuel situation will permit the following aircraft programme, not taking into account (possible losses caused by) bomb damage, transport problems, production losses due to electricity failures, territorial losses etc.[9]
>
> | Month | 3 | 4 | 5 | 6 | 7 | 8 | 9 | 10 | 11 | 12 |
> |--------|-----|-----|-----|------|------|------|------|------|------|------|
> | Me 262 | 350 | 350 | 400 | 550 | 550 | 550 | 550 | 550 | 550 | 550 |
> | Ar 234 | 10 | 20 | 35 | 50 | 50 | 50 | 50 | 50 | 50 | 50 |
> | He 162 | 100 | 100 | 150 | 200 | 250 | 200 | 200 | 200 | 200 | 200 |
> | Ta152 | 20 | 100 | 300 | 450 | 370 | 370 | 370 | 370 | 370 | 370 |
> | TOTALS | 430 | 570 | 885 | 1250 | 1200 | 1170 | 1170 | 1170 | 1170 | 1170 |
>
> To cover losses due to the transport situation, enemy action etc., the following programme, based on the actual fuel supply situation, is suggested :
>
> 1. Me 262 1,000 aircraft monthly with an additional (reserve) capacity of 500 aircraft
> 2. He 162 500 aircraft monthly, additional capacity 1,000 monthly,
> 3. Ar 234 75 aircraft per month
> 4. Ta 152 500 aircraft monthly with an additional 50% factory stocks.
>
> At the same time the following emergency measures should be taken: Immediate suspension and cancellation of the (following) aircraft and engine types from the Emergency Programme:
>
> 1. Bf 109 immediately, including DB 605 production.
> 2. Fw 190 : a final production run of 1,000 aircraft with Jumo 213, distributed over the next four months
> 3. BMW 801 - immediate production stop
> 4. Immediate stop on the Do 335 and Do 635, including their DB 603 engines. (The Ta 152 will be delivered exclusively with the Jumo 213 E). Production capacity for 50 Ju 88 night fighters and torpedo bombers to be maintained. Ar 96/Ar 396 training aircraft and Fa 223 helicopter capacity also to be continued. Reduction of the order for 500 He 162[10] gliders to 50 and (immediate) stop of manufacture of all glider types, except ten Ka 430 aircraft per month.

of Kammler was entirely understandable, for this young, highly intelligent and ruthlessly ambitious man had achieved miracles before with a determination and fanaticism that made even his superiors quake. It had been Kammler, who as Himmler's paladin, had risen from a position of relative obscurity in the Air Ministry to take command of *Amtsgruppe* C of the *SS-Wirtschafts- und Verwaltungshauptamt* (SS-Main Office of Economics and Administration), where he had taken charge of all matters pertaining to SS building and construction projects, including the concentration camps and road building in occupied Russia. Later in the war he was instrumental in the development of the infamous *Mittelwerk* underground V-weapon production facility at Nordhausen in the Harz mountains and then took command of the entire Fi 103 flying bomb and A-4 rocket production and development programme. In the Autumn of 1944, he led the rocket *Blitz* launching more than 4,000 A-4's against targets in Belgium, France and the British Isles.

The *Führer* also ordered that the Me 262 and He 162 were to have priority over the Ar 234.

During March, 231 Me 262 fighters were delivered and nine repaired. Of these, only 120 went to operational units. Eighty-nine went to

JG 7, twelve to KG(J) 54, six to JV 44, six to 10./NJG 11, four to III./KG(J) 6, and three to the TLR. In addition, 20 Me 262 A-1a/U3 short-range reconnaissance aircraft and three Me 262 B-1a/U1 night fighters were converted, the former being delivered to NAG 6 and NAG 1, the latter to 10./NJG 11. Finally, 22 Me 262 B-1a trainers were built or converted, ten of these delivered to III./EJG 2, three to IV./EKG 1, two to II./EKG(J), two to JV 44, two to the *Flieger Überführungs Geschwader*, one to the TLR, one to III./KG(J) 6, and one to III./JG 7.

Meanwhile, development of the Me 262 continued. Apart from experimenting with the use of non-strategic materials such as wood, these included the fitting of new engines, improving aerodynamics and the evolution of advanced weapons.

Right up to the end of the war all production Me 262s were powered by the Jumo 004 B-1 or improved B-4 with air cooled turbine blades. Despite this, improved versions of the engine were being developed. The 1000 kp (2,200 lbs) thrust Jumo 004 C was abandoned and a new variant, the Jumo 004 D, proposed. This introduced a new type of governor which permitted the pilot to adjust engine speed in the lower range much more accurately than with the previous unit. A new acceleration control valve was added to prevent damage to the engine by improper handling. The engine also introduced two-stage fuel valves for fuel injection. This increased thrust at full throttle to 1,000 kp (2,200 lbs). A further development included the Jumo 004 E with afterburning. In this, engine fuel was injected immediately in front of the turbine stator which increased thrust to 1,200 kp (2,650 lbs). After several 100 hour tests, this engine was scheduled to enter series production in July 1945. The Jumo 004 F was to use water injection and the Jumo 004 H was an enlarged engine with an eleven-stage axial-flow compressor designed to produce 1,800 kp (3,970 lbs) thrust. The last two models did not progress beyond the drawing board stage.

On 11 May 1945[11], the Junkers company issued the following figures listing the numbers of Jumo 004 B-1 and B-4 engines manufactured or repaired between August 1944 and March 1945. The production facilities were identified by their official abbreviations:

MSD Junkers Dessau
MZM Junkers Magdeburg
Mulde Junkers Muldenstein
MZK Junkers Köthen
MMW Junkers Leipzig-Taucha
MZZ Junkers Zittau
MZP Junkers Prague

It is interesting that even at the end of August 1944, only 302 Jumo 004 turbojets had been delivered. Many commentators have suggested

Himmler's paladin: SS Obergruppenführer Hans Kammler. On 27 March 1945 Hitler appointed Kammler "Bevollmächtigter der Führer für Strahlflugzeuge" ("The Führer's Plenipotentiary for Jet Aircraft"). The Führer ordered that Kammler was to take over the organisation of jet aircraft from Reichsminister Albert Speer.

New Engines Delivered

	MSD	MZM	Mulde	MZK	MMW	MZZ	MZP	Total
Aug 44	186	13	43	20	3	37	-	302
Sep 44	-	-	143	70	10	17	-	240
Oct 44	-	-	305	201	37	17	-	560
Nov 44	-	-	317	210	15	38	-	580
Dec 44	-	-	310	232	15	53	-	610
Jan 45	12	-	334	240	18	86	-	690
Feb 45	11	5	294	370	25	115	-	820
Mar 45	10	10	280	490	30	120	10	950
Total	219	28	2026	1833	153	483	10	4652

Repaired Engines

	Mulde	MZZ	Lauingen	Total
Aug 44	10	38	-	48
Sep 44	10	53	-	63
Oct 44	-	72	-	72
Nov 44	-	94	-	94
Dec 44	-	104	5	109
Jan 45	-	85	10	95
Feb 45	-	-	10	10
Mar 45	-	-	15	15
Total	20	446	40	506

The three types of aircraft, which in addition to the Me 262, were to form the projected nucleus of the Luftwaffe's offensive and defensive capability for the year 1945. *Above:* With German fears growing of the deployment of American long-range high-altitude strategic bombers, the Ta 152 was intended to perform as a high-altitude, high-speed piston interceptor or "Spezial Höhenjäger". This photograph shows the Cottbus-built Ta 152 V5, W.Nr. 150005, CW+CE, on the compass swing. The aircraft was completed as a Ta 152 H-1.
Right: In September 1944, the RLM issued a specification for an emergency lightweight fighter – or Volksjäger – with bad weather capability, to be powered by a BMW 003 turbojet. The result was the He 162. Here, preparations are being made before the first successful take-off of a production He 162 built at the Heinkel Marienehe works on 25 March 1945.
Below: Arado Ar 234 B-2 jet bombers of III./KG 76 lined up at Burg on a winter's morning in January 1945. In March 1945, Hitler ordered that the Me 262 and He 162 were to have priority over this type.

that the Me 262 could have been brought into service up to a year earlier and, perhaps, without Hitler's interference, smashed the American daylight bombing offensive. There is one major problem with this scenario - its engines. At this time the Jumo 004 was rarely capable of running more than 10 hours without a major overhaul which was too low for general service use. Until this could be improved, its design could not be frozen for mass production. Therefore, it would have been impossible for the aircraft to have been brought into operational service much earlier than it was.

Work also proceeded on the BMW 003 turbojet. Uncompleted developments included the BMW 003 C with seven-stage compressor designed by Brown-Boveri and the BMW 003 D with an eight-stage compressor and two-stage turbine. These engines were designed to produce 900 kp (1,980 lbs) and 1,100 kp (2,430 lbs) thrust respectively, and both may have been intended for the Me 262. The only other engine proposed for installation in the Me 262 was the Daimler-Benz DB 021 turboprop. This was an adaptation of the HeS 11 converted to propeller drive, the development of which was handed over to Daimler-Benz early in 1944. It was designed to deliver 2,000 ehp with 790 kp (1,750 lbs) of residual thrust. The DB 021 was to drive a six-blade propeller, but no prototype was completed by May 1945. Due to its lower fuel consumption, this engine was considered as an alternative power plant for the Me 262 three-seat night fighter.

---

1 Two of the five remaining Bunkerwerke were also to be built in the Landsberg area, code-named Diana 2 and Wallnuss 2 (wallnut 2). The other three were proposed for sites in the Harz Mountains and Muhldorf/Inn, but they were abandoned in December 1944 due to shortages of steel and concrete.

2 Other Bunkerwerke were planned for BMW, Junkers, Daimler-Benz and Focke-Wulf, under the generic code-name "Ringeltaube" (Woodpigeon). Only work on only three sites, "Dora" in the Harz Mountains, Kaufering and Mühldorf/Inn, had been started by the war's end due to shortages of steel and concrete.

3 During the war Gauleiter Fritz Sauckel was responsible for the transportation of five million people from occupied Europe to work as slaves in Germany. Sauckel saw himself as an agent supplying workers for factories and was shocked when arrested by the British in 1945 and put on trial at Nuremberg. He claimed to know nothing of the concentration camps and protested his innocence until hanged in October 1946.

4 The BAL (Bau-Aufsicht Luft) is perhaps best translated at the Aeronautical Inspection Directorate. It was established around 1935 and by 1943 had resident engineers in 107 aircraft manufacturing plants and repair facilities as well as in 57 engine, 15 propeller and more than 100 factories and repair workshops for aeronautical equipment.

5 For further details of Messerschmitt's attitude to the employment of foreign workers, readers are recommended to read Chapter 15 of "Willy Messerschmitt" by Frank Vann published in England by Patrick Stephens Ltd. in 1993.

6 Schnellaktion Prof. Gladenbeck, based at Brandis near Leipzig, was an experimental unit equipped with a small number of aircraft including a Me 262s, three Me 163s, a He 111, a Ju 88 and a high performance sailplane.

7 See Volume Three.

8 Allows for approximately one tonne of J2 per aircraft for factory flight testing.

9 The figures given approximate with those quoted by Generalmajor Diesing at the TLR Amtsgruppenchef discussion held on 12 March 1945.

10 The wooden glider version of the He 162 had been designed for the primary training of young Volksjäger pilots culled from the Hitler Youth.

11 It may seem odd that Junkers could issue a report three days after the German surrender, but this document was prepared for the Americans who were the first Allied forces to occupy the company's facilities at Dessau.

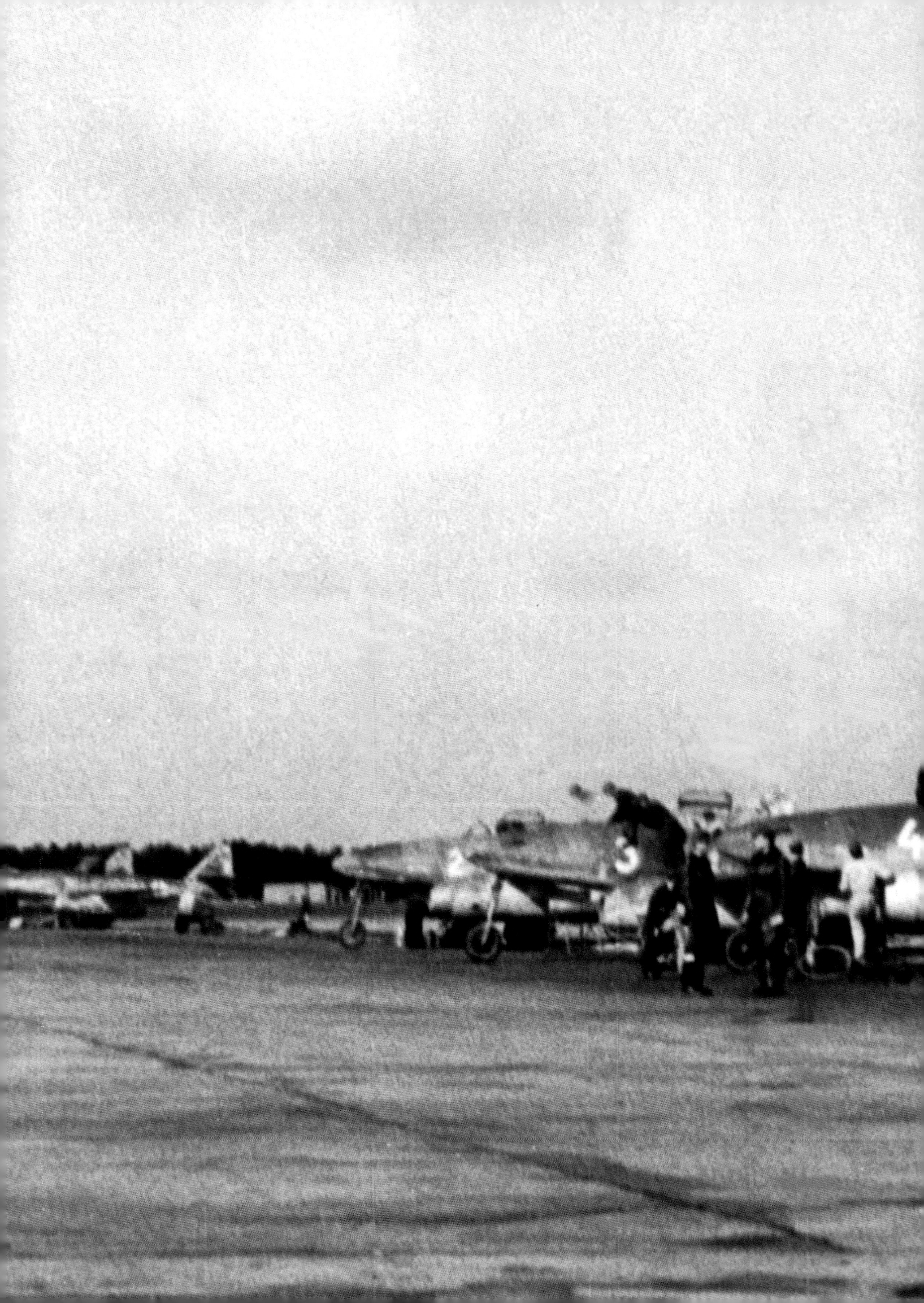

CHAPTER THIRTEEN
"CARELESSNESS AND INADEQUATE TRAINING"

By early November 1944, the *Luftwaffe* had two fully operational Me 262 units. These were *Kommando Nowotny*, a fighter unit based at Achmer and Hesepe and 3./KG 51, a bomber unit based at Rheine. In addition, the experimental unit, *Erprobungskommando 262* was still flying trial interceptions of Allied reconnaissance aircraft from Lechfeld in Bavaria.

Oberst Hannes Trautloft, the Luftwaffe Inspector for Day Fighters, spent several days at Achmer in early October 1944, and made "great personal efforts" to work Kommando Nowotny up to full and effective fighting strength, using competent fighter pilots drawn from other units. Trautloft is seen here at Lechfeld inspecting the controls of an Me 262 B-1a two seat trainer, coded "White 17', belonging to III./EJG 2.

The first operations by *Kommando Nowotny* had already proved less than successful, no fewer than ten aircraft being destroyed or damaged between 4 and 13 October. In an attempt to discover the reason, Messerschmitt dispatched a technical field team *(Technischer Außendienst)* under Fritz Wendel to Achmer. The *Luftwaffe* pilots were convinced that the losses were due to design flaws with the engines and undercarriage but Wendel did not agree. Late in October he issued the following highly critical report which mentioned, in particular, the lack of training.

"*Kommando Nowotny has been in action since 3 October 1944. Up until 24 October sorties had been flown on a total of three days. The Inspector of the Day Fighters, Oberst Trautloft, was at the base during the first days and had made great personal efforts to ensure the success of the first fighter sorties with the Me 262.*

"*He saw to it that several successful fighter pilots were taken from other units to form the core of this unit. The commander,* Major *Nowotny is a successful Eastern Front pilot but is unfamiliar with the present situation in the West and, at 23, is not the superior leader personality necessary to guarantee the success of this vital operation. The following points bear this out:*

"*1. The first day of the operations by the* Kommando *went as follows. A large number of enemy fighters were already over the airfield, but four of the* Kommando's *aircraft took off from Achmer and two more from the unit's second airfield at Hesepe, some 6 km (4 mls) away. Of the aircraft which took off from Achmer, two were shot down on take-off, one on landing. One of the other two was also shot down, probably on landing. Our losses were probably 3 or 4.*

"*Like any other aircraft, the Me 262 is vulnerable during take-off and landing. It must be possible, and it is possible, that take-offs occur when there are no enemy aircraft over the airfield.*

"*2. There is a variety of opinions among the pilots and* Staffel *leaders as to the best tactical employment of the Me 262, indeed there are even contradictory views. Clear tactical objectives and corresponding instruction to the pilots is lacking.*

"*3. The majority of the pilots have received far too little instruction on the Me 262. No sorties were flown during the past ten days due to poor weather. This time should have been used for training, but nothing was done.* Major *Nowotny himself once landed with a less than fully extended nosewheel. The aircraft was heavily damaged in the incident.*

"*4. The first fighter operations should provide the experience necessary to overcome the shortcomings and mistakes in any new design.*

Right: Major Walter Nowotny, commander of Kommando Nowotny, pensively watches proceedings at Achmer, one of the two airfields which served as a base for his unit.

"CARELESSNESS AND INADEQUATE TRAINING" • 409

An impressive photograph showing Luftwaffe ground crews working on a line up of Me 262 A-1as of Kommando Nowotny at Achmer in the autumn of 1944. The truth was that the pilots of this unit – some of whom are seen here in discussion in front of "White 4" – were still struggling to master their new aircraft and there were contradictory views as to the best methods of tactical deployment.

Me 262 A-1a "White 19", Kommando Nowotny, Achmer, October 1944

Although carrying similar markings to the aircraft of Erprobungskommando 262, the Me 262s of Kommando Nowotny had their upper surfaces camouflaged in two shades of green (81 and 82) with pale blue grey (76) beneath. Most aircraft that belonged to this unit had the distinctive sharply defined pattern on the vertical tail surfaces, which judging by the exact duplication on each aircraft suggests the use of a standard stencil for each side. Photographic evidence shows that many of the surviving aircraft retained their tail markings after they were transferred to other units when Kommando Nowotny was disbanded.

During its development, several famous fighter pilots were given the chance to examine the Me 262. Here Major Hermann Graf, is shown the controls of an early prototype, probably the V3, by Messerschmitt flight test co-ordinator, Gerhard Caroli and (with spectacles), test pilot, Karl Baur. Graf was awarded the Diamonds to the Knight's Cross.
On 14 May 1942, he scored seven victories and in one 17 day period shot down 47 aircraft. He was the second pilot to achieve 150 victories, ending the war with a total score of 212. He served as commander of Jagdergänzungsgruppe Ost and also led both JG 11 and JG 52. Despite flying 830 sorties, he never flew the Me 262 operationally.

Below and opposite page:
A sequence of photographs showing aircraft of Kommando Nowotny being made ready for operations. The unit's machines were often distinguishable by their distinctive striped tail markings and some aircraft had yellow cowling rings and fuselage bands. It is interesting to note the variety of airfield support vehicles used by the unit.
Bottom: A fuel bowser and trailer arrive at the dispersal to begin refuelling of "White 4".

The pilots must therefore be trained to recognise the real faults. Failing completely to appreciate this state of affairs, Major *Nowotny has selected the following point, among others, which he considers important. He feels that the electric starter handle, which is located on the starboard side console at present, should be replaced by a button on the instrument panel.*

"The starter is only used once for each engine before a flight. It is totally unimportant whether it is installed on the right or at the front.

"Points 3 and 4 are especially significant as they illustrate the greatest weakness of our air force. This arm, which employs the most modern and complicated machines, in which one man is often responsible for a machine requiring many thousands of hours to construct, is not even conscious of this fact. Pilots lack the necessary technical training. Intensive theoretical instruction is also missing during conversion to new aircraft types. As well as aircraft, this would save a great deal of fuel. As proof the following example:

"Our twin-engined aircraft can be flown and, with some caution, landed following the loss of one engine. There continue to be too many losses (of late with the Me 262 as well), simply because the use of the rudder by the pilots is completely wrong or has been learned wrongly.

"Instruction on the aircraft type is particularly bad with Kommando Nowotny. *The importance given to the technical side may be illustrated by the fact that the* Gruppe Technical Officer at Achmer, Hptm. Streicher, *is not a technician. The* Staffel Technical Officer at Hesepe, *the roughly 19-year-old* Oberfähnrich Russel, *is also a complete layman, who has himself recently destroyed two aircraft as a result of carelessness and inadequate training."*

Wendel's opinions were supported by Horst Geyer, the then commander of *EKdo 262*. He recalled that when Nowotny arrived at Lechfeld for training he made only one familiarisation flight in the Me 262 and seemed quite confident that he could handle any problems that the radical aircraft might present without further preparation.

When *Kommando Nowotny* returned to operations on 1 November 1944, four aircraft attacked a group of P-51 Mustangs from the US 20th and 352nd Fighter Groups. Near Zwolle, in Holland, *Ofäh*. Willi Banzhaff of the *3. Staffel*

shot down a P-51 piloted by Lt. Dennis J. Alison of the 77th Fighter Squadron, 20th Fighter Group. He continued his dive through the American formation but as he attempted to climb, his Me 262 was shot down in turn by a P-51 of the US 352nd Fighter Group piloted by Lt. William T. Gerbe Jr., and a P-47 of the 56th Fighter Group flown by Lt. Walter R. Groce. Banzhaff bailed out and escaped without injury. Next day the *Kommando* claimed three victories, a P-51 and a P-47 by *Fw.* Erich Büttner and a P-47 by *Ofw.* Helmut Baudach. On the debit side *Uffz.* Alois Zollner was killed when one engine of his Me 262 failed on take-off from Achmer, but *Ofw.* Hubert Göbel escaped without injury when his aircraft was damaged in a taxying accident. Three Me 262s were lost on 4 November. *Ofw.* Göbel shot down a P-51 piloted by Flt.Off. Willard W. Royer of the 356th Fighter Group near the Dummer Lake, but his aircraft was then destroyed when attempting an emergency landing at Bohmte. *Ofäh.* Banzhaff was reported missing near Lüneburg, reason unknown, and *Ofw.* Helmut Zander's aircraft was totally destroyed when he attempted a single engined landing at Hesepe. Astonishingly he was flung from the aircraft and survived unhurt.

On 6 November 1944, four more Me 262s from the *Kommando* were damaged, three of them in emergency landings all caused, according to German sources, by running out of fuel. *Lt.* Spangenburg crashed near Lemwerder, *Ofw.* Kreutzer near Ahlhorn and *Ofw.* Heinz Lennartz near Bremen. Each pilot escaped without injury. US sources however claim that Spangenburg was

Below: A Kettenkrad pulls "White 1" away from its dispersal to reveal "White 19" which has an auxiliary 24 volt electrical supply cart positioned by its port wing. The white "S" painted on the rear fuselage of "White 1" below the horizontal tail surface, denotes a "Schulflugzeug", or training machine. This machine was found at Innsbruck's civilian aerodrome in Austria at the end of the war.

Captain Charles E. Yeager (centre) of the P-51 equipped US 357th Fighter Group. On 6 November 1944, he is believed to have shot down Lt. Spangenburg of Kommando Nowotny. As he attempted an emergency landing, being fired at by his own Flak, Spangenburg crashed into a group of farm buildings at Lemwerder, near Bremen, and suffered head and arm injuries. His aircraft, W.Nr. 110389, caught fire and was destroyed.

shot down by a P-51 piloted by Capt. Charles E. "Chuck" Yeager[1] of the 357th Fighter Group. Yeager spotted the Me 262 attempting to land, and dived after it at over 500 mph (805 kph). Braving his way through heavy flak, the American pilot fired a burst from his six machine-guns, and looking back was gratified to see what he thought was the jet crash into a wooded field, one of its wings breaking off. However, the records of the Weserflug aircraft factory at Lemwerder contest Yeager's version of events. At 11.25, *Lt.* Spangenburg's Me 262, W.Nr. 110389, was seen flying around the works airfield at 800-1000 m (2625-3,300 ft). An air raid alarm had just been sounded and the airfield *Flak* defences erroneously identified Spangenburg as an enemy aircraft, whereupon they opened fire. With Yeager on his tail and under fire from the airfield gunners, Spangenburg flew in at high speed and landed two minutes later towards the south west. His jet bounced several times and continued to move at high speed towards some agricultural buildings close to the airfield perimeter. It then careered off the airfield and into an adjacent turnip field, colliding with a horse-drawn farm wagon and eventually crashing into a barn. Flames shot out of the aircraft, but as soon as the machine stopped, the pilot jettisoned his canopy and climbed out.

Fortunately, a group of ground personnel and local civilians attempted to put out the fire and shortly after, a rescue unit arrived and took Spangenburg away in an ambulance. He received emergency treatment for injuries to his face and head and was later sent to a reserve hospital at Bremen-Blumenthal.

It is possible that it was Lennartz's machine that was shot down by Lt. William J. Quinn of the 361st Fighter Group in the Bassum area, south of Bremen. The fourth Me 262, piloted by *Ofw.* Baudach, was damaged in a taxying accident at Hesepe. The only success achieved by the unit on this day was when *Lt.* Franz Schall destroyed a P-47.

On 7 November, a nine-man salvage unit arrived at Lemwerder airfield from Oldenburg to dismantle Lt. Spangenburg's crash-landed Me 262. The crash had resulted in the death of two horses, a farm wagon destroyed and damage to

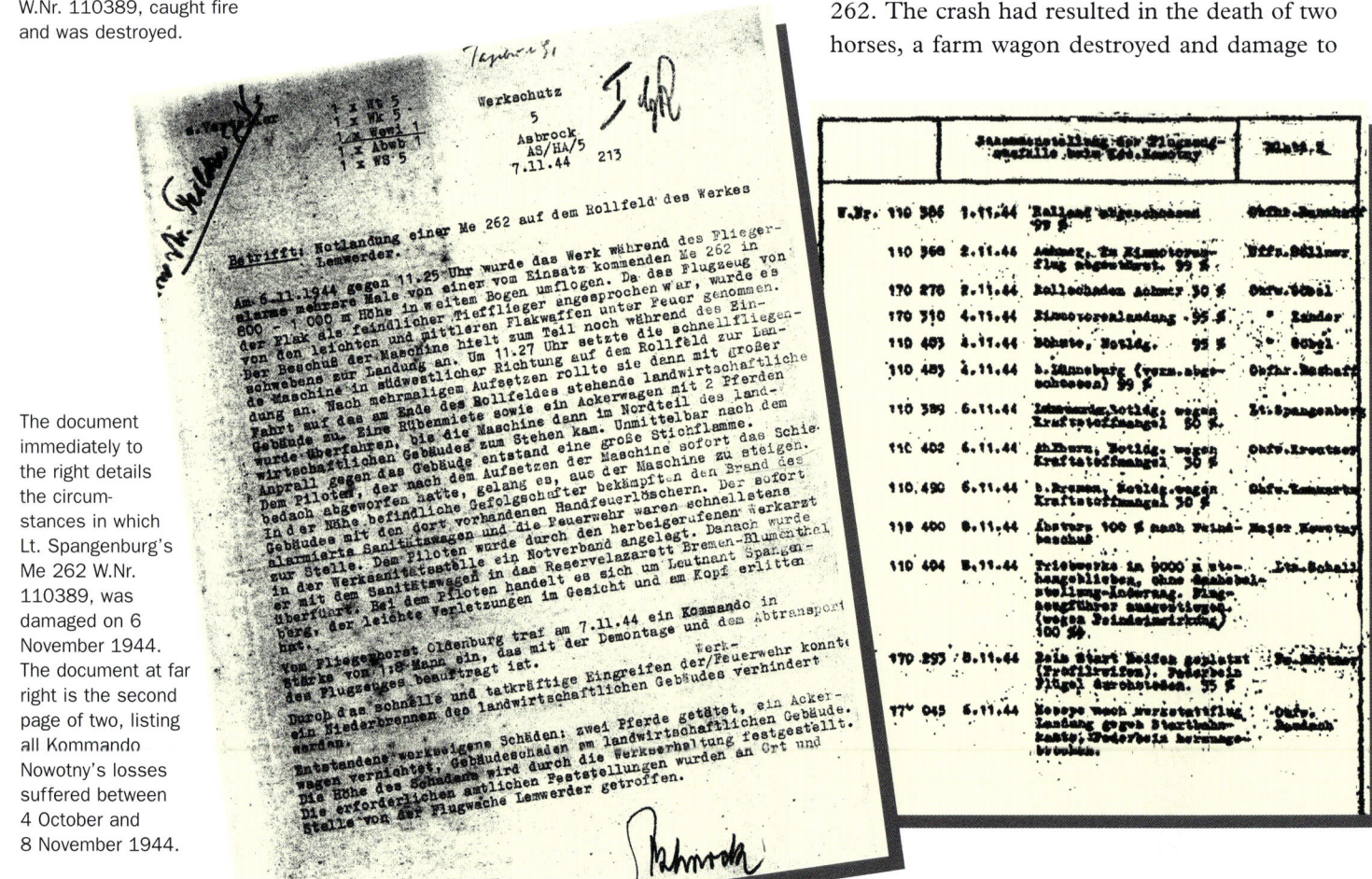

The document immediately to the right details the circumstances in which Lt. Spangenburg's Me 262 W.Nr. 110389, was damaged on 6 November 1944. The document at far right is the second page of two, listing all Kommando Nowotny's losses suffered between 4 October and 8 November 1944.

local agricultural buildings. That same day, *Generals* Keller and Galland arrived to inspect the *Kommando*, the latter already disappointed by the poor showing of the unit. During the late morning of the following day the two senior officers were present as the unit scrambled to intercept an American bomber formation. Two aircraft, piloted by *Maj.* Nowotny and *Oblt.* Wegmann were to take off from Achmer and two, flown by *Lt.* Schall and *Fw.* Büttner, from Hesepe. The engines of Nowotny's "White 8" refused to start, and Büttner's aircraft blew a tyre on take-off, causing slight damage, but Wegmann and Schall engaged the enemy, claiming a P-51 and P-47 respectively.

As the bombers returned during the early afternoon, Nowotny and Schall took off to intercept. Schall claimed two P-51s, but they were in fact both P-47s from the 356th Fighter Group piloted by Lt. Charles C. McKelvy and Lt. William L. Hoffert. Shortly afterwards Schall's engines flamed out and he was caught by a Mustang piloted by Lt. James W. Kenny of the 357th Fighter Group. As Kenny later reported: "Lt. Corwin and I were going home. Corwin had a rough engine. We took up a course of 295 degrees and flew for an hour from the target. We saw a box of B-17s with no escort, so Corwin suggested that we cover them. As we climbed above them to 22, 000 feet, we saw a lone bogey going 180 degrees to the bombers in the vicinity of Osnabruck. We broke into it and identified it as a Me 262. It climbed, turned towards the bombers and passed them. Then it turned and made a pass from five o'clock and I got on his tail with Corwin behind me. I started firing from about 400 yards at 30 degrees to zero degrees deflection. I saw a puff of red smoke come from him and got on his tail again. He was diving very shallowly and I over-shot him twice doing 300 mph. The first time he kept straight ahead, but the second time he made a medium turn to the left. I out-turned him and got behind him again. Then he bailed out at 4,000 feet. Smoke was coming out of the right nacelle. I believe he was out of fuel. Apparently, from my experience today, the Me 262 cannot dive or turn sharply."

Schall only just enough time to bail out before his aircraft exploded in a ball of flame.

Nowotny was not so lucky. After shooting down a B-24 and P-51, he was chased by a large number of Mustangs but after out-distancing them, he disappeared into cloud cover at 7,000 ft (2,000 m). He then turned through 180 degrees which brought him towards a P-51 piloted by Lt. Richard W. Stevens of the 364th Fighter Group. Stevens managed to get behind the Me 262 and gave it a two second burst from 500 yards (450 m). After the jet began to slow, he gave it another two second burst and then followed it over an airfield firing all the time. Suddenly Nowotny's

The villa which served as the staff headquarters of Kommando Nowotny in the village of Pente near Bramsche, close to Achmer airfield. Known as "Wulfhagen", the building was set amidst beautiful parkland.

Below: A line-up of Me 262s on the dispersal line at Achmer.

Me 262 A-1a W.Nr, 130017 "White 4"

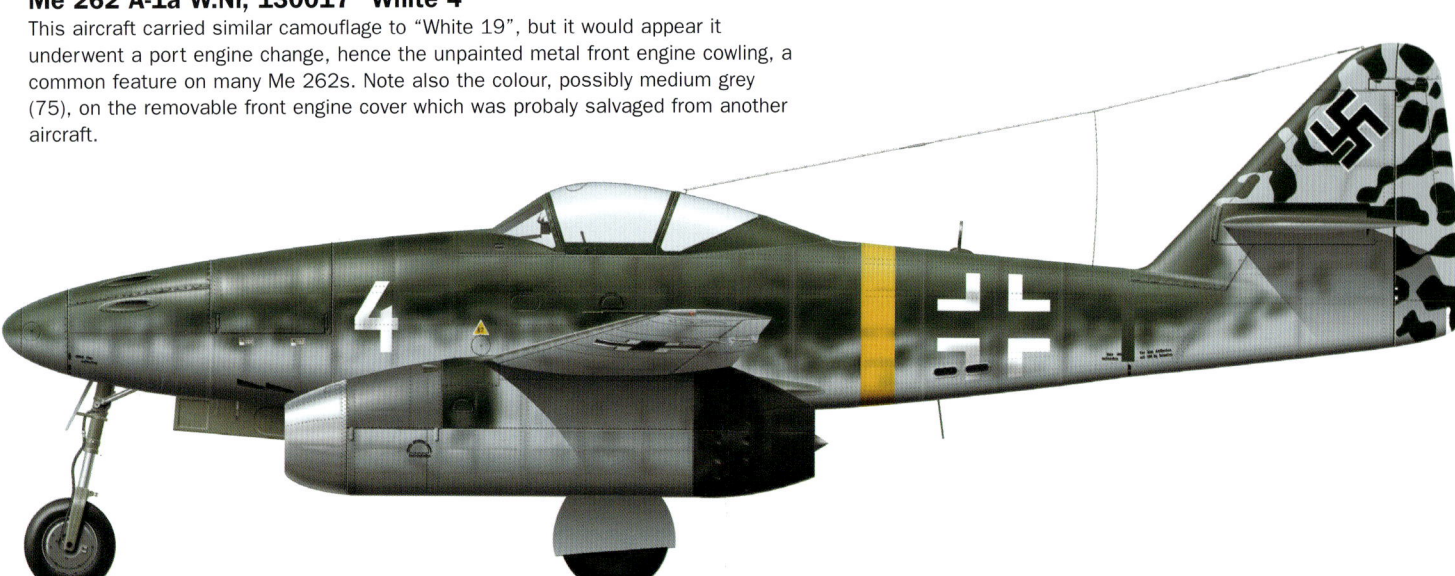

This aircraft carried similar camouflage to "White 19", but it would appear it underwent a port engine change, hence the unpainted metal front engine cowling, a common feature on many Me 262s. Note also the colour, possibly medium grey (75), on the removable front engine cover which was probaly salvaged from another aircraft.

The Me 262 A-1a, W.Nr. 130017, "White 4" was delivered to Erprobungskommando 262 in June 1944. It was damaged in an accident on the 13th, but was repaired to be flown by Fw. Helmut Lennartz on 20 July. It may have been the aircraft in which Lt. Alfred Schreiber claimed to have shot down a Mosquito on 26 July 1944. It was probably later transferred to Kommando Nowotny but was destroyed in a crash on 31 October.

"Carelessness and inadequate training" • 415

Leutnant Franz Schall (on telephone) who joined Kommando Nowotny from I./JG 52 to command the 2. Staffel and later led the 10. Staffel of JG 7. Schall was an accomplished fighter pilot who, in two days in August 1944, claimed 11 and 13 Soviet aircraft shot down respectively. He would fly some 550 missions, and is accredited with the shooting down of some 140 Allied aircraft, the destruction of three tanks, 24 vehicles and one locomotive. He was awarded the Ritterkreuz in October 1944 but would be killed in a Me 262.

Left: On 8 November 1944, Lt. James W. Kenny of the US 357th Fighter Group flying a P-51 Mustang, managed to score hits on a Me 262 piloted by Lt Franz Schall of Kommando Nowotny. *Insets*: Because of the damage sustained, Schall bailed out, leaving Kenny to take a remarkable sequence of photographs of the stricken jet with his gun camera.

Below: Kommando Nowotny's Me 262 A-1a "White 4" makes its descent towards the runway at Achmer following a sortie.

"CARELESSNESS AND INADEQUATE TRAINING" • 417

This page and opposite above: A ubiquitous Kettenkrad tracked motorcycle combination tows Me 262 A-1a W.Nr. 110813 "Green 3 and S" of the staff flight of Kommando Nowotny past the camera. It was standard policy that wherever possible, Kettenkrads (and later in the war, in some cases, oxen), were used to tow aircraft to and from their dispersals in an effort to save fuel.

Me 262 A-1a W.Nr. 110813 "Green 3", Kommando Nowotny, Achmer, September 1944
This aircraft had previously been used in bomb dropping trials before its transfer to Kommando Nowotny with whom it was used as a training aircraft. The aircraft is shown on page 435 during these trials and also at this time it carried the unusual green letter 'S' under the tail unit, which signified that the aircraft was not suitable for combat and was only to be used in a training role. All Me 262s relegated to training had the letter 'S' applied under the tail unit but was normally applied in white. However, JV 44 did have one aircraft carrying a large letter 'S' in red.

aircraft went into a steep left hand turn and disappeared into the overcast. Horrified listeners on the ground heard Nowotny report over the radio: *"Just made the third kill... left jet has failed... been attacked again... been hit..."* and then his Me 262 crashed in flames north of Bramsche before he could bail out.

On 7 November 1944, Generalleutnant Galland (second from left), the General der Jagdflieger, visited Achmer to inspect the men and machines of Kommando Nowotny. It was to prove a fateful visit for he witnessed Nowotny's sudden death and within days ordered the withdrawal of the Kommando for retraining.

Nowotny's death sounded the death knell of the *Kommando*. Although it had claimed 18 confirmed victories, it had lost a total of 26 Me 262s destroyed or damaged. Shortly afterwards it was transferred back to Lechfeld for retraining, *Hptm.* Georg-Peter Eder being appointed temporary commander.

Wendel submitted another critical report. *"The* Kommando *was withdrawn for a refresher course at Lechfeld after four crashes on 8 November.*[2] *This withdrawal was ordered by General Galland who had been with the unit on 7 and 8 November. I have already stressed weaknesses and faults in the leadership and training of this* Kommando *in my last report. The pilots are only partly 'fighter trained' and go into action after only two flights in the 8-262*[3]*. In this respect, they have never altered, and it was only after Major Nowotny was killed after an air battle with a large number of Mustangs, that General Galland gave the order for their 'removal'. The* Kommando *should be back to full strength in 8 to 10 days."*

By the end of October 1944, *Kommando Schenk* had been re-incorporated into I./KG 51. At this time the unit was based variously at Rheine, Hörstel and Hopsten and had the following leading personnel:

KOMMODORE	*Obstlt.* Wolf-Dietrich Meister
I. GRUPPE KOMMANDEUR	
	Maj. Heinz Unrau
I. GRUPPE ADJUTANT	*Oblt.* Harald Hovestadt
1. STAFFEL KAPITÄN	*Oblt.* Pahl
2. STAFFEL KAPITÄN	*Hptm.* Rudolf Abrahamczik
3. STAFFEL KAPITÄN	*Hptm.* Eberhard Winkel

On 20 October the *Gruppe* reported a strength of 31 aircraft, of which 26 were serviceable. Schenk continued to advise the unit on operational tactics, and eventually took over from Meister as *Geschwader Kommodore* on 5 December 1944. Initially the Me 262s of *Kommando Schenk* had carried large black identification letters on their noses but after only a short period of operations they assumed their familiar "9K" fuselage codes of KG 51 with some also carrying the famous *Edelweiss* badge painted below the cockpit.

On 2 November, I./KG 51 flew its first operation when four Me 262s attacked Allied airfields, two aircraft carrying AB 250 anti-personnel bomb containers and two SD 250 semi armour-piercing bombs. The operation was marred by an injury to *Hptm.* Eberhard Winkel, the *Staffelkapitän* of 3./KG 51, when his Me 262, coded 9K+CL, crashed at Grave in Holland. His place was taken temporarily by *Oblt.* Stephan.

Me 262 A-1a "White 15" of Kommando Nowotny is seen here being armed and made ready for flight. Note the white nose cone.

Although it was intended that KG(J) 54 should re-equip with the Me 262, deliveries proceeded very slowly. As a stop-gap the unit was partially equipped with the Fw 190. One of these, an A-5 coded B3+XL, piloted by *Ofäh.* Wolfgang Schneider of the *1. Staffel*, was shot down in a low level attack on 11 November 1944. The first Me 262 to be lost by the unit was W.Nr. 170107 which was destroyed when an engine caught fire on take off from Giebelstadt nine days later. The pilot, *Ofäh.* Richard Schöpe of the *2. Staffel*, was killed. The *Staffel* lost another pilot on 2 December 1944 when *Obgef.* Hajo Mentzel was killed during a training flight south of Gerolzhofen.

Meanwhile, one other unit had received its first Me 262. Early in June 1944, *Obtl.* Herward Braunegg was charged with establishing an experimental jet reconnaissance unit. Establishment of *Kommando Braunegg* began at Lechfeld, but it was not until 26 August 1944, that the first Me 262 reconnaissance aircraft to be completed was transferred to the *Versuchsverband OKL*, which took over overall control of *Obtl.* Braunegg's unit. The *Kommando* was eventually to operate a mixture of standard Me 262 A-1as and a few especially converted A-1a/U3s carrying two Rb 50/30 cameras[4]. The first aircraft to be lost by the unit was W.Nr. 170006 flown by *Fj.Ofw.* Friedrich Shauek. He was killed in a crash near Lissa on 25 October. On 6 November 1944, the *Kommando* transferred from Lechfeld to Rheine. Simultaneously, *Maj.* Heinz Schütze, on the staff of *Gen.Maj.* Karl-Henning von Barsewisch, the *General der Aufklärungsflieger*, gave orders for the formation of a specialised short-range jet reconnaissance *Gruppe* to be known as NAG 6. By 28 November *Kommando Braunegg* had six Me 262s, with three serviceable, and four pilots. Two days later it transferred from Lechfeld to Schwäbisch Hall to operate under *Oberst* Hentschel's *5. Jagd Division* at Durlach.

The loss of Nowotny, and an earlier injury to Horst Götz, of the Ar 234 reconnaissance *Kommando Götz*, led to a decision to give some of these units alternative names. Therefore, at the end of November 1944, *Kommando Braunegg*, received the designation *Kommando Panther*. The unit reported a strength of four pilots and five aircraft on 26 November and four days later transferred from Rheine to Schwäbisch Hall.

As recorded earlier, the remnants of Nowotny's *Kommando* were transferred back to Lechfeld where they were re-united with *EKdo 262*. This unit had meanwhile received the new designation III./EJG 2 on 27 October 1944, although it appears that this name was rarely used by the *Kommando's* pilots. On 16 November *Obtl.* Werner Glomb, *Kapitän* of 11./EJG 2, was killed when his Me 262 A-2a crashed near Unterslauersbach. On the same date the Allied "Ultra" code breaking service reported that III./EJG 2 had a strength of 18 aircraft and 12 crews with 69 pupils. Pilots had been arriving from many defunct *Luftwaffe* units,

The Gruppenkommandeur of I./KG 51, Major Heinz Unrau (right) shares a joke with fellow officers of his unit at Rheine-Bentlage, autumn 1944. Hauptmann Rudolf Roesch is seen centre with Ritterkreuz while to the left is Leutnant Maser. Roesch was reported missing during a meteorological reconnaissance flight west of Helmond in Holland on 28 November 1944.

Left: Hptm. Rudolf Abrahamczik, Staffelkapitän of 2./KG 51, warms his hands in the engine heat of one of the Geschwader's Me 262 bombers at Rheine, autumn 1944. Abrahamczik would be amongst the small group of former bomber pilots who would fly the Me 262 in the ground attack role over Prague with Gefechtsverband Hogeback in the final days of the war.

Me 262 A-2a "9K+YH", 1./KG 51, autumn 1944
Similar in colour to 9K+BH on page 423 and in common with many other
Me 262s of KG 51 at this time, this aircraft had its nose cone and top of
the fin and rudder painted white, indicating the Staffel colour.

"Carelessness and inadequate training" • 421

This page and opposite: A fine sequence of photographs showing Me 262 A-2a, "9K+YH" of 1./KG 51. The "9K+H" part of the code was painted in small black characters with the aircraft's individual letter "Y" in white. Note that this letter is unusual in having a curved tail. The aircraft also bears a white nose and tail tips often carried on aircraft of the 1. Staffel, but the gun ports have been left unpainted. The aircraft has had the heavy oversprayed "scribble" pattern camouflage applied to its fuselage and upper surfaces. It is fitted with two ETC 503 bomb racks beneath the forward fuselage.

A typical scene at Rheine in late 1944, as a Kettenkrad pulls 1./KG 51's Me 262 A-2a, W.Nr. 170096, (9K+BH) from the line-up in readiness for another mission over the western front. All of KG 51's aircraft had dark green camouflage upper surfaces with "scribble" patterns of darker greens oversprayed. In most cases, the tips of the nose and tail, gun ports and individual letters were painted in the respective Staffel colour, white for 1. Staffel, black for 2. Staffel and yellow for 3. Staffel.

Me 262 A-2a W.Nr. 170096, 1./KG 51, Rheine, September 1944

Above: "White B" as seen at Rheine, September 1944, like many aircraft of KG 51 "Edelweiss" it carried the stylised heavy scribble pattern of the two greens (81 and 82) on the upper surfaces with pale blue grey (76) beneath. The unit code "9K+BH" was painted on the fuselage sides, with the "9K" and "H" appearing in small black characters approximately one sixth in height of the individual letter "B", which appeared in white. Like many of KG 51's aircraft of the period, this Me 262 had the tip of the nosecone, fin and rudder as well as two gun ports edged in white, denoting the Staffel colour. The W.Nr. 170096 was applied in black on the fin. This aircraft was badly damaged at Giebelstadt on 2 October 1944 after completing 38 flights totalling 16 hours.

Above: A mechanic from KG 51 fits a wooden engine cover to one of the unit's aircraft. This makes an interesting comparison to the metal "basket" variety as used by Erprobungkommando 262 at Lechfeld in the summer of 1944 and seen in Chapter 8 of this work. The comparative crudeness of KG 51's equipment may be a reflection of the overall problem of supply affecting many frontline Luftwaffe units by late 1944.

Left: A close-up of the nose of an Me 262 A-2a of 1./KG 51. Although this aircraft had four gun ports, only two 30 mm MK 108 cannon were carried in the variant. The glazed port in the extreme nose is for the BSK 16 gun camera.

HERWARD BRAUNEGG

Born on 26 December 1917 in Graz, the son of Generalmajor Alexander Braunegg, an Austrian army officer. Braunegg joined the Austrian Air Force on 30 September 1937 and, after this was incorporated into the Luftwaffe following the Anschluss of 13 March 1938, he became a student at the Luftkriegsschule at Berlin-Gatow. Following training with various Aufklärungs-fliegersschulen (Reconnaissance Schools), he was transferred to Aufklärungsstaffel 1.(H)/41 on 10 December 1939 and to 4.(H)/41 on 14 June 1942. He then served with NAG 9 as Technical Officer and Staffelkapitän flying Bf 109s and Fw 189s, being awarded the Knight's Cross on 26 March 1944. In total, Braunegg was to fly 353 missions during the war. After the conflict he became a doctor of technology and returned to the Austrian Army to become an Oberst in the reserve in 1970. He died on 16 December 1983.

Above: This close-up of 'White 3' shows the standard B2 type Balkenkreuz carried beneath the wing of most Me 262s.

Me 262 A-1a/U3 W.Nr. 500259, "White 3", 1./NAG 6 early 1945
Unfortunately no photographs have so far been discovered of Kommando Braunegg's aircraft, but this machine from its successor, NAG 6, would have been very similar in appearance. This aircraft was flown by Uffz. Heinz Huxold in February 1945.

"CARELESSNESS AND INADEQUATE TRAINING" • 425

Ground crew hitch a ride on a Kettenkrad half-track motorcycle combination as it tows Me 262 A-1a/U3 W.Nr. 500259 "White 3" of NAG 6 from the runway to its dispersal following the execution of another jet reconnaissance mission over the southern half of the western front in the late autumn of 1944. Note that the aircraft carries a narrow yellow fuselage band, a B2 underwing cross and has been fitted with a wooden engine intake cover similar to that used by aircraft of KG 51 seen earlier in this chapter. Apart from the two Rb 50/30 cameras mounted in the nose, the aircraft used by Kommando Braunegg and NAG 6 also carried a single MK 108 cannon mounted in the nose.

This page and opposite: Me 262 A-1a/U3 W.Nr. 500259 "White 3" seen here at Lechfeld around February/March 1945. The photo shows the film magazine being removed from the Rb 50/30 camera for processing. This aircraft, flown by Uffz. Heinz Huxold, performed a reconnaissance mission over the city of Dresden following the Allied bombing raids of 13/14 February 1945. Huxold claimed one P-51 Mustang shot down on this mission.

Messerschmitt Me 262 A-1a/U3 W.Nr. 500259 "White 3", 1./Nahaufklärungsgruppe 6

Though relatively small in terms of aircraft and pilot strength, the Luftwaffe's jet reconnaissance units nevertheless provided the German high command with vital photographic intelligence on Allied troop and armoured movements. As the war progressed and the Allies began to drive deeper into what remained of the Third Reich, so they enjoyed ever increasing air superiority. The speed of the Me 262 in the reconnaissance role thus became of critical importance. The sequence on these pages shows a member of the airfield staff climbing a maintenance ladder to remove the film magazine from one of 'White 3' nose mounted RB 50/30 cameras. The designation Rb 50/30 indicated that the camera had a focal length of 50 cm and a plate size of 30 x 30 cm (11.8 x 11.8 inches).

JOHANNES STEINHOFF

Born on 15 September 1913 at Bottendorf in Saxony. Steinhoff joined the German Navy in 1934 as an officer cadet before transferring to the Luftwaffe in 1936. At the outbreak of war he was Staffelkapitän of 10./JG 26 flying experimental night fighter sorties from Köln-Ostheim. He was transferred to JG 52 in February 1940, commanding this Geschwader's 4. Staffel during the Battle of Britain and the invasion of the Soviet Union. He was awarded the Knight's Cross on 30 August 1941 and took over command of II./JG 52 in February 1942. He scored his 100th victory on 31 August 1942, and was awarded the Oak Leaves on 2 September. He was posted to North Africa in March 1943 to take over command of JG 77 and, on 28 July 1944, was awarded the Swords to his Knight's Cross. In 1952 he returned to the Bundesluftwaffe and within four years became Deputy Chief of Staff, Operations. He was promoted to Brigade-General in 1958 and to Generalmajor in 1962. He retired in 1972 to his home in Bonn where he died in 1994.

Major Erich Hohagen, seen here at Lechfeld in December 1944, wearing a woolen skull cap which partially conceals the scars of his recent head injury. Hohagen received the minimum of jet training at EJG 2 before being transferred to the new III./JG 7 as its Kommandeur. However, he still considers the Me 262 to have been "...the biggest step since the Wright brothers flew an aircraft heavier than air." Hohagen is seen talking to Oberst Hannes Trautloft, the Inspector of Day Fighters. Behind the officers can be seen the two-seat jet trainer, Me 262 B-1a, W.Nr. 170014, "White 17". This aircraft was evaluated in early March 1945 by officers from the weapons testing centre at Tarnewitz, with Fl.Stabsing. Fach test flying it on 3 March with Lt. Harbort.

Geyer's *Kommando* being charged with their retraining. A few operational sorties were flown in November, *Hptm*. Eder claiming the destruction of several Allied aircraft including a P-38 which he rammed.

At an Armaments Conference held between 1 and 4 November 1944, Hitler finally gave permission to begin series production of the Me 262 as a *fighter*, but stipulated that each aircraft "must be capable of carrying at least one 250 kg (550 lb) bomb in case of emergency". This order allowed Galland to begin formation of the first jet fighter *Geschwader* under the designation JG 7. It had been envisaged as early as August 1944 to equip this unit with Bf 109 G-14 piston-engined fighters, but these plans were dropped on 12 November. Seven days later, the remnants of *Kommando Nowotny* were redesignated III./JG 7, with the formation of two additional *Gruppen* planned, all to be equipped with the Me 262. To command JG 7, Galland appointed *Oberst* Johannes Steinhoff, a very experienced fighter pilot with 170 victories to his credit and holder of the Knight's Cross with Swords. The leading personnel were:

Kommodore	*Oberst* Johannes Steinhoff
Technical Officer	*Hptm*. Streicher
III. Gruppe Kommandeur	*Major* Erich Hohagen
III. Gruppe Technical Officer	*Oberinspektor* Grote
III. Gruppe Signals Officer	*Lt*. Günther Preusker
9. *Staffelkapitän*	*Hptm*. Georg-Peter Eder
10. *Staffelkapitän*	*Oblt*. Franz Schall
11. *Staffelkapitän*	*Oblt*. Joachim Weber

Because III./EJG 2 *(EKdo 262)* was already overstretched with Me 262 pilot training, it was decided to redeploy some resources from the bomber wing, KG 1 "Hindenburg", which had just been disbanded. For a short time, the name "Hindenburg" was transferred to JG 7, but soon afterwards it was named "Nowotny" in memory of its fallen leader. It had been proposed that III./JG 7 should receive 40 aircraft by the end of November, but by that time it only had eleven Me 262s.

Flieger Überführungs Geschwader 1 (Aircraft Ferry Wing 1) under *Obstlt*. Zeidler was charged with transporting many newly completed Me 262s from their assembly plants to the operational units. The wing had been formed on 20 May 1942, and by 1944 comprised at least seven different *Gruppen*, each covering a different area of Germany. These were *Nord* (north), *Ost* (east), *Süd* (south), *Süd-Ost* (south-east), *Süd-West* (south-west), *West* (west) and *Mitte* (centre). In addition to *Luftwaffe* pilots who had been transferred from disbanded units or those no longer fit for operational service, the unit also possessed a number of well-known women aviators including Vera von Bissing and Beate Uhse. During the course of its duties, the various *Gruppen* were to lose a number of pilots and Me 262s in accidents or to marauding Allied fighters.

Not long after the formation of III./JG 7, on 27 November 1944, the old Bf 109 fighter unit, II./JG 3, became the *I.Gruppe* of the new *Geschwader*. The leading personnel were:

I. Gruppe Kommandeur
                           Hptm. Theodor Weissenberger
1. Staffelkapitän   *Oblt.* Hans Grünberg
2. Staffelkapitän   *Oblt.* Fritz Stehle
3. Staffelkapitän   *Oblt.* Hans Waldmann

Weissenberger was a very able officer who had been awarded the Knight's Cross with Oak Leaves. He had already claimed 200 victories mainly with JG 5 in Norway and Finland. It was proposed that the unit would convert to the Me 262 at Kaltenkirchen in Schleswig-Holstein.

The 26 November 1944 was quite an eventful day for the Me 262. Three pilots who were undergoing jet fighter training with III./EJG 2, *Major* Rudi Sinner (ex *Kommandeur* of I./JG 27), *Lt.* Fritz R. Müller and *Ofw.* Hermann Büchner, took off to intercept Allied reconnaissance aircraft over Bavaria. Both Sinner and Buchner shot down a 7th Photo Reconnaissance Group F-5 Lightning, the former piloted by Lt. Julius R. Thomas, the latter by Lt. Irvin J. Rickey. Müller also badly damaged a Mosquito from 60 Squadron, South African Air Force. The traffic was not all one way however. *Lt.* Alfred Schreiber, who had claimed *EKdo 262's* first victory[5] but had now transferred to 9./JG 7, was killed in an accident at Lechfeld and *Ofw.* Rudolf Alf of 1./JG 7, was killed while practising low level flying near Fürstenfeldbrück.

Meanwhile, on 18 October 1944, a 28 year old pilot serving with II./NJG 11, *Lt.* Kurt Welter, had been

Left: Born in Frankfurt in 1906, Vera von Bissing was one of a number well-known female pre-war German aviators who later joined Flieger Überführungs Geschwader 1 as a ferry pilot to deliver Me 262s. During the 1930s she had flown as part of an aerobatic team, flying many different types of aircraft including the Messerschmitt M 35b and giving air show performances all over Europe.

Two views of an Me 262 A-2a of an unidentified unit, but probably in the hands of an aircraft ferrying unit with orders to deliver the machine to KG 51. The aircraft carries no tactical or unit markings but is fitted with two ETC 503 bomb racks and the upper gun ports blanked out.

Oblt. Hans Grünberg, nicknamed "Specker", was born at Gross-Fahlenwerder in Pommerania on 8 July 1918. His first operational unit was 5./JG 3 which he rose to command before becoming Staffelkapitän of 1./JG 7 in November 1944. He was eventually to claim 82 victories, five of them in the Me 262 before transferring to JV 44 at the end of the war.

THEODOR WEISSENBERGER

Born on 21 December 1914 at Mülheim. Initially Weissenberger was a very keen glider pilot and instructor, but in the autumn of 1941 he was posted to northern Norway to serve with 1.(Z)/JG 77 which became 6./JG 5 in January 1942. He scored his first aerial victory on 23 October 1941, and destroyed 23 enemy aircraft, 15 locomotives, two flak installations, one radio station and 10 barracks during his service with this unit. He was awarded the Knight's Cross on 13 November 1942, then having 28 victories and, on 15 June 1943, he took over command of 7./JG 5. On 2 August 1943 he was awarded the Oak Leaves to his Knight's Cross, then having 112 victories. The next month he took over 6./JG 5 from Oblt. Heinrich Ehrler, and then II./JG 5 on 26 March 1944. On 4 June 1944 he became Kommandeur of I./JG 5 and within a few weeks had scored 25 victories in operations against the Allied landings, his 200th victim falling on 25 July. During the war, Weissenberger flew over 500 combat missions, scored 208 victories and was nominated for the Swords. He was killed on 10 June 1950 in a motor racing accident at the Nürburgring.

presented with the *Ritterkreuz*. At the presentation he had been asked to experiment with the Me 262 as a night fighter to combat the hated Mosquito fast bomber. Shortly afterwards, Welter transferred to Rechlin-Lärz where he was given a standard Me 262 A-1a. After a number of trials and errors, he shot down his first Mosquito on 28 November, proving that the jet fighter could be used satisfactorily in that role. On 7 December Welter was one of a number of officers who examined a mock-up of an Me 262 night fighter, the aircraft to be equipped with FuG 350 and FuG 218 radar, many cockpit modifications, a K22 autopilot, and armament reduced to two MK 108s.

During December, Welter is thought to have shot down three more Mosquitoes, and on the 11th of the month Göring ordered that three Me 262s and three Ar 234s be made available for the night fighting role. Six days later Welter tested an Ar 234 at night, but was not impressed[6]. On the same day he was asked to form the first specialised Me 262 night fighter detachment under the designation *Kommando Welter*, and by the end of the month, four Me 262 A-1as had been allocated to the unit.

KURT WELTER

Born on 25 February 1916 at Köln-Lindenthal, joining the Luftwaffe as early as 1 October 1934. Welter trained as a pilot but served as an instructor until 2 September 1943 when he joined 5./JG 301 which flew single-engined "Wilde Sau" night fighter operations in the defence of the German homeland. By the beginning of April 1944 Welter had shot down 17 four-engined bombers during only 15 missions. On 7 July 1944 he was posted to 5./JG 300 and shot down two B-17s and three P-51s within the month. Shortly afterwards he was transferred to NJGr 10, and then to 10./JG 300, a Staffel charged specifically with the destruction of de Havilland Mosquito bombers. During his service with NJGr 10 and 10./JG 300, Welter destroyed eight Mosquitoes including one which he rammed. He was awarded the Knight's Cross on 18 October 1944 at which time he had 34 victories and had been transferred to II./NJG 11. For his operations with the Me 262 night fighter, which is detailed in Volume Four in this series, Welter was awarded the Oak Leaves on 18 March 1945. He was killed in a car accident near Leck is Schleswig-Holstein on 7 July 1949.

Kurt Welter, standing left, next to his Fw 190 whilst serving with NJGr 10. There is some evidence from Welter's German contemporaries that he was prone to exaggerate his claims, however, but their accuracy will probably never be finally established.

In the bomber role, I./KG 51 was continuing to fly operational sorties against Allied troops and strongpoints in North-West Germany. In November 1944, II.*Gruppe* of KG 51 under *Major* Herbert Voss began to receive its first Me 262s at Schwäbisch Hall. On 4 December the *Gruppe* reported a strength of 35 aircraft and 54 crews. The *Gruppe's* leading personnel were:

II. *Gruppe Kommandeur*	*Major* Herbert Voss
4. *Staffel Kapitän*	*Oblt.* Chiuruski
5. *Staffel Kapitän*	*Hptm.* Fritz Abel
6. *Staffel Kapitän*	*Oblt.* Wolfgang Bätz

On 13 November 1944 a carpet bombing raid on Rheine caused KG 51 heavy casualties. Among the pilots killed were *Oblt.* Merlau and *Fw.* Hoffmann, with the *I. Gruppe* medical officer, Dr. Denkhaus, badly injured. Bombs also caused many casualties among the men of 5./KG 51 at Hesepe. The I. *Gruppe Stab* was forced to move to Hopsten where it rotated between Hörstel, Dreierwalde and Esch. On 26 November 2./KG 51 reported *Oblt.* Heinz Lehmann killed in a crash 3km south of Kirchwistedt. Two days later, "Ultra" decrypts reported that I./KG 51 at Rheine and Hopsten had a strength of 48 aircraft and 46 crews.

During the day, *Hptm.* Rudolf Roesch, of 1./KG 51 was reported missing during a meteorological reconnaissance flight west of Helmond in Holland. On 30 November *Uffz.* Horst Sanio of 2./KG 51, flying W.Nr. 170120, was shot down by British flak also at Helmond.

In the autumn of 1944, Fritz Wendel, the Messerschmitt test pilot, visited the headquarters of KG 51 at Rheine to assess bombing operations using the Me 262. Wendel is seen here in discussion with Major Heinz Unrau, Kommandeur I./KG 51.

An Me 262 of 1./KG 51 sits on the rain-slick runway at Hopsten, late 1944. Just visible in the photograph is the white nose of the 1.Staffel and what appear to be ETC 503 bomb racks under the fuselage.

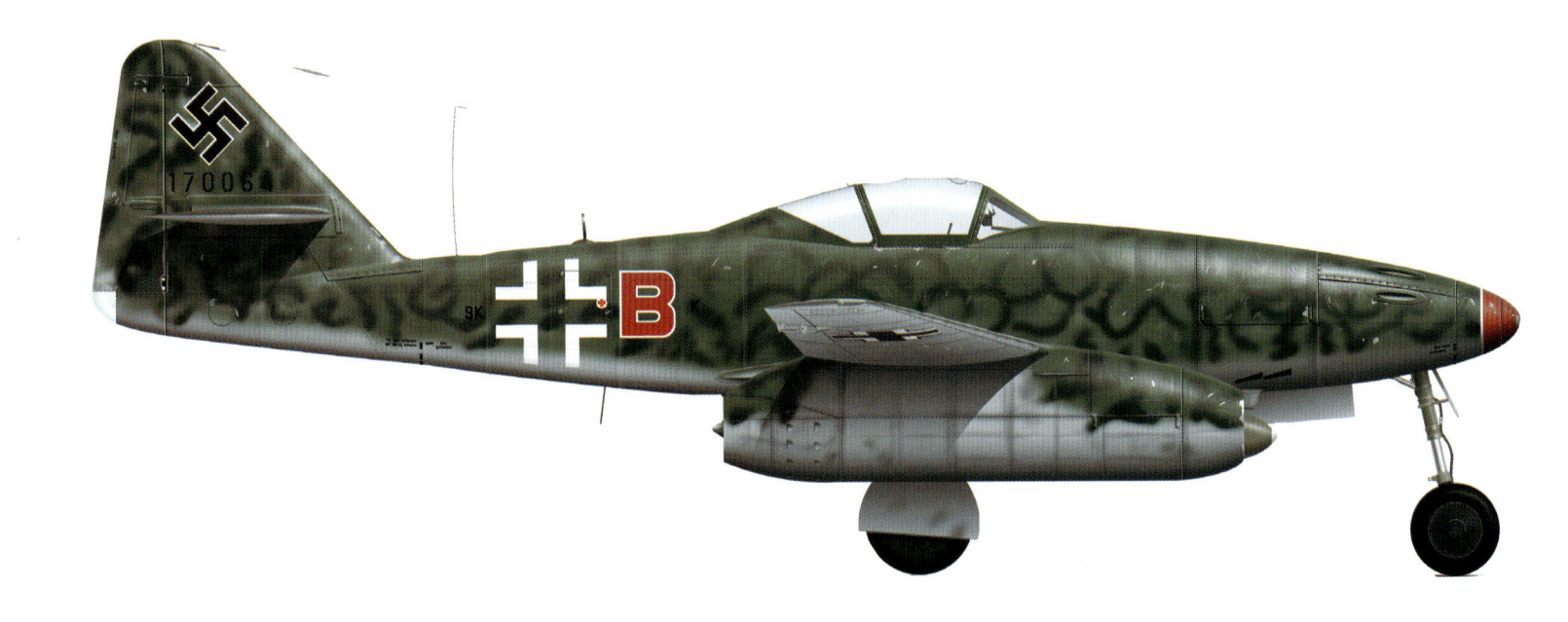

Me 262 A-2a "9K+BK" 2./KG 51 "Edelweiss", Rheine, October 1944
Carrying the "scribble" pattern of the greens (81 and 82) with pale blue grey (76) beneath, this Me 262 of 2./KG 51 had the same camouflage pattern as the aircraft of the 1. Staffel. Part of the unit code, "9K+ K", was painted in small black characters, with the individual letter "B" and the tip of the fuselage nose painted in red, thinly edged in white. Although exact records are lacking, this may have been the aircraft, W.Nr. 170120, in which Uffz. Horst Sanio was shot down and killed by British flak on 30 November 1944.

Below: Me 262 A-2a, "Red B" '9K+BK' of 2./KG 51 is towed out of its camouflaged shelter at Rheine, late 1944. At this time, KG 51's aircraft were flying intensive missions against Allied troops and strongpoints in north-west Germany, Holland and Belgium..

"Carelessness and inadequate training" • 433

Left: British armour enters Geilenkirchen, mid-November 1944. In the foreground is a Churchill AVRE (Armoured Vehicle Royal Engineers) armed with a 290 mm Petard Spigot mortar designed to destroy concrete walls, bunkers and fortifications. The shell weighed over 20 kg and could be fired to a range of 80 m. Such vehicles formed targets for the Me 262s of I./KG 51 at this time.

Below: Photographed by passing British infantry on 30 November 1944, smoke drifts from the wreckage of Uffz. Horst Sanio's Me 262, W.Nr. 170120, in a field on the outskirts of Helmond in Holland, close to the railway to Düren. Sanio of 2./KG 51 was shot down by British anti-aircraft fire. For some time afterwards, British troops were forced to keep onlookers at a safe distance because of the exploding ammunition and fuel carried by the aircraft.

Right and Above: RAF and British Army personnel examine the burnt out remains of the Me 262 W.Nr. 170120 piloted by Uffz. Horst Sanio of 2./KG 51, shot down by anti-aircraft fire at Helmond, 30 November 1944.

Below, right and opposite: This aircraft, W.Nr. 110813, parked amidst the trees somewhere in southern Germany, was used in bomb dropping evaluation trials. It carries two 500 kg bombs on Wikingerschiff bomb racks suspended beneath the forward fuselage. At this time the aircraft already carried the green 'S' under the tailplane and after these trials it was transferred to Kommando Nowotny, where the the bomb racks were removed and the code "Green 3' was applied, although the green "S" under the tailplane (*see opposite*) was retained signifying that the machine continued to be used as a trainer, only this time in the fighter role.

KG 51 "Edelweiss" Geschwader emblem

Below: A Me 262 A-2a of 2./KG 51 fitted with ETC 503 bomb racks, resting on tripods for undercarriage tests. Note the typical camouflage pattern applied to KG 51 aircraft at this time and the red nose cone denoting a 2. Staffel machine. The tail tip has also been painted. Although the aircraft carried the Edelweiss badge of KG 51, it has no national insignia suggesting that it has recently been oversprayed.

Below: Pilots of KG 51 standing in front of one of the Geschwader's aircraft. Note the freshly applied "Edelweiss" Geschwader emblem on the nose.

Some indication of a typical mission flown by KG 51 can be gained from this interrogation of one of its pilots:

"Briefing usually was very short, lasting from 5 to 10 minutes. Information given was concerned only with the target and its location. There was no orientation on flak or other factors affecting the mission. We were left to figure out our routes to and from the target and the altitudes to be flown.

"The deepest penetration Me 262s made with bombs was 250 km (155 mls) flying at an altitude of 4,000 m (13,100 ft). The formation flown to the target was usually of four aircraft abreast with 25 to 30 m (80 to 100 ft) between wingtips. Speed to the target was about 675 km/h (420 mph). The usual altitude was 4,000 m, and each aircraft carried two 250 kg bombs under the nose. Prior to January 1945, Hitler's personal order 7 forbade any Me 262 flying below 4,000 m. The serious effect of this flying altitude on bombing accuracy caused continuous complaints from the pilots, but it was not until the end of January that the order was changed to allow pilots to go down to an altitude they considered safe.

"When Allied fighters were encountered en route to the target, the Me 262s usually increased speed and easily climbed away. Flak was evaded rather easily by weaving from side to side.

"The maximum diving angle of the Me 262 with bombs was 35 degrees. We dived down from 4,000 m to 1,000 m (3,300 ft) but never much lower. Care was taken to prevent the air speed exceeding 920 km/h (570 mph) since the Me 262 was red-lined at 950 km/h (590 mph). Care was also exercised to empty the rear 600 ltr (158 Imp gal) tank before the dive. This was necessary because the release of bombs with a full rear tank caused the nose of the aircraft to pitch up very suddenly, either knocking out the pilot or throwing the machine into an uncontrollable spin. Our pilots used the old Revi bomb sight which was supposedly accurate to within 35 to 40 m (115 to 130 ft). Following release of our bombs, the Me 262s returned home at between 1,000 and 1,200 m (3,300 and 3,900 ft) with a distance of 60 to 90 m (200 to 300 ft) between aircraft."

---

1 Yeager later became the first man to officially break the sound barrier in the Bell X-1 on 14 October 1947.
2 The fourth aircraft to be lost on 8 November may have been that piloted by Ofw. Helmut Baudach who was reported shot down by P-51s. He bailed out safely.
3 All German powered aircraft designations were prefixed with the number '8', gliders using '108', piston engines '9' and jet and rocket engines '109'.
4 See Chapter 9.
5 See Chapter 8.
6 See Monarch Series No.1 on the Ar 234 by J Richard Smith and Eddie J Creek published by Monogram Aviation Publications, page 133.
7 Hitler's order was finally rescinded on 21 December 1944 during the Ardennes offensive.

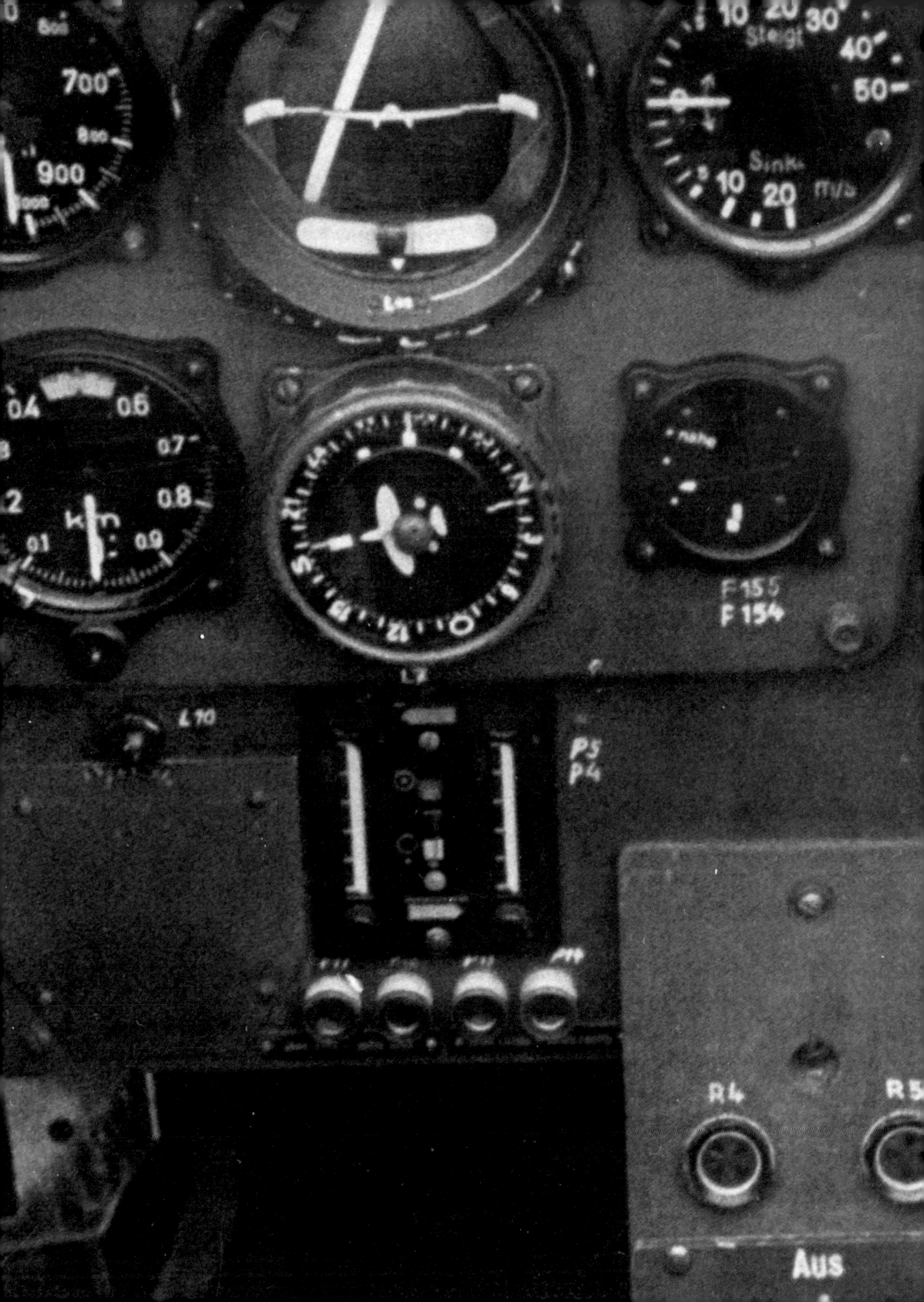
Steigt
m/s
km
F 155
F 154
L 10
P 5
P 4
R 4
Aus

APPENDIX FIVE
CAMOUFLAGE AND MARKINGS

APPENDIX SIX
LUFTWAFFE RANKS AND FLYING UNITS

APPENDIX SEVEN
MESSERSCHMITT ME 262 SPECIFICATION FIGURES

APPENDIX FIVE
CAMOUFLAGE AND MARKINGS

As has been recorded in Appendix One of Volume One, Messerschmitt employed a scheme of undercoating the whole of Me 262 airframes in RLM grey (colour 7120.02). This was followed by a single coat of the undersurface colour blue-grey 7120.76 overall. When the first production aircraft, W.Nr. 130011, was delivered to *Erprobungskommando 262* at Lechfeld it retained this finish with the black four letter code 'VI+AK' painted on both sides of the fuselage and below the wings (see page 182 of Volume One).

All subsequent aircraft delivered to the unit probably had a camouflage pattern of RLM 74 and 75 applied on the upper surfaces of the wings, fuselage and tailplane, over the overall factory finish of 76 which was retained as the underside colour. The pattern was similar to that illustrated on page 199 of Volume One although by this time the colours used had changed. On 1 July 1944, a directive entitled *Sammelmitteilung* (Collected Instructions) had been issued, instructing that:

1) All new new aircraft types whose mission would have called for the use of colours 70 and 71, are from now on to be painted in colours 81 and 82.

2) For types already in production, colours 70 and 71 are to be superseded by colours 81 and 82 as soon as possible.

Available stocks of 70 and 71 are naturally to be used up. As it may be assumed that these colours will not be exhausted simultaneously, and in order to avoid re-orders of small quantities of 70 and 71, the use of residual stocks in the following combinations is authorised.

   Colour 70 (remaining quantity) + colour 82
   Colour 71 (remaining quantity) + colour 81

Delivery of colour-sample cards for RLM shades 81 and 82 is for the present not possible, thus testing the paint for correct colour shade is omitted.

Although this was not to affect the Me 262 which had previously used a camouflage pattern of dark grey (74) and medium grey (75) a later instruction, *Sammelmitteilung Nr.2* of 15 August 1944 stated that:

As a result of the new revision, the following colours will not be used in future: 65, 70, 71 and 74. Colour 70 however is still prescribed for propellers.

The document also made mention of a new colour 83 which is thought to have been a darker green than 82. From this and observation of contemporary colour photos, it would appear that many fighters of the late war period, of which the Me 262 was of course one, often utilised a camouflage pattern of 81 and 82, 81 and 75 or 83 and 75. As already stated, this pattern was applied to the aircraft's upper surfaces with the sides of the fuselage and turbojets together with the vertical tail surfaces being mottled in the same colours, the mottling usually becoming less prominent as it merged with the lower surface blue-grey 76.

Erprobungskommando 262's national markings usually comprised a broad white outline cross or *Balkenkreuz* on the fuselage (type B5[1]), a narrower white outline cross on the upper surfaces of both wings (type B6) and a black cross outlined in white and edged in black (type B2) on the under-surfaces. Most of the unit's aircraft carried a black swastika or *Hakenkreuz* edged in white (type H2a) on both sides if the fin, but at least one aircraft, W.Nr. 170045 'White 5' had an all white swastika (type H3a). A distinctive feature of the *Kommando's* aircraft was the narrow yellow (RLM 04) band painted around the fuselage forward of the fuselage *Balkenkreuz*. The aircraft's individual number was painted on the nose, forward of the wing leading edge, in white outlined in black. The six figure *Werk Nummer* (abbreviated in most German documents as W.Nr.) was usually stencilled on both sides of the fin, directly above the tailplane in black.

Most of the later test series aircraft used this type of camouflage and markings, but often with a large white 'V' or *Versuchs* (experimental) followed by three numbers (these represented the last three digits of the W.Nr.) painted on the nose and sometimes repeated, in black, on the nosewheel door and occasionally also on the rear of the fuselage in white. Rechlin aircraft were either identified by their original four letter radio call sign or, more often, by the code of the individual test programme being carried out with the machine within E-Stelle Rechlin (See Chapter 10 page 317 for a list of Me 262 test aircraft and codes allocated to Rechlin). The codes used were usually painted in black on the fuselage but the camouflage in which the aircraft was delivered was usually retained. The *Werk Nummer* was again painted on the fin above the tailplane, but sometimes in white instead of black.

The aircraft of the first Me 262 bomber unit, *Kommando Schenk*, carried similar camouflage to the fighters (probably 74, 75 and 76), although black and white photos would indicate they may have been somewhat paler. The under wing crosses were usually of the B3 type (without the black edging) and the *Werk Nummer* were sometimes painted on the rear fuselage, beneath the tailplane. Individual aircraft were marked with a black letter edged in white painted on the fuselage forward of the wing leading edge. This letter was also usually repeated, in black, on the front of the nosewheel door.

When *Kommando Schenk* was incorporated into KG 51, this unit's aircraft employed similar camouflage to that previously described, but a heavy mottling was introduced and often applied in continuous streaks in a type of "scribble" pattern obviously applied with a spray gun. National insignia were similar to those used by the previous units, usually the type B2 crosses beneath the wings. Unlike the previous units however, KG 51 carried the standard four character bomber unit code system adopted by all *Luftwaffe* operational units with the exception of fighters and ground attack aircraft on 24 October 1939.

In this the first two characters (always made up of a letter and a figure), applied to the left of the fuselage *Balkenkreuz* identified the *Geschwader* to which the aircraft belonged. The third character, positioned immediately to the right of the fuselage cross was the aircraft's individual identification letter, and the last letter identified the *Staffel* or *Stabschwarm*. The official German painting guide, Der *Flugzeugmaler* (The Aircraft Painter) of 1944 detailed how these codes should be applied - the following is a literal translation:

"Aircraft are to be marked in block characters irrespective of whether letters or numerals are used. An even thickness of the characters used is of special importance. Characters are defined by their height, width, thickness and the the space between each character. Spacing of the characters has to be even otherwise they will appear distorted. The letters C, E, F, J and L will be narrower, since they would otherwise appear too wide. M and W appear much wider.

Centre line of characters is parallel to the Balkenkreuz centre line. It runs parallel to the horizontal plane in flight, not to the fuselage centre line. On and under the wings, the centre line is at right angles to the direction of flight. Codes such as numbers and letters, are not to be applied to the upper surfaces of military and combat aircraft. The third letter is, however, to be applied to the undersurfaces of combat aircraft, centred between wingtip and Balkenkreuz.

KG 51's Geschwader identification code was 9K and, like most *Luftwaffe* bomber units, it had three *Staffeln* in each *Gruppe*. The *Stabschwarm* and *Staffel* letters used by these units are shown below:

Geschwader Stab   A   (green)

I. Gruppe Stab	B	(green)	II. Gruppe Stab	C	(green)
1. Staffel	H	(white)	4. Staffel	M	(white)
2. Staffel	K	(red)	5. Staffel	N	(red)
3. Staffel	L	(yellow)	6. Staffel	P	(yellow)

III. Gruppe Stab	D	(green)	IV. Gruppe Stab	E	(green)
7. Staffel	R	(white)	10. Staffel	U	(white)
8. Staffel	S	(red)	11. Staffel	V	(red)
9. Staffel	T	(yellow)	12. Staffel	W	(yellow)

By the time KG 51 became operational with the Me 262, the application of the four character code had changed. The *Geschwader* code (the first two characters) and the *Staffel* identification (the last letter) were painted in black approximately one-fifth the size of the individual letter. The individual letter itself was painted in the *Staffel* colour. The origins of these colours can be traced back to those used by the old German Imperial Army: white for the first sub-unit, red for the second, yellow for the third, blue for the fourth, green for the fifth and brown for the sixth.

Geschwader Stab	Blue (RLM 24)
I. II. III. IV. and V Gruppe Stab	Green (RLM 25)
1. *Staffel* within a *Gruppe*	White (RLM 21)
2. *Staffel* within a *Gruppe*	Red (RLM 23)
3. *Staffel* within a *Gruppe*	Yellow (RLM 27)

In KG 51's case, the white and yellow letters were usually outlined in black with the red letters edged in white. Apart from these markings, KG 51's Me 262s also often had the tips of fuselage, rudder and fin painted in the *Staffel* colour with a similar contrasting edging. Some aircraft of KG 51 also had their famous *Edelweiss* emblem[3] painted on the fuselage sides forward of the cockpit.

The first fully operational German jet fighter unit, *Kommando Nowotny*, carried very similar camouflage and markings to those used by *Erprobungskommando 262*, even down to the yellow rear fuselage band. Some aircraft have been quoted as having yellow cowlings to the front part of engine but it is more likely that these parts were left in bare metal finish due to an engine change as the front of all Jumo 004 engines came as part of the unit and was included in any replacement. The one distinctive feature of the unit's aircraft was the vertical tail camouflage pattern, which appears to be the same on all Me 262s when the unit was formed. In common with other Me 262 units, some of the *Kommando's* aircraft carried a white (and in at least one instance a green) letter 'S' on the rear fuselage, aft of the *Balkenkreuz* indicating that they were a *Schulflugzeug* or training aircraft not fit for combat. Legend has it that the aircraft in which Walter Nowotny was shot brown, W.Nr. 110400, was possibly coded 'White 8' and had a large green heart painted beneath the cockpit, but this has yet to be confirmed by photographic evidence.

Unfortunately, no photos of the reconnaissance unit, *Kommando Braunegg*, have yet been discovered, but they are thought to have been very similar to its successor, NAG 6. This unit had much darker green uppersurface camouflage than most me 262s, possibly utilising RLM colour 81 only. NAG 6 also had yellow rear fuselage bands and individual aircraft were identified by numbers painted in the Staffel colour on the fuselage, forward of the wing leading edge.

---

1   Readers are referred to "JV 44" by Robert Forsyth published by Classic Publications in 1997 Page 324 for references to German National Markings.
2   See Page 317 for full list of Me 262 test aircraft and codes allocated to Rechlin.
3   See page 434

APPENDIX SIX
LUFTWAFFE RANKS AND FLYING UNITS

RANKS

The table below lists the wartime *Luftwaffe* ranks together with their equivalent in the Royal Air Force and the US Army Air Force:

Luftwaffe	Royal Air Force	U.S.A.A.F.
Generalfeldmarschall	Marshal of the RAF	Five Star General
Generaloberst	Air Chief Marshal	Four Star General
General der Flieger	Air Marshal	Lieutenant General
Generalleutnant	Air Vice Marshal	Major General
Generalmajor	Air Commodore	Brigadier General
Oberst	Group Captain	Colonel
Oberstleutnant	Wing Commander	Lieutenant Colonel
Major	Squadron Leader	Major
Hauptmann	Flight Lieutenant	Captain
Oberleutnant	Flying Officer	First Lieutenant
Leutnant	Pilot Officer	Lieutenant
Oberfähnrich	(leading cadet)	(leading cadet)
Fähnrich	(cadet)	(cadet)
Stabsfeldwebel	Warrant Officer	Warrant Officer
Oberfeldwebel	Flight Sergeant	Master Sergeant
Feldwebel	Sergeant	Technical Sergeant
Unterfeldwebel	-	-
Unteroffizier	Corporal	Staff Sergeant
Hauptgefreiter	-	Sergeant
Obergefreiter	Leading Aircraftman	Corporal
Gefreiter	Aircraftman First Class	Private First Class
Flieger	Aircraftman	Private

In addition, the *Luftwaffe* used the term "*Hauptfeldwebel*". This was not a rank. A *Hauptfeldwebel* (colloquially called "*Spiess*") was the NCO administrative head of a company or corresponding unit (*Staffel*, battery etc.). His rank could be anything from *Unteroffizier* to the various *Feldwebel*.

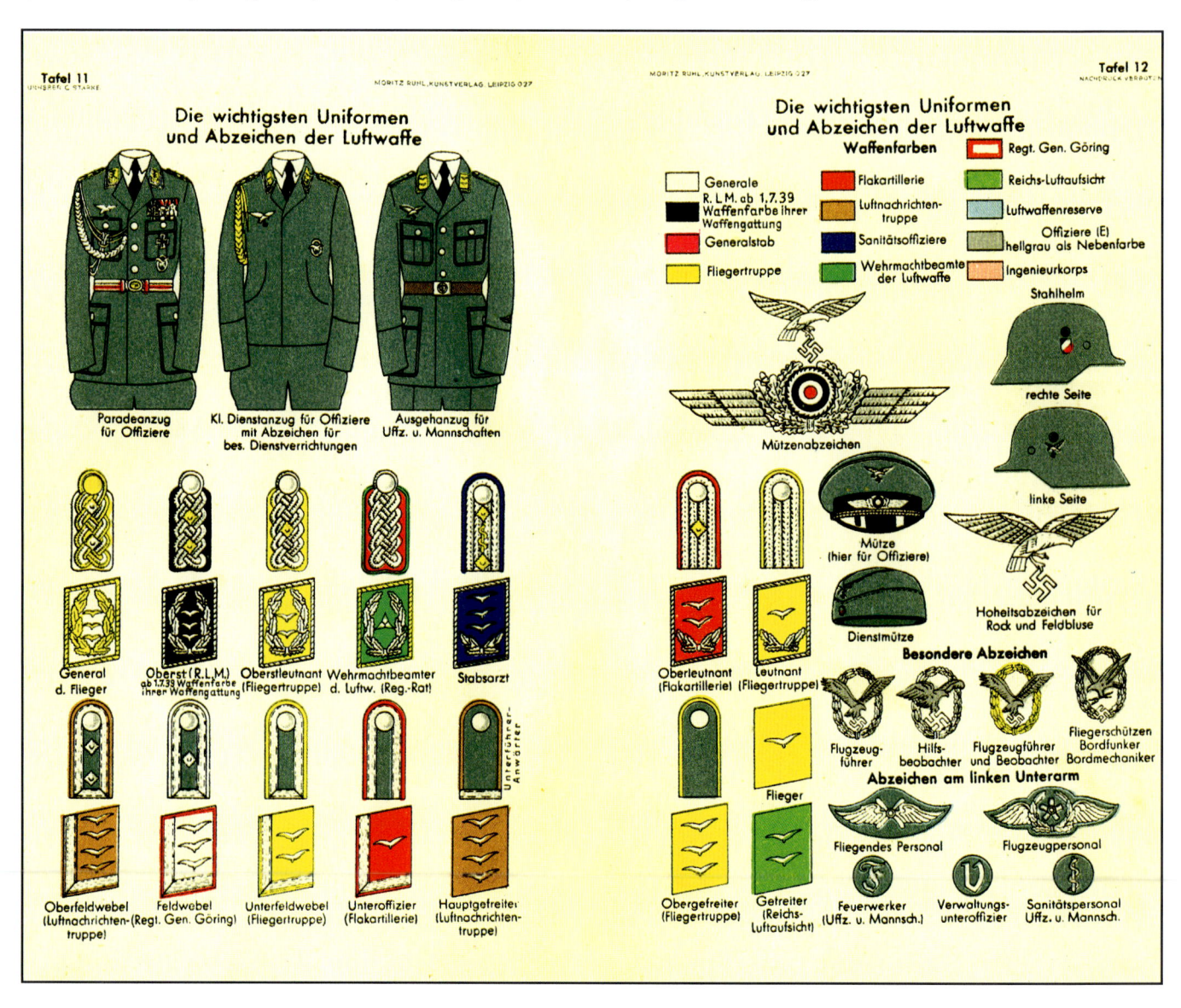

Flying Units

The basic *Luftwaffe* flying unit was the *Staffel* or squadron which was normally made up of between 9 and 12 (usually 16) aircraft. It was led by a *Staffelkapitän* who normally had the rank of *Hauptmann* or *Oberleutnant*. The *Staffel* was always identified by an Arabic number - for example, the 5. *Staffel*. The dot which followed the number had the same meaning as "th" in English - this the Fifth *Staffel* in the above example. Apart from the aircraft and aircrew, the *Staffel* had a ground organisation of various vehicles and about 150 men.

Three or four *Staffeln* could be combined together to form a *Gruppe* or Group. This could be autonomous, usually in the case of reconnaissance units, (when it was identified by an Arabic numeral), or as part of a *Geschwader* or Wing (when it was identified by a Roman number). For example *Nahaufklärungsgruppe* 6 or the III. *Gruppe* of JG 27. The *Gruppe* also contained a *Stab* (literally "staff") or Headquarters Flight which included such persons as the as the *Gruppen Kommandeur* (usually a *Major* or *Hauptmann*, the *Gruppe Adjutant* and the *Gruppe Technische Offizier* (Technical Officer).

As with the *Staffel*, three, four or occasionally five *Gruppen* could be combined together to form a *Geschwader* or Wing. These were always identified by an Arabic numeral. Like the *Gruppe*, the *Geschwader* contained a *Stab* made up of the *Geschwader Kommodore*, (usually an *Oberst*, *Oberstleutnant* or *Major*) and other personnel such as *Adjutant*, TO, Ia (operations officer), Ic (intelligence officer), and *Nachrichten* Officer (signals officer).

When the Second World War began, the make up of a typical *Geschwader* was as follows:

Geschwader Stab

I. Gruppe	II. Gruppe	III. Gruppe
1. Staffel	4. Staffel	7. Staffel
2. Staffel	5. Staffel	8. Staffel
3. Staffel	6. Staffel	9. Staffel

During the autumn of 1944 (and in the case of JG 2 and JG 26 the summer of 1943) many Fighter Wings (*Jagdgeschwader*) were expanded to have four *Gruppen* of four *Staffeln* each. The typical fighter *Geschwader* of this period would appear thus:

Geschwader Stab

I. Gruppe	II. Gruppe	III. Gruppe	IV. Gruppe
1. Staffel	5. Staffel	9. Staffel	13. Staffel
2. Staffel	6. Staffel	10. Staffel	14. Staffel
3. Staffel	7. Staffel	11. Staffel	15. Staffel
4. Staffel	8. Staffel	12 Staffel	16. Staffel

The major type of *Geschwader* were:

German	English	Written as
Jagdgeschwader	Day Fighter Wing	JG
Kampfgeschwader	Bomber Wing	KG
Kampfgeschwader (Jagd)	Bomber Wing on Fighter operations	KG(J)
Nachtjagdgeschwader	Night Fighter Wing	NJG
Schnellkampfgeschwader	Fast Bomber Wing	SKG
Schlachtgeschwader	Ground Attack Wing	SG
Sturzkampfgeschwader	Dive Bomber Wing	St.G
Transportgeschwader	Transport Wing	TG
Zerstörergeschwader	Destroyer Wing	ZG

Common types of autonimous *Gruppen* were:

German	English	Written as
Aufklärungsgruppe	Reconnaissance Group	Aufkl.Gr.
Fernaufklärungsgruppe	Long-range Reconnaissance Grp	FAG
Nahaufklärungsgruppe	Short-range Reconnaissance Grp	NAG
Nachtschlachtgruppe	Night Ground-attack Group	NSG

Other *Luftwaffe* units mentioned in these Volumes are the *Erprobungskommando* and the *Kommando*. These were both experimental tests units, the former charged with developing a particular aircraft, weapon or weapons, the latter with developing operational tactics. *Erprobungskommando* were identified by an Arabic numeral, a *Kommando* either by its commander's name or codename.

Left: Two pages taken from an official German document, dated circa 1939, illustrating the majority of rank and insignia badges as well as the various Arms operating within the Luftwaffe organisation together with their colour identification.

APPENDIX SEVEN
MESSERSCHMITT Me 262 SPECIFICATION FIGURES

For details on armament and other loads, see Chapter 9.

	Me 262 A-1a fighter		Me 262 A-1a fighter-bomber with SC 500 bomb	
Wing span	12.56 m	41 ft 2.5 ins	12.56 m	41 ft 2.5 ins
Wing area	21.7 sq m	233.58 sq ft	21.7 sq m	233.58 sq ft
Overall length	10.6 m	34 ft 7.25 ins	10.6 m	34 ft 7.25 ins
Wheel track	2.33 m	7 ft 5.25 ins	2.33 m	7 ft 5.25 ins
Height	3.83 m	12 ft 6.75 ins	3.83 m	12 ft 6.75 ins
Equipped weight	4,120 kg	9,083 lbs	4,150 kg	9,149 lbs
Crew	100 kg	220 lbs	100 kg	220 lbs
Ammunition	304 kg	670 lbs	304 kg	670 lbs
Fuel (2 x 900 ltrs)	1,330 kg	2,932 lbs	1,330 kg	2,932 lbs
Additional fuel	220 kg	485 lbs	220 kg	485 lbs
Take-off weight	6,074 kg	13,391 lbs	6,604 kg	14,559 lbs
Rockets with fuel	300 kg	661 lbs	300 kg	661 lbs
Total	6,374 kg	14,052 lbs	6,904 kg	15,220 lbs
Maximum speed at sea level	800 km/h	497 mph	718 km/h	446 mph
at 6,000 m (19,685 ft)	870 km/h	541 mph	750 km/h	466 mph
at 9,000 m (29,528 ft)	845 km/h	525 mph	685 km/h	426 mph
Climbing speed at sea level	19.3 m/sec	63.3 ft/sec	14.9 m/sec	48.9 ft/sec
at 6,000 m (19,685 ft)	10.0 m/sec	32.8 ft/sec	7.0 m/sec	23 ft/sec
at 9,000 m (29,528 ft)	5.2 m/sec	17.1 ft/sec	3.0 m/sec	9.8 ft/sec
Climbing time				
to 6,000 m (19,685 ft)	7.0 mins	7.0 mins	9.3 mins	9.3 mins
to 9,000 m (29,528 ft)	14.0 mins	14.0 mins	19.9 mins	19.9 mins
Service Ceiling[1]	11800 m	38,714 ft	10,500 m	34,449 ft
Normal range at sea level	290 km	180 mls	270 km	168 mls
at 6,000 m (19,685 ft)	520 km	323 mls	475 km	295 mls
at 9,000 m (29,528 ft)	644 + km	400 + mls	—	—
Maximum range at sea level	360 km	224 mls	330 km	205 mls
at 6,000 m (19,685 ft)	600 km	373 mls	550 km	342 mls
at 9,000 m (29,528 ft)	710+ km	441+ mls	—	—
Endurance at 100% thrust at sea level	0.36 hours	0.36 hours	0.36 hours	0.36 hours
at 6,000 m (19,685 ft)	0.72 hours	0.72 hours	0.71 hours	0.71 hours
at 9,000 m (29,528 ft)	0.92 hours	0.92 hours	—	—
Maximum Endurance at sea level	0.75 hours	0.75 hours	0.75 hours	0.75 hours
at 6,000 m (19,685 ft)	1.35 hours	1.35 hours	1.21 hours	1.21 hours
at 9,000 m (29,528 ft)	1.30 hours	1.30 hours	—	—
Take-off run 100% thrust	920 m	3,018 ft	1,050 m	3,445 ft
with two 500 kg RATO	540 m	1,772 ft	630 m	2,067 ft
Landing speed	182 km/h	113 mph	182 km/h	113 mph

1 Service ceiling for the Me 262 A-1a was calculated at 5,100 kg (11,243 lbs) and for the Me 262 A-1a fighter-bomber at 5,500 kg (12,125 lbs)

Glossary

Abteilung	Battalion, department, section, detachment	Kommando	Unit, Detachment or Command – usually autonomous
Aufklärer	Reconnaissance Aircraft	Kommodore	Title given to the commander of a Geschwader
Baubeschreibung	Project Description		
Behelfsaufklärer	Interim Reconnaissance Aircraft	Luftflotte	Air Fleet
Behelfsnachtjäger	Interim Night Fighter	Nachtjäger	Night Fighter
Blitzbomber	Fast Bomber	Panzerflugzeug	Armoured Aircraft
Bomberkanzel	Bomber Nose	Projektbüro	Project office
Bunkerwerke	Bunker (underground) factory	Protokoll	Record or report
Diplom-Ingenieur	Academic degree in engineering subject	Oberstabsing.	Senior Staff Engineer
		Reichsminister	Reich Minister
Einsatzkommando	Operational unit, detachment or command	Reichsluftministerium (RLM)	Reich air ministry
Ergänzungs	Operational Conversion and Training	REIMAHG	Reichsmarschall Hermann Göring Works
Erprobungskommando	Test/experimental unit	Ritterkreuz	Knight's Cruise
Erprobungsstelle (E-stelle)	Test centre	Ritterkreuzträger	Holder of the Knight's Cross
Experten	Ace Pilots	Rotte	Element of two aircraft
Flieger/Flugzeug Überführungs Geschwader	Aircraft Ferrying Wing	Rüstsatze	Field Equipment Addition/Conversion Packs
Fliegerdivision	Flying Division		
Fliegerkorps	Flying Corps	Schlechtwetterjäger	All Weather Fighter
		Schnellstbomber	Fast Bomber
General der Aufklärer	General of the Reconnaissance Arm	Schulflugzeug	Trainer
General der Jagdflieger	General of the Fighter Arm	Schwarm	Element of two Rotten (see above)
General der Kampfflieger	General of the Bomber Arm	Stabsing.	Staff Engineer
Geschwader	Wing	Staffel	Squadron
Gruppe	Group	Staffelkapitän	Squadron commander
Heimatschützer	Home Defender	Technisches Amt	Technical Office
Industries Schutz Schwarm	Industry Defence Flight	Versuchs	Trials
Interzeptor	Interceptor	Waldwerk	Forest Factory
Jagd Division	Fighter Division	Wikingerschiff	"Viking Ship" – name given to type of bomb rack fitted to Me 262
Jagdgeschwader	Fighter wing		
Jäger	Fighter		
Jägerstab	Fighter Staff		

INDEX

PERSONALITIES

Abel, Hptm. Fritz 431
Abrahamczik, Hptm. Rudolf 418
Alf, Ofw. Rudolf 429
Alison, Lt. Dennis J. (USAAF) 411
Althoff, Karl 306
Banzhaff, Ofw. Willi 410
Barsewisch, Gen.Maj.. Hans-Henning 272, 337, 419
Bätz, Oblt. Wolfgang 431
Baudach, Fw. Helmut 234, 258, 261, 411, 412
Baur, Karl 308
Beaudrault Capt. Valmore J. (USAAF) 373
Behrens, Maj. Otto 314, 360
Bissing, Vera von 429
Bley, Oblt. Paul 235, 238, 251, 262
Bornemann, Dipl.-Ing. Kurt, 339
Böttcher, Obstabsing. 314
Braunegg, Oblt. Herward 419
Brown, Lt.Cmdr. Eric 346
Büchner, Ofw. Hermann 429
Buttmann, Hptm. Hans-Christoff 373
Büttner, Fw. 265, 411, 413
Caroli, Dipl.-Ing. Gerhard 233
Churchill, Winston 248
Cole, P/O Bob (RAF) 373
Coningham, Air Marshal Sir Arthur (RAF) 248
Corwin, Lt. (USAAF) 413
Croy, Lt. Manford O. (USAAF) 369
Cuno, Obstabsing. 320
Degenkolb, Gerhard 399
Delange, Obstabsing. 320
Delatowski, Uffz. Edmund 374
Diesing, Obst. Ulrich 337, 375
Dodd, Flt.Lt F.L. (RAF) 257
Drew, Lt. Urban L. (USAAF) 262
Dryland Flt.Lt. (USAAF) 375
Duff Flt.Lt. (USAAF) 375
Eder, Maj. Georg-Peter 262, 418, 428
Eichhorn, Fw. Erwin 234
Eisenbach, Obstlt. Volprecht Riedesel Freiherr von 377
Engelmann, Obstabsing. Dr. 393, 396
Fingerloos Fw. Joachim 373
Flachs, Uffz. Hans 235, 240
Fleming, Sqdn.Ldr. (RAF) 261
Foster, Lt Hugh O. (USAAF) 374
Francke, Uffz. Gerhard 373
Galland, Genlt. Adolf 245, 376, 413, 428
Gärtner, Oblt. Werner 371
Geyer, Hptm. Horst 249, 251, 259, 261
Gerbe, Lt. William T. (USAAF) 411
Glomb, Oblt. Werner 419
Göbel, Ofw. Hubert 235, 261, 411
Göring, Hermann 238, 272, 388, 399
Götz, Horst 419
Greim, GFM Robert Ritter von 259
Groce, Lt Walter R. (USAAF) 411
Haffke, Ofäh. Erich 262
Hallensleben, Obstlt. Rudolf von 371
Hauteville, Obstabsing. Von 320
Herget, Maj. Wilhelm 274, 393, 396
Herlitzius, Fw Heinz 235, 240, 330
Herrmann, Obst. Hajo 376
Hoffert, Lt. William L. (USAAF) 413
Hilborn, Lt. Robert (USAAF) 261
Hitler, Adolf 235, 272, 314, 330, 348, 363, 370, 401,402, 428
Hohagen, Maj. Erich 428
Holzbaur, Flugkapitän Siegfried 348
Hovestadt, Oblt. Harald 418
Jones, Lt. William A. (USAAF) 261
Junghaus, Fj.Fw. Edgar 374
Kaiser Fhr, Herbert 249
Kammler, SS Obergruppenführer 401, 402
Kappus, Dipl.-Ing. Peter 310
Keitel, GFM Wilhelm 238
Keller, Gen. 413
Kenny, Lt. James W. (USAAF) 413
Kesselring, GFM Albert, 240
Kleinrath, Genlt. Kurt 393, 399
Kobert, Lt. Gerhard 262
Kogler, Obstlt. Johann, 240, 245
Koller, Gen.der Flg. Karl 235
Kramer, Dr. Max 341
Kreipe, Gen. Werner 238, 330
Kreutzberg, Ofw. 257
Lamb, Lt. Huie H. (USAAF) 374
Lange, Otto 392
Lauer, Ofw. Hieronymous 363, 373
Leigh-Mallory, Air Chief Marshal Sir Trafford 248
Lennartz, Fw. Helmut 234, 257, 262, 265, 411, 412
Lindner, Gerd 298, 308, 341, 346
Lobban, Flg.Off. A.S. (RAF) 245
Lockhart-Ross, Lt. Archie (SAAF) 251, 252, 256
Lüthner, Obering. 265
Marienfeld, Obst. Walter 377
Mayer, Hptm. Egon 234
McDowell, W/Cmdr. Andrew (RAF) 263
McKelvey, Lt. Charles C. (USAAF) 413
Meister, Obstlt. Wolf-Dieter 418
Mentzel, Ogef. Hajo 419
Messerschmitt, Prof. Wilhelm 258, 399
Mosbacher, Stabsfw. 314
Müller, Lt. Fritz R. 429
Müller, Oblt. Hans-Günther 235, 238, 251, 257
Myers, Major Joseph (USAAF) 369
Nowotny, Maj. Walter 259-263, 408, 410, 413, 418
Oppel, Hptm. Karl-Friedrich von 377
Peltz, Generalmajor Dietrich 234, 375, 376
Pienaar, Capt Saloman (SAAF) 251, 252, 256
Preusker, Lt. 257, 428
Quinn, Lt. William J. (USAAF) 412
Recker, Ofw, Helmut 235
Rickey, Lt. Irvin J. (USAAF) 429
Roesch, Hptm. Rudolf 431
Rottmann, Lt. 369
Royer, Flt.Off. Willard W. (USAAF) 411
Russel, Ofäh. Heinz 262, 265, 410
Ruther, Fl.Stabsing. 310
Sanio, Uffz. Horst 431
Sauckel, Fritz 385, 388
Saur, Hauptdienstleiter Karl-Otto 314, 360, 388, 399
Schall, Lt. Franz 262, 265, 412, 413, 428
Schauder, Uffz. Herbert 371
Schenk, Maj. Wolfgang 360, 399
Schneider, Ofäh Wolfgang 419
Schnörrer, Lt. Karl 259-261
Schöpe, Ofäh Richard 419
Schreiber, Lt. Alfred 235, 248, 261, 429
Schürfeld, Stabsing. 320
Schütze, Maj. Heinz 419
Schwarz, Ofw. Kurt 377
Shauek, Fj.Ofw. Friedrich 419
Seiler, Friedrich 399
Sinner, Maj. Rudi 429
Sommer, Lt. Erich 369
Spangenburg, Lt. 411,412
Späte, Hptm. Wolfgang 234
Speer, Albert 240, 314, 330, 383, 401
Steinhoff, Obst Johannes 428
Stephan, Oblt 419
Strathmann Ofw 235, 240
Streicher, Hptm 410, 428
Teeter, Lt. Robert (USAAF) 373
Teumer, Oblt. Alfred 262
Thierfelder, Hptm. Werner 234, 245, 249
Thomas, Lt. Julius R. (USAAF) 429
Tizard, Sir Henry 248
Uhse, Beate 429
Umbers, Flt.Lt. (USAAF) 375
Unrau, Maj. Heinz 418
Voss, Maj. Herbert 431
Walker, Lt. John A. (USAAF) 261
Wall, Flt.Lt. A.E. (RAF) 245
Weber, Lt. Joachim 235, 257, 261, 265, 428
Wegmann, Oblt. Günther 235, 251, 261, 262, 265, 413
Weidemann, Lt. Rolf 369
Weiss, Hptm. Robert 263
Weissenberger, Hptm. Theodor 429, 430
Welter, Lt. Kurt 430
Wendel, Fritz 361, 363, 370, 408, 418
Whittle, Frank 248
Wigmann, Stabsing. 320
Winkel, Oblt. Eberhard 360, 418
Wörner Oblt. 234
Yeager, Capt. Charles E. 412
Zander, Ofw. Helmut 411
Zeidler, Obstlt. 428

UNITS

III./EJG 2 261, 382, 399, 403, 419, 428, 429
EKG(J) 399, 403
Erprobungskommando 262 234, 240, 245, 248, 249, 251, 257, 261, 294, 314, 408, 418
Flieger Überführungs Geschwader 382, 392, 399, 428
Gefechtsverband Hallensleben 371
JG 2 234
II./JG 3 429
III./JG 6 261
JG 7 337, 382, 392, 399, 403, 428, 429
JG 11 234
JG 54 259, 263
I./JG 400 261
JGr 10 337
JV 44 282, 321, 346, 399, 403
KG 1 428
KG 51 294, 337, 360, 361, 363, 369, 371-375, 382, 418, 419, 431, 435
KG 54 294, 337, 376, 377, 392
KG 76 382, 392
KG 101 348
KG 254 376
KG 255 360
KG(J) 6 399, 403
KG(J) 54 376, 392, 399
KGr 806 376
Kommando Braunegg 392, 419
Kommando Götz 419
Kommando Panther 419
Kommando Nowotny 262, 263, 265, 408, 410, 418
Kommando Schenk 314, 361, 363, 369, 371, 373, 375, 418
Kommando Welter 392, 435
NAG 1 406
NAG 6 382, 403
NJG 11 399, 403, 430
NSG 1 372
NSG 2 372
NSGr 20 372
Versuchsverband OKL 419
II./ZG 1 259
ZG 2 234
III./ZG 26 234, 235, 240, 257-259, 261

ARMAMENTS AND EQUIPMENT

AB 250 Weapons Container 283, 418
AB 500 Weapons Container 363, 373
BMW 003A Turbojet 300, 301, 310, 405
BMW P.3395 Rocket Engine 300, 301, 306
BT 200 Torpedo Bomb 283, 320
BT 400 Torpedo Bomb 341
ETC 70/C-1 Bomb Rack 341
ETC 503 Bomb Rack 268, 283, 294, 307, 321
ETC 504 Bomb Rack 286, 292
EZ 42 Gunsight 268, 274, 321, 346, 348
FPL Remotely Controlled Gun Barbette 352, 354
FuG 25a IFF 268, 370, 372
FuG 16Z 272, 293, 346, 370, 372
FuG 125 VHF 272, 321
FuG 218 Neptun Radar 339, 430
FuG 350Zc Naxos 307, 430
FuG 353 293
K22 Auto Pilot 346, 430
Lotfe 7H Bomb Sight 286
MG 213C 337
MK 103 Cannon 269, 337, 352
MK 108 Cannon 269, 272, 274, 282, 286, 292, 293, 307, 348, 452, 354, 357, 430
MK 112 Cannon 273, 274, 352
MK 213 Cannon 269, 337
MK 214 Cannon 273, 274, 306, 337, 348, 352
MK 412 337
R4M Orkan Rocket 274, 307, 337, 339, 348
R100bs Rocket 307, 339
RA 55 Automatic Rocket Dispenser 306, 339
Rb50/30 Camera 272, 293
Rb75/30 Camera 272
Revi 16b Gunsight 268
Ruhrstahl X-4 Rocket 307, 341
SC 50 Bomb 320
SC 250 Bomb 268, 283, 307, 320
SC 500 Bomb 268, 283, 307
SD 1 Bomb 373
SD 4 373
SD 10 Bomb 363
SD 250 Bomb 268, 283, 307, 373, 418
SD 500 Bomb 268, 283, 307
SG 116 Zellendusche 337
TSA 2D Bomb-Aimer 285, 307, 346
Walter HWK R11/211 (109-509) Rocket Engine 297, 300, 306, 357
WGr 21 cm Mortar 337, 339